Paved with Gold

Paved with Gold

Discovering the West End of London

David Long

Fort Publishing Ltd

First published in 2015 by Fort Publishing Ltd,
Old Belmont House, 12 Robsland Avenue, Ayr, KA7 2RW

All black-and-white photographs courtesy of David Long and Esther Simpson.
Colour photographs by Simon Kennedy and Simon Murrell
Maps © www.helenstirlingmaps.com 2015. Contains Ordnance Survey data.
© Crown Copyright and Database Right 2015
Original artwork by Doreen Shaw

Printed by Bell and Bain Ltd, Glasgow

Graphic design by Mark Blackadder

Typeset by 3btype.com

ISBN: 978-1-905769-44-5

To: H. J. C. and I. D. A.

Contents

Preface

George VI made a good point when he observed that 'It is not the walls that make the city, but the people who live within them' – not least because at the time the walls were taking a lethal pounding from German bombers. But it is also hard not to agree with the Martin Amis character (in *God's Dice*) who declares, 'It is hard for me to believe that a city is anything more or other than the sum of its streets.'

Certainly much enjoyment can be had from watching the more than eight million Londoners who crowd the city today, and of course in a very real sense it is they who help make the capital the lively, colourful and exhausting place which attracts so many visitors. But of course there is much more to London than the here and now, and in exploring its long history one needs to take in the fabric as well as the inhabitants, not to mention all those other Londoners – born or adoptive – who filled the streets and squares during past centuries when the West End was taking shape.

It would be an exaggeration to suggest that every one of them has a story – or at least not one that is worth hearing. But walking the streets in the heart of London, from Belgravia to Bloomsbury, Covent Garden to Westminster and Whitehall, one is overwhelmed by the number of buildings old and new that are not just interesting in their own right but even more so once you know who lived or died in them or made their name whilst eking out a living behind its otherwise anonymous front door.

That's the point of this book. Not to ignore the famous landmarks (which are also described here with much historical detail and quirky anecdote) but to take the reader down side streets and into corners that even Londoners tend to miss. Peeling away the many layers of history that lie behind the modern offices and too-familiar shop façades – and explaining why and how a whole new London developed to the west of the Roman-walled medieval city – it is an attempt to present within the confines of a single volume an authoritative and engaging account of London's beating heart.

David Long
July 2015

MAYFAIR

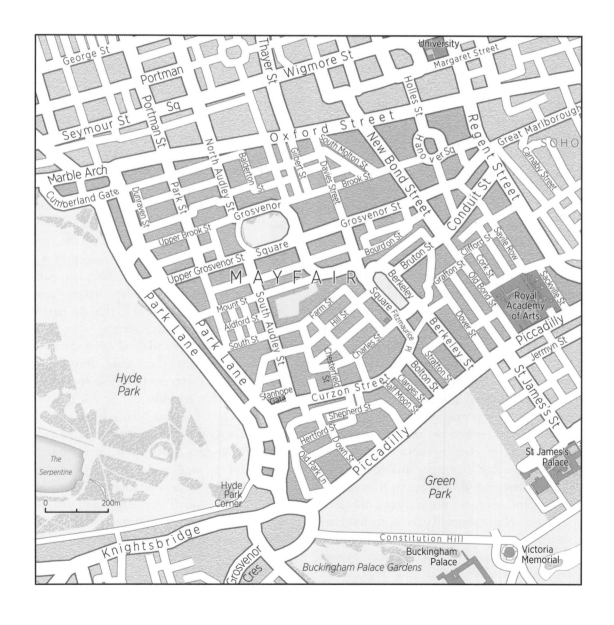

There are few areas in London with such firm boundaries that even the most pretentious estate agent must abide by them, but Mayfair is one such. A parallelogram neatly delineated by Park Lane, Oxford Street, Regent Street and Piccadilly – beyond which frontiers nowhere can sensibly be described as Mayfair – it is a small and expensive yet surprisingly diverse neighbourhood. Like Belgravia and Pimlico it owes both its existence and its present form to the fortuitous marriage in 1677 of an energetic Cheshire landowner to the young heiress Mary Davies (see panel p. 18). Sir Thomas Grosvenor's heir, the 6th Duke of Westminster, owns much of it still – only Pimlico was sold when the 2nd Duke quietly reordered his affairs in 1953 – and like the best of his forebears Major General Gerald Cavendish Grosvenor KG has worked hard to preserve the area's unique character, its charm and its mixed, yet distinctive, architectural heritage.

The name is taken from the annual May Fair, a wild and boisterous two-week affair that in 1686 transferred from Haymarket to the area around what is now Shepherd Market. Lively and hugely popular from the start it very quickly succumbed to the kind of 'loose, idle and disorderly crowds', which, historically, were the fate of every such gathering in the capital. With no police force to control it the fair routinely got out of hand, and, in the 1760s, as the neighbourhood gradually moved upmarket and became more socially desirable, the revels were banished to the East End. Thereafter they were suppressed altogether when the 'drunkenness, fornication, gaming and lewdness' got truly out of hand.

The carefully planned development of the Mayfair we see today had actually begun in the south-east corner around a century earlier with a small cluster of very large houses on land given by Charles II to his aristocratic friends. From there it advanced westwards along Piccadilly before spreading north towards the Oxford road so that by the 1850s the neighbourhood was entirely built over. Its proximity to both the sovereign (at St James's Palace) and the royal parks did much to encourage its growth; so too did the general movement of the population (or at least its better-off members) from east to west as first the City and then Covent Garden and Soho gradually lost status.

Probably by a combination of good fortune and careful arrangement, Mayfair's original landlords managed mostly to develop their respective estates in harmony with each other. New streets and terraces politely attended on neighbouring ones so that vistas were maintained and a visitor traversing Mayfair would not necessarily be unduly aware that he was leaving, say, Lord Grosvenor's territory and entering that of Lord Scarborough or Lord Berkeley. Today much the same is true, and with only a few exceptions – notably Park Lane and Piccadilly, and parts of Berkeley Square – building heights have been restricted in order not to ruin the largely eighteenth-century streetscape.

Clearly based around three great squares – first Hanover, then Grosvenor, and, finally, Berkeley – development proceeded on a more or less regular grid-like pattern, with some variations for example where large aristocratic residences remained standing. As well as these attractive squares and typically broad, straight streets for the well-to-do, the early developers and their builders intelligently provided for the many small tradesmen and artisans needed to service the larger houses. The broad streets were required by a growing taste among the rich for carriages, but such was the Georgians' skill in arranging such things that today much of modern Mayfair's very real charm depends on the survival of the myriad small alleyways, lanes, mews and yards set that were set aside for their businesses.

Mayfair was nevertheless always intended primarily to be residential rather than commercial, and it remained so until the late 1940s when many of those who had moved out to escape the war declined to return or were no longer alive or rich enough to do so. At that point new commercial and retail leases were written to enable businesses to move into the neighbourhood in far greater numbers than before. This was important, as the war had destroyed a good deal of office accommodation further east, and before long two-thirds of properties were no longer residential. However, with these same leases now expiring – and unexpectedly large numbers of wealthy individuals (many from abroad) keen to live in central London – Mayfair is once again returning to its residential roots, which in the 1980s and 1990s might not have been forecast.

Of course aside from its central location another aspect that makes Mayfair so attractive, both to residents and visitors, is its largely domestic architecture. This manages somehow to combine great variety with a reassuring consistency, something that unifies the neighbourhood as one moves from street to square to street. Thus, while a surprisingly high proportion of (on the whole) chaste Georgian terraces and townhouses still typifies the neighbourhood, elsewhere one can enjoy the distinctive, more decorated terracotta frontages and tiles of late-nineteenth century Mount Street – an economical material which was readily cleaned and highly resistant to pollution – some lovely Edwardian and Arts and Crafts touches in nearby Mount Row and a profusion of 1930s neoclassicism.

More recently, particularly towards Oxford Street, Mayfair has admittedly suffered with the rest of London at the hands of the developers of the 1960s and 1970s. But even here there are good signs that when their work is pulled down the tendency has been, and continues to be, to replace it with something very much better and usually a good deal more sympathetic to the Mayfair the 1st Duke of Westminster would have recognised.

Albany

An elegant, private and almost cloistered courtyard towards the circus end of Piccadilly, this intriguing mansion of the 1770s was built by the great Palladian, Sir William Chambers (1723–96), for the 1st Viscount Melbourne. While technically now a block of flats, albeit decidedly upmarket ones, its chaste façade of mellow brown brick and stone dressing is unchanged and exudes the perfect aura of a first-rate Georgian

Albany

nobleman's London residence. On such a busy thoroughfare the place appears surprisingly secluded and is a delicious anachronism in an age and area in which every other building of a similar size and quality has been taken over by a gentleman's club, discreetly redeveloped as offices, or, more commonly, torn down.

Albany takes its name from a later, royal owner, George III's second son Frederick, Duke of York and Albany (1763–1827) who ran up huge debts while struggling to pay a heavy mortgage with the banker Thomas Coutts. Finally, in 1802, he surrendered the house, which was skilfully converted by Henry Holland into smart chambers for bachelors. Thereafter it provided the perfect base for young blades around town, an address even then enjoying a slightly raffish reputation and one famously described as slightly disreputable and yet entirely enviable.

Two hundred years later it still is very much the latter, and today on the rare occasions when one is offered for sale a set or apartment in what the historian Macaulay called this 'luxurious cloister' is still highly sought after. This is little wonder, with the traditional pleasures of clubland and St James's literally a stone's across Piccadilly, and at Albany's discreet rear entrance in Vigo Street the expensive amenities of Savile Row and Mayfair.

Not a single blue plaque has been allowed to disturb the lovely façade, but the list of former residents is illustrious. Besides Henry Holland, leading architects who chose Albany as a London base included Basevi and Smirke. Today their ghosts walk the same corridors as a raft of statesmen such as Canning, Palmerston, Gladstone and Sir Edward Heath. Albany was also once home to the lords Snowdon and Clark, two giants of the arts

in post-war Britain, Sir Thomas Beecham, numerous writers including Greene, Macaulay himself, Huxley, Priestley, Rattigan and Dame Edith Evans – and two of the more notable diarists of our own times in Sir Harold Nicolson and the political *enfant terrible*, Alan Clark MP. The poet Lord Byron lived in apartment 2a for a while; where he liked to box.

Albemarle Street

London's first ever one-way street takes its name from the 2nd Duke of Albemarle as it was laid out behind the site of his London residence, Clarendon House. Eventually considered surplus to requirements by his heirs this magnificent double-pile mansion by Roger Pratt had been acquired in the 1680s by a syndicate of developers, described by the diarist John Evelyn as 'rich bankers and mechanics'. They included the financier and courtier Sir Thomas Bond (see Bond Street) at a time when the area to the north of Piccadilly was still largely market gardens and open fields.

Built for Edward Hyde, 1st Earl of Clarendon (1609–74) – grandfather to Queen Mary II and Queen Anne – Clarendon House had in its day been the finest of the West End mansions, a central section nine bays wide between two side wings each of three bays. Behind it were a generous eight acres of gardens, with a magnificent courtyard fronting onto the quiet lane we now call Piccadilly and a view down St James's Street to St James's Palace. On Clarendon's death his heirs had sold the house to the Duke of Albemarle for £26,000, and eight years later His Grace reached an accommodation with the aforementioned syndicate. Its members promptly pulled the great house down to

Albemarle Street: The Royal Institution

make way for a scheme that was to include Dover Street and Bond Street.

Today the street is associated with two very different scandals, the first involving Oscar Wilde and the second Lord Byron. On 17 May 1824 a collection of Byron's personal papers were deliberately incinerated in the fireplace at no. 50, the offices of his publisher John Murray whose personal opinion was that the contents of said papers would cause irreparable harm to the late poet's reputation. Prior to this Byron had much to thank the publisher for, including an estimated £20,000 in royalties during his lifetime – and indeed the publication of his second book, *Childe Harold's Pilgrimage*, after

which, as Byron himself noted, 'I awoke one morning and found myself famous.' The burning of the papers, in the presence of a small group of Byron's friends and his executors, is still looked upon as a uniquely shocking case of cultural vandalism. It remains a source of very considerable frustration to readers and Byronic scholars alike, knowing that the contents of the missing papers can now never be revealed.

Oscar Wilde's personal decline and lonely death in Paris began in a very real sense at 13 Albemarle Street and the day on which John Sholto Douglas, 9th Marquess of Queensberry, publicly accused Wilde in writing of 'posing as a somdomite' [sic]. The accusation was made in 1895 on the premises of the Albemarle Club – now defunct – prompting Wilde, foolishly, to sue the nobleman for libel. Wilde subsequently withdrew from the proposed court action, after learning that Queensberry intended calling a number of male prostitutes as witnesses. But it was too late and in so doing he left himself open to a charge of gross indecency, which was eventually proven. His reputation lay in ruins but the club survived the scandal before falling on hard times in the 1930s and closing its doors in 1941. A number of other clubs met in Albemarle Street, including for a while the Royal Thames Yacht Club and two dining clubs – the parliamentary Grillons at no.7 and the X Club, which was founded by the naturalist Thomas Huxley for supporters of Darwin's theories of evolution and other radical scientific ideas.

However, the most famous establishment is the Royal Institution, which still survives at nos. 20–21 and is the oldest scientific research body in the world. Founded in 1799 and given its royal charter a year later, the classical Grade 1 listed building, with its fourteen giant Corinthian columns, is home to an organisation dedicated to 'diffusing the knowledge, and facilitating the general introduction, of useful mechanical inventions and improvements; and for teaching, by courses of philosophical lectures and experiments, the application of science to the common purposes of life'. Such has been its influence in scientific research that many important discoveries were either made within its walls or announced from here.

The premises originally comprised two eighteenth-century houses, one an extraordinary structure twelve bays wide but just a single room deep, which were acquired in 1799 and remodelled by Thomas Webster. Its present appearance dates back only to 1838, however, when Lewis Vulliamy created the unifying screen of columns and modified the window openings to regularise the building's appearance. The interior has also been much modified, particularly during the inter-war period, although many original features survive including an eighteenth-century staircase and a late-eighteenth-century lecture theatre. An attractive chimneypiece in no. 20 was removed from the Soho Square home of the explorer and pioneering naturalist Sir Joseph Banks (1743–1820). From the start such was the popularity of the regular talks given at the Royal Institution – and the eminence of the speakers including Michael Faraday, Sir Humphry Davy and more recently a number of Nobel laureates – that a decision was taken to restrict the traffic outside, sending carriages in one direction only in order to reduce the congestion that would otherwise have resulted.

Faraday's importance to the Royal Institution, and to science, cannot be overestimated. Born in south London, in 1791, to a poor family, he received only a rudimentary education, but, always the autodidact, he read voraciously and in the process was able to master a wide range of scientific subjects. After hearing Humphry Davy lecture at the R. I. he wrote to the great man, who found him a job as a chemical assistant. He benefited greatly from his close association with Davy, himself a great scientist, but of whom it is said that 'his greatest discovery was Faraday'. The young man flourished, undertaking groundbreaking research in the fields of electromagnetism and electrochemistry. In 1831, in the Royal Institution's basement, he discovered electromagnetic induction, the principle behind the electric transformer and generator. This discovery was crucial in turning electricity from a curiosity into a technology that would help shape the modern world. Faraday was also a brilliant lecturer and during his time at the R. I. he founded the Friday Evening Discourses and the Christmas Lectures, both of which continue to this day. His contribution is recognised by the Faraday Museum, which is located on the lower floors of the R. I. and includes Faraday's magnetic laboratory as it was in the 1850s.

Over the years the street has had many eminent residents, including the courtier and Great Western Railway chairman Major Victor Spencer, 1st Viscount Churchill (1864–1934), who was born at no. 32. Anne Lister (1791–1840) for a while lodged at no. 29, a rich Yorkshire landowner who travelled widely before dying in the Caucasus. Lister left extensive diaries, running to more than four million words and written in a code of her own design. Based on Ancient Greek and algebra, this was not finally deciphered until almost a century after her death and revealed intimate details of her sex life, which was shown to be exclusively lesbian. Whilst unusual at the time this was not a complete surprise: in 1834 she had claimed to have 'married' a wealthy heiress called Anne Walker, and, among her Yorkshire neighbours, Ms Lister was generally referred to as 'Gentleman Jack'.

Aldford Street

Formerly known as Chapel Street before being renamed after a village on the Duke of Westminster's Cheshire estate, Aldford Street was once home to the dandy's dandy, George Bryan 'Beau' Brummell (1778–1840). He lived at no. 18 before his lifestyle and spiralling debts forced him to flee to a lonely and demented death in northern France. The house at no. 23 also marks the sight of another historic flight, as it was from here that the sixteen-year-old Harriet Westbrook departed in 1811 when she eloped with the poet Percy Bysshe Shelley.

In 1945 the street was briefly home to John Gilbert Winant (1889–1947), a former governor of New Hampshire who became United States ambassador to the Court of St James's under President Franklin D. Roosevelt. Highly energetic in his pursuit of justice and truth – and by all counts a warm and pragmatic personality – Winant became a familiar figure on the streets of wartime London, offering comfort and aid to many of those affected by the air raids. The death of his friend Roosevelt hit him badly, however, financially and emotionally, and after resigning his post he moved to no. 7. Reportedly a broken man, within a few months he had decided to return to the US where he shortly afterwards killed himself. In 1982 it was decided to commemorate Winant's time in London and the positive impact he had made on so many Londoners' lives, with an official Greater London Council blue plaque.

MARY'S FIVE FIELDS
AND THE
DUKES OF WESTMINSTER

The Duke of Westminster's Grosvenor Estate is by no means Britain's largest private landowner – the Duke of Buccleuch's acreage is almost certainly twice the size – but it is certainly the most valuable. In large part this is due to the fortuitous marriage in 1667 of his ancestor Sir Thomas Grosvenor to 12-year-old Mary Davies. Mary brought to the marriage a parcel of land to the west of London that she had inherited from a great uncle, Hugh Audley. 'A loftily respectless and peremptory' lawyer, Audley was a City scrivener who lent money at a rate of interest and bought property with the proceeds. Mary's share was described at the time as 'five fields', most of it swampy meads or meadows.

Sir Thomas was already a substantial landowner, the family claiming descent from a Norman, Gilbert le Grosvenor, and then Robert le Grosvenor who received a grant of land in Cheshire in the 1170s from Hugh of Kevelioc, Earl of Chester. But over the next three centuries Mary's inheritance was to provide the foundation for the creation of a vast fortune and for what is now an international property empire owned and controlled by the family trusts of the 6th Duke. The family's social advancement was to be no less spectacular. In 1622 a baronetcy was conferred on Richard Grosvenor, MP for Cheshire, and the Earldom of Grosvenor created for the 7th Baronet Sir Richard Grosvenor in 1784. In 1831 his son, also Sir Robert, was elevated to the Marquessate of Westminster, and then in 1874 Hugh Lupus Grosvenor, the eldest surviving son of the 2nd Marquess, was made Duke of Westminster by his sovereign, Victoria.

In 1677, even so, Audley's Ela or Ebury estate had not been a particularly impressive possession, around five hundred acres of mostly very poor grazing land and much of it the haunt of footpads. The expansion of London helped change all that, but that it is now so valuable is largely down to the skill and management of the Grosvenor family, even though the descendants of Sir Thomas and the new Lady Grosvenor did little with it until development began in Mayfair in 1720s. Thereafter the 1st Earl Grosvenor obtained a special Act of Parliament (in 1826) to drain the remainder of the five fields and to develop the areas we now know as Belgravia and Pimlico. And while it is true that other aristocratic families similarly developed land close to the capital, and that many still own portions of this, none has come close to matching the Grosvenors' estate in terms of its scale, value and longevity.

The family base never moved from Cheshire, however, and the latest incarnation of Eaton Hall, the seat of the Grosvenors for more than five hundred years, still stands at the heart of a traditional rural estate of many thousands of acres. The family now has several other agricultural and sporting estates as well – in Lancashire, Sutherland and Spain – and a large international portfolio; but with its high rents and rocketing values London has long provided the power for the growth and prosperity.

The family's London acreage is even now what differentiates Major-General Gerald Cavendish Grosvenor KG from his fellow dukes, many of whom count themselves lucky to own a few thousand Highland acres even when, typically, these cost more money to maintain than they can ever earn back. But London too has been fortunate, for it is hard to imagine how else the charm of Mayfair might have survived – or the consistency of a planned neighbourhood such as Belgravia not been compromised – without a single, unified ownership structure with the wealth to take only the longest view, and the personal determination to see this through.

The sense of duty and the commitment to good stewardship of his estates is also evident in the current Duke's personal life. Gerald Grosvenor joined the TA as a trooper in 1970 and when he retired in 2012 – as a two-star major general and deputy-commander land forces – he had forty-two years of soldiering under his belt, making him by some distance the longest-serving member of that force. He is a tireless and highly effective campaigner for the TA and for the rights of his former colleagues, especially in assisting them with finding employment, an often difficult task given that a deployment of six months at a time is not uncommon. In 2011, the Duke spent more than £6 million on a 358-acre estate in the East Midlands, which includes a stately home called Stanford Hall, and plans to create a national rehabilitation centre on the site for wounded soldiers.

Berkeley Square

Still more picturesque than Hanover Square, and laid out on a more human scale than Grosvenor Square, Berkeley Square retains its charm despite the crass and unsympathetic monoliths that dominate two of its four sides. The land beneath the two-hundred-year-old plane trees in the rectangular central garden originally formed part of the estate of a Royalist commander in the Civil War, Lord Berkeley of Stratton (1602–78). The surrounding area was developed between 1700–37, initially not as a square at all, but with houses only on the west and east sides. This was done in order not to spoil the view from the Duke of Devonshire's mighty house on Piccadilly.

It is regrettable that today no early buildings remain on the east side and south sides, which now mostly comprise offices and car showrooms. On the western side a number of significant houses have survived, although none is any longer a private residence. In fact rising prices meant that Berkeley Square ceased to be residential in 1953, when the last private house was sold for £27,000. Ahead of this Sir Winston Churchill lived for a while at no. 48 whilst another prime minister, George Canning (1770–1827), occupied no. 50. The latter is now the premises of Maggs Bros., London's most august antiquarian bookshop (established 1853) and said to be the most haunted house in Mayfair. Canning claims to have witnessed strange goings-on in

Berkeley Square gardens

the house (a young woman is said to have thrown herself from the attic storey). At other times there have been reports of a white-clad figure and a malevolent brown 'mist', and any numbers of wagers involving people sleeping overnight on the premises, but nothing substantial since the bookseller occupied the building in the 1930s.

The victor of Plassey (an 1857 battle in India), Lord Clive of India (1725–74), lived at no. 45 in somewhat palatial surroundings for the mere son of a Shropshire squire; but then he had done well for himself and for his country. In fact his occupation was somewhat episodic: having shown the way for British rule in India, he spent a good deal of time there as the governor of Bengal and commander-in-chief of the Army. His wife Margaret remained in Berkeley Square, however, and the young Mozart is known to have played at her musical soirées. Returning here in later life Clive was accused of corruption and embezzlement, and though acquitted succumbed to depression and killed himself with laudanum in this house. For decades afterwards his descendants refused to consider marking the place with a commemorative plaque, but one was finally affixed to the building in 1953.

The house at no. 44, designed by the architect William Kent in 1742, was two hundred years later described by the architectural historian Sir Nikolaus Pevsner as 'the finest terraced house in London'. Few authorities have chosen to argue, and it is certainly the finest single building on the Berkeley estate. It was built for a royal maid of honour, Lord Burlington's niece Lady Isabella Finch, and its distinctive but restrained exterior gives little away to the outside world but for the heavily pedimented first-floor windows and the immense

Gibbs surround to the doorway. In fact it conceals a vast staircase of substantial grandeur and technical ingenuity, which rises through an interior of considerable magnificence. Horace Walpole thought this feature to be 'as beautiful a piece of scenery . . . as can be imagined'.

Unfortunately access has for many years been restricted to members and friends of the exclusive Clermont Club – the late Lord Lucan among them – which was founded by the gambler and zookeeper John Aspinall in 1962. For this Lady Isabella's bedroom, a tour de force by Henry Holland, was transformed into a baccarat room while a 'gothic' gazebo was built over the garden to serve as a dining room. The celebrated nightclub Annabel's opened a year later in its commodious basements, its founder Mark Birley being encouraged by Aspinall's belief that his high-rollers would appreciate somewhere to

Berkeley Square: the Clermont Club

party into the early hours. Birley's hunch proved to be correct because Annabel's has become arguably the most famous such establishment in the world, celebrating its fiftieth birthday in 2013. It is the only night-club to which the Queen has paid a visit during her reign, the occasion being a 2003 party, when she reportedly had a gin martini with no lemon. Annabel's has always been a haunt of the A-list celebrity and in the early days regulars included Frank Sinatra, Gregory Peck and Aristotle Onassis, while, more recently, even Mick Jagger agreed to put on a tie to gain entry. Its longevity has been astonishing and much credit goes to founder Robin Birley, who named it after his wife, Lady Annabel Vane-Tempest-Stewart, daughter of the Marquess of Londonderry. Birley, who died in 2007, helped give the club its exclusive, yet raffish, reputation. Membership lists are kept secret, photographers are persona non grata and members who are also journalists are lent on not to disclose what goes on there, the lack of information adding greatly to the mystique.

For more than thirty years, some one hundred properties in and around the square were owned by the BP pension fund, but the portfolio was sold to a Middle Eastern investor in 2001 for more than £300 million. BP had originally paid just £12 million.

Bolton Street

Documents dated 1696 show that the Duke of Bolton was seeking permission to lay new sewer pipes to what was then a semi-rural property he owned in this area. A decade later the street that takes his name still marked the western extremity of what was then London, meaning a visitor walking into the sunset would have encountered no more

buildings until he reached the outlying village of Knightsbridge. Today the street provides a typically Mayfair mix of office and residential use, with fragments surviving of the eighteenth-century streetscape although in many cases only the buildings' façades have been retained behind which extensive development and remodelling has taken place. In earlier times Bolton Street was home to two notable writers, Fanny Burney and Henry James.

Frances Burney (1752–1840) – otherwise Madame d'Arblay – lived at no. 11, a building now marked by one of London's earliest official plaques. (Under the auspices of the Royal Society of Arts this was installed in 1865. It is only the second such plaque for a woman after one put up in Baker Street to the actress Mrs Sarah Siddons.) Burney's success came early, very soon after the family moved to London from France, with her first novel, *Evelina*, being lauded by the likes of David Garrick and Samuel Johnson (and latterly Virginia Woolf, who called her the mother of English fiction). Well connected in both literary and social circles – for a number of years she was second keeper of the robes to Queen Charlotte – Madame d'Arblay moved here following the death of her husband in 1818. It was to be the first of four Mayfair houses she was to occupy before her death in 1840, and where most of her three-volume *Memoirs of Doctor Burney* was completed.

Moving to London in 1876, the great American novelist Henry James (1843–1916) took lodgings at no. 3 Bolton Street and while reportedly horrified by the 'uglinesses and hypocrisies' of England – and the 'deadly wooden-faced' mien of his own landlady – he chose to stay. The English, he felt, were every bit as greedy and grasping as the French yet lacked the 'grace to glaze it over'. Eventually, if somewhat grudgingly, the man of letters nevertheless admitted that he had taken 'possession of London; I felt it to be the right place' and this part of Mayfair was to remain his principal home for more than ten years.

Bond Street

Together comprising what is perhaps London's premier retail street, and unique among Mayfair thoroughfares in that they traverse the entire neighbourhood from top to bottom, the conjoined Old Bond Street and New Bond Street were built partly on land acquired by Sir Thomas Bond and his associates (see Albemarle Street) and to the north on a section of the Corporation of London's Conduit Mead estate.

Sir Thomas did not live to see the completion of the street which bears his name – the consortium actually went bankrupt before finding enough tenants – but he is today remembered as the supposed ancestor of the fictional James Bond. (The two men share a family motto: *orbis non sufficit*, the world is not enough.) Following his death the new street was described as lacking anything, architecturally speaking, of any real quality – and in that regard not much has changed. The address is certainly a prestigious one, and it is an expensive square on the Monopoly board; but its international fame and enduring status both depend almost entirely on the opportunity to shop. The buildings, surprisingly, are still largely nondescript, and the traffic quite appalling.

Admiral Nelson lived for a while at no. 147 and at no. 103, with his lover Lady Hamilton moving in later life into no. 160, by which time (1811) she was penniless and facing

imprisonment for debt. Sadly, the latter two buildings have been torn down and rebuilt, a fate shared by so much of the street. With its atmosphere so changed it is today impossible to picture Charles James Fox promenading here with the Prince of Wales (and winning a bet about whether the street's cats would prefer the sunny side or the shade).

The novelist Laurence Sterne (1713–68) died in his lodgings at no. 41, of consumption, having written at breakneck speed the first eighteen chapters of *The Life and Opinions of Tristram Shandy, Gentleman* but then slowed almost to a halt when early drafts fell on stony ground with his would-be publishers. Shortly afterwards the painter Sir Thomas Lawrence (1769–1830) moved into a studio at no. 24 and then to no. 29, when his appointment as painter-in-ordinary to His Majesty George III marked the beginning of a meteoric rise to the presidency of the Royal Academy. Samuel Johnson's celebrated biographer James Boswell is also known to have lived in the street, although like so many of those who moved on so soon after moving in it is no longer possible with any accuracy to identify the site of his lodgings. Others who remained here only briefly include Pitt the Elder, the lyricist of 'Rule Britannia' James Thomson and the historian Edward Gibbon, but again the buildings no longer stand.

We know about Guy Burgess, however. How he took flight to Moscow in May 1951 after a last visit to the Royal Automobile Club in Pall Mall – lunching with fellow traitor Donald Maclean, the relative anonymity of this large club would have suited both parties – and his leaving forever the pokey, three-room flat at 10 New Bond Street, which had been home since the 1940s. One can probably also guess what Churchill thought of him, the great man being depicted further down the street in *Allies*, a delightfully informal work by sculptor Lawrence Holofcener which shows him in animated conversation with Franklin D. Roosevelt who has joined him on a park bench.

Opposite the spy's former home, Asprey dates back to 1781, and since 1848 this luxurious emporium has occupied what was one of Victorian London's first iron-and-plate-glass buildings. In 2004 the premises were modified by architects Foster & Partners, the most striking feature being a large atrium with a sweeping spiral staircase linking the front and rear of the store.

Despite its worldwide reputation for high-quality retailing, many of the most interesting buildings on Bond Street are not shops at all, however, but offices, galleries and an auction house. At nos. 34–35 Sotheby's

dates back even longer than Asprey, to a sale of 'several hundred scarce and valuable books' in March 1744. This makes it the oldest auction house in the country, but very much a babe in arms compared to the bust of Sekhmet, an ancient lion-deity, which is mounted above its main entrance. Carved in diorite or black basalt, Sotheby's *Sekhmet* is thought to be the oldest privately owned monument in London. Carved in Egypt around 1320 BC, it is certainly its oldest outdoor sculpture. For well over a century its likeness has served as the company's unofficial mascot or muse, having arrived at the firm's old Wellington Street premises in the late 1800s as part of a fairly random collection of Egyptian artefacts consigned for sale. It was eventually knocked down for £40 but never collected, and after a while the orphaned goddess was informally adopted

Asprey, Bond Street

Sotheby's, Bond Street

by the staff and brought here when the company moved in 1917. Today few passers-by seem to notice it, but in 1966 it was the subject of a learned article 'The Bust of Sekhmet' which was published in *Ivory Hammer 4: the Year at Sotheby's & Parke Bernet*. The piece included a brief contribution from the young Bruce Chatwin (1940–89), at the time employed as a cataloguer for Sotheby's. As the late novelist and travel writer's first published work copies are now highly collectable.

With a screen of four panels by Henry Moore, the 1953 Time-Life Building on the corner of Bruton Street is a brutal five-storey addition by Michael Rosenauer (see Arlington Street, St James's) although the interior features work by the artist Ben Nicholson OM, Sir Hugh Casson and Sir Mischa Black, the creator of Westminster's now iconic street signage. Pevsner considered its Portland stone façade and marble plinth at the time to be 'uninspired, but acceptable'; and indeed its clean, uniform design has enabled it to mellow over the succeeding decades although the Moore panels are too high properly to be appreciated from the street.

The Fine Art Society at 148, a firm of art dealers although the name disguises this, has occupied the same building since 1876. The façade was modified by Edward Godwin five years later, but with its Venetian detailing and pillared entrance the building was designed expressly as a gallery where most such premises in Mayfair tend to be converted from houses and retail premises. It is generally accepted that the Society pioneered the concept of the one-man show, with an exhibition of Venetian sketches by Whistler in 1880.

Bourdon Street

Originally a narrow lane in the midst of a network of mews, stables and alleys serving the grand houses of Grosvenor Street, much of the charm of Bourdon Street depends on the survival of a number of Victorian structures on the north side, including St George's Buildings and the Grosvenor Buildings. Perhaps surprisingly, in an area that has never surrendered its reputation for exclusivity, both were built for working-class families and as such represent models of socially mixed housing which our own age has never come close to matching. Away from the noise and bustle of Davies Street it is also good to see that several of the older stables and coach-houses are still standing, albeit most of them now converted into bijou residences or to provide what could well be some of the most expensive private car-parking in the world.

Brook Street

The brook in question being the Tyburn, one of London's 'lost' rivers which crosses Mayfair at this point, Brook Street straddles the aforementioned Conduit Mead landholding and the Duke of Westminster's historic Grosvenor estate. Development began in the 1720s, the street shortly afterwards being described as 'for the most part nobly built and inhabited by People of Quality'. Today and in common with much of Mayfair (many of whose residents fled during the war and never returned) it is largely offices and hotels although a number of distinguished buildings can still be identified.

In 1968 Jimi Hendrix (1942–70) moved into a top-floor flat at no. 23, which he considered to be 'my first real home of my own'. Delighted to learn that it was next door to the former residence of the king's kapell-meister, George Frideric Handel (1685–1759), he is then said to have rushed out to buy a copy of the *Messiah*, elements of which have subsequently been identified as possible influences for some of his riffs. In fact in Handel's day nos. 23 and 25 would have been two halves of the same building, Handel paying £60 a year for the whole where Hendrix paid £30 a month for his small portion. Today the building is open to the public, London's Handel House Museum commemorating the great composer's near forty-year Brook Street tenancy, and his death in a bedroom on the first floor. It is by no means the only Georgian survivor, although much of the street was redeveloped in the 1850s.

Other survivors include no. 39, which the architect Jeffry Wyatt designed for himself and occupied from 1804–40. (As Sir Jeffry Wyattville he is best known for his substantial remodelling of Windsor Castle, a £1 million commission secured after beating Robert Smirke, John Nash and Sir John Soane in a fiercely fought competition.) Another architect Colen Campbell (1676–1729) – the Scot widely credited with popularising Classical forms in this country – built the house at no. 76 and lived in it for the last three years of his life. With the tragic demolition in 1824 of his greatest work (Wanstead House in Essex) he is today best remembered for *Vitruvius Britannicus*, an epic three-volume illustrated work setting out the essential principles on which it is said 'the whole of Palladianism in England was to depend'.

Nos. 66 and 68 were similarly designed and built by Edward Shepherd, of Shepherd Market fame, the latter being home to Pitt the Elder in the 1750s. Shepherd himself preferred to remain at no. 47 – occupied by another prime minister, Henry Addington, from 1787–90 – and during the Second World War no. 68 enjoyed a quite different lease of life when it became a secret spy training school for the new US Office of Strategic Services (oss).

In 1940 Benito Mussolini had joked that the Americans must have the best secret service in the world because no-one knew who was in it or where it was. In fact no such organisation existed until the formation two years later of the oss, which was at first based at 40 Berkeley Square but grew to occupy as many as a dozen buildings across Mayfair. Like the us Army, which in 1939 was reportedly smaller than Yugoslavia's, the service rapidly expanded and an estimated two thousand or more 'Oh So Secret' agents are thought to have passed through no. 68 during the course of just three years. Many would have been involved in producing so-called black propaganda, while others dropped by to be fitted for clothing and equipment needed for operations in occupied Europe.

Since the 1920s, 69 Brook Street has been home to the Savile Club, the opulent model for the pleasantly garrulous Greville in *A Handful of Dust*, a novel written by one of its members, Evelyn Waugh. Prior to this it was acquired by Walter Burns, the wealthy brother-in-law of American plutocrat John Pierpont Morgan. Knocked through to no. 71, which he also owned, in 1890 its interior was lavishly fitted out in the fashionable Louis xv style by the Paris-based Dutch architect W. O. W. Bouwens van der Boijen.

On 17 July 1945 a much smaller portion of Brook Street – suite 212, at Claridge's – was temporarily ceded to a foreign power in order that any child born to the wife of the King Peter II of Yugoslavia could legally be said to have been born on home soil. She was a guest at the hotel, and at his birth the new Crown Prince Alexander was duly declared a Yugoslavian citizen. It turned out to be a fruitless exercise: the following November, his father was formally deposed by the country's new constituent assembly rendering the ruse redundant. King Peter was one of several exiled monarchs who sought refuge at Claridge's during the war years, the hotel – London's oldest – having been considered an acceptable home-from-home for visiting royalty since 1860 when Empress Eugénie entertained Queen Victoria to tea here. The obnoxious King Zog of Albania may have preferred the newer, glitzier Ritz – and was rumoured to have paid for an entire floor using bullion stolen from the state bank in Tirana – but many other heads of state, including George II of Greece (who signed in as 'Mr Brown') Wilhelmina of the Netherlands, the Grand Duchess Charlotte of Luxembourg, Haakon VII of Norway and the president of Poland, found the quiet charm of Claridge's more to their liking. For the 1953 coronation the hotel was similarly honoured, and with the names of no fewer than fourteen crowned heads on its guest register it was said that anyone telephoning to the hotel and asking for His Majesty was met with the frosty response, 'Which one?' It is hardly surprising that Claridge's is sometimes known as the 'extension to Buckingham Palace'.

Claridge's, Brook Street

Commoners – albeit extremely wealthy ones, as the most expensive suites run to £7,000 a night – have also found Claridge's to their taste. It is especially popular with entertainers and everyone from Burton and Taylor to Mick Jagger and Lady Gaga have at one time or another walked through its hallowed portals. Pampering is an art form: any time Dame Barbara Cartland was on her way to tea the hotel asked her secretary to confirm whether she was wearing pink or turquoise so that her table could be laid in matching colours. More recently, when a Japanese pop star demanded a Jacuzzi in her suite the general manager replied 'It doesn't have a jacuzzi . . . but it will have in about four days,' a promise that of course was kept. It is no wonder that the great American actor, Spencer Tracy, once sighed, 'When I die I don't want to go to heaven, I want to go to Claridge's.'

Yet the hotel's origins were rather less grand. In 1812, James Mivart started a small boarding house at 49 Brook Street, selling it on in 1854 to William and Marianne Claridge, who owned adjoining property in Davies Street. Thanks to its uncompromising standards of service Claridge's prospered and expanded, and in 1893 was bought by Richard D'Oyly Carte, theatrical impresario and owner of the rival Savoy Hotel in the Strand. He promptly closed Claridge's for a year to allow for major refurbishment, introducing modern facilities such as lifts and walk-in bathrooms. That commitment to excellence was again evident in the 1920s, when the renowned architect and art deco pioneer, Basil Ionides, was commissioned to redesign the restaurant and several suites. In the 1930s his work was enhanced by British designer Oswald P. Milne, who is responsible for the magnificent art deco lobby with

its stunning black-and-white marble floor. Future modernisation projects were conceived to ensure that the art deco aesthetic was sympathetically maintained. More curious, perhaps, is the fact that the first ever demonstration of four-wheel-drive pioneer Harry Ferguson's famous 'little grey Fergie' – the TE20 tractor – took place at the hotel, in the less than demanding environment of its splendid ballroom.

Bruton Street

Developed in 1738 and named after the Somerset estate of the aforementioned Lord Berkeley, Bruton Street has a number of eighteenth century survivors (such as nos. 23–33) although, once houses, these now have shop fronts fitted at street level.

In April 1926 the house which then stood at no. 17 was occupied by the 14th Earl and Countess of Strathmore and Kinghorne. On the twenty-first of the month their daughter, then Duchess of York, gave birth to a girl, who was christened Elizabeth Alexandra Mary. A decade later (according to secret papers not released until 2003) Guy Marcus Trundle, an 'adventurer' and car salesman living at 18 Bruton Street, was under police surveillance as he was thought to be conducting an affair with Mrs Wallis Simpson. It was of course as a consequence of the latter's marriage to Edward VIII that the young Elizabeth Alexandra Mary was later to accede to the throne as Queen Elizabeth II.

The traveller and writer Lady Mary Coke (1727–1811) lived at no. 27 and was possibly born there, while the butterfly collector and pioneering entomologist Frederic Moore (1830–1907) is popularly supposed to have been born at no. 33. Unfortunately, as the building at the time formed part of a menagerie and museum run by the Zoological Society, this last claim sounds rather too good to be true.

Frequently finding himself pursued by creditors the dramatist Richard Brinsley Sheridan (1751–1816) was another resident of Bruton Street, as was the aforementioned George Canning. Unfortunately, changes in numbering, and the vagaries of history, mean it is no longer possible to identify precisely where either house stood. The location of the milliner's shop in the street has similarly been lost, where in 1769 Sarah Metyard and her daughter tied up a servant for three days until she starved and died of dehydration. Both eventually went to the gallows after the younger of them unwisely entrusted to friends the grisly details of what they had done.

Charles Street

On the corner with Hay's Mews, and originally known as the Running Horse, what became the longest pub name in London (and reputedly the second longest in England) the I Am The Only Running Footman was renamed in the 1770s by the 4th Duke of Queensbury in honour of a manservant who was said to be able to keep up a respectable eight miles per hour. Charles Street itself, with its unexpected kink and narrowing at the western end, is only slightly older than this, building work on this section of the Berkeley estate having begun around 1745. A number of houses and features date from that time, including nos. 10 and 16–18 on the north side, 39–41 and 48 on the south side, many of the attractive ironwork lamp-holders and the slender kerbside stone obelisks. Other buildings are more recent but still attractive, such as the home of the

English Speaking Union at no. 37, known as Dartmouth House, which dates from only 1890. It was formed from three smaller dwellings originally brought together for the banker 'Ned' Baring, 1st Lord Revelstoke (1828–97) who achieved the distinction of a name check in Gilbert and Sullivan's *Iolanthe*.

The ESU itself was established in 1918 by the newspaper editor and proprietor Sir Evelyn Wrench who sought to 'bring together and empower people of different languages and cultures' and it moved to its current home in Charles Street in 1926. A charitable organisation much concerned with debating and education, it received its royal charter in 1957 and now has sister organisations in more than fifty countries. It works, firstly, to foster education in the English-speaking countries of the world, and, secondly, to promote English as a shared international language. Sir Evelyn is also the founder of the Royal Over-seas League (see Arlington Street, St James's.)

From 1766–8 the prominent potter and industrialist Josiah Wedgwood rented a modest two rooms at no. 5 as his first West End showroom, and the writer and critic John Ruskin lived at no. 6 for a few months in 1853 while working on the third volume of his influential tome, *The Stones of Venice*. The 5th Earl of Rosebery was born at no. 20

English Speaking Union, Charles Street

in 1847, succeeding William Gladstone as prime minister less than fifty years later, but by far the most distinguished resident of the street was HRH the Duke of Clarence. In 1826 he was living at no. 22, and four years later came to the throne as William IV, 'the Sailor King'. When he died in 1837 he left eight surviving children but, as all were illegitimate, he was succeeded by his niece, Victoria.

Chesterfield Street

Until its demolition in 1937 Chesterfield House was one of the sights of Mayfair. It was also briefly home to royalty in the person of Mary, Princess Royal (1895–1967) following her marriage to the 6th Earl of Harewood. In 1747 its creator Philip Stanhope, 4th Earl of Chesterfield (1694–1773) had hinted at its magnificence in a letter describing how he was 'at present ruining myself by building a fine house . . . which will be finished in the French style with an abundance of sculptures and gilding'. Fronted by an immense colonnaded courtyard 177 feet by 94, the interior included marble columns and an enormous ceremonial staircase. This had been salvaged at great expense from Canons Park in Edgware, the vast palace which had earlier bankrupted the unfortunate 2nd Duke of Chandos whom George II described as 'a hot headed, passionate, half-witted coxcomb'.

Showing what were, in Stanhope's day, open fields to the west of London – deer were still being hunted in Hyde Park until 1768 – early prints of Chesterfield House

Chesterfield House, Chesterfield Street

Georgian terraces, Chesterfield Street

illustrate its relatively remote location. However, new developments in and around this part of Mayfair meant the Earl soon found the number of his neighbours growing, and the houses on the west side of Chesterfield Street would once have backed onto his lordship's garden.

The destruction of Chesterfield House was and remains a sad loss for London, although the street that bears its name is arguably one of Mayfair's least spoiled. Very little altered from the eighteenth century – it comprises two complete Georgian terraces, of brick not stucco – for such a central location it is also a surprisingly peaceful thoroughfare. Today it looks much as it must have done when Beau Brummell entertained his 'Dandiacal Body' of foolish acolytes at no. 4, and when W. Somerset Maugham lived at no. 6. It was while living at Chesterfield Street from 1911–19 that Maugham wrote

his most successful novel, *Of Human Bondage*, and contracted to marry the talented interior designer Syrie Wellcombe, daughter of the Barnardo's charity founder. Unfortunately it was also at this time that he began his long relationship with his lover, Gerald Haxton, with whom eventually he moved to France. The marriage failed.

Clarges Street

Once memorably described as a 'mountebank prototype-cast for the role of tippling lecher' the actor Edmund Kean (1789–1833) lived at no. 12 for almost a decade during which time he faced a charge of having a criminal conversation, a euphemism for an adulterous affair. The man he cuckolded sued him for £2,000 and won £800, Kean's love letters being read out in open court while, outside the building, chancers sold lewd ballads about a man who needed a woman before every performance and once had three before stepping onto the boards to play Richard III. Appropriately perhaps he later collapsed on stage (and subsequently died) with a line from *Othello* on his lips: 'Villain be sure thou prove my love a whore.'

In 1803 a rather different kind of rogue lived at no. 46, the politician Charles James Fox being such an inveterate gambler that his father once had to settle debts for him amounting to £120,000. Even with such generosity Fox nevertheless contrived to go bankrupt twice more, and by the end of his life was said to have lost £200,000 at the tables of St James's, equivalent to £20 million in today's terms. At other times residents of the street included Nelson's Lady Hamilton at no. 11 and at no. 3 the historian Thomas Babington Macaulay although by 1840 the latter had taken a set of chambers in Albany (see separate entry).

Clifford Street

Whilst St James's remains very much the heart of traditional clubland, the odd establishment has flourished north of Piccadilly, and arguably none more so than Buck's at 18 Clifford Street. The original home of the Naval and Military Club (see Piccadilly and St James's Square) the building itself is one of several splendid eighteenth-century survivors in the street. This was first laid out in 1719 on land acquired half a century earlier by the Earl of Burlington for his palatial home on Piccadilly. Nos. 4, 5, 8 and 9 on the north side are particularly fine – no. 7 has been demolished but was home to Henry Addington after his spell as prime minister (1801–4) – as are nos. 16, 17 and 18 on the opposite side of the street.

Buck's, Clifford Street

Occupying the last of these, Buck's was founded only relatively recently, an officer in the Blues (the Royal Horse Guards) deciding to establish a new club in London whilst fighting in France during the First World War. Assuming he was fortunate enough to survive the slaughter, Captain H. J. Buckmaster wished to create a place for 'officers of the Household Cavalry and their friends' to relax, somewhere which was less stuffy than the more traditional service clubs. He was also keen for it to have a cocktail bar, something that at the time was considered an innovation too far by many of the deeply conservative denizens of clubland.

His new home-from-home duly opened in June 1919, and was an immediate success. Today it is frequently considered to be the equal of the seventeenth- and eighteenth-century clubs of St James's Street – Boodle's, Brooks's and White's – at least in terms of its atmosphere, exclusivity and membership, if not the quality of its architecture. The cocktail bar was also a big draw in the early days, the club's barman – a McGarry or MacGarry – being credited with the invention of the Buck's Fizz as well as the Sidecar, a variation on the Brandy Daisy. PG Wodehouse clearly liked the atmosphere too, mentioning Buck's several times in his novels, and in part modelling Bertie Wooster's beloved Drones on it while ensuring that the fictional club also had a barman called McGarry. Evelyn Waugh produced another version of it for the page, again in *A Handful of Dust*, which this time he called Brat's, and he describes it as having been founded 'in the burst of bonhomie immediately after the war'. For his part the eponymous Buck lived in a flat upstairs and remained in charge until well into his eighties. The baton was only passed to the next generation in 1966 when he graduated to that other great club in the sky.

Conduit Street

As long ago as the fifteenth century, the City of London authorities had acquired land in this area in order to secure a supply of fresh water, and for the next three hundred years the Lord Mayor and his Corporation would regularly ride out to hunt hare and fox on either side of what is now Oxford Street. The hunt was a particular pleasure, to be enjoyed by the assembled company after an official inspection of the medieval pipe or conduit which gives the modern street its name.

9 Conduit Street

Traditionally, a banquet was held following the revels, for which the Corporation commissioned 'a good hansom room . . . for the receipt of their Lord Mayor and their Company, and for the hansom dressing of their meat'. This banqueting house survived until 1736 but by then was in a ruinous state. It was demolished and the site known as Conduit Mead used instead to graze cattle.

Development of the new residential street began shortly afterwards, although only three buildings survive from that era at nos. 42, 43 and 47. The finest building is slightly later, however. Once occupied by the British offshoot of Christian Dior and now the Sketch Gallery restaurant, no. 9 was designed by James Wyatt in 1779 for a prosperous

Lincolnshire MP. The narrow three-bay façade with its Tuscan entrance, arched and rusticated ground floor and giant Ionic pilasters is a surviving, early exercise in working with 'Higgin's cement,' a form of stucco. Some indication of its quality can be assumed from its use as an exhibition space for the (now Royal) Institute of British Architects before this crossed Oxford Street in 1966 and moved to new premises in Portland Place.

Charles James Fox was born in a house on this street in 1749, although it is no longer possible to determine its precise location, and in 1798 Colonel John Cockerell of the Bengal Infantry died in Conduit Street having disinherited his wife, the Indo-Portuguese Estuarta who is now thought to have been one of the first Asians to live permanently in England.

Cork Street

Another early eighteenth-century development on what had been the gardens of Burlington House, the name is derived from the earldom of Cork in Ireland, a subsidiary title belonging to the earls of Burlington. Now almost entirely occupied by shops and art galleries, none of the buildings is earlier than 1814 and most are Victorian or later. Galleries have increasingly become a feature of Cork Street as a consequence of its proximity to the Royal Academy. The first to open was the Mayor gallery in 1925, owned by the eponymous Fred Mayor, showing works by Klee, Miro and Paolozzi as well as homegrown talents such as Henry Moore and Paul Nash. Others quickly followed, such as the Medici gallery and the Waddington gallery, many of which have cooperated with each other to organise charitable and promotional functions such as the annual Cork Street Open Exhibition.

There is no doubt that today Cork Street is the leader in its field in Britain, perhaps even in Europe; for many it is to art what Savile Row is to tailoring. Its galleries continue to innovate and promote art, both foreign and domestic, by new and established artists. In recent years, for example, the Mayor has shown works by the likes of Warhol, Rauschenberg and Twombly, while the Medici mounts ten exhibitions a year. It is therefore alarming for the art collector and connoisseur that a proposed new housing development, mooted in 2012, might threaten the street's place at the heart of national culture.

For more than a decade from 1725 a house at no. 5 was occupied by the 1st Lord Masham and his wife Abigail, a close confidante of Queen Anne. She was also a cousin to Sarah Jennings, Duchess of Marlborough and the first and most formidable chatelaine of Blenheim Palace. She was thus able to observe at close quarters the gradual breakdown in the close relationship between duchess and sovereign, and able eventually to manoeuvre herself into a position where she could replace her cousin in Anne's affections and assume her role as Keeper of the Royal Purse. In 1739 the poet and satirist Alexander Pope was living at no. 7, but, like no. 5, this has been rebuilt at least once since his day.

Curzon Street

One of the main arteries of Mayfair, although with such substantial office developments (particularly at the Berkeley Square end) it is hard to credit that for more than a century the north side was largely open and comprised little more than the well-tended private gardens of Chesterfield House and Crewe House. The latter is still standing, and presents one of the most astounding sights in the whole of the west end. A vast Georgian mansion, complete with carriage drive and gate lodges, portico and porte cochère, its stucco front, bow windows and sweeping lawns would be impressive enough in a country setting. Here, in the heart of w1, they almost defy belief.

With Chesterfield House long gone, and Lansdowne House cruelly cut about (see Fitzmaurice Place), there is in fact nothing comparable to this anywhere in central London save, perhaps, Lord Palmerston's noble house, the erstwhile home of the Naval and Military Club at 94 Piccadilly. It is true that the slightly-too-pristine finish of Crewe's gleaming cream exterior can make the whole confection seem at times slightly dreamlike, even artificial, but while it looks like a film set, particularly at night when it is floodlit, the Marquess of Crewe's immense palace is most definitely the genuine, late-Georgian article.

It was built around 1730 by Edward Shepherd for himself, but in 1813 it was altered

Crewe House, Curzon Street

and extended for the 1st Lord Wharncliffe. The addition of columns, two attractive bow-fronted wings and a substantial central pediment meant the simplicity of Shepherd's original 'white garden house' was to some extent sacrificed to a more obvious idea of expensive Georgian grandeur. Today passers-by can even so marvel at its striking seven-bay front with its two-and-a-half storeys, and still get a reasonably good impression of how the most successful nineteenth-century magnates – and a very few of the richer aristocrats – would have lived during their months in town for the London season.

Unfortunately, and unlike the Wallace Collection's Hertford House in Manchester Square, Crewe House is emphatically not open to the public and so can be viewed only through the railings or from the pavement outside. Its future is at least in safe hands, however, as having survived a number of years with less sympathetic commercial and institutional owners – during the war it was home to the Ministry of Propaganda – in 1980 the freehold was acquired by King Fahd for the new embassy of the Kingdom of Saudi Arabia.

Not much else of Georgian Curzon Street still stands, although the graceful curve as it marches away from Park Lane is still an attractive sight. As well as nos. 18–23, the buildings at nos. 28, 29 and 30 are perhaps the finest survivors – the last named includes some remodelling by Robert Adam dating back to the 1770s – while nos. 47 and 48 date from around 1840.

Until 1899 Crewe House looked out over the infamous May Fair Chapel, in which many thousands of couples contracted semi-legal marriages under the auspices of Reverend Alexander Keith. Without banns read or licences issued, these ceremonies were controversial; anathema to the church authorities but still hugely popular. There were around seven hundred of them in 1742 alone, and Keith continued to officiate even after being excommunicated and imprisoned. But eventually the Marriage Act (1754) put his actions wholly beyond the law, although not before he had officiated at the marriages of the aforementioned 2nd Duke of Chandos (to a woman he had 'bought' from an allegedly abusive husband) and the 2nd Duke of Hamilton who was in such a hurry that his bride had to make do with a curtain ring in place of a real one.

Some distance away in the City of London, in quiet Frederick's Place EC2, official plaques commemorate the life of 'Edwin Waterhouse, Eminent Accountant' – nowhere but the Square Mile, you might think – and that of Benjamin Disraeli. The latter briefly worked there in the law but soon left to commence his political career when a lady acquaintance advised him in 1821 'You have too much genius for Frederick's Place – it will never do.' She was correct, of course, and after serving twice as prime minister, in 1868 and from 1874–80, 'Dizzy' eventually came to Curzon Street to die. In 1881 he spent his last night at no. 19, a house he had acquired with the royalties from his novel *Endymion*. Days before the street outside had been covered with straw in order that the passing horses would not disturb his final hours.

More recent deaths here include those of 'Mama Cass', aka Cass Elliot, of The Mamas and the Papas, and drummer Keith Moon of The Who. The pair died four years apart but in the same two-bed apartment: flat 12, 9 Curzon Place, which was at the time let to a third iconic musician, Harry Nilsson. (Curzon Street's other great rock connection, more cheerfully, is that until it was

closed down by the Marine Offences Act in 1967 the 'pirate' broadcaster Radio London was based at 17 Curzon Street where it was said regularly to draw an extraordinary twelve million listeners.) Other notable occupants of the street have included the novelist Nancy Mitford (1904–73) who spent three of the war years working at the bookseller G. Heywood Hill Ltd, which is still trading at no. 10, and the 1st Marquess of Reading who lived on the other side of the street at no. 32. Both buildings have official blue plaques.

Ordinarily, Miss Mitford's plaque would have been erected in Bloomfield Terrace, Maida Vale which is where she lived for much of the war; but such was the importance of the bookshop as an informal salon for writers of the period that the decision was taken to mount a plaque here instead. Regulars at the shop during Mitford's tenure included her great chum Evelyn Waugh as well as Anthony Powell, Osbert Sitwell and Patrick Leigh Fermor. Mitford herself earned £3 a week for her duties during the time that the shop's proprietor was absent on military service.

Rufus Isaacs, 1st Marquess of Reading (1860–1935) was an English jurist and politician, the first Jew to be appointed to the cabinet (Disraeli had Jewish parents but was baptised) and the last ever Liberal foreign secretary. He was subsequently appointed ambassador to the United States and Viceroy of India, one of his predecessors in this latter post being the first and last Marquess of Curzon, a skilled political entrepreneur whose eighteenth-century ancestor Nathaniel Curzon owned much of the land on which the modern street is built.

Frequently voted one of London's favourite cinemas, the Grade II-listed Curzon

Curzon Cinema, Curzon Street

Bourdon House, Davies Street

at no. 38 was built in 1934, originally as a single-storey building, but then reconstructed thirty years later by the firm of Sir John Burnet, Tait & Partners to incorporate an underground car park, shops and apartments above. Unusually, it has two royal boxes and two screens – the latter respectively among the largest and most intimate in London – and is still family owned. With a showing of *La Ronde* by Max Ophuls in 1950 it became one of the first cinemas in London to screen foreign-language films.

Despite its authentic Robert Adam detailing and exceptionally fine first-floor ballroom, the nearby Crockford's Club at no. 30 is not to be confused with the eighteenth-century original which was in St James's (see Chapter 2).

Davies Street

Named after Mary Davies, the heiress whose 1677 marriage to Sir Thomas Grosvenor provided the foundations for a valuable ducal estate, the street was laid out from 1720s onwards although little from that period now survives. Never grand, then as now most of the buildings were small scale

and intended for craftsmen and tradesmen. In the 1780s, the Grosvenors established a small market in the street but this was a rare failure in an area that is still to this day largely retail and commercial.

By far the most interesting building is also the oldest, Bourdon House being now a showroom for menswear retailer Alfred Dunhill but for much of its three-hundred-year history a handsome and detached residence with a rare walled garden. Built in 1725 it was subsequently extended and remodelled for 'Bendor' otherwise Hugh Grosvenor, 2nd Duke of Westminster (1879–1953) who retained it for his own use following the sale and demolition of Grosvenor House (see Park Lane). Whilst still comfortably accommodated in Mayfair, his descendant, the 6th Duke, chooses to keep a far lower profile.

Dover Street

One of Sir Thomas Bond's partners in developing Mayfair was a royal favourite and sometime MP for Bury St Edmunds: Henry Jermyn, 1st Earl of Jermyn (1604–84) one of whose subsidiary titles was Lord Dover. The street that bears this name today is busier than many in Mayfair, but retains some of its later, Georgian dignity in buildings such as nos. 25–27 on the east side. By far the most exceptional building, however, is Ely House at no. 37, which was built in a severe but attractive Palladian style for the Bishop of Ely in 1772. This move to Mayfair followed a decision to abandon the bishopric's historic London residence, a once vast complex of buildings off Holborn that it had occupied since the thirteenth century when a row with the powerful Knights Templars meant having to abandon riverside premises in the Temple.

The bishops of Ely remained in Dover Street until 1909, after which their splendid townhouse was taken over by the Albemarle Club. It joined the Arts Club (which, much changed, is still at no. 40) and the Bath Club at no. 34, where the ballroom of what had been the Marquess of Abergavenny's town-house was skilfully converted into a swimming pool. When the latter was badly damaged by enemy action during the war the club's members decamped to the Conservative Club in St James's Street – the combined entity was rudely nicknamed the Lava-Tory – but the Bath lost something in the move, haemorrhaging members and momentum and eventually closed.

At no. 37 the Albemarle fared little better. The club had recovered from the Queens-berry-Wilde scandal (see Albemarle Street above) but struggled for years before grinding to a halt in 1941. An attempt was made to revive it, and in the 1960s it was particularly popular among cricketers, with members including Peter May, Sir Len Hutton, Subbah Row and Colin Ingleby-Mackenzie, but this incarnation also collapsed. If recalled at all these days the place is remembered by clubmen of a certain age only for its morning 'mashie', an exceptionally potent pick-me-up

Ely House, 37 Dover Street

of gin, absinthe, egg white, lemon juice and distilled aniseed.

Elsewhere in the street development and redevelopment mean it is often impossible to say who lived where, but Dover Street residents are known to have included the diarist John Evelyn, the brewer Samuel Whitbread (1720–96) who at his death was said to be worth a million, and Fryderyk Chopin who relocated to London from France following the 1848 Revolution.

A few years earlier a former manservant called James Brown had opened his eponymous hotel at no. 23, a wonderful establishment that today spreads over a several elegant houses on the east side. As well as providing a cheeky shortcut through to Albemarle Street (where a later proprietor bought a rival hotel and joined the two together) Brown's Hotel has provided the backdrop to a number of intriguing historical events.

In 1876 a guest called Alexander Graham Bell made Britain's first successful telephone call – to the hotel owner who was a few miles away in west London. A decade later another guest, Theodore Roosevelt, left the hotel to walk to his wedding in Hanover Square before returning with his bride Eleanor and remaining at Brown's for the duration of the honeymoon. (Kipling did likewise, and is thought to have worked on *The Jungle Book* in a suite overlooking Albemarle Street.) In the 1930s, George II of the Hellenes began his long exile from Greece at the hotel before moving to Claridge's, and in another suite in 1941 the Dutch government-in-exile formally declared war on Japan.

Down Street

A pretty but undistinguished street running downhill into Piccadilly, for a short while during the war years Down Street played a pivotal role when one of London's so-called ghost stations was converted into a secure underground bunker for Winston Churchill. The distinctive ox-blood tiling (by Leslie Green) of the station entrance at no. 24 still marks it out today, although what was only a very short-lived stop on the Great Northern Piccadilly & Brompton Railway (now simply the Piccadilly Line) closed many decades ago.

When a second war with Germany seemed likely the disused station was commandeered, officially to provide a secure administrative headquarters for the Railways Executive Committee although it subsequently emerged that it was intended to house Churchill's wartime cabinet rooms. 'A considerable underground office in Piccadilly,' is what Sir Winston called it, 'seventy feet below the surface and covered with high strong buildings.' Reportedly his home for

Down Street station

forty days and nights, it was here that the PM chaired meetings in its deep bunker until the new, even more heavily protected Cabinet War Rooms beneath Storey's Gate enabled him to move back to Whitehall. What is commonly held to be Churchill's bathtub is still in situ, near the stairs at one end of the platform. Also a number of old telephones and other communications equipment, some of it for the London Midland and Scottish Railway and the remainder vital to prosecute Churchill's war against Germany and Japan.

Dunraven Street

In May 1840, at what was then 14 New Norfolk Street, a Swiss valet called François Courvoisier stripped off his clothes, crept into his master's bedroom in the dead of night and slit Lord William Russell's throat using Lord William's own razor. The crime was discovered the following morning, whereupon Courvoisier reportedly feigned surprise. When various missing items of household silver were discovered at a hotel near Leicester Square, and a link made between the valet and hotel staff, Courvoisier's fate was nonetheless sealed. Russell may have had a reputation as something of a martinet, but his status as a Member of Parliament (and brother to two dukes) meant the hapless foreigner was bound to hang. He duly did on the sixth of July the same year, outside Newgate gaol and before a frenzied crowd of some forty thousand.

The street was renamed in 1940 after Windham Thomas Wyndham-Quin, 4th Earl of Dunraven and Mount-Earl (1841–1926) a war correspondent, politician and sportsman who lived at no. 27. On behalf of the *Daily Telegraph*, Dunraven covered the Anglo-Abyssinian War in 1868, while sharing a tent with the explorer Stanley, and in 1871 he reported on the Siege of Paris. In 1919 he witnessed the signing of the Versailles Treaty, and between times found the leisure to win the 1893 America's Cup with his magnificent gaff-rigged cutter *Valkyrie II*. Unfortunately, this vessel sank barely a year later and when *Valkyrie III* failed to retain the cup in 1895 her owner caused a good deal of bad feeling by accusing the Americans of cheating.

At no. 17 a blue plaque records the intermittent occupation of the house by Mr and Mrs Pelham Grenville Wodehouse, the great 'Plum' and Ethel moving in and out of the undistinguished, late-nineteenth century neo-Georgian house several times between 1927 and 1934. Over this period he wrote ten books, most of them in his bedroom, including *Summer Lightning*, *Thank You Jeeves* and *Right Ho Jeeves*.

Farm Street

When the part of Lord Berkeley's estate known as Hay Hill Farm was built over in the mid-eighteenth century the name was neatly commemorated in Hay's Mews, Hill Street and Farm Street. Now thought exclus-ive, Farm Street was never especially smart, much of the development providing little more than stabling with accommodation for household servants above.

Today the buildings of most significance are Farm House and the Church of the Immaculate Conception, the latter an important component of twentieth-century Catholic life in central London, the former once home to a Hollywood starlet. For many years the English headquarters of the Society of Jesus or Jesuits, the church had its origins in the Catholic Emancipation Act of 1829, which, after a long hiatus, allowed Roman Catholics once again to build their own churches. A decade and a half after the Act passed the architect J. J. Scoles was commissioned to build a new house of worship in Farm Street, for which he chose a Decorated-gothic style modelled on the cathedral at Beauvais and inspired by Carlisle Cathedral.

With an altar designed by Pugin, communion rails of marble and lapis lazuli, and

Church of the Immaculate Conception, Farm St.

Venetian mosaics, the rich interior and traditional Jesuit teaching attracted a fashionable following among the Mayfair elite which in truth it still enjoys. The future Cardinal Manning received instruction in Farm Street, Evelyn Waugh was received into the Catholic Church here, and when Disraeli was dying he sent for one of the fathers (although in the event the priest arrived in Curzon Street too late). In the 1880s the Prince of Wales attended a requiem here for an Austria archduke, and when Lloyd George attended another mass he was ticked off by the sacristan for being inappropriately dressed.

Farm House, meanwhile, though never actually a farmhouse, is a pretty divergence from the more conventional architecture of this part of Mayfair. A somewhat laboured but nevertheless enjoyable half-timbered pastiche it is not quite as old as it looks, despite a mention in the deeds of a right of way that allows sheep to pass straight through its middle. In fact what we see now was substantially rebuilt in the early twentieth century, the creation of a Mrs Stakosch, who favoured a rural-Gothic style with some heavy panelling within. Happily she somewhere found genuine medieval doors and period fixtures to give her home an authentic feel and – while the original stone-flagged floors have since been covered up or removed – a century later it is hard not to enjoy the result. The impressive oak front door is carved both sides with the heads of the apostles, the oriel window is striking and the Jacobean internal doors all close against original linen-fold panelling.

Its most famous occupant is almost certainly Gloria Swanson (1899–1983) and in the 1970s a Carl Jasper mural was uncovered in the dining room depicting the lady in

Farm House, Farm Street

several of her films. In the 1920s the house was owned by Gloria Vanderbilt's twin, Thelma, Lady Furness, who enjoys the distinction of having been a mistress to the Prince of Wales until she made the mistake of introducing him to Wallis Simpson.

Fitzmaurice Place
Something of busy rat-run linking Berkeley Square to Curzon Street, Fitzmaurice Place was driven through only in the 1930s, a move that required a genuinely regrettable case of architectural vandalism. To make way for increased road traffic Fitzmaurice House was 'set back' by about forty feet, a quietly callous euphemism which conceals the fact that the front of this magnificent Adam mansion was brutally hacked off and a new façade attached to the remaining portion. In order to achieve this, the dining room was dismantled and is now in New York's Metropolitan Museum, and the principal drawing room was similarly dispatched to the Museum of Arts in Philadelphia. More of the interior was simply discarded, and the building eventually sold to the Lansdowne Club which still inhabits what remains.

A picture dating from before the Great War shows what has been lost, a magnificent

Lansdowne Club, Fitzmaurice Place

Palladian house of seven bays with two wings of three. As late as 1908 this could still be described as 'secluded', so extensive were its private railed gardens at the foot of Berkeley Square. Adam's client for what is now sadly become just 9 Fitzmaurice Place had been the fabulously rich Marquess of Bute (1713–92). This country's first Scottish prime minister, he withdrew from London and sold the (unfinished) house after accusations that he was building it using the proceeds of public office. The buyer was William, Earl of Shelburne who renamed the house after himself when he was created Marquess of Lansdowne.

The price sounded steep at £22,500, although it was said that the hapless Bute was selling at a loss. The new owner continued to pour money into it, however, commissioning Joseph Bonomi to create a new library which was later remodelled by George Dance the Younger and then again by Sir Robert Smirke. Today it is stylistically one of the club's more successful rooms, much of the remainder having been remodelled in 1935 in the then-fashionable Art Moderne style by White Allom, the firm responsible for the interiors of the great Cunard liners RMS *Queen Mary* and RMS *Queen Elizabeth*.

Like Bute, Shelburne served a term as prime minister, and is today commemorated by a blue plaque at this address. So too is the celebrated store owner Harry Gordon Selfridge (1858–1947) who leased the house from 1921–9 while conducting a somewhat scandalous affair with two Hungarian-American cabaret artistes called the Dolly Sisters. His lifestyle as the great house's last tenant was extravagant in the extreme, an epitome of pre-war partying, and after spending freely for years on fleets of Rolls-Royce cars, racehorses and country houses, Selfridge eventually slipped into debt. He lost control of his retail empire and died a poor man in a small flat in Putney.

Grafton Street

Essentially an L-shaped extension to Dover Street, Grafton Street marks the southern extremity of the City of London's old Conduit Mead estate. In 1723 a portion of this was acquired by Charles Fitzroy, 2nd Duke of Grafton (1683–1757) and those of his neighbours keen to prevent any new building compromising the views from their townhouses. By 1771 the 3rd Duke had decided to develop the land himself, however, and nos. 3–6 with their substantial stone door-cases and Tuscan columns are survivors of his scheme (nos. 4 and 5 still have the arms of the City Corporation on their facades).

Across the road, nos. 21–23 are smaller and later buildings, mid-Georgian, but with Venetian windows on the first floor nevertheless highly attractive adornments to what is now a street of shops and offices.

A blue plaque on the side wall of Asprey (see Bond Street) commemorates the life of John Henry Brodribb, a Somerset man who found fame in London treading the boards as Sir Henry Irving (1838–1905). An associate of Ellen Terry and Bram Stoker, Irving moved into a first and second floor flat at 15a after separating from his wife. She had never shown anything but contempt for his chosen profession, and without her he reportedly lived a typical bachelor existence, in (as one visitor put it) a 'perfect example of the confusion and neglect of order in which the artistic mind delights'.

Green Street

Named after a jobbing builder who died after falling down a well, and in the early days not at all a fashionable place to live, Green Street forms part of the Duke of Westminster's Mayfair estate. It was first laid out between 1720 and 1760, although Hampden House at nos. 60–61 is the only survivor from this period. The most remarkable building in the street is somewhat newer, however, no. 32 having been designed in 1897 for the 4th Lord Ribblesdale. The architect was Sidney Smith (no relation of Revd Sidney Smith, who also lived in Green Street for a time) and it was for many years the Brazilian embassy until its sale in 2013 to a developer for a reported £40 million.

Ribblesdale was a man whose aristocratic mien so impressed the Prince of Wales that in 1890 he prevailed upon John Singer Sargent to paint his now celebrated full-length portrait. Thereafter the future Edward VII nicknamed him 'the Ancestor', the *New York Times* on Ribblesdale's death in 1925 likening his lordship to 'a particularly fine type of British aristocrat, blending in appearance and bearing the modernity of this century with all that was courtly and gracious in the Victorian period'. A master of buckhounds, he was sadly left without an heir following the death of both his sons, one in the Somaliland expedition of 1904 and the other at Gallipoli.

William Blake lived at no. 23 in the early 1780s, and from 1934–40 the house at no. 46 was occupied by Thomas Octave Murdoch Sopwith (1888–1989), more commonly just 'Sir Tommy' and a notable aviation pioneer and aircraft builder. Haunted by a family tragedy – as a child he had accidentally

32 Green Street

43

discharged a shotgun killing his own father – Sopwith was an international ice-hockey player before discovering the joys of flight.

His first venture, the Sopwith Aviation Company, produced upwards of eighteen thousand aircraft for Britain and her Great War allies, including the superb Sopwith Pup and the charismatic if demanding Camel. By 1934, after being declared bankrupt, he had taken the helm of Hawker Aircraft Limited, joining forces with test pilot Harry Hawker and later merging with the Armstrong Siddeley automotive group. With a new war against Germany he rode to his country's aid once again, the company's outstanding Hurricane never quite matching the emotional appeal of the Spitfire but seeing action in literally every theatre from 1939–45 and accounting for a far greater proportion of kills during the Battle of Britain than its Supermarine rival.

Grosvenor Square

This square is very much the heart of the Duke of Westminster's Mayfair estate, and the centrepiece of an immense development which by 1891 had led to suggestions that the Grosvenors were now to be considered the richest family in Europe. For a long while it had a reputation as the grandest address in Mayfair – meaning, conceivably, in the whole of London – and until well into the twentieth century more than half of householders on the square were titled.

The square itself is enormous, second only to Lincoln's Inn Fields, and so were the houses, which, in the 1720s, boasted five or even seven bays and were selling for as much as £7,500. From its inception until 1939 it sat at the epicentre of London society, its houses chiefly occupied only during the par-

liamentary season (winter and spring) with owners retreating to their country estates for the remainder of the year. Today, sadly, only three houses predate 1900 and with much of the square now flats and hotels (and at the time of writing the entire west side still taken up by Eero Saarinen's American embassy) it is hard to get a flavour of the eighteenth-century original.

In part due to the square's repeated redevelopment there is only one blue plaque, as it happens to another aviation pioneer and manufacturer. For the last decade of his life Sir Frederick Handley-Page (1885–1962) kept a flat in a 1930s building at no. 18, and died there at the age of seventy-six. The square has another aviation connection too, namely a memorial to the Eagle squadrons of fighter pilots who crossed the Atlantic as volunteers before America joined the Second World War.

To the delight of many who enjoy Mayfair, Saarinen's aforementioned embassy building is now scheduled for demolition and is likely to be replaced by more residential and hotel accommodation. Stylistically, it was never well-suited to its site, being too short to fill one side of the square and entirely out of keeping with the other four sides. Whilst a reasonably strong design on a bomb-damaged site (the Portland-stone facing is merely decorative) it also somehow lacks the necessary authority and gravitas. Were it instead a few hundred yards to the north it could readily be mistaken for one of several Oxford Street department stores, and even now it lacks the self-confidence and sense of certainty that is seen in other Saarinen pieces such as the St Louis arch and his technical-centre building for General Motors in Warren, Michigan.

The presence of the embassy has seen this

part of Mayfair nicknamed either Little America or Eisenhower Platz and with good reason. It is true that in the 1960s Londoners celebrated the triumph of London's pigeons over the vast gold eagle mounted on Saarinen's unsympathetic behemoth – it needs frequently to be cleaned of droppings – but the 'special relationship' between our two countries is nevertheless seen to good advantage in and around the square. In the centre of the gardens stands a statue of one president – Franklin Delano Roosevelt, a rare honour for a foreigner – whilst another, John Adams (1735–1826) is known to have lived at no. 9, one of the surviving houses but now radically altered. In 1942 a third moved into the building now occupied by no. 20. As supreme commander of the Allied Forces in Europe, Dwight D. Eisenhower used the square as his headquarters when planning and implementing Operation Torch, the invasion of North Africa ('Ike', as he was invariably known, is also commemorated a by a statue here as the photograph shows). The presence of the American embassy has also, inevitably, made Grosvenor Square the focus of demonstrations by a plethora of anti-war and anti-nuclear campaigners; with perhaps the most celebrated such event occurring in 1968, as the associated panel shows.

As befits such a prestigious address Grosvenor Square has been referenced in a number of literary works, including *Pride and Prejudice*, several Oscar Wilde plays – *The Importance of Being Earnest*, *An Ideal Husband* and *Lady Windermere's Fan* – and Charles Dickens's *Little Dorrit*. More surprising, however, is the lyric to the song 'Scarlet Begonias' by the Grateful Dead, the protagonist of which, in another nod to Little America, is recorded as 'walkin' 'round Grosvenor Square'.

Finally no. 39 (now demolished) was the venue for a dinner in February 1820 at which Prime Minister Lord Liverpool expected to sit down with his entire cabinet. Knowing this a plan was hatched by a group of anarchists to assassinate them during the dinner, but this was foiled and the following May – after first being hanged – five of the so-called Cato Street Conspirators enjoyed the dubious distinction of being the last criminals to be publicly beheaded in London.

Eisenhower statue, Grosvenor Square

45

THE SIEGE OF GROSVENOR SQUARE

Modern London is well used to political demonstrations and marches of all kinds, many of them violent like the poll-tax riots of 1990 in Trafalgar Square. However, in 1968, such lawlessness was relatively rare and it therefore came as a shock to the British public when a demonstration outside the American embassy saw police officers being attacked by protestors. It had all started so peacefully that March morning when a crowd of around ten thousand gathered in Trafalgar Square to protest about Britain's support for America's war in Vietnam. Many luminaries of the left were present, including a young Tariq Ali and actress Vanessa Redgrave, who had flown in from Rome to add her voice to the throng. The demonstration in London was part of a whole series of such events across the West, as students, left-wing groups and peace campaigners came onto the streets in huge numbers. The good humour of the marchers did not last for long. As the demonstration snaked up to Grosvenor Square, violence erupted. Stones and clods of earth from the garden in the square were lifted and used as missiles against police lines, while others hurled firecrackers and smoke bombs. Fighting erupted, resulting in many officers and demonstrators being taken to hospital. Despite the best efforts of a thousand of London's finest to keep the situation under control, they were pinned back by the sheer weight of numbers and the protestors, after a siege that had lasted nearly two hours, were now within a hundred yards of the embassy.

Fearing that the situation might get completely out of control, resulting in the embassy being breached, senior officers ordered the mounted units to charge. As the horses galloped across the square the demonstrators threw not only firecrackers and smoke bombs but also thunder-flashes. Amid the confusion, however, it soon became clear that the decision to charge was the right one. Gradually, order was restored and the square cleared of protestors. The panic was over.

The country, however, had had a rude awakening. In a statement to the House of Commons, James Callaghan, at that time home secretary, deplored the violence and noted that 246 demonstrators had been charged, with 117 police officers and 45 demonstrators receiving medical treatment. He took the view that the police had 'showed considerable restraint and self-discipline in the face of severe provocation'. Callaghan caught the mood of the public well because there is no doubt that the sympathy of most people was with the authorities: *The Times* reported that many people had phoned Scotland Yard expressing their support for the police.

Many MPs were worried about the co-ordination of the violence by extremists, many of whom, they believed, were foreign. There is certainly something in this and several papers reported that radical student leaders from Germany, France and Holland had been at the demo. Others were concerned about the increasing militancy among British university students, noting that the Grosvenor Square debacle had come just twelve months after the famous sit-in at the London School of Economics, the purpose of which was to secure more power for students in the counsels of the university.

There is a quite charming footnote. The children of St Chad's primary school in Birmingham put together a special book, illustrated by themselves, as a tribute to the brave police officers. The children, who were all aged between five and seven, also enclosed ten shillings they had collected and asked Sir Joseph Simpson, commissioner of the Metropolitan Police, to buy sugar lumps for the horses. In their letter the pupils said 'they were sad and angry with the cruel people who hurt our policemen and horses in London yesterday'.

Grosvenor Street

While Eisenhower was active in Grosvenor Square his countrymen were busy in nearby Grosvenor Street, establishing the afore-mentioned Office of Strategic Services as the wartime predecessor to the CIA. The OSS at that time had its headquarters at no. 70, although it quickly spilled over to fill at least eight other central London addresses. At the back of no. 70, for example, was a secret print shop that produced false papers for agents crossing into occupied Europe. The agency took the unusual step of recruiting only legi-timate engravers, doing so on the grounds that convicted forgers were by definition failures. It was nevertheless said that even this honest crew never lacked for a cigarette as they soon became adept at forging ration stamps during their spare time. More legit-imate documents were artificially aged by being worn under the armpit and trampled underfoot on the office floor.

Entirely rebuilt, no. 70 is now the head-quarters of a quite different organisation, namely the Grosvenor Group, the Duke of Westminster's large and highly successful property-development company. The loca-tion for such an important part of his inher-itance is perhaps only to be expected, His Grace having chosen a prime site on what in

Grosvenor Group offices,
70 Grosvenor Street

the 1730s was described as 'a spacious well built street, inhabited chiefly by People of Distinction'.

At that time the street would have been entirely residential, and more uniform than today when only approximately twenty of the original seventy-four houses survive in some form. Unsurprisingly, none is any longer a single residence, but a brief résumé of the occupants of just one house gives one a good flavour of who those 'People of Distinction' were. Built in July 1725, and last altered during the Great War, 33 Grosvenor Street was at different times home to Baron Sparre, the Swedish envoy, a son of 3rd Earl of Sun-derland, the 1st Marquess of Stafford, the 1st Earl Spencer of Althorp, the 8th Earl of Northampton and a Dowager Duchess of Beaufort, the 7th Earl of Chesterfield, the 8th Viscount Doneraile, a daughter in law of the 5th Duke of Richmond and Lennox, the 7th Baron Rodney, Princess Hatzfeldt (for-merly Miss Clara Huntington of Detroit, Michigan) and, finally, the 6th Earl Cadogan who moved out in 1928.

In 1824 *The Asiatic Magazine* reported that a new members club was opening at no. 16 for members 'of rank and talent connected with our Eastern empire' many of them business-men or 'boxwallahs' rather than officers of the East India Company or in the army. (Called the Oriental Club it subsequently moved to Hanover Square, where three pet hedgehogs were put on the staff to control a plague of black beetles in the kitchen, and then to its present home on Stratford Place.) For more than twenty years another club, the Sesame at 49 Grosvenor Street, provided a somewhat eccentric home for poet and critic Edith Sitwell, while the Casanova Club, a 1960s casino at no. 52, was a popular haunt of Princess Margaret and her set.

The street also has a couple of official blue plaques, to an actress and a film producer. Few now remember the name Anne Oldfield (1683–1730) but she lived at what is now no. 60 for the last five years of her life. Prior to this she had become one of the leading ladies of the early-eighteenth-century theatre, joining the Drury Lane company aged sixteen at the recommendation of the architect-dramatist Sir John Vanbrugh and appearing in more than one hundred plays. Accorded what at the time was the unique distinction of a burial in Westminster Abbey, the actress was also the mistress of General John Churchill whose son later took on the property. Now only its façade remains.

Across the street nos. 21–22 was the workplace of Sir Alexander Korda (1893–1956) the celebrated Hungarian-Jewish director and producer. As a young man he made films in his native country as well as in Germany and Hollywood, but he was at his most fruitful after relocating to Britain in the 1930s. Soon after arriving he built Denham Studios in Buckinghamshire, said at the time to have had the best facilities in Europe, and he was knighted in 1942 for his film work and an important undercover role with British intelligence services during the early years of the war.

Half Moon Street

Running from the Third Church of Christ, Scientist on Curzon Street into Piccadilly – and immortalised in a film of the same name based on Paul Theroux's short novel *Doctor Slaughter* – Half Moon Street has for so long comprised apartment blocks, hotels and offices that it is no longer possible to say with certainty where many of its former residents lived. A number of fine Georgian houses still

stand, however, including an attractive range at nos. 7–15, and nos. 14 and 26, which have elegant Regency additions. One can only guess in which of them Sapper's Bulldog Drummond and Bertie Wooster were supposed by their creators to live; where James Boswell lodged in 1768; and which house was home to the scandalous Lola Montez in 1849. A famous 'Spanish dancer' in Victorian England (but actually Irish, and born Eliza Gilbert) Montez had affairs with Franz Liszt and Ludwig I of Bavaria before contracting a bigamous marriage to one George Heald. He fortunately died almost immediately, thus saving her from prison but doing nothing to rescue her reputation.

Hanover Square

Laid out shortly after the accession (as George I) of the Elector of Hanover in 1714, the square therefore predates both Berkeley and Grosvenor. The landowner was the 1st Earl of Scarborough, a staunchly Whig supporter of William III whom he had fought for at the Battle of Boyne. Today the square is noisy and much changed from when the Earl first began selling leases here in 1717, although a few Georgian houses still stand including nos. 16, 20 and 24. The sociable French statesman Prince Talleyrand (1754–1838) was living at no. 21 in 1835, and always a popular figure around town was accorded the honour of a personal handrail on the staircase at the Travellers' Club in Pall Mall when his health began to fail. (This is still in place.)

Two buildings in particular made the square more than usually fashionable: the church of St George at the southern end and the Hanover Square Rooms at no. 4. The latter were the creation in 1775 of the Swiss-

Italian Sir John Gallini, a series of concert rooms in which J. C. Bach, Josef Haydn, Felix Mendelssohn, Hector Berlioz, Niccolò Paganini, Franz Liszt and Gallini himself performed before their closure in 1900. The Mayfair parish church of St George Hanover Square was no less fashionable, a Commissioners' church built in 1721–5 by John James – one of Wren's assistants – on a plot of land given by General William Steuart.

It is now thought to be the first church in London to have a classical portico, in this case with six mighty Corinthians columns. Completed at a cost of £10,000, its design and corner site posed a number of problems and the conjunction of a short square tower

St George church, Hanover Square

and what is stylistically a Roman temple is perhaps not entirely successful. The Maddox Street façade is however particularly handsome and strong, and the interior a delight with its Grinling Gibbons reredos framing a 1724 *Last Supper* by William Kent, and an east window of four-hundred-year-old Antwerp glass. The two dogs sheltering under the coffered portico ceiling are thought to be by Sir Edwin Landseer.

Among the many aristocrats and society figures who married here mention should be made of Theodore Roosevelt, Samuel Parkes who won a Victoria Cross during the Charge of the Light Brigade, and the architect John Nash. Lady Hamilton also tied the knot at St George's, as did the poet Shelley, Benjamin Disraeli and George Eliot, and Herbert Asquith with another five prime ministers in the congregation. George Frideric Handel was a regular worshipper in the church during his long years in London (see Brook Street), and Boswell in his diary for 1762 admits to having paid less attention than he might to the service because the Duchess of Grafton 'attracted his eyes too much'.

Hertford Street

Once fashionable but now largely offices, narrow Hertford Street dates from around 1760 and still contains a number of good early houses, including nos. 10–13, 17–19, 36–39 and 45–46. The first of these includes interior work by John Adam (1721–92) and unusually it has two blue plaques: one to a soldier; the other to the dramatist Richard Brinsley Sheridan (1751–1816). The soldier, General John Burgoyne (1723–92) was also something of a dramatist and whilst serving as commander-in-chief of Ireland penned a number of plays that were staged by David Garrick. Like those of the most famous soldier-dramatist Sir John Vanbrugh these are rarely performed these days, but they were successful at the time with Horace Walpole describing *The Heiress* as 'the best modern comedy'. Aged seventy, Burgoyne died in the house after an enjoyable evening at the theatre, suddenly and quite unexpectedly. He left behind five children – four of them illegitimate – one of whom followed his father into the army, rose to the rank of field marshal and lived long enough to see his own son awarded the Victoria Cross after an action in the Crimea.

Sheridan moved into no. 10 some three years after Burgoyne's abrupt passing. Recently remarried to 'Hecca' Ogle, he stayed in Hertford Street for nearly seven years. During this period he wrote *Pizarro*, established himself as a leading Whig and a famously good parliamentary orator, and steered the Theatre Royal Drury Lane through what is now acknowledged to have been a golden period for stagecraft in London. His attempts to manage his own finances were markedly less successful, however, and in 1802 bailiffs arrived at Hertford Street and not for the first time Sheridan was forced to move on.

Hill Street

Always one of the better streets in an exceptional area, in 1900 the visiting writer and caricaturist Max Beerbohm admitted that a stroll down Hill Street was all it took to make him feel 'very well-bred . . . and though not clever very proud'. Development of this part of the Berkeley estate began in 1745, and particularly towards Berkeley Square where elegant fanlights and wrought-iron balconies proliferate one is still left with a good

impression of Mayfair's mid-eighteenth-century streetscape. This is so even though little if anything remains except in somewhat altered form, with externally at least no. 36 perhaps the best surviving house.

Substantially remodelled for a law firm, nos. 29–31 is the former home of the Georgian bluestocking and arts patron Mrs Elizabeth Montagu (1718–1800) although only a few decorative features survive from her time. In the 1770s the house was a leading salon, regular members of Mrs Montagu's circle including many literary, artistic and dramatic luminaries such as Samuel Johnson, Sir Joshua Reynolds, Edmund Burke and David Garrick. Another member, Horace Walpole, was already well established but protégées of this formidable hostess were to include Fanny Burney (see above), Hannah More, Anna Barbauld and Sarah Fielding. Delighted to find she was distantly related to the novelist Laurence Sterne (see Bond Street) Mrs Montagu also offered to look after his personal papers when he fell ill.

The Whig anti-slave-trade campaigner and sometime Lord Chancellor Henry Brougham, later Lord Brougham and Vaux (1778–1868) lived at no. 5. Though not especially rich – until he found a rich widow to marry, his north-country estates extended to little more than two thousand acres – Brougham had a sharp intellect, a quick wit and a legendary ego. Sometimes addressing the Commons as many as three hundred times in a single session, he still holds the record for the longest speech ever delivered in the House after remaining on his feet for six hours on 7 February 1828. Somehow he also found time to design the four-wheel horse carriage which still bears his name, to publish a number of learned papers on light and colour through the Royal Society and to engage in more popular journalism, which he used to support his lively private life. (When the latter attracted the attention of the scandal-monger Harriette Wilson he quickly paid up to secure his anonymity in her *Memoirs*, unlike the Duke of Wellington who famously told her, 'publish and be damned'.)

Hill Street also has two delightful maritime connections. These are the modest but friendly Naval Club at no. 38, and no. 6 at the corner of Hill Street and Berkeley Square, which, until his execution for 'failing to do his utmost,' was home to the ill-fated Admiral John Byng. In happier times Byng (1704–57) had installed a device at the house which by a system of rods, cams and pulleys linked a dial downstairs to a weather vane on the roof, thereby indicating the wind direction at all hours of the day. In this way Admiral Byng could estimate the likely progress and direction of the fleet, or indeed the enemy.

Unfortunately, after the loss of Minorca to the French in the Seven Years War, the hapless Byng was relieved of his command and court-martialled. Found guilty he was then shot by a firing squad on board his own ship, HMS *Monarch*, in order – as Voltaire put it – *pour encourager les autres*. Although the charge was one of personal cowardice and disaffection, and carried a mandatory sentence of death, George II could have used

The Naval Club, 38 Hill Street

his royal prerogative to prevent the sentence being carried out. In the event – after a good bit of political manoeuvring, much of it designed to protect Admiralty interests – His Majesty chose not to and Byng died at the hands of his own marines.

Hyde Park Corner

London's most handsome roundabout is dominated by what at various times has been known as the Wellington, Constitution and occasionally even Green Park Arch. (Even with these three names Decimus Burton's 1828 design still gets mistaken by tourists for Marble Arch at the other end of Park Lane.) It was intended as a ceremonial entry to the Iron Duke's Apsley House before increasing traffic levels required its removal to its present island site in 1883.

Originally it was topped by a mighty bronze by sculptor Matthew Cotes Wyatt and his son, depicting the old soldier on his favourite horse Copenhagen. More than thirty feet high and weighing in excess of forty tons this was unfortunately so ugly that on seeing it a Frenchman reportedly declared '*Nous avons été vengé*' ('we have been avenged'). Even Queen Victoria thought it an eyesore and agreed it should be removed, but she sensitively suggested the operation should wait until Wellington was dead. In 1883 it was taken down and carted out to Surrey where, in the opinion of the Prince of Wales, its erection in Aldershot would be 'highly regarded by the Army'.

Its replacement was another, smaller bronze of the Duke, and a second, *The Angel of Peace Descending on the Quadriga of Victory*. Created by Adrian Jones and more commonly called the Quadriga, this is widely regarded as one of the most successful and elegant groups of

*Wellington, or Constitution, Arch,
Hyde Park Corner*

its sort in the country. The cost this time was met by Herbert Stern, 1st Lord Michelham, who presented it in 1912 in memory of his friend Edward VII. His own son provided the model for the figure, a winged representation of 'Peace' pulling at the reins of the four spirited horses, inside one of which the sculptor famously hosted a dinner for eight upon the completion of his masterwork.

Apsley House, happily, still stands, and is open to the public although the Iron Duke's descendants retain a private apartment in the building. The presence here of the Wellington Museum makes its affiliation to the great man clear, although the house was originally constructed by Robert Adam in the 1770s for Lord Chancellor Apsley (1714–94). In 1807 it was acquired by Wellington's brother although financial difficulties forced him to sell it to his sibling ten years later. Shortly after this it was enlarged and given a new facing of Bath stone and a Corinthian port-

Apsley House, Hyde Park Corner

ico by Benjamin Dean Wyatt. Curiously, the interior is largely French in style, and at the foot of the main staircase Napoleon, naked, is depicted as 'Mars the Peacemaker' by the sculptor Antonio Canova. In Wellington's day, before the later rerouting of Park Lane, the house stood at the end of Piccadilly and as the first house passed by anyone approaching the capital from the west it soon became known as 'No. 1 London'. Strictly speaking it is 149 Piccadilly, although it is now quite isolated on an island site.

Marble Arch

Designed by John Nash, Marble Arch too has been moved from its original position. In 1827, the £10,000 structure was made to stand in the courtyard in front of Buckingham Palace beneath a statue of George IV. Modelled on the Roman Arch of Constantine it features reliefs by Richard Westmacott and E. H. Baily, the latter now largely forgotten despite having carved perhaps the most famous sculpture in London: Nelson at the top of his column. Like Nelson the statue of George IV somehow found its way to Trafalgar Square, and in 1851 the Arch was moved without him to the northern end of Park Lane.

It now stands on what has become one of London's busiest traffic islands with the gates at its centre remaining mostly locked. This is because, a charming legacy of its original purpose, only senior members of

Marble Arch

the royal family are allowed to pass beneath the arch and the King's Troop Royal Horse Artillery when its officers and men are engaged in their ceremonial duties.

Mount Street

A map engraved by George Vertue in 1738 shows a 'Plan of the City and Suburbs of London as fortified by Order of Parliament in the years 1642 and 1643.' Describing the fortifications designed to repel a Royalist attack on the capital, it includes a series of defensive earthworks and batteries, one of which – Oliver's Mount – is thought to explain the name of the street built on the site nearly eighty years later.

The street at that time was largely commercial and unpretentious, most of the shops and dwellings being relatively small and with the street dominated on one side by a parish workhouse for around six hundred paupers, which stood where no. 103 is now. From 1880 onwards much of this was torn down by the new Duke of Westminster. It was rebuilt in the familiar red-pink terracotta Queen Anne style which His Grace very much favoured at the time, and which still characterises much of the Grosvenor family's Mayfair estate. The workhouse was removed to Pimlico, which at that time was also owned by the Duke, and around this time Fanny Burney's erstwhile home at no. 112 quietly disappeared.

The Duke took the opportunity substantially to reorder the street, so that the portion on the park side west of South Audley Street was set aside for private residences. Commercial interests were thus restricted to the eastern end. Inevitably this plan has not survived intact, although at nos. 68–69 and 78–79 it is still possible to see the kind of large houses the Duke commissioned from his estate surveyor, Eustace Balfour.

By far the most impressive address in the street is no. 54, however, which since 1940 has been the official residence of the His Excellency the Brazilian ambassador. It was designed by Fairfax B. Wade in 1896 for Lord Windsor, later first Earl of Plymouth (1857–1923). A notable connoisseur and patron of the arts who was especially keen on architecture – in 1913 he acquired Crystal Palace for the nation – Lord Plymouth bought a double corner plot in Mount Street where he conceived an opulent and exuberantly appointed townhouse. On completion the new Plymouth House was certainly that, with vast service basements covering a larger area than the house itself, two floors of entertaining rooms and advanced mechanical lifts to bring wine and coal into the principal chambers. As well as a magnificent terrace,

the house was also fitted throughout with stunning marble walls, floors and pillars, much of the stone coming from Plymouth's own quarries in Penarth. A real hidden Mayfair gem, it is widely regarded as the most spectacular diplomatic building in the capital.

Originally the Coburg until Great War antipathies led to it being renamed after HRH the Duke of Connaught (1850–1942), the present Connaught Hotel on the corner with Carlos Place dates from 1897. Since that time it has had just six general managers, suggesting – as its owners and their guests would wish – an establishment where the focus is very much on tradition and conservative values as well as luxury and exclusivity. The elegant curved façade of the six-storey building is by Lewis Isaacs and H. L. Florence. It is largely of red brick with stone dressings in a style best described as 'free Jacobean-Renaissance' and like the hotel

Brazilian Embassy, Mount Street

Connaught Hotel, Mount Street

itself is quiet and discreet. It has, however, continued to invest heavily: a £70 million refurbishment programme in 2007 included a new wing and spa, a new art deco ballroom was opened in 2009 and the water feature (see photograph) outside the main entrance was created in 2011 by Japanese architect Tadao Ando.

Old Park Lane

Park Lane proper retains its reputation as a prestige address, but for all that it is one of the largest, widest, busiest and noisiest thoroughfares in central London. Old Park Lane perhaps gives a slightly better idea of what it once was, however, although it too is unfortunately now dominated by a pair of large and uncompromising structures in the Metropolitan and Four Seasons hotels. On the eastern side, at least, a quantity of faux 'Queen Anne' redbrick, some pretty bay windows and the Rose and Crown give it some character.

Oxford Street

Marking the northern boundary of Mayfair the south side of Oxford Street could be said to fall within the neighbourhood although nothing about what was once the Roman road from Hampshire to Suffolk – its scale, noise, crowds or atmosphere – really conforms to any sensible notion of a prestigious, mixed-used neighbourhood such as Mayfair.

Park Lane

Once no more than that – a narrow lane running along the walled boundary to a private royal park – development of Park Lane began in earnest in the 1760s with a handful

of vast aristocratic mansions on its eastern side. Now mostly gone, at that time many of them faced into Mayfair rather than towards Hyde Park, or, like nos. 93–99, were set back from the carriageway. Because of this it was to be another half-century before Park Lane itself became a prestigious address.

The turning point was probably in the mid-1820s when the wall around the park was taken down and replaced by railings, and the young Decimus Burton (1800–81) was commissioned to provide a stylish new entrance to the park (from Buckingham Palace) with his Ionic screen at Hyde Park Corner. Other equally impressive entrances were created at Grosvenor, Stanhope and Cumberland Gates, and with a number of the aforementioned mansions remodelled to face the other way Park Lane suddenly found itself the height of fashion.

Decimus Burton gates, Hyde Park Corner

Of the surviving houses, no. 93 was Disraeli's home from 1839–72, while Rufus Isaacs (see Curzon Street) was at no. 96 from 1903–10. Dating back to 1823, no. 99 was built for Sir Moses Montefiore (1784–1885) a great philanthropist who retired from the City at the age of forty and spent the next sixty-one years travelling widely and working on behalf of Jewish communities at home and abroad. Montefiore lived long enough to see his hundredth birthday, and on what would have been his two-hundredth the President of Israel, Chaim Herzog, travelled to London to unveil a blue plaque affixed to the house.

The larger and much grander houses that grew up along Park Lane have now mostly gone, with several of the most spectacular being replaced by the hotels bearing their names. Of these the Duke of Westminster's Grosvenor House, with its famous gallery, went in 1927; Dorchester House, which had been modelled on Rome's Palazzo Farnese, came down in 1929; and the double-fronted Londonderry House as recently as 1962. The reality was that since the 1880s onwards the old Park Lane aristocrats were gradually being supplanted by a generation of new men, in particular the so-called Randlords – the fabulously wealthy magnates whose new fortunes were being made in the gold and diamond fields of South Africa. By the Great War even the richest of the old guard, Bendor, 2nd Duke of Westminster, seemed to recognise that the era of London's great aristocratic residences was drawing to a close, and other owners were hit hard by new taxes and a shortage of servants. It was nevertheless a sad sight to see so many of these private palaces torn down.

Several of the hotels that replaced them were at least highly luxurious and not without distinction. In 1928 the Grosvenor House, for example, was the first hotel in London to have a swimming pool (and an ice-rink, beneath what is now the ballroom) while the creators of the Dorchester famously sound-proofed the bedrooms using dried seaweed. Wimperis, Simpson & Guthrie, architects of the former, succeeded to a degree in disguising the hotel's very considerable bulk – 478 bedrooms and more than 150 apartments – by creating four densely-packed blocks, set at an angle to Park Lane beneath decorative belvederes designed by Lutyens who was brought in as a consultant.

Admittedly, not even he could prevent the side elevation badly compromising Upper Grosvenor Street, but on Park Lane clever details like the disappearing pilasters and a screen of Corinthian columns at first-floor level do much to enhance the way the hotel

The Dorchester, Park Lane

blends into its surroundings in a way in which others (such as the Hilton to the south) do not. Despite the fact that it is only two years younger, the Dorchester was always intended to be more conspicuously modern, although one of the architects Sir Edward Owen Williams nevertheless resigned when attempts were made to soften the initial plans. Construction was handled by the company founded by its co-owner, Sir Robert Alpine, widely known as 'Concrete Bob' because of his faith in that particular material.

The same material enabled the top eight storeys to be built in less than three months, these being supported on a three-foot slab of concrete which formed the roof to the first floor. The design also made the structure immensely strong, with its faïence finish and curved entrance façade cleverly mitigating any suggestion of its monolithic bulk. During the war the hotel benefited from the widely held presumption that it was safer and more bomb-proof than its rivals, although the management was forced to ban the song 'Boomps-a-Daisy' from the dance floor as so many patrons, being serving British and Allied officers, were carrying revolvers in their hip pockets.

It is also amusing to reflect how the Dorchester attracted so many foreign agents at this time, as well as Lord Halifax, the foreign secretary, who used the hotel to entertain a mistress he shared with Mussolini's London representative. Because of this MI5 decided to keep the place under special surveillance, but unfortunately the man it charged with doing the job was one Guy Burgess, subsequently revealed as a Soviet spy. It is even so hard not to regret what has been lost to make way for the hotels, one good example being the magnificent marble main staircase at Dorchester House. This had cost

£30,000 to build in 1859 yet brought a bid of just £273 when it was knocked down for salvage seventy years later.

Sadly now just one great house survives, the Earl of Dudley's at no. 100 with its distinctive cast-iron conservatory on the first floor. As Dudley House it was never quite in the first rank, however, and unfortunately it has twice been altered after being severely bomb-damaged in 1940 and then again thirty years later when it was converted into offices. Nor, regrettably, is there any trace left of no. 13 in the cellar of which in 1872 a Madame Riel was done to death.

Riel called herself an actress but was actually the mistress of the 3rd Earl of Lucan, the Crimean War commander who had ordered the fateful charge of the Light Brigade and was implicated in the savage evictions during the Irish famine. She retained a servant girl – a Belgian called Marguerite Diblanc – but after a row gave her only a week's wages when serving her with a month's notice. In revenge the girl broke into the house, tied a rope around her erstwhile employer's neck and dragged her down to the basement where she finished her off.

Diblanc somehow escaped to France with a quantity of money and some jewels, but was quickly caught, brought back and charged with murder. It was naturally a capital offence but, following a trial in which to his embarrassment Lord Lucan was ordered to take the stand, she received a life sentence. Clearly outraged by the high-handed way in which the girl had been treated, the jury had put in a plea for clemency and, unusually, this was heeded.

Piccadilly (north side)

In 1612 a rich tailor called Robert Baker built himself a large country house in what is now Soho. Locally this was known as Pickadilly Hall after the source of his wealth, the manufacture and sale of picadils, a 'kinde of stiff collar' then much in fashion among members of the Stuart court. The name stuck and when development began along what had been an ancient thoroughfare leading out into the country it quickly supplanted its official title, Portugal Street, which had been chosen for Charles II's wife, Catherine of Braganza.

From the start the north side was always the more heavily developed, early plots being leased or sold for the construction of a series of aristocratic townhouses giving their owners proximity to St James's Palace and largely rural views to the south. Only three now survive in any recognisable form. Of these Burlington House is much altered as the home of the Royal Academy of Arts and other learned bodies, Albany is as described elsewhere in this chapter, while at the time of writing Cambridge House (no. 94) looks very sad after many years of lying empty.

No longer properly visible from the street thanks to a messily Italianate nineteenth-century arched screen, the first of these, Burlington House, is most closely associated with 20-year-old Richard Boyle, 3rd Earl of

Royal Academy, Piccadilly

Burlington. In 1715, when he returned from his first trip to Italy, he commissioned Colen Campbell to extend and remodel an old family property, the opening salvo of a life-long campaign to persuade English architects and their clients to adopt a stricter adherence to the precepts of Classical building. Campbell based his seven-bay design on Palladio's Palazzo Porto Colleoni, with a rusticated ground floor, Ionic orders above, large Venetian windows and careful Inigo Jones detailing.

Finished in Portland stone, it has since been much modified, in particular by Robert Smirke – who added a storey after the Royal Academy of Arts took on the lease of the building in 1867 – and Norman Foster who created the new Sackler Galleries in 1991. Because of this it is necessary to refer to the original drawings to get a true idea of what Campbell – and Burlington – had in mind, and to appreciate how radical their creation would have been at the time. The photograph here is of the facade on Old Burlington Street.

For some years, from around 1812, Burlington House was owned by Lord George Cavendish (1754–1834), a younger son of the 4th Duke of Devonshire who commissioned his architect Samuel Ware to build a covered arcade (of the sort then popular in France) on empty ground to the west of his property. Officially, Burlington Arcade, the first of its kind in London, was 'for the sale of jewellery and fancy articles of fashionable demand, for the gratification of the publick and to give employment to industrious females'. Unofficially it was said that Cavendish wished merely to prevent passers-by throwing oyster shells and other rubbish over the wall and his courtyard and garden.

In commercial terms it was an immediate

Burlington Arcade, Piccadilly

success and has remained so, helped in the early days by Mayfair's growing population and a shift among the rich from east to west London. For a while it provided somewhere for the better class of prostitute to display herself, many of whom rented rooms above the shops. In part to disrupt this activity a new storey was added in 1911, when the opportunity was also taken to build a new entrance onto Piccadilly. Unfortunately the architect E. Beresford Pite returned twenty years later to remodel this last feature, in doing so achieving little but the ruination of his original work and prompting the *Architectural Review* to claim that 'the whole appearance of the Arcade is spoiled'.

These days Piccadilly is much concerned with retail but for much of its history the street boasted many noblemen's mansions, several the equal of Burlington's. The most tragic losses among them include the destruction of the aforementioned Clarendon House by Sir Thomas Bond and his associates, and later Berkeley House. This was gutted by fire in 1733 when a workman foolishly left a pot of glue boiling whilst they had breakfast. By that time it was in the possession of William Cavendish, 3rd Duke of Devonshire (1698–1755) who decided to rebuild.

The renamed Devonshire House was the work of William Kent, its refreshingly plain and severe exterior contrasting strongly with an interior so opulent that the solid-silver epaulettes of the footmen appeared entirely in keeping. With a private orchestra and a picture gallery large enough to serve as a theatre (Edward Bulwer-Lytton's *Not So Bad as We Seem* debuted here before Queen Victoria, and at other times Dickens and Wilkie Collins both performed in the house), the dukes' London domain was an important centre of cultural, political and society life for more than 150 years.

Hit by heavy death duties following the demise of the 8th Duke (and still struggling with the substantial debts incurred by the 7th) the 9th Duke decided to dispose of the house in 1920. He received £750,000 and by 1926 the house and its spacious courtyard had been replaced by a large commercial development. Like its latest incarnation this was also called Devonshire House, and today nothing of the original survives save the entrance gates. With the courtyard long gone these now stand on the opposite side of Piccadilly forming an entry into Green Park.

Slightly smaller but still decidedly grand, with its carriage drive and white façade, Cambridge House was designed by Matthew Brettingham for Lord Egremont in the 1750s. Originally named for him it was renamed a century later when it was occupied by HRH

Prince Adolphus (1774–1850) 1st Duke of Cambridge and seventh son of George III. Lord Palmerston took it on for a decade from 1855, after which it was remodelled for the Naval and Military Club, which is still known as the In and Out after the lettering on the gate piers. The Naval and Military remained in situ until 1999 – A. E. W. Mason began writing *The Four Feathers* beneath a tree in the rear courtyard – when its members acquired a rare freehold complete with garden and mews house in St James's Square.

With its views across Green Park the western end of Piccadilly has long been the more prestigious, and whilst many of the buildings have been rebuilt it is still possible to identify the locations of several houses and their occupants. Nelson's mistress Lady Hamilton lived at no. 99 with her husband Sir William from 1800–3 and Lord Byron at no. 139 after his marriage to Anne Isabella Milbanke in 1815. The arrangement seemed doomed from the start. By all accounts a high-minded and deeply moral woman, within a year she had had enough of the poet's philandering and generally poor treatment of her and after little more than a year they separated.

In 1857 the death was announced from no. 110 of Hester, Viscountess Keith, otherwise known as 'Queenie' Thrale. A leading intellectual of her day, she is known to have corresponded with Samuel Johnson (who had known her mother) and Fanny Burney. In 1923, perhaps because of this literary connection, Dorothy L. Sayers appropriated the address for her character Lord Peter Wimsey who lived at 'No. 110a', by which time it was described as 'a new, perfect and expensive block'. Among others who favoured the western end were the Rothschilds, with Nathaniel, the first Lord Rothschild (1840–

1914) moving into his father's tall and gloomy Victorian house at no. 148. His brother Alfred Rothschild lived around the corner at 1 Seamore Place and a third (Leopold) was at 5 Hamilton Place just off Park Lane. Sadly none of these is now extant, however, having been lost when the southern end of Park Lane was rerouted and widened in the 1960s.

By then, but for Albany at the far end, no wholly residential buildings were left standing in Piccadilly, and today the most interesting survivors are the clubs. These include the former St James's Club at 106, in which much work by Robert Adam survives, the Cavalry and Guards (which, in 1987, took over no. 127) and the Royal Air Force next door at no. 128. None would be confused with the private houses which once occupied their buildings, but traditional clubs of this sort continue to provide a respectful, appropriate and more sympathetic use for such places than other more commercial alternatives.

Regent Street (west side)

An important part of John Nash's sweeping plans to link the Prince Regent's park to his palace overlooking the Mall, work on what was at first known simply as New Street required the wholesale destruction of a mass of streets and alleyways and caused enormous disturbance to residents before it was completed in 1825. By way of consolation existing tenants were offered the opportunity to purchase new ninety-nine-year Crown leases, but many would have been unable to afford this option. Then as now Regent Street (as it soon became) was intended from the start to be highly commercial and decidedly upmarket. Development was instead left to large-scale private developers – including Sir John Soane, C. R. Cockerell and Nash

himself – although with the exception of the latter's All Soul's north of Oxford Circus no building from the period remains.

In part this was because Nash's own buildings were not of especially high quality. Shifting patterns in retail, particularly in the late Victorian and Edwardian periods, also called for quite different building types and resulted in much larger department stores being erected over the foundations of countless smaller shops and offices. Today, as a result, no building on the west side of the street is of especial merit although with the Crown Estate once again redeveloping this may change in future years.

Sackville Street

First laid out in the 1670s the street takes its name from Captain Edward Sackville, a younger brother of the 5th Earl of Dorset who leased a house on the western side. Until 1690 it was still occasionally known as Chip or Chipps Street, but since this time has been so comprehensively redeveloped and renumbered that very little early work remains. A Robert Adam ceiling survives at no. 29 and the house at no. 36 is thought to have been designed in 1732 by Henry Flitcroft. (Together with Henry Holland, Flitcroft was largely responsible for rebuilding Woburn Abbey a decade later for the 4th Duke of Bedford.)

As a result of this, whilst we know the addresses of many former occupants, it is not possible accurately to match contemporary street numbers to those that would have been relevant when, for example, the actor Charles Kemble (1775–1854) lived at no. 6, or when the architect Charles Barry jnr. spent the best part of a decade living at no. 27. Elsewhere in the records one finds several nineteenth-century MPs living in Sackville Street, and a surprising number of eminent Georgian medics. These include Sir Gilbert Blane who introduced lemons and limes to the Royal Navy (to prevent scurvy) and served as physician-in-ordinary to both George IV and William IV. As it happens the street's most celebrated former resident was also an eminent doctor: John Snow (1813–58). His story is best left to the Soho chapter, but an official plaque records his occupancy of no. 18 from 1853–8 and his landmark work on the spread of cholera in urban areas.

Savile Row

Sometimes described as a club, the reality of Savile Row is that it is more of a village, with everything that such a description implies. The first impression on visiting is definitely one of self-containment, while the locals peering out through their windows during quiet periods of the day seem neither to welcome visitors nor any signs of change. Like many small communities the residents also value their traditions and incomers are still described that way – which is to say as outsiders – for literally decades after they first arrive.

Ironically, for such a masculine enclave, the Row is named after a woman: Lady Dorothy Savile was the wife of the 3rd Earl of Burlington. When first planned in the 1730s it was intended to be a residential street and a number of original dwellings can still be seen at nos. 3, 11–14, 16 and 17. All are on the east side because, until the nineteenth century, much of the west side comprised the gardens of houses in Old Burlington Street. No. 14, incidentally, is where Sheridan passed away in 1816 having finally exhausted his luck, health and money.

The street's tailoring connections are surprisingly modern. The premises at no. 1, for example, with its William Kent ceiling, belonged to the Royal Geographical Society long before it was taken over by Gieves & Hawkes and is where the body of the great missionary and explorer David Livingstone lay before his burial in Westminster Abbey. Nor is Gieves & Hawkes quite as venerable as its international fame might suggest, the two halves having come together as recently as the mid-1970s. As separate entities they had clothed both Wellington and Nelson, but the first to arrive in the Row was Henry Poole, in 1846. Poole's father, James, had opened a drapery in Brunswick Street in 1806 and became known for his beautifully made military uniforms. He later moved to Old Burlington Street, and, on his father's death in 1846, Henry Poole enlarged the premises by building a splendid new showroom with an entrance onto the adjoining Savile Row. Eight generations later his firm is still here, at no. 15, its list of clients including the Queen, Tsar Alexander II, Sir Winston Churchill, Charlie Chaplin and even Buffalo Bill. Such has been Poole's influence on tailoring that, in 1996, an exhibition was mounted at the

Henry Poole & Co, Savile Row

Victoria and Albert Museum chronicling the history of the firm and displaying many of its finest creations.

Poole's origins are in fact typical. The splendid firm of Huntsman at no. 11 was similarly a gaiter and breeches maker at first, while Henry Maxwell, once the street's most famous boot maker, started out fashioning spurs using a forge in his own back garden. Indeed only one of the big names, Hardy Amies in Sheridan's old house at no. 14, could have claimed a truly illustrious back story. He chose not to, however, saying little if anything about his distinguished war as a secret agent with the Special Operations Executive. After the war Amies was set up in business by the first Mrs Cary Grant, and very soon acquired the chilly hauteur of his neighbours.

Mention must be made of the many innovations pioneered by the tailors of Savile Row and their predecessors in other parts of Mayfair. In 1808, Beau Brummell, dandy and unofficial sartorial adviser to the Prince Regent, introduced trousers to fashionable London. Brummell, often described as the 'intellectual godfather' of Savile Row, was also responsible for a completely new style of dress for the upper-class male, one that emphasised simple elegance and muted colours as opposed to the extravagant fashions favoured before the French Revolution. In 1850, the firm of James Lock (located in St James's Street, but part of this area's great tailoring traditions) invented a Savile Row classic: the bowler hat, which was designed to protect gamekeepers against falling pheasants and the poacher's stick. The first dinner jacket made its appearance in 1860 when Bertie, the Prince of Wales and future Edward VII, ordered a short smoking jacket to be worn at informal dinner parties.

One of Bertie's successors as Prince of Wales can also vouch for the quality of Savile Row's esteemed gentleman's outfitters. In early 2013 Prince Charles visited his tailor, Anderson and Sheppard, for the first time. Although now located in Burlington Street, the firm was in Savile Row for more than a century and embodies the traditional values of its spiritual home. The Prince, who normally has his fittings done in Clarence House, was at his tailor with the twin aim of encouraging the use of British wool and apprenticeships. During his visit it was noted (by the *Daily Telegraph*) that his Anderson and Sheppard suits have lasted for decades and in the event of frayed cuffs or tears can be expertly repaired on the premises. His famous doubled-breasted herringbone tweed overcoat, which he dons every winter, was made for him in 1987. Known in Anderson and Sheppard documentation as 'Charles Smith' to protect his privacy, Prince Charles is living testament to the craftsmanship of Savile Row.

The aura projected by these exclusive shops serves to conceal how, in the early days, the men of Savile Row were definitely 'in trade' – and fairly low trade at that. These days their

Huntsman, Savile Row

reputation (and dare one say it their prices) mean many would-be customers feel nervous about walking through the doorways of what after all are merely shops, and it is easy to forget how the street must once have been before the cutters and stitchers moved in. For example, long before Huntsman arrived at no. 11 it was home for nearly thirty years to Richard Bright (1789–1858). A medical lecturer and researcher at Guy's Hospital, to the medical profession Bright is widely thought of as 'the father of nephrology' for his pioneering work on kidney disease.

The historian George Grote (1794–1871) lived next door at no. 28, whilst compiling his magisterial *History of Greece*, which runs to twelve volumes. And from 1839–49 the architect Lewis Vulliamy was living at no. 13, some of which time he spent creating a new front for the Royal Institution in Albemarle Street. Another architect, George Basevi, the designer of Belgrave Square, lived at no. 17 from 1826–45.

Shepherd Market

Built in 1735–46 on the site of the old May Fair to serve the large aristocratic houses on Piccadilly, the architect and developer Edward Shepherd's small precinct of shops and taverns still retains something of its small-scale, domestic, eighteenth-century feel. It does so even though, almost without exception, the aristocratic mansions are long gone; together with the servants who would once have thronged these passageways while collecting their provisions.

When it was primarily residential the West End would have had several such places, built expressly to serve the clusters of first-quality houses being thrown up by the various commercial and aristocratic developers. At one such Robert Seymour (in his 1735 *Survey of the Cities of London and Westminster*) observed 'country butchers, higglers and the like' selling goods at a handsome premium to 'stewards of the People of Quality, who spare no price to furnish their Lord's Houses with what is nice and delicate'. Inevitably the majority have now gone or been so altered as to be unrecognisable, and Shepherd Market is now the sole reminder of the amenities which would been drawn to the stable yards and kitchens of London's best addresses. As such it is also a unique and precious reminder of how adept the Georgians could be when it came to executing attractive but practical town plans.

Shepherd himself was quick to realise that, although the riotous and disorderly May Fair had been suppressed, in the absence of a police force the best way to prevent its return was simply to build over the land. With this in mind he erected a two-storey structure with a butcher and other shops below and an informal theatre in the great room in the space above. Around this grew a tightly drawn grid of narrow streets and alleyways, a surprisingly intimate little enclave which today is best entered via the covered passageway at 47 Curzon Street.

Shepherd's market building is now long gone, as is his duck pond. However, Ye Grapes still stands and it was in rooms opposite this that the Armenian writer Dikran Kouyoumdjian (1895–1956) chose to live in the 1920s. Changing his name to Michael Arlen he published *The Green Hat*, using Shepherd Market and its environs as the setting for a racy bestseller about a young widow with a shady past and a love of fast cars and faster men. A rich mix of high and low life – as indeed was Shepherd Market until quite recently – Arlen could himself have stepped straight out of the novel's pages, with his sharp suits, quick wit and ostentatious yellow Rolls-Royce. Today visitors are more likely to see another fast man in the area, Sir Stirling Moss, who has been a resident since the 1960s.

South Audley Street

Very much a street of two halves, its name is taken from Sir Hugh Audley whose land-holdings in this part of London were acquired by the Grosvenor estate through marriage to Audley's heiress, Mary Davies. Today there is plenty of character towards the lower half of the street, which was always grander and more obviously residential, but precious little charm above South Street. Here, historically, the tenants were mostly shopkeepers and tradesmen, and late-Victorian development has swept away nearly all that went before.

An obvious exception to this is the Grosvenor Chapel, which was completed in 1731. Its modest design and plain building style became the model for the many North American churches it now seems to resemble, and most appropriately during the war years the congregation made every effort to welcome American servicemen to its Sunday services. Regular worshippers at that time

Grosvenor Chapel, South Audley Street

included General Dwight D. Eisenhower, and at others Florence Nightingale, the novelist Rose Macaulay and John Betjeman. The writer and traveller Lady Mary Wortley Montagu (1689–1762) is buried beneath the chapel together with the radical and pamphleteer John Wilkes (1725–97) and the Duke of Wellington's parents, the 1st Earl and Countess of Mornington.

Travelling southwards the street becomes considerably more interesting, the loss of Chesterfield House obviously regrettable although there are attractive survivors from the 1730s at nos. 9–16 and 71–75 which were almost certainly built by Edward Shepherd (see above). Some still have sumptuous Georgian plasterwork interiors, although a painted ceiling in a room at no. 75 was removed to the National Gallery in the late 1960s after being identified as being by Giovanni Battista Tiepolo (1696–1770).

This extraordinary find is thought to be connected with Henry Louis Bischoffsheim, a successful banker and art connoisseur who lived in the house from 1873–1908. His wife sat for Millais, and he is assumed to have installed the Tiepolo during his time in South Audley Street. An earlier resident of the same house was the 3rd Earl of Bute, briefly prime minister from 1762–3. Between times the street was home to the sculptor Sir Richard Westmacott who lived at no. 14 from 1818–56 having previously occupied 24 Mount Street (and spent much of his youth next door, at no. 25).

The womanising Comte d'Artois (1757–1836), the younger brother of Louis XVI and Louis XVII, lived for nine years at no. 72 before the fall of Napoleon enabled his return to France. Eventually acceding to the throne as Charles X, and thus the last Bourbon king, his reign from 1824–1830 was deeply unpopular and his forced abdication marked the final flourish of a remarkable 250-year dynasty. His house has fared better but, whilst still of the 1730s, it has been substantially altered since his day.

As it happens, 77 South Audley Street was also briefly a royal residence, when another exile, Caroline of Brunswick, returned to London from Italy in 1820. She came to assert her position as Queen Consort to the newly crowned George IV, but barred from the coronation she died three weeks later and her body was returned to Brunswick for burial. Her house is no longer standing.

South Molton Street

With no known connection to the eponymous Devon village, the name remains something of a mystery although the street remains one of the more popular thoroughfares in Mayfair for shoppers and visitors alike. Development of this part of the City of London's Conduit Mead estate began in the 1750s, and the City Corporation's arms can still be seen on no. 63. With its original ground-floor windows this is one of several buildings which have survived the fairly wholesale redevelopment of the street around 1900.

The numbering is not thought to have altered since then, however, so that the building at no. 17 almost certainly occupies the site of William Blake's lodgings in 1803 when the artist-poet-visionary and his wife were described as 'still poor [and] durtyer than ever'. More surprising, perhaps, is the former occupier of no. 34. From 1931 until his death twenty years later the trade-union baron and Labour cabinet minister Ernest Bevin kept a flat here in Mayfair, presumably seeing no contradiction between such an

elevated address and his own reputation as a socialist and man of the people.

South Street

Nothing remains of the eighteenth-century streetscape, when the best of the houses would have enjoyed an enviable prospect of Hyde Park. South Street is nevertheless notable for no. 38, Aberconway House, the only substantial dwelling to be built in this area between the wars and inarguably the last truly great private house to have been constructed in Mayfair. Built in the 1920s in an imposing neo-Georgian style for the industrialist Henry McLaren, 2nd Baron Aberconway, it is the work of Grosvenor Estate surveyor Edmund Wimperis, his partner W. B. Simpson and – substantially – of the young J. M. Easton who went on to design the Royal Horticultural Society's New Hall (see Westminster, Vincent Square). With a 90-foot frontage on to the street it is an immense house, with a 65-foot entrance hall largely of black marble, palatial reception and entertaining spaces, an adjoining 8,000-square-foot guest house at no. 40, and, to the rear, access to one of Mayfair's

Aberconway House, South Street

loveliest and most private gardens. This was laid out by Wimperis in 1914 as a communal benefit for the larger houses of South Street and Hill Street, none of which is any longer residential.

The Duke d'Orléans, cousin of King Louis XVI, lived intermittently at no. 2 from 1788–93. Calling himself Philippe Égalité, he rather surprisingly, yet enthusiastically, supported the French Revolution but was guillotined nevertheless and so did not live to see his son crowned the last king of France. The 1st Marquess of Cornwallis, the commander at Yorktown, lived at no. 4 from 1766–8, and the Duke of Sussex, a younger son of George III, spent more than a decade at no. 12 from 1832 onwards. Prime Minister Lord Melbourne lived at no. 18 from 1830–48 – like many nineteenth-century political grandees he preferred to make his own arrangements rather than moving into Downing Street – and in 1903 another prime minister, Alec Douglas-Home, was born at no. 28.

Almost certainly the street's longest-established resident was Florence Nightingale. She moved into no. 10 in 1865, having already taken a lease next door at no. 8. She remained there until her death in 1910, living on very favourable terms from the 1st Duke of Westminster after protesting that a rent increase would compel her to 'go to Onslow Gardens or South Kensington which would be a public injury'. Unfortunately the house itself no longer stands, and the blue plaque erected in 1978 is affixed to a 1930s apartment block.

Stanhope Gate

Built in the shadow of the 4th Earl Stanhope's Chesterfield House, and for a while known as Great Stanhope Street, this short but broad

Former home of Lord Fitzroy Somerset: 5 Stanhope Gate

thoroughfare links South Audley Street and Park Lane. It contains a number of the original houses of 1760, though sadly none is any longer residential.

The two buildings of most interest are the bank on the corner with Park Lane, an exuberant if somewhat overdone exercise in Victorian Gothic Revival, and the house at no. 5, which for twenty years was home to Field Marshal the Lord Fitzroy Somerset, 1st Baron Raglan (1788–1855). Refaced and given at least one extra storey shortly before the Great War, it is nevertheless one of the original mid-eighteenth-century houses. Somerset, as he then was, served alongside Wellington for more than forty years, lost an arm at Waterloo, and in 1814 married his niece, Emily Wellesley-Pole.

The couple moved to Stanhope Gate in

1834 and while he was to post some important victories as the British commander in the Crimea – notably at Inkerman and Alma – his reputation suffered after his involvement in the disastrous Charge of the Light Brigade in October 1854. He died, exhausted, the following year while still on operations.

Stratton Street

Until 1924 and the demolition of Devonshire House (see Piccadilly) Stratton Street – named for the seventeenth-century landowner, Lord Berkeley of Stratton – was a cul-de-sac constrained on one side by the wall surrounding the Duke of Devonshire's palatial townhouse. Once this was removed the street was pushed through, across what had been the ducal garden to Berkeley Street. This and subsequent developments mean that none of the original late seventeenth-century houses – all of them 'gentilely built, and well inhabited' – still stands. Instead, dominated by large office blocks and the May Fair Hotel, no. 6 is the oldest building in the street. It is at least a hundred years younger, however, but with its raised bay window supported on a cast-iron column must once have had a good view of the Duke's otherwise reasonably private three acres.

Because of this it is impossible to place with any certainty the former homes of Lord Lynedoch (1748–1843), the exceptionally long-lived Peninsular War commander, or that of Baroness Burdett-Coutts (1814–1906) at what was then no.1. Described as the richest woman in England after inheriting £3 million from her banker grandfather in 1837 – and by Edward VII as 'after my mother the most remarkable woman in the kingdom' – Angela Burdett-Coutts built markets, schools,

soup kitchens and homes for the downtrodden of London, endowed bishoprics in the colonies and established the National Society for the Prevention of Cruelty to Children. She had many influential friends, including Charles Dickens and the Duke of Wellington, and worked with them on a wide range of philanthropic ventures. She was herself childless, remaining single until the age of 67 when she married her 29-year-old secretary. When Baroness Coutts died in December 1906 her body lay in state for two days in 1 Stratton Street, with an astonishing thirty thousand people passing through the doors to pay their respects to the 'Queen of the Poor', as she had become known. She was buried in Westminster Abbey.

Unfortunately, the loss of her house means she has no blue plaque in Stratton Street, nor at her country house in Highgate, which has also been demolished. In fact the only resident commemorated in the street is Benjamin Baruch 'Bert' Ambrose (c.1896–1971) a dance-band leader. He performed nightly at the May Fair Hotel from 1927–40, apparently after being tempted back from New York by the Prince of Wales. His new contract allowed him a flat above the hotel, and time off to broadcast and to record. At his peak his band was producing more than eighty records a year and he claimed to have discovered the young Vera Lynn. But after a year of war he retired to the Home Counties when the persistent air-raids became too much to bear.

Upper Brook Street

After thirty years of building work the Grosvenor Square to Park Lane extension to Brook Street was completed in 1759, by which time a quarter of the houses were occupied by titled families. Thereafter, never losing its prestige, it remained almost entirely residential until the outbreak of the Second World War. Even now almost two dozen eighteenth-century houses survive, albeit with many of their number refaced, extended or remodelled. Of these, nos. 33, 35 and 36 are the finest. The first, with its distinctive late-eighteenth-century Tuscan column and arched openings on the ground floor, is the work of Sir Robert Taylor (1714–88) whose pupils included John Nash and Samuel Pepys Cockerell. After failing as a sculptor he enjoyed considerable success as an architect, succeeding Sir William Chambers as Architect of the King's Works and preceding Sir

John Soane as architect to the Bank of England before dying of a chill caught at friend's funeral.

With their strongly delineated string-courses of stone, vermiculated keystones over the windows and characteristic Gibbs surrounds to the doors, nos. 35 and 36 are early Georgian and externally among the best preserved houses of this period on the entire Grosvenor estate. Built very much as a pair – and modified as such when the first-floor windows were lengthened and a balcony added in the nineteenth century – they have a long history of aristocratic occupation. Including the Duchess of Atholl (wife of 2nd Duke, 1746–8) followed by her

Georgian splendour at 35–36 Upper Brook Steet

son-in-law the 20th Earl of Crawford, the 1st and 2nd Viscounts Dudley and Ward (1742–80), the 2nd and 3rd Viscounts Harberton (1827–31), the 12th Earl of Home (1872) and sometime Lord Chancellor the Earl Jowitt (1922–42) it is an impressive list but by no means exceptional for this part of the Duke of Westminster's demesne.

As Lord Ashley, the future 7th Earl of Shaftesbury (1801–85) lived at no. 49, during which time he campaigned tirelessly to improve the lot of slaves, factory workers, chimney-sweeps and others oppressed individuals (see the *Eros* section of Piccadilly Circus for a more detailed account of Shaftesbury's career). Unfortunately, his unusual passion for what he termed 'Christian Zionism' led to the formation of the Society for Promoting Christianity among the Jews. This controversial move showed no regard for the traditions of this most ancient religion, and instead sought to convert Jews before shipping them off to Palestine to serve the Empire. Through its efforts a single Polish rabbi, called Ginsberg, was reborn as the somewhat unlikely sounding Rev. Crichton-Ginsberg, but even in a good year (1862) the Society managed to recruit just three individuals to its highly questionable cause.

Upper Grosvenor Street

Despite much of the Grosvenor Square to Park Lane section of Grosvenor Street being badly compromised (by the glowering side elevations of the Grosvenor House Hotel on one side and the Saarinen's US Embassy on the other) it remains one of the principal crossings of the ducal estate. It is also still in parts an attractive one, with as many as two dozen houses surviving from the early 1720s when it was first laid out. It is hardly a

surprise that none has remained unaltered: approximately half of them were given new stone fronts in the years before the Great War, and, as with so many of the larger streets in Mayfair, the remainder have long since been converted to apartments and offices. Before this the street had a number of distinguished residents, although in many cases the buildings have been swept away.

For example, today a small 1930s apartment block covers nos. 39–40 on the south side, but for almost fifty years it was the London home of John Walter (1818–94) the Liberal politician and proprietor of *The Times*. After his father and grandfather he was the third John Walter to hold this position, the fourth – his son – drowning on the family's Berkshire estate before he could take the reins. At around the same time no. 41 was extended for the banker Thomas Baring (1799–1873) to accommodate a collection 'upwards of three hundred pictures, distributed through the apartments, and filling a moderately sized gallery which has been erected expressly to display some of the larger works'. And, from 1937–66, no. 44 was the London home of William Waldorf Astor, 3rd Viscount Astor, known as Bill, whose reputation was sullied by the 1963 Profumo scandal when he was accused of having an affair with Mandy Rice Davies.

On the north side, nos. 1–5 were pulled down as part of the clearance of a massive site needed for the American embassy. Of the survivors no. 9 still retains its early Georgian appearance despite new storeys being added in the nineteenth century along with a new portico. From 1759–64 it was home to William Tryon, a future governor New York and North Carolina. No. 13 was home to the 8th, 9th and 10th dukes of Somerset, from 1752–93, while no. 15 was occupied by Captain David Beatty, later Admiral of the Fleet Earl Beatty (1871–1936).

The latter was a controversial character under whose command at Jutland the Royal Navy's losses were higher than the enemy's although this did not prevent Germany being adjudged the loser. Beatty is recalled for an almost comical comment – 'There seems to be something wrong with our bloody ships today' – after several battle cruisers exploded and sank under heavy German fire. He lived in the house in Upper Brook Street from 1903–10, and like Sir Robert Taylor in Upper Brook Street died after attending the funeral of a friend (Admiral Lord Jellicoe). He was buried in St Paul's Cathedral despite his express wish to join his wife in a double plot at Dingley Hall in Leicestershire.

A blue plaque at no. 16, another early house (c. 1730) which was refaced 150 years later, marks the occupation for more than two decades of Sir Robert Peel (1750–1830), the industrialist father of a second Sir Robert (1788–1850). In fact the son would have spent relatively few years living in Upper Grosvenor Street (he was twelve years old when they moved in) but it is now the sole surviving residence of this former prime minister and founder of the Metropolitan Police.

While he gained a plaque Sir Robert Peel was by no means the only resident of the street to align himself so closely with issues of public safety. In 1890 Stewart Graham Menzies was born at no. 46, although this is nowhere advertised. For years he was known only as 'C' – clearly providing the model for James Bond's superior 'M' – a deliberately shadowy character who as head of the Secret Intelligence Service (MI6) during and after the war has more than once been described as the greatest British spymaster in history.

ST JAMES'S

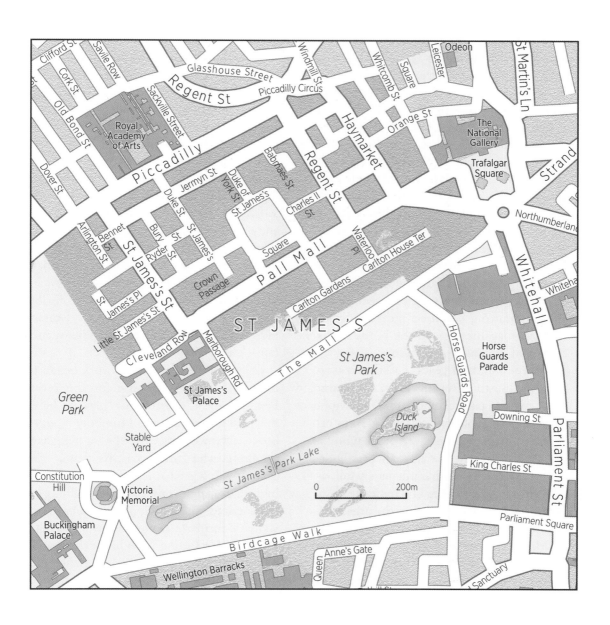

Another notorious quagmire transformed into an elegant and expensive residential enclave, St James's continues to enjoy a reputation as a somehow more masculine place than Mayfair despite its unlikely beginnings as a charitable refuge for fourteen 'leprous maidens'. For a long time the only building in the area was a hospital dedicated to St James the Less. Deliberately placed in a remote spot a safe and respectable distance from Whitehall, this had been founded in the early twelfth century by Queen Matilda but was pulled down in the 1530s and rebuilt as a 'goodly manor', a retreat for Henry VIII from the formality of the Palace of Whitehall.

Before its destruction in a final, devastating fire in April 1691, the palace had extended to more than one-and-a-half-thousand rooms, making it larger than either the Vatican or Versailles. St James's Palace was never intended to match it in either scale or grandeur, and was instead a much more homely building of wonderfully mellow Tudor brick. Fate intervened, however, with the loss of Whitehall. It meant that what was originally intended as no more than a comfortable hunting box for a pleasure-loving monarch became instead the home of the kings and queens and remained so for the next three hundred years. For this reason, from the Restoration onwards, the shared histories of palace and neighbourhood become inseparable with the area we now call St James's expressly conceived by a handful of speculative developers as a kind of prestigious *faubourg* or royal suburb immediately following the return from exile of Charles II.

Here the decisive move in the area's elevation was the 1660 grant of land from Charles II to his friend and courtier Henry Jermyn, 1st Earl of St Albans (1605–84). Jermyn's master plan involved the creation of the aforementioned *faubourg*, building as close as possible to the palace and with its centre on St James's Square (see below). As the first such development in the West End, the new square was intended solely for 'Noble men and other Persons of Quality'; but other similarly prestigious developments followed hard on its heels – including a number of vast mansions overlooking St James's Park and Green Park, several of which still survive – so that the area has never lost tone.

As with Mayfair the extent of the neighbourhood they created was and has remained clearly delineated as the developers were limited on two sides by Piccadilly and Haymarket and on the other two by the immovable boundaries of the royal parks. The intended clients for the large and spacious houses were from the first noblemen, diplomats and courtiers, all of them powerful individuals keen for proximity to the crown and able to pay handsomely for it. And very quickly they arrived in droves, attracted by the opportunity to get close to the Crown, by developments which were uniformly new and grand, and by the King's decision to further adorn the neighbourhood by landscaping Henry VIII's old hunting ground between St James's and Whitehall.

Long before 1783, when work began on the lavish Carlton House for the future Prince Regent, the area had become by far the most fashionable in all London – today it boasts an embarrassment of blue plaques to celebrated and famous past residents – and even now it has what is almost certainly the highest concentration of listed buildings in the country. These include a number of surviving Georgian townhouses, some venerable clubs (including in White's the world's oldest), a clutch of authentically eighteenth-century shops and even offices. Indeed in recent years so many hedge funds have been attracted to the latter (the nature of their business means such companies do not need large, modern buildings) that according to the *Economist* 'more money is managed in St James's than in Frankfurt'.

Arlington Street

In 1681 the King made a significant grant of land to the north of his palace, this time to another favourite, Sir Henry Bennet, Earl of Arlington (1618–85), who had sustained a wound to the nose fighting in the Civil War before following the royal family into exile in France. Sir Henry was also the builder of the first Arlington House, incidentally, which in time was to be extended, completely re-modelled and renamed Buckingham Palace.

The street that bears his name today (together with the adjacent Bennet Street, see below) was developed shortly after the grant was made. Albeit on a smaller scale than the Earl of St Albans, Arlington planned to build 'an *enclave de luxe* for the Nobility' on his six precious acres, and by 1728 its location overlooking Green Park saw it being described as 'one of the most beautiful situations in Europe, for health, convenience and beauty'. Within a very few years it was even better known by the nickname 'Ministerial Street', so numerous were the members of the cabinet who kept houses here to be close to the Crown. Of these the most prominent was Sir Robert Walpole (1676–1745) Britain's first prime minister who lived first at no. 17 and later at no. 5, where he eventually died. After leaving Mayfair in 1804 Charles James Fox spent two years at no. 9, and no. 16 was home to another prime minister, Lord North, and to Prince Frederick, Duke of York and Albany, George IV's

22 Arlington Street

heavily indebted younger brother who died here in 1827. An unidentified lodgings in Arlington Street is also thought to be where Lord Nelson and his wife had their final, parting row, the former Frances 'Fanny' Nisbet having issued an ultimatum over Christmas 1800 demanding the distinguished sailor choose between Lady Hamilton and herself.

Today the street includes the entrance used by most visitors to the Ritz (see Piccadilly, south side) but architecturally speaking the side elevation to this hotel is by no means its chief treasure. That honour goes to no. 22, a deceptively large house designed by William Kent in 1740 on what was, and arguably still is, the prime site on the street. With a court-yard in front, and to the rear views across Green Park, it was able to take full advantage of a location in which the house stood 'in the midst of the hurry and splendour of the town' while 'the back is in the quiet simplicity of the country'. For many years its exuberant Grade II* interiors were beautifully maintained but lost to the public as it was occupied by an insurance company, but in 2005 the house was acquired by the new owners of Ritz and it is now used as an annexe for parties and receptions.

Its neighbours have been less fortunate

and indeed the best of them has disappeared completely. Known as Pomfret Castle this was a large but charming Gothic folly of a house designed twenty years later by Sanderson Miller, a talented gentleman-amateur. With a full complement of turrets, crenellations and even a separate gatehouse it sounds improbable for central London but it looked quite wonderful until its twentieth-century demolition. A near contemporary still stands at no. 21, but this has changed a good deal since Giacomo Leoni designed its simple and austere Palladian façade. Asymmetrical but comprised of regularly spaced pedimented windows and a refined Ionic door case, like the Kent house it faces the park, and it too is set back behind an enviably spacious courtyard. No. 16 is slightly earlier, a small but solid-looking gatehouse with a rusticated archway and now Grade I listed. It was completed in 1736 for Lord North whose son, as prime minister, steered Britain through the American War of Independence.

For many years Arlington Street was also home to the magazine publisher and night-club owner Paul Raymond (1925–2008). Working over many years he assembled an unrivalled property portfolio comprising as much as seventy acres of Soho – the largest private London estate of the twentieth century – but he chose to live quietly in a penthouse on the other side of Piccadilly. Located in a 1930s block designed by the Viennese-born architect Michael Rosenauer, the penthouse was previously home to the newspaper proprietor William Maxwell Aitken, 1st Lord Beaverbrook (1879–1964) following the destruction of his house in nearby Cleveland Row.

Babmaes Street

More a cul-de-sac than a street the name commemorates Baptist Mae, a friend and confidant of Charles II and his Keeper of the Privy Purse. Originally it would have provided access to what was once extensive mews accommodation situated to the rear of the large houses in St James's Square. Today only one of the original mews houses still stands. Situated at the far end, this precious survivor forms part of the house and garden to 4 St James's Square and so belongs to the Naval and Military Club. With the exception of the Three Crowns pub the quiet street is otherwise now offices and bleak.

Bennet Street

A street of relatively little interest now with the original houses all torn down, no. 4 occupies the site of the lodgings occupied by Lord Byron from 1813–14 when he was engaged in writing *The Corsair* and *The Bride of Abydos*. Since 1984 the spacious Portland Gallery at no. 8 has specialised in modern British and contemporary art, both painting and sculpture.

On the corner with Arlington Street the name of the Blue Posts, a somewhat later replacement for the tavern mentioned in 1667 by the Restoration dramatist George Etheredge, is a reference to the sedan chairs whose operators used to ply for hire from the street. At that time a pair of blue bollards mounted on the kerb or in the yard of an inn would have functioned to signal to would-be customers the presence of what was in effect a type of early taxi rank.

Bury Street

Whilst still in its entirety Crown property, Bury Street formed part of the land granted to Henry Jermyn in 1660 and takes its name from Bury St Edmunds in Suffolk. This is close to the Jermyn family seat at Rush-brooke Hall, and ahead of his advancement to the earldom of St Albans Jermyn was ennobled as Baron Jermyn of St Edmunds-bury. For a while the street was even so known as 'Berry Street' and in 1720 was described by the historian John Strype as being 'a handsome open street'. A newspaper adver-tisement of that time describing a house for sale made much of the location, in particular the 'Commodiousness of the Situation, being near St James's Church, Chapel, Park, Palace, Coffee and Chocolate Houses'.

Unfortunately, none of the original houses now survives – there was a large fire in 1755 when Horace Walpole observed that 'an officer jumped out of window, and is much hurt' – and indeed scarcely a building in the street is more than a hundred years old. Today it is very much dominated by the *Economist* building to one side, which prop-erly belongs to St James's Street, and by some fanciful terracotta bow windows down towards King Street. Otherwise, viewed from Ryder Street, the mansion block at no. 10 is a cheerful exercise in Edwardiana, a faux Georgian design of 1910 by G. Thrale Jell.

Renumbering since Walpole's day means it is not possible to place any of the street's several illustrious residents, but these are known to have included Dean Swift in 1710, when he was paying eight shillings a week for 'the first floor, a dining-room and bed-chamber'. The Irish essayist and politician (and co-founder of the *Spectator*) Sir Richard Steele lived in Bury Street from 1707–12, and for a while a favourite of George III, the future Earl of Liverpool (1727–1808) had lodgings at the corner of Bury and Jermyn Street in a building now occupied by royal shirt makers Turnbull and Asser.

Carlton Gardens

A later extension by John Nash to Carlton House Terrace (see below) this pleasantly quiet street runs between the Mall and Pall Mall, dates from the 1820s and is perhaps central London's most conspicuously mag-nificent backwater. Short and wide it con-tains only very few houses (there is a small modern apartment block on the north side) although each is immense and the roll call of residents singularly impressive. Most of the work belongs to John Nash, with no. 3 being by Decimus Burton and no. 4 sadly demol-ished in 1929 and replaced by something larger and inferior.

From 1839–40, 1 Carlton Gardens was leased to Prince Louis Napoleon (1808–73), Bonaparte's nephew and heir who served as the president of the French Second Republic and (as Napoleon III) as the ruler of the Second Empire after mounting a coup d'état in 1851. In the latter role he was not unsuc-cessful at home, but his surrender at Sedan in 1870 was a disaster, and both a personal and national humiliation. Returning to England he died at Chislehurst in Kent less than three years later (see King Street). Today the building serves as the official residence of the foreign secretary, who might thus be regarded as enjoying rather better accom-modation than either the prime minister or the chancellor of the exchequer in Downing Street. The statue outside is of George VI, and at the foot of the steps either side of this two large friezes commemorate the long life of his Queen, Elizabeth the Queen Mother.

Foreign Secretary's residence, 1 Carlton Gardens

No. 2 is also now a government building, and is used by the Privy Council, but for the first two years of the Great War it was home to Field Marshal H. H. Kitchener, 1st Earl Kitchener of Khartoum (1850–1916). Lord Kitchener was popular and highly visible figure around London, not least because he had his Rolls Royce painted bright yellow so that police constables would see him coming and clear the route ahead. The house was later acquired by the 9th Duke of Devonshire who made some attempt to remodel the interior in the style of the old Devonshire House (see Mayfair chapter) before letting it to the newspaper proprietor Lord Northcliffe. Lauded as the father or modern journalism the owner of *The Times* died in the house in August 1922, having formed the curious habit of retreating to a small monk's cell of a hut he had erected on the roof. This has since been removed.

For many years no. 3 was occupied by MI6, and indeed may still be. Long used for interviewing prospective recruits, in 1961 it was the scene of George Blake's interrogation after the suspected Soviet double agent had been flushed out by a Polish defector called Michael Goleniewski. With his guilt never in much doubt Blake looked certain to receive the maximum sentence for spying in peacetime, which, at the time, was fourteen years. Instead he was given three such terms to run consecutively, the Lord Chief Justice, Lord Parker of Waddington, choosing to punish separately three different episodes in three different countries. This left Blake with a record sentence for a British court, forty-two years in all, and one that remained unbroken until 1986. The length of the sentence was shocking to many, but in so far as they are known so were Blake's crimes. Blake himself freely admitted that he could not recall what was handed over 'because it was so much,' and estimates of the number of friendly agents he exposed run as high as four hundred. Many of these disappeared and one must assume they were executed.

But for those who were appalled at the sentence there were also some very uncomfortable comparisons to be drawn between the treatment meted out to the working class Blake and the much softer handling of the more obviously middle-class and better-connected members of the Cambridge University 'ring'. In part because of this disparity and its perceived unfairness a plan was hatched by three anti-nuclear protesters to spring Blake from Wormwood Scrubs and help him on his way to Moscow. Incredibly the plan worked, and in 1966 by the simple expedient of throwing a length of rope over the prison's east wall Blake was freed and then driven to East Germany hidden in a campervan. In 1989 in an intriguing postscript – one of the three having died in the interim – two of the conspirators were then arrested and charged after publishing a book on the subject. Deciding to defend themselves in court, both emphatically denied condoning Blake's crimes but insisted his sentence was vicious, inhuman and hypocritical. The jury seemed to agree and found both men innocent of all charges. At the time of writing Blake continues to live somewhere in Russia, reportedly on a full KGB pension.

Insensitively rebuilt in 1932 by Sir Reginald Blomfield, no. 4 is clearly too tall for its surroundings, faced in stone instead of stucco, and indeed led to questions being raised in Parliament. It replaced a previous building that was home to three foreign secretaries: Lord Palmerston from 1847–55, A. J. Balfour from 1874–91 and in 1898 George Nathaniel Curzon, 1st Marquess Curzon of Kedleston (see Carlton House Terrace). One of the original marble fire surrounds with its grate has survived, however, and is in the Victoria and Albert Museum. Today a large plaque on the building's façade records the presence from 1940–4 of officers of the Free French Forces and includes the transcript of the famous speech broadcast to the French people by Charles de Gaulle after the fall of France in 1940. A statue of the general was installed opposite the building, and unveiled by the Queen in 1993. William Gladstone lived at no. 6 from 1838–41, but is commemorated at Carlton House Terrace where his tenancy was much longer (see below).

General Charles de Gaulle, Carlton Gardens

Carlton House Terrace

The name of course commemorates the great palace built by the Prince Regent starting in the 1780s, but now sadly entirely demolished. Its history began thirty years earlier, in 1732, when Frederick Prince of Wales acquired a house originally built for the Anglo-Irish politician Henry Boyle, Lord Carleton (1669–1725). This was enlarged by the prince's widow following his death in 1751 and their son, George III, subsequently agreed to his own son taking on the lease providing he meet the costs of 'all repairs, taxes and the keeping of the gardens'. The gardens, which at that time were extensive, were by William Kent and were said to be impressive. But the house was markedly less so, and having admired Henry Holland's new Brooks's Club (see St James's Street) the architect was summoned by the prince and asked to rebuild it in the fashionable neoclassical style. Beginning around 1783 the work was to take almost three decades with John Nash soon joining Holland to work on the interior. As the project expanded to incorporate the sites of neighbouring houses, which were bought and even pulled down, Prince George was forced to admit that the cost was 'enormous'. As lavish within as it was spectacular without, opinions varied widely when it was finally completed, with one architect comparing the result to Versailles while another insisted it was merely 'overdone with finery'.

Fitted out with marble from Italy and the finest French furniture, it was to be the scene of countless lavish celebrations. Among these was one in 1811 to mark the prince's appointment as Regent, another three years later to celebrate Wellington's triumph over Napoleon and a third in 1816 on the occasion of the wedding of its owner's only child. Sadly,

Princess Charlotte was later to die in childbirth, aged just twenty-one. When the Regent finally succeeded his ailing father in 1820, his coronation as George IV costing an unprecedented £243,000, the creator of this beautiful extravagance decided it was nevertheless insufficiently grand. Within five years Carlton House was no more. The columns from its Corinthian portico went to the National Gallery, and a number of fireplaces and door cases were reused at Buckingham Palace and Windsor Castle. The remainder disappeared completely, and in its place John Nash was commissioned to build the creamy terraces we see today. These are widely admired, typifying the quietly plain and dignified restraint of the best of Regency architecture, and in the opinion of Nikolaus Pevsner likely to rank as 'the greatest terrace houses ever built in Britain'.

With the private gardens behind the Athenaeum, Reform and Travellers' Club now making up much of one side of the street, Nash's original plan had been to link the two blocks of terrace houses with a large domed fountain, reusing the columns from the old house and closing the vista from Regent Street. He failed to get approval for this part of his scheme, however, and instead a flight of steps was built down to the Mall and later surmounted by Benjamin Wyatt's Tuscan granite column and Sir Richard Westmacott's bronze statue of the Duke of York. Even without the fountain, having been designed as a single architectural entity when viewed from St James's Park, the two rows nevertheless represent a successful example of unified street architecture. This effect is enhanced by the end house to each block being carried up above the roof of the main façade, giving an impression of a matched pair of vast pavilions. Similarly, to the rear, the Park being much lower ground, the basement rooms were uniformly extended

Carlton House Terrace

out to the Mall where immense Grecian Doric columns support a balustraded parapet with the houses standing on top of this vast podium.

Today the two rows (each of nine houses) are almost without exception occupied by institutions. These include the Turf Club at no. 5 (which famously once numbered an impressive sixteen dukes among its members) the Royal Society at nos. 6–9, the British Academy at nos. 10–11 and at no. 12, slightly paradoxically housed in such traditional surroundings, the Institute of Contemporary Arts. Until 1939, however, Carlton House Terrace was largely still residential, a fashionable address that for a long time attracted a number of notable occupants. From 1840–6, the house at no. 5 was occupied by Lord Palmerston, with another prime minister, Earl Grey, at no. 13 from 1851–7 and then again two years later. An early London County Council plaque on no. 11 marks the residency of a third prime minister: William Ewart Gladstone, the great Liberal having earlier lived at no. 4. As previously noted, Lord Curzon also lived in the terrace, occupying the house at no. 1 from 1905–22 following his time as Viceroy of India.

By far the most controversial tenant, however, was Joachim von Ribbentrop, Germany's reviled ambassador to Britain from 1936–8. Starting with the Prussian Legation in 1849 German embassy staff occupied no. 9 until the outbreak of the Second World War, by which time it had been combined with no. 8 and possibly remodelled by Hitler's favourite architect, Albert Speer. Prior to von Ribbentrop's arrival the death of his predecessor Dr Leopold von Hoesch (1881–1936) led to the extraordinary spectacle of Nazis goose-stepping along the Mall, the normal protocols for an ambassador dying in office

8 and 9 Carlton House Terrace

requiring the host country to mount what was almost a state funeral. While von Hoesch was by all accounts a reluctant Nazi (his death was officially put down to a stroke but he may well have been murdered on the orders of Berlin) the proceedings included a nineteen-gun salute, British cabinet ministers leading the mourners and a detachment of Grenadier Guards marching alongside Nazi troops. These were to accompany a ceremonial gun limber on which the swastika-draped coffin was borne to Victoria Station and then back to Germany. Today, so close to Waterloo Place – and with statues commemorating the polar explorer Captain Robert Falcon Scott, the wartime 'defender of London' Air Chief Marshal Sir Keith Park and so many other Imperial heroes – the Nazi connection is hard to believe. Indeed it might well be but for the existence of a tiny

Carlton House Terrace: London's only
Nazi memorial

headstone hidden in the shadow of a large plane tree here in Carlton House Terrace. Officially, the headstone is London's only Nazi memorial; it is the grave of Giro (*Eine treuer begleiter*, 'a true companion'), the late ambassador's faithful hound who died in an accident during his time in London.

Charles II Street

Largely a story of loss, what until 1939 was simply 'Charles Street' is of little interest today having been much rebuilt and cut short by the creation of Lower Regent Street by John Nash in 1819. In fact that end of the street was never the most prestigious; its proximity to the old St James's market meaning the accommodation was markedly smaller and cheaper than at the St James's Square end. At what is now no. 29 once stood a large early-eighteenth-century house built for the Earls of Galloway. This was later occupied by the Earl of Liverpool (1770–1828) when the future prime minister was Secretary of State for War and the Colonies, but demolished in 1912.

Linking the street to Pall Mall, the vaulted Royal Opera Arcade was designed by Nash in 1816 and like Burlington Arcade (see Mayfair chapter) conformed to a generally Parisian design. The small and attractive bow-fronted shops are on one side only, the other side being occupied by the premises of Her Majesty's Theatre. Once the Haymarket or Italian Opera House this too had been designed by Nash, with colonnades on three sides and the arcade on the fourth. The present building, designed by Charles J. Phipps in a lavish French Renaissance style in 1897, is traditionally renamed His or Her Majesty's each time a new monarch ascends to the throne. Its design was intended to complement that of the Carlton Hotel on Lower Regent Street but this was demolished after being badly bombed in 1940.

The former Charles Street was also home to the Junior United Service Club (see Pall Mall), its clubhouse designed by Sir Robert Smirke and described as being 'Grecian' in style rather than 'Greek'. The members moved in during 1819 but unfortunately the new building was never much liked and soon moves were afoot to sell it to the members of the Travellers' Club. When they declined to take it on, Decimus Burton was brought in to improve things. To a point this worked, but eventually the club authorities abandoned it and sensibly merged with the United Service Club on Pall Mall. The clubhouse was duly pulled down, and in 1958 replaced by new premises for the United Kingdom Atomic Energy Authority. This still stands and fronts onto Lower Regent Street.

Cleveland Row

Barbara Villiers (1640–1709), born into the aristocracy, was regarded by historians and gossips alike as the most materialistic and acquisitive of Charles II's several mistresses. In her earlier years she took a rope dancer at Bartholomew Fair as a lover, but lived to see five of her six offspring acknowledged by the King and ennobled by him. (She was herself made Countess of Castlemaine and then Duchess of Cleveland.) Tall, voluptuous and auburn-haired, she was variously described as 'the uncrowned queen' and the 'curse of the nation' for the influence she was thought to hold over the throne. In 1688 Charles bought a large property for her close to his own palace, built in the 1620s for the Earl of Berkshire but soon renamed Cleveland House and much extended by the avaricious Duchess. That house stood on this site until the mid-nineteenth century, hence the name of the street, but it was subsequently renamed Bridgewater House after a later owner, the canal-building 3rd Duke of Bridgewater. The Duke again extended the old house to include a huge top-lit gallery for his important collection of pictures, and his nephew and heir – the 1st Duke of Sutherland (1758–1833), historically to be counted among Britain's greatest territorial magnates with an estimated 1.3 million acres in the Highlands – continued its restoration for some years. By the late 1830s, however, the old structure was nevertheless considered dated and somewhat hazardous, and the architect Sir Charles Barry was commissioned to create the vast Italianate palace that occupies the site today, with the carcase finished in 1848 and the interior by 1864. The scale is impressive and it is, as Pevsner notes, 'a colossal presence in such a modest street'.

The most striking feature of Barry's Bridgewater House was its immense central hall, a glazed courtyard or *cortile* rising through the full height of the building and surrounded on all sides by domed and vaulted arcades giving onto the ground and first-floor corridors and staterooms. The decoration was mostly by the German, Jakob Götzenberger, but entirely Italian in its influences. In particular, Götzenberger drew heavily on designs by Raphael: most notably the famous loggia he created at the Vatican; and also the house Raphael designed for Cardinal Guilio de Medici, the Villa Madama – an influential Renaissance structure on the slopes of Monte Mario near Rome. Lavish use of coloured marble, and richly painted and gilded vaulting continued as far as the owner's private apartments.

The new house also incorporated a long, narrow, picture gallery with Corinthian screens at either end, which, despite being private was regularly opened to the public. Unfortunately, it was badly damaged by a direct hit in the 1940s, with two of the greatest works – Titian's *Diana and Actaeon* and his *Three Ages of Man* – later resurfacing in the National Gallery of Scotland. After this, Bridgewater House was sold to an insurance company and later to a firm of engineers.

Bridgewater House, Cleveland Row

Incredibly, what is by far the largest house in central London was then brought back into private ownership (in 1980) and at the time of writing Bridgewater House is still owned by the family of a Greek shipping tycoon.

With the exception of St James's Palace (see separate entry) no other building in Cleveland Row comes close to rivalling Bridgewater House in either scale or magnificence, although several older properties still stand in an attractive row opposite. In the 1820s the novelist Frederick Marryat (1792–1848) – usually bylined 'Captain Marryat' – lived at no. 5, some years before resigning his Royal Navy commission to write *Mr Midshipman Easy* and *Children of the New Forest*. On the north side the little L-shape of Russell Court still gives an impression of a nicely unspoilt central London mews.

Overlooking the park, Stornoway House was constructed around 1790 by Samuel Wyatt, but in the 1950s it was substantially rebuilt within the original walls after sustaining heavy aerial damage during the previous decade. Early occupiers included the Whig George Grenville, who served as prime minister from 1763–5 and Miles Peter Andrews (1742–1814), a largely forgotten figure who uniquely combined in one person the professions of munitions manufacturer and playwright. From 1926 until its near destruction by the Luftwaffe the house was occupied by the aforementioned Lord Beaverbrook who lived here during his time as Minister for Aircraft Production. Appointed by Churchill personally – the combative pair were great friends – the significance of the position was perhaps most clearly expressed by the American *Time* magazine when a 1940 cover story noted that 'this war is a war of machines. It will be won on the assembly line.'

Crown Passage

A narrow and slightly dark but wonderful cut-through from King Street to Pall Mall, Crown Passage is not architecturally distinguished but has successfully escaped the fate of so many central London alleyways. Whilst these have declined into dank hangouts for the homeless (and the worst kind of informal stopping-off places for drunks caught short) Crown Passage still buzzes from dawn to dusk with a cheerful jumble of independent shops, bustling cafés and even an historic pub, the only building in the passage of any distinction.

While the passage dates back to 1673 the present Red Lion is merely Georgian, although its black timber frontage and leaded lights clearly hint at a much earlier building on the same site. So too do the sturdy brackets for gas lighting outside, and indeed the pub (which has been owned by the same brewer for more than two centuries) has a good claim to possess the second oldest liquor licence in the West End. Once a year, on the last weekend in January, cavaliers in full rig crowd into the main bar to lament the execution on 30 January 1649 of their beloved monarch, Charles I. Also to ponder yet again the existence of an old subterranean tunnel, which is rumoured either to have linked the pub to nearby St James's Palace or to the site of Eleanor 'Nell' Gwyn's old house on the other side of Pall Mall.

Sadly neither seems at all likely, but even without the legend Crown Passage is charming and like the old markets which grew up alongside the large houses it continues to provide services of real value to those living and working in this corner of the West End. Years ago it was said that without leaving it, one could hire a chimney sweep, be measured for a suit and have a hat made, buy the week's groceries and a daily paper, get a hair-cut and organise the dry cleaning. Today you still can, most of it anyway, and while with its famous names and royal warrants Jermyn Street undoubtedly remains this neighbour-hood's premier shopping street even that distinguished thoroughfare would be hard-pressed to match the sheer range of goods available in Crown Passage.

Duke of York Street

By chance the other truly memorable pub in St James's is also called Red Lion, this time a perfect Victorian gin palace in miniature and an exemplar of that era's over-developed taste for interior decoration. Lush and plush, a riot of elaborate carved and deeply pol-ished mahogany, its cheerfully cramped but characterful interior boasts an abundance of etched and bevelled glass panels, glittering cut-glass mirrors; even a genuine 'Lincrusta' ceiling of embossed decorated paper.

The street itself was named in honour of Charles II's brother and heir, the Duke of York, who came to the throne in 1685 as James II. Development began around the same time, providing a view from St James's Square to Wren's church of St James's on Piccadilly. At that time it is thought to have

Red Lion, Duke of York Street

comprised just five houses on the west side, and three opposite. None has survived and today the Victorian tavern – a handsome replacement for one that occupied the same site in the eighteenth century – is the most interesting building in the street. The dis-tinctive covered doorway beneath a Tuscan porch at the foot of the street on the western side (actually a side door to 10 St James's Square) provides another point of interest. Until recently so too did the semi-derelict but charming premises of the old Wheeler's fish restaurant in the adjacent Apple Tree Yard, but sadly this was torn down in 2013.

Duke Street St James's

A companion street in that it too is named after the Duke of York (1633–1701) this is another development to have been built on Henry Jermyn's land. Completed in the 1680s it was the first street in this part of the West End to have a paved pathway on one side for pedestrians. Although there were always lodgings here it was from the outset decidedly commercial rather than residen-tial, and by 1749 it was a busy thoroughfare with a number of small craftsmen, two chandlers, a stocking maker, an upholder (upholsterer) selling soft furnishings and a peruke- or wigmaker. As this list of trades-men suggests it was not a particularly smart street, although among those who lodged here at this time six described themselves as gentlemen, and Dr Robert Young was a well-respected surgeon.

Somewhat less respectable were its female contingent, including Charlotte Kelly, who moved into no. 30 in 1765. Her 'House of Civility' was the haunt of a 'bevy of beauties' although male clients were also free to enter-tain their own doxies on the premises if they so wished. Nor was Mrs Kelly alone in this endeavour, as her neighbours included Lucy Seales, a 'very genteel and well-made lass' but one who (as a guide to such services put it at the time) 'has not seen much service yet [as] she shows little passion in her work'.

Today many of the buildings look older than they are, but some are attractive. Nos. 2–4, for example, is a curious Edwardian ensemble but with its arcaded ground floor, prominent aedicule or tabernacle framing to the first-floor windows and positively Roman second-floor windows it is clearly intended to echo a much earlier style.

Haymarket (west side)

The derivation of its name being somewhat obvious, the presence of such a market here would have depended on the proximity of the Kings Mews – also known as the Dunghill – which from the thirteenth to the nineteenth century stood on the site now occupied by Trafalgar Square. In 1661 Charles II appointed a market inspector to oversee the sale of hay, straw and fodder, and the following year agreed that a levy should be payable on all sales to underwrite the cost of improving and maintaining the site. The market nevertheless soon became a filthy place and it was swept away by his successor. On coming to the throne James II insisted on its removal to a new site north of Piccadilly, where in time it developed into the large and unruly May Fair. (See Mayfair chapter.) Many small hay and straw sellers managed to stay on, however, and it was not until 1830 that they were finally banished.

Historically, the whole of the west side had belonged to Queen Henrietta Maria, although in 1661 she granted a lease to her friend, the developer Henry Jermyn (1605–

Her Majesty's Theatre and New Zealand House, Haymarket

84), who quickly started building. By 1720 John Strype's *Survey of London* found here 'a spacious street of great resort, full of inns and houses of entertainment' – meaning theatres as well as the inevitable brothels – and it was in one of the taverns, Long's, that the 7th Earl of Pembroke killed a man in a duel. For this he served a month under guard in the Tower of London, afterwards dying of drink and syphilis (aged just thirty) after being found guilty of killing two more men.

Haymarket's seedy reputation endured – in Victorian times it was still a 'great parade ground of abandoned women' – but most of its buildings have not. The present Her Majesty's Theatre by Charles John Phipps (1835–97), for example, is the fourth theatre on this site, the latest replacement for the 1705 original, which was built for Sir John Vanbrugh. With rich, but small-scale,

Victorian detailing it is typical of Phipps, a man whose extraordinary portfolio includes around fifty theatres, among them the Queen's, Vaudeville, Prince's, Strand, Garrick and the Savoy which in 1881 was the world's first public building to be entirely lit by electricity. The great Victorian actor-manager and theatre impresario, Sir Herbert Beerbohm Tree, called Her Majesty's 'beautiful, beautiful', while another admirer, George Bernard Shaw, felt compelled to congratulate the architect for eschewing the usual tendency of Victorians to make such places 'panelled, and mirrored, and mantel-pieced like the first class saloon of a P&O liner or a Pullman drawing-room car'. Instead beneath its great dome Phipps created something grand but restrained, inspired by the opera house at Versailles rather than seeking to ape it. With a similar triple tier of boxes and Corinthian columns of marble the interior is delightful, and outside too its layers pile atop each other like a wedding cake but without sacrificing anything in terms of scale or style.

Architecturally, New Zealand House is the only other building of note on the St James's eastern boundary, and inevitably it towers over the theatre in a manner that is not entirely happy. It is nevertheless an unusually striking and elegant eighteen-storey monolith of glass and concrete, and as such a worthy replacement for the aforementioned, bomb-damaged Carlton Theatre. It was designed in the late-1950s by Robert Matthew, and opened by the Queen in 1963, the tower positioned above a four-storey 'podium' with a combination of Belgian marble and Portland stone cladding. Especially generous glazing, carefully chosen proportions and features such as the densely planted inner courtyard on the second floor made it clear from the start that this was no ordinary commercial office development. In consequence, fifty years on, it is still an outstandingly handsome building in a way that so many 1960s rivals are not. For many years the view from the top floor Martini Terrace was considered the eighth best in London, and today at 225 feet it provides the best possible view across St James's.

Jermyn Street

Dismissed by jealous rivals as 'fat, opportunistic, and full of soup and gold,' Henry Jermyn did well out of his friendship with the Crown, in part it was said because he had secretly married the King's mother. Such a charge is possible but unlikely now to be proved, although for years a bas relief on the Bury Street façade of 73 Jermyn Street showed the happy outcome of their relationship. This depicted the day in 1661 when Charles II assigned to Jermyn the title deeds to forty-five acres of poor quality land together with the necessary permissions to make of them what he could. The plaque was unfortunately thrown into a skip by builders a few years ago and is now lost. In creating what amounted to London's first aristocratic suburb, Jermyn recognised that to be properly self-contained his new community of great houses needed to include the sort of modest courtyards, shops and markets that today make St James's such a pleasure to stroll through. Its immediate proximity to the Court guaranteed the prestige of St James's Square, which was soon home to half a dozen dukes (and an even greater number of earls) while Jermyn Street quickly established itself as a fashionable shopping street – as it still is today – as well as a place to live.

The western portion of the street was always the more fashionable, and while none of the original buildings have survived John Churchill, 1st Duke of Marlborough (1650–1722) kept a house here from 1675–84. His neighbours would have included Charles Beauclerk (1670–1726), the product of the relationship between Charles II and Nell Gwyn, and subsequently the 1st Duke of St Albans.

A blue plaque at no. 87 records that for a while it was home to Sir Isaac Newton. However, renumbering since the eighteenth century, and the fact that so many people lodged here rather than building fine homes, means many former residents can no longer be placed with any accuracy. Lord Nelson certainly lived in Jermyn Street for a while, as did Sir Walter Scott and Sidney Smith. There was also at least one future prime minister in W. E. Gladstone, who, when first summoned to Westminster, was living above a corn chandler's here. Thomas Wall (of sausage and ice cream fame) was actually born here in 1846, at no. 113, and the poet Thomas Gray was in the habit of lodging in Jermyn Street at 'Roberts's the hosiers, or at Frisby's the oilman' both of which must be assumed to have been at the poorer, eastern end of the street.

By 1815 Jermyn Street included 'a whole range of hotels [where] all the articles of consumption are of the best; and the accommodations, much to the injury of taverns and lodging-houses, combine all the retirement and comforts of home'. Much the same is true today, and indeed some of the best-known names in the street would have been there at this time even if the buildings they occupy have since been demolished and rebuilt. Companies like J. Floris, for example, royal perfumers since the arrival in London from Minorca of Juan Famenio Floris in 1730. This ninth-generation family concern is still

using the attractive mahogany display cases and counters that were commissioned to show off their colognes and toiletries at Prince Albert's Great Exhibition in 1851. Further along the pavement R. E. Tricker has been making traditional English shoes since the last days of George IV, and Messrs. Paxton & Whitfield, the celebrated cheese-monger and provisions merchant, moved here as long ago as 1797 having already spent at least half a century running a successful stall at Clare Market.

Sadly, many other notable enterprises have gone. Wall's original butchers shop at no. 113, for example, eventually became a restaurant, and the Turkish baths at no. 76 failed to reopen after being bombed flat in 1941. (Impressively, a similar establishment at no. 92 survived until 1976.) In many ways an even greater loss, however, was the unique interior to hat maker Edward Bates at no. 21. For more than a century this was barely altered from when the shop first opened in 1898. With row upon row of decorative hat-boxes, and fading yellow newspaper cuttings of the great and the good sporting their new Bates hats, caps and panamas, surveying it all was the preserved remains of Binks the cat. Apparently, the handsome tom wandered in as a stray more than ninety years ago, and, 'admired and loved by everyone', he never left. He was stuffed and mounted following his death around the time of the 1926 General Strike, and remained at the shop until its closure was forced by redevelopment in 2009. You can still buy a Bates hat today – they sell them at Hilditch and Key at no. 73 – but somehow, even though Binks is there too, in a glass case with his top hat and cigar – it is not the same.

Until the aforementioned development (ongoing at the time of writing) the shop next door at no. 20 was arguably even more impressive, the premises of Geo. F Trumper. With its dark panelling, brass fittings and gleaming glass-fronted cabinets, the ambience was clearly intended to be more senior club library than mere barbers shop, but then was nothing 'mere' about George Trumper. Appointed court hairdresser to Queen Victoria, Empress of India, his family was similarly honoured throughout five subsequent reigns, and has now happily found a new home in Duke of York Street.

In October 2009, as Bates and Trumper were boxing everything up to move, Jermyn Street saw no fewer than ten dukes – Leinster, Wellington, St Albans, Norfolk, Rutland, Northumberland, Bedford, Somerset, Argyll and Montrose – coming together for lunch in what is thought to have been the largest gathering of their Graces since the Coronation in 1953. The venue for this historic decaducal event was Wilton's at no. 55, a restaurant that proudly proclaims a heritage stretching back more than 250 years. Surprisingly, even with this history, it cannot claim to be London's oldest restaurant, which, in fact, is Rules (see Covent Garden chapter). The reason is that what is now London's finest fish-and-seafood restaurant was in 1742 merely a stall selling oysters, shrimps and cockles in the Haymarket. Business prospered, however, and by 1805 the founder's nephew was able to take a lease and open his new Wilton's Shellfish Mongers and Oyster Rooms in Cockspur Street. Several royal warrants followed, and while the address changed several times Wilton's sensibly chose to remain in St James's. It very nearly closed in its bicentenary year, in 1942 when a German bomb landed on the nearby Wren church, and the owner decided she had finally had enough. Happily, one of her regulars was in that day, the banker Olaf Hambro, who looked up from his oysters and asked for the restaurant to be added to his bill. His family owns it still.

Equally happily, and despite all the redevelopment, there are still some lovely architectural touches to be seen elsewhere in Jermyn Street. No. 106 is a nice turn-of-the-century Jacobean pastiche with Art Nouveau touches, while nos. 93 and 97 are two of the best examples of traditional mid-Victorian London shop fronts in London. The crested capitals outside Turnbull and Asser at no. 71 look as brightly decorated as any ship's figurehead, and no. 53, with its elegant curved glass façade, leads the eye nicely into the charming Piccadilly Arcade. The adjacent statue of Beau Brummell is recent (2002, by Irena Sidiecka) but is a nice reminder of the days, not that long ago, when it could still be said that, while Bond Street was for the ladies, Jermyn Street was definitely a place for gentlemen.

Piccadilly Arcade, Jermyn Street

Beau Brummell, Jermyn Street

King Street

Another named for Charles II, King Street was completed in 1682 – two years before Henry Jermyn's death – but again no seventeenth-century buildings remain among the modern blocks. The Golden Lion tavern is thus one of the few older buildings in this part of St James's and the most interesting, a colourful and richly decorated Victorian replacement for a tavern that stood here as long ago as 1762 and possibly much earlier. The adjacent block replaced the St James's Theatre which – in the face of many objections – was demolished in 1957 to make way for a decidedly pedestrian office development. Among the protesters were the future Lord Olivier and his then wife Vivien Leigh, both actors being then commemorated in an attractive frieze affixed to the side of the new

building in a move that could be seen as both cynical and vaguely insulting.

The St James's, which opened in the 1830s, was for a while managed by Mrs John Wood, a former child actor. Oscar Wilde's *Lady Windermere's Fan* and *The Importance of Being Earnest* both had their premieres here, as did *The Second Mrs Tanqueray* by Sir Arthur Wing Pinero (1855–1934). The theatre's demolition became something of a cause célèbre, and it was subsequently agreed by the authorities that henceforth no London theatre would close without a replacement building being found. It had been built on the site of Nerot's Hotel, which opened in 1776 and was where Nelson met his wife after returning from his victory over Napoleon in the Battle of the Nile in 1798. (In a curious twist, exactly fifty years later Bonaparte's nephew, Napoleon III, was living down the street at no. 1c, a fact commemorated by the oldest surviving blue plaque in the capital and the only one to incorporate the French imperial eagle.)

For all that, the theatre's neighbour was arguably more interesting still, having once been the premises of Almack's Assembly Rooms, the fashionable eighteenth-century haunt, which opened in 1765. The proprietor was an incomer who called himself William Almack after coming south, having (it was rumoured) arrived at the name by modifying the rather too Scottish-sounding name of MacCall. A place for gambling and for elaborate balls, membership was exclusively upper class, Almack relying on a number of society ladies (known as the Seven Patronesses) to advise him as to who should and should not be admitted. The dress code was strict (the Duke of Wellington was once refused entry for wearing trousers instead of knee breeches) but the entertainment such premises was leased to an auctioneer, and the building was largely destroyed by enemy action in the Second World War.

Although one block at the corner of St James's Square was recently converted to apartments, King Street remains largely commercial with Christie's at no. 8 perhaps the most prominent of the firms accommodated here. The present building is not interesting – only the 1893 façade survived the Second World War – but is the principal London saleroom of the fine-art auctioneers, an enterprise that traces its origins to a former midshipman, James Christie, who set up shop in Pall Mall in 1767. Initially, the company would sell anything that came in, but by the turn of the century the firm had begun to specialise, Christie forming close friendships with painters such as Gainsborough (his next-door neighbour) and Sir Joshua Reynolds. In 1823 the company moved to the present address, by which time Christie's son, also James, had taken the reins. The last Christie to control the company retired in 1889, and exactly one hundred years later its annual turnover was reported to be £1 billion.

Little St James's Street

Once a passageway no more than ten-feet wide, what in 1680 was called Catherine Wheel Yard after a long-gone tavern of that name provided a link between St James's Street to a private stable yard on the boundary of Green Park. At that time it extended over what had once been the gardens of Cleveland House, but much of it was swept away when the much larger Bridgewater House was built on the same site (see Cleveland Row). By 1722 the remaining portion of the passageway had been widened and renamed Little

The Golden Lion, King Street

that a ticket of entry was considered to be 'the seventh heaven of the fashionable world'. Its success lasted for more than half a century, but by 1835 the fashion (and fashionable) had moved on. In 1893 part of the

St James's Street and in the 1840s it was extended at right-angles with a new section running north–south along the high wall of Bridgewater House. This still occupies almost one whole side of the street, its magnificent carriage entry firmly locked but with a splendid brass bell pull for visiting coachmen. Unfortunately a modest eighteenth-century terrace on the other side, built by Thomas Dance who later designed the main block of Guy's Hospital, has long since disappeared, although an attractive Georgian mews building (backing on to Russell Court) still survives.

Curiously, so too does the name Catherine Wheel Yard, although this now refers to a small cobbled cul-de-sac that lies between Bridgewater House and Spencer House (see St James's Place) at the right angle in Little St James's Street. It was originally owned by 'John Underwood, citizen and leather seller of London' and like nearby Blue Ball Yard it is still an attractive and pleasantly private corner of this part of the capital.

Marlborough Road

For many years a private access road from palace to park, Marlborough Road was opened to public traffic – meaning then mostly equestrian – only as recently as 1856. The Crown's reluctance to do this earlier is easy to understand, since the modern road (whilst not especially busy) effectively cuts off the Tudor St James's Palace from its delightful classical Queen's Chapel.

Bringing a taste of sixteenth century Italy to seventeenth century England, the chapel was designed by Inigo Jones, originally for a Spanish princess, but then for a French queen when negotiations with representatives of the Iberian throne faltered and collapsed.

The Queen's Chapel, Marlborough Road

Difficulties had arisen in 1623 because traditional European religious rivalries meant that Spain was not convinced that once back in London Charles I would honour an agreement to allow the Infanta Maria Anna to have sole charge of their children for the first twelve years, together with her own chapel. (She was also to have a bishop and twenty priests, who would be exempt from English law.) Unable to persuade the Spanish that he would keep his word, the King was forced to find another bride and by good fortune, in France, Henrietta Maria's spiritual guardians were easier to deal with.

As Queen, Henrietta too asked for and got her own chapel, a building that together with the architect's other iconic, light-coloured designs – the Banqueting Hall of 1619, the Queen's House, Greenwich (1616–35) and St Paul's in Covent Garden (1631–8) – must have conspired to make the mellow brick jumble of Tudor London look very old fashioned. The chapel's full-width Venetian window overlooking the street is also thought to be the first one in the country, an attractive repudiation of the Perpendicular Gothic that had for so long held sway in this country among the ecclesiastic authorities. Alongside the Tudor palace this small box of a building combines beauty and simplicity in a manner that today one might term minimalist. Plain, chaste and wonderfully unassertive, its rendered exterior makes little if any compromise to its situation or surroundings and instead adheres as closely as any building in this part of London to the precepts of the Classical Revival.

Sadly it is never open to the public except during services, but beneath its vaulted ceiling of white and gold the chapel appears largely original although the gallery, stalls and lectern are slightly later additions. Perhaps unsurprisingly, given that it was built by a Protestant king for a Catholic queen, the chapel has paid host to an unusually wide range of worshippers over the years. Not just the Queen Consort's Catholic masses, but also Dutch Reformed services for William and Mary, Lutheran services for several generations of Hanoverians, and, more recently, Danish rites for Edward VII's Queen Alexandra. To further confuse the situation, from the eighteenth to the early twentieth century, even the name was changed and for a while it was known as the German Chapel Royal.

Mason's Yard

Entered via a covered opening from Duke Street, Mason's Yard is surprisingly spacious and shares its origins with nearby St James's Square. In Henry Jermyn's day it was known as West Stable Yard and provided stabling for horses and standing space for carriages serving or visiting the large houses on the square. Until 1845 it enjoyed direct access into the square, but this was lost when new premises for the London Library were constructed in the north-west corner.

The name Mason commemorates Henry Mason, who lived on Duke Street in the 1730s and opened a tavern (called the Mason's Arms) on the site of what is now the Chequers. By then the yard behind was occupied mostly by artisans and workshops, but, since 2006, it has been dominated by the White Cube Gallery, a West End offshoot of the prestigious East End pioneer. The gallery's striking and uncompromisingly modern space was designed by MRJ Rundell & Associates, and, with its characteristic 'glass-box' top, replaced an electricity substation

White Cube Gallery, Mason's Yard

93

that had blighted the appearance of the yard for many years.

Ormond Yard

Connected to Mason's Yard by a narrow and sharply angled footpath, Ormond Yard is markedly smaller and commemorates what was the largest house in Jermyn's St James's Square development. In 1682 this was purchased by the socially ambitious Anglo-Irish military commander, James Butler, 1st Duke of Ormonde, together with a small vacant lot behind it on which he built his own private stables. The purchase of such a house in St James's was a crucial consideration for Butler and his family, the Duke's own son noting 'how ill it would look now you are an English Duke to have no house there'. On the death of His Grace in 1688 the house passed to a grandson, the 2nd Duke, who remained in the house until 1715 when he was forced to flee to France after being impeached for treason. In his absence he was attainted, his estates forfeited and his honours extinguished, but when the house was put on the market it proved simply too big to sell. In 1736 it was pulled down and replaced by a new development of six smaller properties – the present extent of nos. 9–11 St James's Square and nos. 4–6 Duke of York Street giving a good indication of its size – with the yard behind now the only surviving fragment of the ducal domain.

Pall Mall

As early as the 1590s many European cities had tree-shaded avenues on which the leisured classes could play croquet-like games with long mallets of lance-wood and boxwood balls. Mary Queen of Scot played a version of it,

known variously as *palamaglio*, *palo a maglio* or *palle maille*, and it was her son James I who introduced it to London society after coming to the throne of England in 1603. Charles II also took it up with great enthusiasm, initially playing the game here, when lime trees would have provided the shade, and later creating a new and improved gaming *allée* on what is now the Mall.

When first opened to traffic it was intended to be called Catherine Street (in honour of the Queen) but the old name endured while its location between St James's Square and the Palace ensured it was never anything but a highly fashionable address. It was first lit by gas in 1807, to celebrate the birthday of George III, and today it is still almost entirely Crown property. No. 79 is the sole exception to this on the south side, the freehold to this property having been conveyed through trustees from Charles II to his mistress Nell Gwyn and her descendants. To the modern eye the interest lies almost entirely in the clubs and converted houses on the south side. There is little but shops and offices opposite, although Pall Mall was once very much the centre of the London art scene with the premises of the Royal Academy, Christie's and the nascent National Gallery all briefly here in the 1800s.

Walking from St James's Palace (see panel) the first building of note is sadly cut off from view by a high wall and the uncompromising bulk of an office block by Sir Edwin Lutyens at no. 68. Now somewhat lost behind this unfortunately tall monolith, the eighteenth century Marlborough House was designed in red brick by Christopher Wren the Younger for the 1st Duchess. Much modified, it is the home of the Commonwealth secretariat, hence the very visible security measures, but for many years it was an important royal residence. The birthplace of George V it was also home to Albert Edward, Prince of Wales, Queen Alexandra and Queen Mary with the two queens taking up residence here as widows. (There are memorials to both around the corner in Marlborough Road.) Largely invisible from the Mall, the best view of the building these days is to be had from the two bedroom floors of the Oxford and Cambridge Club at no. 71, although access to this large and striking neoclassical building by Sir Robert Smirke is of course also restricted to its members and their guests.

Described after its recent restoration and redecoration as having emerged 'from the shadows as one of London's richest essays in Greek Revival architecture' the Oxford and Cambridge's eclectic yet coherent façade is today one of the delights of Pall Mall. It was designed to reflect the educated sensibilities of the club membership – the seven reliefs are based on designs by Smirke's Royal Academician father – and certainly it more than holds its own among several architecturally distinguished neighbours. Inside it is equally impressive, Smirke's cool, elegant, Grecian interiors having survived the war (when a bomb landed in the kitchens but failed to detonate) as well as a number of early-twentieth-century alterations.

Further along the street Schomberg House at nos. 80–82 could not provide a stronger contrast to Smirke's work, a rare survivor of seventeenth-century townhouse façade, executed in beautiful brown brick with red decorations. The house was built in 1698 for the 3rd Duke of Schomberg, whose father had been William III's second-in-command during the Glorious Revolution a decade earlier. It was originally much larger

(the east wing was torn down in 1850) and Thomas Gainsborough rented rooms here from 1744–88, although reconstruction behind its lovely façade means that nothing within survives from his time.

At no. 89 the Royal Automobile Club has long been nicknamed 'the Chauffeurs Arms'. This is a slightly sneering reference to it being the least exclusive of the traditional gentlemen's clubs, although with its Turkish baths, a doubles court for squash, a private post office and London's most beautiful swimming pool its facilities are the best of any West End club. Occupying the site of the old War Office – some internal features of which were reconstructed within the clubhouse – it was completed in 1911 by Charles Mewes and Arthur J. Davis, the medal-winning star pupils of the École des Beaux Arts in France, who also designed the Ritz (see Piccadilly, South Side). In technical terms the building was hugely advanced for its time, built on a heroic scale with 60-foot foundations and an eight-storey, 2,000-ton steel matrix supporting the 228-foot-long Portland stone façade we see today. Its arrival on such a prominent site in clubland was not entirely welcomed, however, with members of its older, more conservatively minded rivals deploring what one of their number described as 'a furred, goggled, spare-tyred and cigar-smoking' crowd.

Rivals then and now would have included the Athenaeum, Travellers' and Reform, three clubs that have long been the pride of Pall Mall and which must be counted among its finest buildings. That said, the first of them is described in the section on Waterloo Place, as this is where it has its entrance. Next door, the Travellers' Club – members of which were required in the early days to have travelled the equivalent of five hundred

(left to right) Former United Services', Athenaeum, Travellers' and Reform clubs, seen from Pall Mall

miles in a straight line from London – is a charming, early essay in club architecture by Charles Barry. Though smaller than its neighbours it remains a highly significant building in its own right. The first of its kind to adopt the increasingly fashionable style of the Italian Renaissance, when it was completed in 1832 it proved highly influential. Quite modest, its asymmetrical façade of stucco, not stone, and just five bays wide, Barry's design replaced what had been a 'shabby low-roomed house' at a cost of £64,189. With the principal rooms arranged around a *cortile* (see Bridgewater House above), the Travellers' provided a pattern that was rapidly copied elsewhere in clubland although as at the Reform (see below) its imitators frequently worked to a larger

scale and with marked emphasis on show rather than comfort or practicality. The Pall Mall elevation is naturally the most familiar but the garden front is in the opinion of many even more attractive. Venetian in style it can be seen through the trees from Carlton House Terrace, and the best room in the club is the first-floor library, which in recent years has featured in many films and television series.

The Reform is also by Barry, and is regarded as his masterpiece. The design was again inspired by the Italian Renaissance and the finished structure bears more than a passing resemblance to the Palazzo Farnese, which Michelangelo completed in 1589, and which Barry had closely studied. Much wider than the Travellers', it has nine bays on three floors and the windows on the two main floors are enclosed in their own aedicule, each of which resembles a mini-building made up of two columns and a pediment across the top like a roof. The façade is in Portland stone, and, like the Travellers', it is arranged around a large central hall. This rises through to a glass canopy and is exceptionally richly decorated, the surrounding cloisters largely of warm yellow marble and red decoration. The upper gallery is supported by twenty Ionic columns, from which a corresponding range of Corinthian columns rise; the gallery is served by a magnificent tunnel-vaulted staircase. Like the Travellers', the Reform has a magnificent tripartite library where members may sleep and read.

The club was founded in 1836 in the wake of the groundbreaking Representation of the People Act 1832, usually known as the Great Reform Act. It was intended as a meeting place for the successful and newly enfranchised business class, a class which (just as it had been denied the vote) had found itself excluded from the aristocratic and socially much smarter clubs of St James's Street. Specifically to differentiate themselves from the Regency rakes and dandies, these 'new' men had looked to their architect to create something entirely new for their club. A departure from the coffee-house origins and country-house ambience of the likes of White's, Brooks's and Boodle's, the style chosen was explicitly modern for the times. The building was also to be very large and self-consciously magnificent, a move to underline the success and progressive beliefs of the membership, and their arrival in Pall Mall. The Reform was also the first club in London to have bedrooms, its members paying heavily to retain the services of Alexis Soyer (who at this time was arguably the most famous chef anywhere in the world) and employing the very latest technologies to warm the dishes and turn the spits using the power of steam. The point was well-made although it is doubtful the denizens of St James's Street expressed much concern.

The Reform was for many decades the ex-officio headquarters of the Liberal Party, with party meetings convened, general elections planned and plots hatched. However, politics, perhaps inevitably, split the membership and by the 1920s it had evolved into a social club, although one that is still characterised by a progressive outlook. This was evident in 1981 when the Reform agreed to accept lady members, long before any of the traditional gentlemen's clubs had even considered such a move.

On the north side the modern block of the venerable Army and Navy Club replaced a similar, even loftier and even larger Renaissance-style *palazzo*. The members voted to demolish in 1963, but only when it became apparent that the expense of its upkeep could literally ruin them. Its replacement is not especially attractive: it looks more like an office than a traditional club, but the members clearly like it and they enjoy using it. Had several other clubs in the area taken a similarly pragmatic view, it is possible that they too might have been saved from extinction. As it is they have gone, and so, sadly, have their clubhouses. That said the neighbouring Junior Carlton Club attempted just such a move in 1968, and it failed disastrously. The new building's ceilings were too low to be grand, the colour scheme and fixtures too modern for comfort and in less than a decade the members abandoned the building and wound the club up.

THE LONDON CLUB

Gentlemen's clubs are a peculiarly English institution and, moreover, a peculiarly London one. As Anthony Lejeune notes in his wonderful book, *The Gentlemen's Clubs of London*, they are a 'reflection of an indestructible old England'. While other countries have attempted to copy the concept, none has come close to recreating the special atmosphere to be found in the many establishments that grace the West End of the city. More than three centuries after the development of the first recognisable gentlemen's club the ethos that brought like-minded people together in a convivial atmosphere is as relevant today as it ever was.

While often elegant structures, designed by the leading architects of the day, the best clubs are much more than mere bricks and mortar. They embody the character of the members, who must be gentlemanly, agreeable, and, if possible, sparkling conversationalists. In short, they must be 'clubbable'. As one member of the Garrick wrote in the 1870s, 'It would be better that ten unobjectionable men should be excluded than that one terrible bore should be admitted.' That intolerance of the bore – a person recognised by everyone, but not by himself – is invariably a key criterion when judging membership applications, not least because the presence of the bore is likely to drive out other members.

There is another quality that the best clubs share: the members are kindred spirits, often sharing a similar background, profession, outlook or temperament. This is accurately reflected across the pantheon of West End clubs. Sometimes the name gives it away: the Army and Navy, the National Liberal, the Farmer's, the Traveller's, the Caledonian. Other clubs, however, give no such clue, meaning that it is necessary to dig a little deeper. It might be reasonable to conclude that the Garrick has a strong thespian background, which, of course, it has but the origins of other establishments are not so easy to discern from their names. The Athenaeum, for example, was formed for those of a more intellectual bent, while Brooks's was a young man's haunt in its early days and the headquarters of a fast set of young dandies nicknamed the Macaronies. Buck's came into being in 1919 after Captain H. J. Buckmaster and some of his former comrades, back from the Great War, decided to follow up on their wartime idea for a club that was less formal and stuffy than the existing West End establishments. The

Beefsteak (on Irving Street) as the name suggests, grew out of eighteenth-century all-male dining clubs, whose members venerated this dish.

Clubland can be traced back for centuries. It is said that Shakespeare and Donne were members of a club set up by Sir Walter Ralegh, which met at the Mermaid tavern. In the seventeenth century the clubs became more political in their outlook, often growing out of the coffee and chocolate houses that catered to the wealthy and well-connected. The best example of this is White's, which today is located in St James's Street, but was founded as White's Chocolate House in 1693 by an Italian immigrant called Francesco Bianco. As more clubs opened many were in essence a centre for gambling, gossip and camaraderie, but politics too was an important factor for some, with Brooks's being increasingly associated with the Whigs and White's with the Tories.

The influence of politics took on a new significance in the nineteenth century as 'new' money in the shape of the businessmen enriched by the Industrial Revolution vied for control of Parliament with 'old' money, the aristocracy and owners of landed estates. Perhaps the most political was the Carlton Club, which was formed to rally opponents of the Great Reform Act of 1832; a piece of legislation that significantly extended the franchise and in consequence was seen as a threat by many in the establishment. For its first fifty years the Carlton performed, as Lejeune observes, 'many of the functions now performed by the Conservative Central Office'. By contrast, the Reform Club, set up by Edward Ellice, a Liberal politician, had as its raison d'etre the promotion of the principles outlined in the Act. It is therefore hardly surprising that, a century-and-a-half later, in 1981, the Reform became the first of the traditional clubs to allow ladies to become members.

The West End club has long been a source of inspiration for writers. In the novel *Around the World in Eighty Days*, by Jules Verne, the hero Phileas Fogg begins and ends his epic journey at the Reform Club. While Fogg, the fictional traveller, was granted entry to the hallowed portals a real-life counterpart, Michael Palin, was refused admission after recreating Fogg's journey for a 1989 BBC television series of the same name. It is thought that Palin's 'crime' was that he was not wearing a tie, a strict requirement of gentlemen visiting the Reform, although others take the view that it was because the club was closed for a function. White's appears, albeit heavily disguised, in the novels of Evelyn Waugh, while writers from P. G. Wodehouse to Anthony Trollope have drawn on the great traditions of clubland in their work.

Behaving like a gentleman is still essential for the club member. This is the unbreakable thread that connects the seventeenth century to the twenty-first. Even the most powerful men in the land have felt bound by the strict propriety of clubland. During the period in which Stanley Baldwin was prime minister he arrived one night at the Carlton for dinner with his wife, wearing day clothes. When a club servant advised him of the impropriety of being so attired, Baldwin made a point of going round all the members present to apologise for his oversight. Nor is possession of a royal title a guarantee that the owner of said title will get his own way: in the mid nineteenth century, the Prince of Wales, the future Edward VII, was so annoyed at being told off for smoking by a servant at White's that he stormed out and helped to found a new club, one in which smoking was permitted in every room.

The modern obsessions with political correctness and social justice might have proved hazardous for the gentlemen's club. In addition, the West End has seen a new wave of clubs being opened, expensive to join, but more relaxed than the old-guard establishments on Pall Mall, and another potential threat to traditional clubland. In fact the opposite has proved true. An article in the *Financial Times*, from December 2012, makes it clear that not only are clubs surviving but also that they are thriving. Many have grown membership numbers, while others have long waiting lists.

The older clubs have also moved with the times, without jettisoning the standards that have made them what they are, perhaps because the vast majority are still owned and controlled by their members. Thanks to new and highly trained chefs the food is now immeasurably superior to the often stodgy and unimaginative fare of the past. Capacious wine cellars, stocked with good champagne, white burgundy and claret sold at prices below restaurant levels is another attraction. And while the club may no longer be the cockpit of power of days gone by, the powerful and well-connected still use them to discuss contentious issues in a wholly discreet atmosphere. The traditional London club will be with us for a long time to come.

Park Place

This was developed in the 1680s on land owned by the aforementioned Duchess of Cleveland, although no buildings survive from that time. The earliest still standing are almost certainly nos. 12 and 13, although even here the original eighteenth-century façades have been modified with mid-nineteenth-century balconies and iron work. The most interesting is no. 14, however. Also eighteenth century, this is the premises of Pratt's Club, a small and cluttered but cosy basement, entry to which is jealously guarded.

The club traces its origins to an evening in 1841 when the 7th Duke of Beaufort, 'bored with his usual haunts,' dropped in on the home of his erstwhile steward, William Nathaniel Pratt. The Duke and his friends quickly acquired the habit of visiting regularly, sitting in Pratt's kitchen, conversing and gaming in a manner that has continued uninterrupted ever since. Owned by successive dukes of Devonshire since the 1930s, the club opens in the evening and closes only when the last guest has gone home. To avoid confusion the servants are all known as 'George' and with just one table fourteen diners are seated as they arrive thereby encouraging conversation among members who might not otherwise know each other particularly well.

A quite different club is the Royal Over-Seas League at the park end of the cul-de-sac. Considerably larger, with as many as twenty-thousand members and eighty bedrooms, this occupies part of a 1736 property that was built by James Gibbs (1682–1754) for Lord North. (Curiously its gatehouse is now to be found at 16 Arlington Street, although this portion no longer forms part of the club.) The League itself was established in 1910 by the proprietor of the *Spectator*, Sir Evelyn

Pratt's Club, Park Place

Royal Over-Seas League, Park Place

Wrench, to foster greater understanding and cooperation between the peoples of the British Empire. Today, entirely supported by its members' subscriptions, and with reciprocal clubs and branches in more than seventy countries, it supports 'the ideals of the Commonwealth' by encouraging friendship, cultural exchanges and welfare programmes around the world.

Piccadilly (south side)

As badly abused over the years as the other side of the street (see Mayfair chapter) the south side of Piccadilly was despite its proximity to the Crown never as favoured and today boasts nothing to rival even the small handful of aristocratic mansions which have survived in Mayfair. On the approach from Piccadilly Circus the first building of any real interest is the former Simpson's clothing store (now Waterstone's) one of several with a reasonable claim to be Britain's first welded-steel building. Completed in 1936 it was designed by Joseph Emberton although with its large windows and excellent proportions it looks far more contemporary. One of the first window dressers employed in the store is said to have been the artist László Moholy-Nagy, and while the interior has been completely refitted for the sale and display of books some period fixtures have survived. The main staircase is particularly good.

The quietly polite brick and stonework of St James's Piccadilly – Wren's only London church outside the borders of the Square Mile – gives little clue to its tranquil and sumptuous interior. The church was begun in 1676 to serve the residents of the new developments being created by Lord St Albans, and when it was built Jermyn Street was a far more significant thoroughfare than

St James's Piccadilly, seen from Jermyn Street

Piccadilly. This explains why today its principal entrance seems to be at the rear, but perhaps not why it took nearly a decade to complete given the importance at this time of churches in the urban landscape. Inside one finds splendid lime wood carvings by Grinling Gibbons, the same artist's elaborate and beautifully worked marble font (at which both Pitt the Elder and the poet William Blake were both christened) and Doric pillars beneath Corinthian columns which rise majestically to a richly plastered, barrel-vaulted ceiling. The organ is also of such quality that when it was first installed in 1691 the incumbent felt sufficiently confident to ask Henry Purcell to test it. Some 150 years later craftsmen repairing this same organ found inside it a miniature carved wooden coffin containing the body of a songbird.

The church fortunately survived a serious

fire bombing in the 1940s, which destroyed the vestry and the original spire. Fortunately, the aforementioned wood carvings survived, having been removed to safety, but after seventy years the spire is still a glass-fibre replacement. Perhaps the most striking thing about the church, however, is how light and airy it is inside. Two rows of large windows, and a large open interior said to have a capacity of nearly two thousand worshippers, make this a uniquely wonderful space and one well suited to the concerts and other cultural highlights with which it has long been associated.

Overlooking the churchyard (now given over to a crowded but charming market) the former Midland Bank is by the young Lutyens, a building Pevsner describes as 'a very successful hors d'oeuvre' although the equally eminent architectural historian Sir John Summerson is said to have considered it impudent and illogical. Lutyens preferred to characterise its lively exterior decoration and fenestration as 'Wrennaissance' – a term that has taken on a life of its own – and with its walnut-and-limed-oak interior it is still one of the more attractive buildings on Piccadilly.

Architecturally, the premises of Fortnum and Mason at no. 181 are not remarkable, but the shop still is, a place Dickens described as 'a blossom of lobster salad' and which has a delightful history. In 1705 Hugh Mason had a small shop further south at St James's Market and rented a room above it to William Fortnum, who was then employed as a footman to Queen Anne. The latter insisted on new candles daily, and given responsibility for replacing them each morning, Fortnum started selling the half-used candles on his own account. By 1707 he had accumulated sufficient savings to go into business with Mason. Purveying 'hart's horn, gableworm seed, saffron and dirty white candy' the two

Fortnum and Mason, Piccadilly

were well placed to influence and profit from the changing tastes of their wealthy, aristocratic neighbours.

The business quickly prospered, proving itself to be an exceptionally smart innovator by introducing both a postal service for customers (in 1794, almost half a century before the General Post Office) and an early form of profit-sharing. The shop was also the first in Britain to sell tins of American baked beans (bought from a Mr Heinz, in 1886) and takes credit for inventing the Scotch egg. It also provisioned the first Everest expedition, the hunt for Tutankhamun's tomb and officers fighting the Peninsular and Crimean wars. (Similarly, during the Second World War a special officers department offered silver-plated 'sporks' for eating trench suppers single-handed, and even special nickel-silver bayonet tips.)

Today the Piccadilly store is probably the most famous food emporium in the world, although it does stock a wide range of other goods. People from all backgrounds flock to the food hall on the lower-ground floor – it is said to be a favourite of the royal family – where one can find the finest comestibles from across the globe. Particular mention must be made of the Fortnum and Mason hamper, which is world renowned, having been dispatched to every corner of the world from Everest to the Epsom Derby, and eulogised by innumerable writers including Charles Dickens. The first hampers were provided in the eighteenth century to well-heeled travellers visiting their country estates or taking the waters at Bath. The tradition grew, with hampers becoming an integral part of society events such as the Henley regatta and Cowes week, while on Derby Day carriages queued from four in the morning to satisfy the appetite of hungry race-goers. Soldiers at the front also took comfort from their Fortnum and Masson hampers, and, during the Crimean War, Queen Victoria was moved to send one to Florence Nightingale to help her feed the wounded.

Barring an entrance to Green Park underground station, the last building on this side of Piccadilly is the immense block of the Ritz Hotel, which was opened by the Blackpool Building and Vendor Company in 1906. It was designed by the most fashionable architects in London at that time, Mewes and Davis, whom we met in Pall Mall, and the name references the celebrated hotelier César Ritz, although by this time he was retired. In design terms its style was entirely new to London: lavishly Louis XVI within and a slightly forbidding combination of Portland stone and Norwegian granite without. The impressive arcading at street level was also French in style, successfully evoking the Rue de Rivoli, although for many years the main entrance to the hotel has been around the corner in quieter Arlington Street.

For many years the Ritz was a byword for luxury, and in the early days the entrance was even equipped with a bell the doorman could use to alert staff inside of the arrival of royalty. Even so, the truth was that many aristocratic visitors and crowned heads preferred the quieter, more discreet charms of older establishments such as Claridge's and the Connaught, and in the 1970s the hotel fell on such hard times that it was sold to an industrial conglomerate for considerably less than £3 million. More recently it has undergone a hugely expensive restoration and today features such as the main dining room, the Long Gallery and the celebrated Palm Court bear comparison with any of the world's greatest hotels. Its position overlooking Green Park is also something its rivals can only envy, and the cool Art Deco design of the new Rivoli Bar is one of the most successful in London.

In 2012 London finally marked the unequalled sacrifice of the men of Bomber Command during the years 1939–45 by erecting a fitting memorial at the end of the street (it is actually on a slip road rather than Piccadilly itself). Remembering the courage and sacrifice of the 55,573 crewmen who lost their lives during the war years, the memorial, which cost £6 million, was designed by Liam O'Connor and is built in Portland stone. Attention to detail is evident throughout, especially in the roof, which has aluminium sheets recovered from a crashed Handley Page Halifax III shot down over Belgium in May 1944.

The wonderful centrepiece, by sculptor Philip Jackson, is a bronze sculpture of the thousand survivors and family members who came from as far afield as Australia and New Zealand. After the unveiling, the Battle of Britain Memorial Flight Avro Lancaster overflew the park, dropping thousands of poppies which drifted across the capital in a silent and deeply moving tribute to the lives lost but for so long overlooked.

Ryder Street

Captain Richard Rider was master carpenter to Charles II, and what was originally Rider Street is still entirely Crown property. The land formed part of the original grant to Henry Jermyn, but nothing remains from his original development and the oldest building today is the former Dieudonné's Hotel at no. 11. Dating back to 1865 it is the work of John Norton, a highly original and idiosyncratic design that incorporates both Gothic and Renaissance elements as well as unusual round-headed windows. The red-and-black brickwork is similarly unorthodox for this part of London, as was the arrangement of upstairs bedrooms which – Dieudonné's being something of a notorious *maison de rendez-vous* – were all linked by internal doors. Perhaps fittingly given all this it was the home of the Eccentric Club from 1914 until its demise in 1986 (although throughout this time the building remained the property of Christie's whose headquarters back onto it). Traditionally popular among actors and theatrical artistes, the club possessed a small museum of music-hall mementoes and the clock above the bar ran backwards. Despite a tradition of raising impressive sums for a number of charities the members were sadly unable to prevent their own club from going into liquidation and Christie's has since reoccupied the building.

Ritz Hotel, Piccadilly

seven-man crew of a heavy bomber, a work that took him two years to complete and involved him borrowing flying suits and equipment from the RAF museum to ensure that every aspect in the piece was perfectly recreated. In the sculpture five figures look to the skies, searching in vain for planes that will never return, while two look down at the ground, thinking about the terrible ordeal they have endured.

Next to the memorial is a yew tree, donated by the people of Germany, a tribute not only to the German civilians who died in the bombing raids but also a recognition of the role played by the men of Bomber Command in freeing their country from Nazi tyranny. Following a long-running appeal for funds – which was spearheaded by the late Bee Gees singer, Robin Gibb – the Bomber Command memorial was unveiled on 28 June 2012 by the Queen in front of some five

ST JAMES'S PALACE

For centuries it was possible for members of the public simply to walk through the imposing redbrick gateway with its polygonal turrets and decorative mock battlements. Today, unsurprisingly, heightened security rules this out, meaning sightseers can no longer enter the little courtyard behind and are instead restricted to admiring those parts of Henry VIII's 'goodly manor' that can be seen from Cleveland Row and Marlborough Road. One is nevertheless left with an impression of somewhere charming and intimate, quite unlike a palace and extraordinarily modest for an era when even a moderately successful Tudor courtier would have sought to build or buy a home capable of impressing visitors with its wealth and decoration. Recognising this Daniel Defoe called the place 'low and mean' and in 1776 the social reformer Sir John Fielding was complaining that his sovereign's palace 'reflects no honour on the kingdom, and is the jest of foreigners'.

Of course, in part, the reason is that it was never really intended to be a palace. When Henry VIII coveted the aforementioned leper house he just wanted it for a hunting box, a convenient place from which to ride out into what are now St James's Park and Green Park. Henry VI had long ago given the property to his newly established Eton College, which was prevailed upon to exchange it for others owned by the Crown, and Henry VIII certainly used it often once it had been rebuilt. His monogram can be found on the gatehouse (and is intertwined with Ann Boleyn's above at least one Tudor fireplace) and two of his children died here, Mary I and the illegitimate Henry FitzRoy, 1st Duke of Richmond and Somerset, whom he briefly considered setting on the throne. But it was only in 1698 under William and Mary that St James's became the administrative centre of royal life in the capital, replacing Whitehall Palace following one last, disastrous fire a few years previously.

Prior to this it served a useful role as a royal maternity wing, so that all nine children of Charles I and Henrietta Maria were born in the palace, including Charles II and James II. Mary II was born here too, as were George IV and Queen Anne. Charles I spent his last few nights in what by then had been converted into a Cromwellian barracks, taunted by the soldiers guarding him ahead of his execution, or at the very least ignored by them, which would have amounted to much the same thing. It is also where George IV spent his wedding night in a fireplace having, according to Queen Caroline, drunk so much that she decided to leave him there.

It is inevitable that since those days a good deal has changed: the sash windows above the main entrance are clearly Georgian; no attempt was made to replace many of the parts ravaged by a fire in 1809 that destroyed that portion of the palace providing a link to the Queen's Chapel on what is now Marlborough Road; and much of the remainder was remodelled in the nineteenth century at the request of Queen Victoria and redecorated by William Morris. Fortunately, enough of the old palace survives for it to have remained a familiar landmark, and for as many as fifteen or sixteen generations. This includes some interiors by Wren and Kent, and externally

features, which, to even the most untutored eye, are clearly Tudor and provide plenty of evidence of that dynasty's enthusiasm for building in brick. Among them are the gatehouse and several turrets, with the state apartments also boasting two surviving Tudor rooms dating from the time of Henry VIII. The Chapel Royal clearly dates from the time of Henry VIII; indeed it was built by Henry in honour of his marriage to Anne of Cleves. Although much of the chapel was reformed by Sir Robert Smirke in the 1830s, the remarkable ceiling is assuredly Tudor, dated 1540, and consisting of interlocking octagons, crosses and elongated hexagons. This where Queen Mary I lay in state prior to her burial in 1558 and it is also where Queen Victoria was married to Prince Albert in 1840. Reflecting its royal connections, the Chapel Royal has also had a distinguished list of organists, among them Thomas Tallis, William Byrd and George Frideric Handel.

Today the Palace is as busy as ever it was, housing the offices of the Royal Collection Department, the Marshal of the Diplomatic Corps, the Central Chancery of the Orders of Knighthood, the Chapel Royal, the Gentlemen at Arms, the Yeomen of the Guard and the Queen's Watermen, as well as providing some grace-and-favour accommodation for a fortunate few. That it also remains the *official* royal residence, meaning that 175 years after Victoria moved into Buckingham Palace foreign ambassadors are still formally accredited to the Court of St James's, also imbues St James's Palace with a sense of timelessness and continuity that is entirely missing from Hampton Court Palace or Kew.

St James's Place

Originally called Rossington Street (after the master builder responsible for much of the construction) this quiet, L-shaped residential street was completed in the 1690s when those living here were reportedly enjoying 'fresh air out of the park'. Some houses from that period remain, although all have been substantially altered. Otherwise its two most important buildings could not contrast more strongly with each other: the eighteenth century Spencer House and a 1961 apartment block by Sir Denys Lasdun, which replaced a house by James Wyatt after this had been destroyed in the Blitz. The Wyatt house is obviously a regrettable loss, but the apartment block is impressive and has often been described as first building of its type of any real quality to have been built in London after the war. The materials used externally are exceptionally good, granite and bronze, while the strong horizontal banding enabled Lasdun to convey a sense of grandeur entirely in keeping with the building's prominent position overlooking the park. Inside high ceilings achieve a similar effect, making these perhaps the most covetable apartments in this part of London and certainly more so than others of a similar vintage.

Inevitably, Spencer House makes an even greater impact on the viewer, particularly when seen from the park. A large, double-fronted, nobleman's mansion, the entrance façade in St James's Place is quiet and dignified, while that overlooking the park is markedly more public and exuberant. With a rusticated ground floor and an upper floor of engaged Tuscan columns beneath an immense portico, it appears above the trees as a pretty as a palace and deserves to be regarded as such. It is, even so, much altered from the time it was built for the 1st Earl Spencer, John Vardy's original plan having been substantially reworked by Robert Taylor and Henry Holland. In 1758 James 'Athenian' Stuart, author of the influential *Antiquities of Athens*, the first accurate survey of ancient Greek architecture, was also brought in to decorate the three principal rooms in his newly fashionable Grecian style.

St James's Place apartments, by Denys Lasdun

Spencer House, St James's Place

A decade later a visitor observed how 'no expense was spared by the noble owner, and neither the brightest fancy nor the correctest judgement wanting'. It is perhaps not surprising that Pevsner rates Spencer House as 'the finest C18 London mansion remaining'.

From 1948 onwards, stripped of many features, this great building was let as offices and occupied by a number of organisations. Then, in the early 1990s, a major restoration was completed under the current owner, the 4th Baron Rothschild. Spencer House is occasionally opened to the public, and a visit is not to be missed. Whilst the entrance is plain and austere, elsewhere in the house elaborate carving, rich gilding and some highly novel decorative touches – such as the tree motifs and the mythical creatures in the Palm Room – make this one of the most exciting interiors anywhere in the capital. Conceived as a showcase of classical design by a family at the peak of its wealth and power, its restoration has taken more than ten years to complete and is stunning.

Two private hotels in the street are also worth noting. These are the Stafford, which has been at nos. 16–18 since 1912 with additional accommodation behind in the delightful Blue Ball Yard, and Duke's which overlooks its own private courtyard at no. 35. The building was originally conceived as a set of luxury chambers for well-heeled bachelors, and it still has that air today.

St James's Square

The centrepiece of the Earl of St Albans's prized *faubourg*, and for centuries its most prestigious address, St James's Square was originally designed around three sides of a piazza so that those buildings to the south – by far the least interesting – are strictly

St James's Square looking towards the Naval and Military Club

speaking part of Pall Mall. After nearly 350 years it is London's most regular seventeenth-century square as well as its most unspoilt and as a consequence by far the most attractive. That said: no house survives from the Earl's original plan, nor are there any longer six dukes and seven earls in residence. A combination of prestigious company headquarters and traditional clubs – all now mixed – nevertheless means the square retains a distinguished air which is unusual if not unique in twenty-first-century London.

The Naval and Military Club at no. 4 occupies what is substantially the oldest house still remaining; it was rebuilt in 1726 after a disastrous fire, and is thus the oldest clubhouse in St James's. Until 1908 this large and important Palladian corner house was still owned by the descendants of the 1st Duke of Kent, whose father had first occupied it, and it is unique today in having both its large garden and original mews still intact (see Babmaes Street). The architect was almost certainly Edward Shepherd, although there are suggestions that Rysbrack, Giacomo Leoni and even Nicholas Hawksmoor may have had a hand in its creation as the Duke was an enthusiastic patron of these and other artists. Lutyens is thought to have designed the garden. The Naval and Military acquired the house at the turn of the last century, having previously occupied Cambridge House on Piccadilly, where the writing on the gate pillars led to it being nicknamed the 'In and Out'. It was founded by a group of infantry officers in 1862 and past scions have included Scott of the Antarctic, Earl Mountbatten and William Gordon VC, who was killed at the club when it was bombed during the war. Today approximately a third of its members actively serve or have done so, with a further third being their offspring. A blue plaque on

Naval and Military Club, St James's Square

the front of the house records the long tenure of Nancy Astor, and it is tempting to wonder what this famously feisty (and teetotal) individual would have made of her home becoming a gentlemen's club with no fewer than three separate bars.

No. 5 is a later rebuilding, by Matthew Brettingham the Elder in 1748, of a house built in 1711 for the 3rd Earl of Strafford whose family still owns the freehold. In 1984 it was occupied by the Libyan Embassy and the scene of an anti-Gaddafi demonstration in which WPC Yvonne Fletcher was fatally shot. A memorial to her stands on this corner of the central garden (see panel, p.113).

Among the most attractive facades on the square, nos. 9–11 by Henry Flitcroft replaced a large house built for the 1st Duke of Ormonde (see Ormond Yard) and today all three are occupied by the Royal Institute of

*WPC Yvonne Fletcher Memorial,
St James's Square*

International Affairs, a think tank otherwise known as Chatham House. No. 10 was home to no fewer than three prime ministers, William Pitt (Earl of Chatham), the Earl of Derby and Gladstone. No. 12 is notable for its blue plaque to Ada, Countess of Lovelace (1815–52), the sole legitimate child of the poet Byron and one of the first women to be so honoured. Her brief but astonishing career as a writer and mathematician places her as one of the pioneers of modern computing, even perhaps the world's first computer programmer. The house itself is the work of Thomas Cubitt (see Belgravia).

No. 13 is an earlier Brettingham design of the 1730s, was once home to the 3rd Duke of Roxburgh and his famous library, and until 1941 was occupied by the Windham Club. Next to it we find the London Library, founded by Thomas Carlyle in 1841 and now

possessor of more than a million volumes dating back nearly five hundred years. Today it extends a long way back into Mason's Yard, and enjoys a reputation as the world's oldest and largest private-subscription library with around eight thousand members. Like no. 13, its glassy Victorian façade pays due respect to the architecture of the square but the interiors of both buildings have been substantially and repeatedly remodelled, in the library's case to accommodate more than fifteen miles of shelving and rooms where writers may work in comfort and undisturbed.

If no. 4 is the oldest house in the square, no. 15, Lichfield House, is architecturally the most distinguished. The first house on the site was built by the speculator Richard Frith around 1679 and in the early days was home to Frances Stewart, Duchess of Richmond and Lennox (1647–1702), who provided the inspiration for Britannia on British coins and famously rebuffed the advances of Charles II. Some forty years after her death the house was remodelled for the MP Thomas Anson, ancestor of the present Earl of Lichfield, who commissioned James 'Athenian' Stuart to design the magnificent and original house we see today. Behind its stone façade there have been many changes over the years, the building having been at different times a private home, a temporary clubhouse for the Army and Navy Club and an insurance office. At the time of writing the Grade I building is being converted back into a single dwelling, an extraordinary project – plans exist for a swimming pool in the basement – which will see the first private home in the square since the 2nd Viscount Astor and his politician wife Nancy moved out of no. 4 in 1942.

Since 1850 the East India Club has

occupied no. 16, its members acquiring the house next door shortly afterwards. Both were then rebuilt by Charles Fish, in 1865, to create the substantial clubhouse we see today. Prior to this, for more than sixty years, no. 16 had been home to Lady Elizabeth Germaine, whom the Duchess of Marlborough thought 'very ugly' and unlucky although she inherited a vast fortune and was largely popular. The house was also the scene of an extraordinary incident in 1815 when guests were surprised by the arrival of a bloodstained Major the Hon. Henry Percy, clutching the French imperial flag. This he laid at the feet of the Prince Regent, while announcing England's victory at Waterloo, although the hostess was reportedly much annoyed to have her party upstaged in this way.

Like nos. 16–17 the offices at nos. 20–21 give an appearance of unity, but only the former is original: a house, three-bays wide, which was built in 1771–5 by Robert Adam for Sir Watkins Williams Wynn, a rich Welsh politician. The childhood home of Queen Elizabeth the Queen Mother, in 1935 it was bought by a drinks company together with the adjacent plot, which been occupied by the townhouse of the eighty-ninth Bishop of Winchester. Following the demolition of the latter a new building was created by Mewes and Davis with an identical façade to no. 21. Linked by a matching seventh bay, the two buildings are now fully incorporated with each other.

There is little to say of the buildings on the Pall Mall side of the square, but continuing round the square no. 31 occupies the extensive site of the old Norfolk House, the London home of the dukes of that name from 1722 until the 16th Duke sold up in 1938. The property was briefly rented to Frederick, Prince of Wales when he was evicted from St James's Palace by George II (who thought him 'the greatest ass and the greatest liar') and provides a second royal connection for the square as it is where George III was born in 1738. When the house was demolished exactly two hundred years later the music room was preserved and can be seen in the Victoria and Albert Museum. A plaque on the wall of its replacement, also called Norfolk House, records its tenure as the London headquarters of Dwight Eisenhower's 1st Allied Army. Two critically important wartime operations, Torch and Overlord – the invasions of French North Africa and Normandy – were planned and launched from this building.

Rather unusually, the gardens at the centre of the square are open to the public during the day, although they are still privately owned by the freeholders of the houses. The statue at the centre is of William III, and the base includes a representation of the molehill over which his horse stumbled with fatal results in 1702. (The anniversary of this incident was marked for many years by Bonnie Prince Charlie's men, each drinking a cheerful toast to 'the little gentleman in the black velvet waistcoat', although some historians insist that his demise was as a result of complications arising from the fall.) In the 1730s, when the square was still cobbled, this part was occupied by a large central water basin and surrounded by an octagon of iron railings. In the nineteenth century the pool was filled in and replaced by the gardens we see today. The basic plan for this was by John Nash, who also built the small gazebo on the southern side, and the lime trees were planted around 1825.

THE MURDER OF PC YVONNE FLETCHER

It was 1984 and Libya was going through yet another bout of political turbulence. The Libyan dictator, the late Colonel Muammar Gadaffi – a constant thorn in the side of western governments and nicknamed 'mad dog' by US president Ronald Reagan – was cracking down on political dissidents at home and abroad. London, inevitably, became the locus for opponents to launch protests against his regime and it was outside the Libyan embassy in St James's Square, on 17 April 1984, that one of the most heinous crimes in British history was perpetrated.

Police Constable Yvonne Fletcher had harboured a lifelong ambition to join the force. However, at only five-foot two in her stocking soles she was a full two inches under the height requirement. That did not deter Yvonne: she applied, and then reapplied, until senior officers, impressed by her drive and determination, gave in and offered her a place in the Metropolitan Police. Posted to Bow Street, the 25-year-old soon found personal happiness to add to professional fulfilment: she met a fellow constable at the station, Michael Liddle, and they became engaged. When the anti-Gadaffi protests in St James's Square started it was natural that police officers from nearby Bow Street would be assigned to keep the peace.

The demonstration organised by the National Front for the Liberation of Libya was on the small side, with no more than seventy people involved. The publicity it generated, however, was clearly more than just a minor irritant to the Gadaffi government, which had recently murdered a number of dissidents in Britain and in other countries. It has now become clear that, after getting orders from the powers-that-be in Tripoli, the embassy staff responded with deadly force. Within seconds PC Yvonne Fletcher lay dying, cut down by shots that had come from the direction of the Libyan embassy.

A British witness had been standing close to the scene and he later gave a vivid account of what happened to *The Times*:

> I saw Yvonne Fletcher fall . . . within seconds her white shirt turned to red with blood. I saw her little cap lying in the road. It was a pathetic sight. There was a splattering of blood a few yards away. The [reinforcing officers] carried her to Charles II Street to await an ambulance. She looked in a grave way, ashen white with her eyes closed.
>
> On a sunny day in the centre of London, it was pure madness. It was just an insignificant little demonstration.

As fate would have it, the first person at Yvonne's side was her fiancé, PC Michael Liddle, who had also been on duty in the square. He reached her within seconds and went with her to Westminster Hospital where, despite the best efforts of doctors, she died of her wounds. The effect on Liddle and the Fletcher family was devastating; at a sombre press conference Yvonne's mother, Queenie, fighting back tears, said that her daughter had wanted to be a police officer from the age of three.

Home Secretary Leon Britain described the machine-gun assaults as 'barbarous' and there was deep public anger at what had happened. However, despite the fact that a serving police officer had been brutally murdered, the British government's hands were tied. Thanks to the principle of diplomatic immunity, the police could not enter the embassy without being invited in either by the embassy staff or the Libyan government. Nor could accredited diplomats even be interviewed without consent. There was also a highly credible threat from Colonel Gadaffi to contend with: although he issued a statement regretting the death of Yvonne Fletcher, in the same breath he said that British citizens in Libya would be taken hostage if the SAS, who were on stand-by, stormed the embassy. As if to emphasise the seriousness of the threat, a bomb went off in Heathrow airport two days later, which, on examination, was shown to be the same type used by the

Libyan regime against dissidents elsewhere. In spite of surrounding the embassy for almost ten days, all that the British government could do was to order the Libyans to leave and to sever diplomatic relations. The Met suspected that the gun used to kill their colleague was concealed in one of the diplomats' suitcases.

The funeral of PC Fletcher was held in Salisbury Cathedral on 27 April 1984, near to her home village of Semley. Her mum, dad and three sisters were in church, along with other family and friends, six hundred serving police officers and Leon Brittain. At the back of the coffin rested her police hat, which had lain close to the embassy in St James's Square for ten days during the standoff with the Libyans until a brave policeman took a chance and retrieved it. The hat was taken to the service by her colleagues, which was their mark of respect for the tiniest officer in the force.

There has still been no justice for Yvonne Fletcher. Hers is the only police murder of the last thirty years to go unsolved, although there is a possibility that the killer will be brought to justice. New information has emerged since the overthrow of the Gadaffi regime in 2011, and the alleged gunman has even been named in several newspaper reports. With the cooperation of the new Libyan government, British police visited Libya in the summer of 2012 for what were described as 'preliminary discussions' about the case. Further, albeit slow, progress has been made with reports in 2014 suggesting that the killer (who may be hiding in Egypt) is under constant surveillance by MI6.

St James's Street

One of the oldest thoroughfares in the area, dating back to Henry VIII's acquisition of the old lazar house, St James's Street was paved as early as 1662. It soon became the fashionable place for gentlemen to meet, the coffee and chocolate houses in which they assembled providing the prototypes for the gentlemen's clubs which adorn the street today. By far the most venerable is White's at nos. 37–38, the oldest club in the world, with a foundation date of 1693, and a reputation among its even now mostly patrician members as 'an oasis of civilisation in a desert of democracy'. As the only seventeenth-century survivor in clubland, its only possible rivals are Brooks's at no. 60 – a Whig club when White's was still Tory – and Boodle's at no. 28, although both were founded decades later. White's was founded by an Italian immigrant, Francesco Bianco (Francis White in English), and after his death it was named Mrs White's Chocolate House. His establishment sold chocolate concoctions to its members, chocolate at the time being a luxury that only the wealthy could afford. In time it became a fully fledged gentlemen's club, the most fashionable in London and the unofficial headquarters of the Tory party. White's became well known for its Betting Book, in which many outrageous and controversial wagers were made: Lord Alvanley, a member of the Prince Regent's inner circle and a noted wit and dandy, laid a bet of £3,000 on which of two raindrops would reach the bottom of the club's famed bow window first; while, in a gamble with much more serious consequences, one member wagered £1,000 that a human could live underwater for twelve hours and hired a proxy to undertake the stunt, which, not surprisingly, ended with the unfortunate soul drowning.

White's moved to its current location here in 1755, a mansion built by Edward Villiers in 1674. Much reconstruction has taken place since, notably by James Wyatt in 1787–9. Authentically exclusive and surprisingly small – besides the bar and coffee room, its members have the use of little more than a room for cards and a room occupied by a billiards table and the television – White's is an attractive clubhouse but compact and quite discreet. The bow window to the left of the entrance was where the dandy George 'Beau' Brummell would sit and be observed by the public. Today it is still very exclusive and a piece in the *Financial Times* in December 2012 notes that 'A recent visitor to White's, the venerable gentlemen's club housed in 18th century splendour in London's St James's, walked up to the bar to find it occupied by three dukes. "It's the one place in town where they feel totally at home," he said.' That said there are London clubs with even more ducal members than White's.

Brooks's is the most distinguished clubhouse of the three, a country house in miniature, which was designed by Henry Holland and once memorably described as being 'like a duke's house – with the Duke lying dead

White's, St James's Street

Brooks's, St James's Street

Boodle's, St James's Street

upstairs'. Some idea of how little the place has changed in the last two centuries may be assumed from the knowledge that when the club's Great Subscription Room was badly damaged by fire in the 1970s the restorers referred to a painting of the room by Thomas Rowlandson (b.1756) in order to ensure they correctly matched the colour of the walls to the original. Situated across the street Boodle's, from the outside at least, is nevertheless a more obviously striking building, the large and elegant fan-shaped window the work of John Crunden, a largely forgotten eighteenth-century architect and designer. Other clubs in the street include the Carlton at no. 69, the Conservative at no. 74 (now offices) and the Thatched House at no. 86 (likewise). No. 50 was the celebrated Crockford's until its demise in 1845, and, substantially rebuilt, it served for a while as the Jamaican High Commission before reopening as a casino.

The remainder of the street is largely shops and offices, but several of these are outstanding. Towering over Boodle's, the Economist building by Alison and Peter Smithson was the first 1960s structure – more correctly, three hexagonal towers on a raised plinth – to be given listed status. By way of a contrast a short walk south brings some wonderful eighteenth-century survivors: the premises of Lock's the hatters, almost certainly the oldest shop in London (it has been at no. 6 since 1765); and the celebrated wine merchant Berry Bros. & Rudd. The latter is still family owned after more than three hundred years and backs onto Pickering Place, London's smallest square. It was reputedly the scene of last fatal duel to take place in the capital, the houses built by William Pickering, son-in-law of the 'Widow Bourne' who established the grocers that the Berry brothers subsequently took over.

Stable Yard

Sadly not accessible to the public, Stable Yard now falls within the protective cordon thrown around St James's Palace, Clarence House and Lancaster House. These last two may, however, be glimpsed from the Mall and Green Park respectively, or by peering past the police barrier on Cleveland Row. Elegant and stuccoed, Clarence House dates back to 1828 and was built by John Nash for the duke of that name before the latter acceded to the throne as William IV. With Buckingham Palace still a work in progress, and St James's Palace too small, His Majesty chose to remain at Clarence House until his death in 1837. To maintain a connection with St James's Palace a passage (still extant) was built linking Clarence House to Ambassadors' Court. During the Second World War, Clarence House was used as a headquarters by the Red Cross, but has otherwise remained an important royal residence.

Stable Yard

Queen Victoria's mother, the Duchess of Kent, lived here from 1840–61, and the Duke of Edinburgh from 1866–1900, during which time a new storey was added. Victoria's third son, the Duke of Connaught, occupied it from 1900 until his death in 1942, and Queen Elizabeth the Queen Mother spent her long widowhood here. Technically a part of St James's Palace, it is now the official London home of the Prince of Wales, the Duke and Duchess of Cambridge and Prince Henry of Wales.

Across Stable Yard, Lancaster House is used by the government for entertaining and occasional high-level international conferences. It was previously known as York House and then Stafford House, a vast building of Bath stone originally designed by Sir Robert Smirke until he was replaced – at the instigation of George IV – by Benjamin Wyatt and later still by Charles Barry. Already immense it was extended for a new owner, the 1st Duke of Sutherland in the 1830s, Queen Victoria observing its vast staircase and central hall and commenting that she had come 'from my cottage to your palace'. She continued to visit, however, and in 1848 heard Chopin performing here at a private concert in front of the Duke of Wellington. Immediately prior to his death in 1913 the 4th Duke of Sutherland sold the house to the industrialist Sir William Lever. He immediately renamed the house after his home county and presented the remaining portion of its Crown lease to the nation. Until 1946 part of it housed the London Museum (before this was formed into the Museum of London and relocated to the City) and in 1953 it was the venue for the Queen's Coronation banquet. It is not open to the public.

The Mall

Replacing Pall Mall as a gaming *allée*, the creation after the Restoration of the Mall was an important component of Charles II's plan to develop this part of Henry VIII's hunting ground into a new St James's Park. The design has been attributed to the great landscape architect André le Nôtre, a designer much admired by Charles II on his return from France. However research suggests that, reputedly an admirer of English parks, the Frenchman eventually declined to tinker with what he saw. The original Mall may well thus have been built along the lines suggested by the King. For a while it appeared on maps of London as Pall Mall, our own Pall Mall being at that time being called Catherine Street, after the Queen. For well over a hundred years it was a fashionable and pleasant place to promenade, a Prussian visitor to the city observing in 1733 that even the royal family joined the crowds 'attended by only half a dozen Yeoman of the Guard'. By this time it seems that ball-and-mallet games were no longer played beneath the shade of the lime trees, and in 1820 the daily promenades were reportedly also a thing of the past.

The Mall we see today is therefore very much a twentieth-century creation, conceived as part of a national processional route commemorating the long reign of Queen Victoria. With her memorial on a *rond-point* at one end, and Admiralty Arch at the other, it lies just south of the original mall, which today is used for parking and by pedestrians. An impressively wide avenue between lines of trees, in detail and execution the new Mall was largely the creation of Sir Aston Webb (1849–1930), the architect responsible for the façade of Buckingham Palace, and, indeed, for Admiralty Arch. Aside from these two,

its most dominant features are the backs of Carlton House Terrace on one side and on the other the forbidding, vine-clad bulk of the wartime Admiralty Citadel.

Waterloo Place

The southern extremity of Regent Street, Waterloo Place – as perhaps its name suggests – is something of a national pantheon to British and Imperial heroes, with memorials to explorers Scott of the Antarctic (by his wife) and Sir John Franklin, Air Chief Marshal Sir Keith Park, Field Marshal John Fox Burgoyne (see Mayfair chapter) Florence Nightingale, and others. The cast-iron lamp stands are also exceptionally good. Architecturally, Waterloo Place's stars are both clubs, however, although the first of these – the United Services (known to clubmen as 'the Senior') collapsed in 1964 and is now occupied by the Institute of Directors. It was designed by John Nash around the time his Carlton House was being demolished but then remodelled by Decimus Burton in a Victorian-Italianate style. The Pall Mall façade boasts a broad porch with coupled Roman Doric columns, and on Waterloo Place visitors can still see a horse-mounting block reputedly installed at the behest of the Duke of Wellington, a member of this and a number of other clubs.

Directly opposite – as Nash had always intended – the Athenaeum is an altogether more successful design. It too has a porch of paired Doric columns, but placed beneath a blue and white frieze, a fine and finely proportioned first-floor balcony and a gilded figure by E. H. Baily of the goddess Pallas Athene, it is a far more distinguished example of the Classical Revival. Notwithstanding the clumsy attic storey (a much later addition) the restrained yet majestic appeal of the exterior is more than matched by the spacious elegance of the club within and – it must be said – by the intellectual eminence of the members of this, the most establishment of establishment clubs.

Even by the elevated standards of St James's, the Athenaeum is in short a quite exceptional building, if perhaps not quite enough to deflect the stinging criticism that the club itself is one in which (as was once said) 'all the arts and sciences are understood – except gastronomy'. The rather sniffy quote alludes to the explicitly eminent nature of its members, for this is a club founded as an 'association of individuals known for their scientific and literary attainments'. Even now a special dispensation allows for certain applicants to be elected immediately – the Speaker of the House of Commons, the president of the Royal Society, either of the

two archbishops – but generally the election procedure was intended (and continues) to weed out anyone who is not genuinely distinguished in their field. The original membership committee, for example, included both Michael Faraday and Sir Humphry Davy; and of the first intake of members no fewer than eight went on to become prime minister.

Many important works have been drafted and redrafted in its great library, including books by Dickens, Darwin, and Trollope, the latter having famously if reluctantly killed off one of his characters after hearing two of his fellow members discussing after lunch how boring they found her. After their great row at the Garrick (see Covent Garden chapter) the Athenaeum is also where Dickens and Thackeray healed their long rift – shaking hands on the steps going up to the entrance after fifteen years.

Athenaeum, Waterloo Place

FITZROVIA

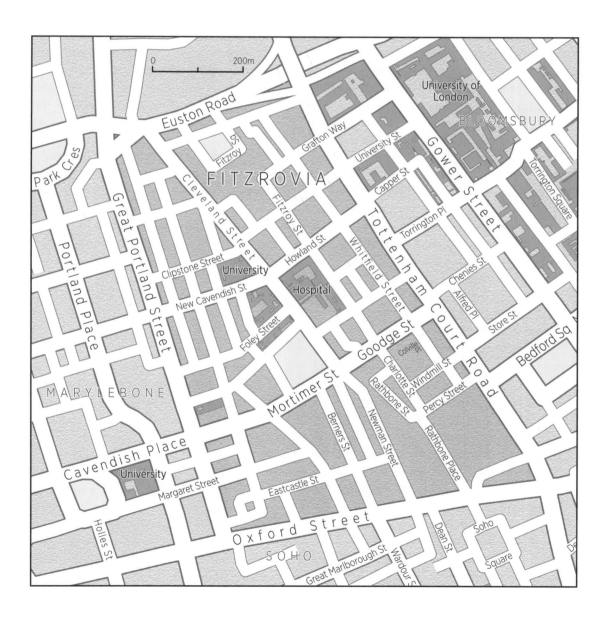

Occasionally described as North Soho (but never Noho), it is possible that the term Fitzrovia was coined as recently as 1940, when it made its print debut that year in the 'William Hickey' gossip column in Lord Beaverbrook's *Daily Express*. At the time, the identity concealed by the newspaper's celebrated *nom de gossip* was Tom Driberg MP, the erstwhile Communist, likely KGB double-agent and – whilst enjoying a high profile career in the Labour Party – dangerously promiscuous homosexual adventurer. Fitzrovia took a while to catch on but today the term is to be found on Ordnance Survey maps following a successful campaign by local residents. The derivation of the name stems from the decorative Fitzroy Tavern in Charlotte Street, a popular meeting place for artists and intellectuals in the years during and after the war. The FitzRoys of the title were and are the Dukes of Grafton, a dynasty descended from one of Charles II's several bastards, and who, until the 1920s, owned considerable acreage in this area. Nearby Euston station, for example, is named after the family seat, Euston Hall in Suffolk, and the heir is traditionally known by the courtesy title, Earl of Euston.

Although the name is now widely known, Fitzrovia is a relatively small neighbourhood and falls within a tapering quadrangle bounded by Euston Road, Tottenham Court Road, Oxford Street and Great Portland Street. The last of these was probably the first street to be planned, beginning around 1720, after which development spread north and east and doing so in a fairly piecemeal fashion as numbers of small landholders spotted an opportunity and decided to build.

With the exception of Fitzroy Square none of the developments was to be especially grand, and fighting a losing battle from the start with the westward migration of London's rich and respectable a good many of the developers' better terraces were very quickly subdivided into flats and workshops. This was done to accommodate the writers, artists and other traditionally impecunious craftsmen-types who were soon flooding into the area to take the place of the more socially ambitious residents as they decamped to Mayfair and Belgravia.

Among the earliest to arrive were furniture makers from France and elsewhere in Europe, and by the eighteenth century two very familiar names were active in the area: Thomas Chippendale and the painter John Constable, who kept a house here but spent a good deal of time at his country home in Hampstead. Fitzrovia was later to become more strongly associated with writers and artists than craftsmen, and the likes of George Bernard Shaw, Walter Sickert, Augustus John and Dylan Thomas helped to cement its reputation as a decidedly bohemian, if somewhat seedy, hangout for English society's creative nonconformists. Driberg, indeed, may well have borrowed the term 'Fitzrovia' from Augustus John, one of the regulars at the aforementioned Fitzroy Tavern, who is thought to have been the first to refer to the neighbourhood in this way.

Today the area is still surprisingly residential, but home as well to many commercial interests including a cluster of advertising and media companies in and around the main artery of Charlotte Street. Despite its useful central location and high rents, the local population is nevertheless considered by the Office of National Statistics to have levels of deprivation above the national average. The reason is that Fitzrovia's lively café culture and stylish film and television-company premises blind visitors to a long history of immigration from Greece and Italy, and latterly from as far afield as north India and Nepal. A recent piece in the *Daily Telegraph*, for example, characterised the neighbourhood as a place where 'it is rare to see a house without an English Heritage blue sign' before going on to describe one of several illegal squats. Listing a number of eminent former residents – all the usual suspects: GBS, Virginia Woolf and Lord Salisbury, who was prime minister on three occasions – the writer lent weight to this by naming some of the more recent incomers, such as novelist Ian McEwan, Madonna's ex-husband Guy Ritchie (whose two houses were at the time being illegally occupied by protesters) and the television presenter Griff Rhys Jones.

But in fact with the notable exception of Fitzroy Square, its elegant and most obviously privileged centrepiece, Fitzrovia never enjoyed much if any time at the top of the tree. Like many of London's inner-city neighbourhoods it quickly became a heavily mixed area and one where, even now, a wide disparity of wealth and living conditions are to be found. Much of the available property is council-owned, in the hands of housing associations or fairly low-quality private-rented-sector accommodation, despite nearly forty years of campaigning for better conditions. The sense of deprivation is, if anything, reinforced by the lack of public open space in the area – the central garden in Fitzroy Square, for example, is generally kept under lock and key – making Fitzrovia rather more akin to neighbouring Soho, say, than to well-ordered Bloomsbury on the other side of Tottenham Court Road.

Charlotte Street

First laid out in 1763 – and named for Charlotte of Mecklenburg-Strelitz who had married George III two years earlier – Charlotte Street was briefly residential but soon turned commercial and since the 1980s has enjoyed a reputation as the home of the advertising world and its allied trades. Very definitely a street of two halves, the portion lying to the north of the Goodge Street junction has been more obviously redeveloped than the southern half with much larger buildings such as a headquarters building for the Saatchi & Saatchi media

Saatchi and Saatchi, Charlotte Street

group (at no. 80) and at no. 99 the unattractive Astor College. Purpose-built as a hall of residence for University College London, this last named occupies most of an entire block. Its construction unfortunately required the demolition of a number of period properties, including one associated with an especially gruesome murder of the early twentieth century.

On 2 November 1917, a road sweeper on the far side of the Euston Road came upon two loosely wrapped packages that had been thrown over the railings into a private garden. Peering into one he discovered the body and arms of a female, and in the other the police found the unfortunate woman's legs. Even in this pre-forensics age the trail quickly led to a butcher's basement at 101 Charlotte Street – the body had been expertly cut-up, and wrapped in meat-seller's muslin – where they found the victim's head and hands concealed in a barrel owned by a Frenchman called Louis Voisin. The victim turned out to be his former lover, Emilienne Gerard, who had been beaten to death when she stumbled upon her replacement, one Berthe Roche, enjoying a quiet evening in with Voisin. Roche served only eighteen months for the murder, before being deemed insane, but after having disposed of the body in such a brutal manner, Voisin was hanged at Pentonville the following March. Having so carelessly discarded Mme. Gerard's remains, with no attempt at concealment, it is hard to believe that either of them expected to get away with such a violent crime.

The street's more illustrious occupants have included a number of eighteenth-century landscape painters, including John Constable, George Morland and Richard Wilson, and the illustrator Daniel Maclise. Constable had a studio at no. 74 from 1822–37, during which time he painted his celebrated *Hampstead Heath*, a work that now hangs in the Fitzwilliam Museum, Cambridge. Sir Robert Smirke similarly spent much of his youth at no. 81, while no. 36 was occupied by his fellow architect John Nash in 1824. None of these houses still survives, although the street continues to have a substantial resident population, albeit mostly in flats above the shops and cafés at ground-floor level.

The aforementioned Fitzroy Tavern is still thriving on the corner with Windmill Street, the building by W. M. Brutton opening in the 1880s as a coffee house before obtaining a licence as a public house known as the Hundred Marks. The present name dates from shortly after the Great War, at which time with the forceful but likeable Judah 'Pop' Kleinfeld as landlord it became well

The Fitzroy Tavern, Charlotte Street

known as a hangout for London's literary *demi-monde*. In part this may have been a consequence of its proximity to Broadcasting House where several of the pub's commercially more successful habituées – George Orwell, for example, and Dylan Thomas – occasionally had cause to be. Its reputation – much boosted by the memoirs of the shabby but talented and attractively louche Julian Maclaren-Ross and others – lasted until the 1950s, by which time the celebrity clientele had mostly started drinking elsewhere, for example in the aforementioned Wheatsheaf, which tended to keep longer hours. Today, inevitably, it is popular with students from UCL.

At the junction with Tottenham Street until it was demolished in 1970, the Scala Theatre occupied the premises of the eighteenth century King's Concert Rooms. This was a popular haunt of George III, and perhaps it was he who persuaded the resident directors of Concerts of Ancient Music to move closer to his palace and into what is now Her Majesty's Theatre in 1794 (see Haymarket, St James's). Rebuilt as the Scala, it hosted some of London's earliest screenings of colour films during the run up to the Great War, and in the 1960s several scenes were shot here for The Beatles movie *A Hard Day's Night*. In 1947 bystanders on the pavement outside witnessed the cold-blooded shooting in broad daylight of father-of-six Alec de Antiqui. This was one of a rash of gangland killings that followed post-war demobilisation, when thousands of former servicemen returned home with the weapons they had neglected to turn in.

Cleveland Street

Six dukedoms descend from the illegitimate offspring of Charles II, with no fewer than three of them belonging to the children of Barbara Villiers. She also managed to secure for herself the titles Countess of Castlemaine and Duchess of Cleveland. One of several streets in the capital named after her, Cleveland Street was for many years at the southern end dominated by buildings associated with the Middlesex Hospital until this was closed and largely demolished in 2008. Founded in 1745, the hospital chapel with its lavish marble and mosaic interior has been left marooned in the middle of what, at the time of writing, is a vast building site. Together with the now empty-eyed façade of the west-facing range on Nassau Street, it is the only part of the hospital still standing.

From 1812–15, no. 141, now a church club, was home to the American inventor Samuel Morse. Also a keen and talented painter, Morse moved to England specifically to be at 'the very centre of all the artists in London'. For a while he studied under one of the founders of the Royal Academy, a man who was for twenty-eight years its president, the Anglo-American artist Benjamin West (1738–1820).

Today, however, the most interesting building in the street is a former workhouse that was built on the east side around 1778. Originally called the St Paul Covent Garden Workhouse (and later the Central London Sick Asylum) this was scheduled for demolition along with the bulk of the Middlesex Hospital but has been saved after a vociferous and well-run campaign conducted by locals and other defenders of London's built environment. Built on an H-plan to house a substantial number of paupers, around two hundred, it was later modified and extended by Thomas Hardwick (father of Philip) to accommodate considerably more than this number. Externally, the building we see today is not substantially altered from a description of it dated 1856, but its importance to London is by no means merely architectural. In recent years it has been asserted that this building almost certainly provided the inspiration for the workhouse in *Oliver Twist* as that book's author, Charles Dickens, is known to have lived at what is now 22 Cleveland Street in 1815–16 and then again as a teenager from 1828–31.

Cleveland Street's other hold on posterity is the Cleveland Street Scandal of 1889, an infamous affair that was ignited by a raid on what in previous decades would have been described as a 'molly-house', or homosexual brothel, at no. 19. Among those named as clients of the establishment were: the Duke of Beaufort's son, Lord Arthur Somerset, equerry to the Prince of Wales; the Prince's son, HRH Albert Victor; and Henry James FitzRoy, Earl of Euston. The latter successfully sued for libel after his name was mentioned in the press, but the equerry fled abroad before he could be arrested and later died at his new home on the French Riviera. Prince Albert Victor was never called to account for his movements, but the scandal did much to perpetuate the myth that homosexuality was a largely aristocratic crime that saw innocent working-class boys corrupted for money.

Workhouse, Cleveland Street

Clipstone Street

In April 2011 great excitement attended the discovery on the corner of Clipstone Street and Cleveland Street of a large piece of graffiti by the street artist Banksy. Now protected by a perspex barrier, this depicts a large rat beneath the caption: IF GRAFFITI CHANGED ANYTHING IT WOULD BE ILLEGAL, which is a reworking of an old anarchist slogan. It apparently appeared between midnight and the early hours of Easter Monday, the excitement perhaps a commentary on the fact that Clipstone Street itself has little else to detain the visitor. The name comes a village on the estate of the Dukes of Portland, a former mining community in north-west Nottinghamshire. The painter George Frederic Watts OM (1817–1904) is the street's most illustrious former resident – he lived at no. 1 as a youth and later at no. 14 – but today the street and the neighbouring (and ill-named) Clipstone Mews is dominated by unattractive post-war flats and offices.

Colville Place

A characterful narrow eighteenth-century oasis connecting Charlotte Street and Whitfield Street, what was originally called Colville Court was originally laid out as two rows of modest dwellings, one facing the other. The two-bay houses are three storeys tall, with plain parapets to conceal their rooflines, and iron lamp stands down the centre of the line providing both decoration

Banksy graffito, Clipstone Street

and illumination. The houses date from 1766, and were built for the leaseholder William Franks by a carpenter called John Colvill (*sic*) hence the name. Colvill however was bankrupted by the project, and many of the houses on the east side were all but destroyed by German bombers in the 1940s. Today, despite having no gardens, the survivors are nevertheless much sought after, particularly those like nos. 5, 6 and 10 with their fluted pilasters and decorated cornices, and command high prices by local standards.

Fitzroy Square

Marrying off her 9-year-old son Henry to the 5-year-old daughter of a neighbour in St James's, Barbara Villiers secured for him a dowry that included the manor of Tottenham Court (see Bloomsbury chapter) as well as the aforementioned estate at Euston in Suffolk which said neighbour – the 1st Earl of Arlington – had settled on his only daughter, Isabella Bennett. Fitzroy Square was developed by the young couple's great-grandson Lord Southampton, and is the only London square to have been developed by the Adam brothers. Robert Adam was personally responsible for the design of the east and south sides which were constructed in Portland stone from 1793–8, the plastered north and west sides taking another thirty-five years to complete. (The south side of the square is in fact a 1957 recreation as Adam's work had been almost entirely destroyed by enemy action during the previous decade.)

Perhaps unsurprisingly, this east side is the most successful, a range Nikolaus Pevsner describes as a 'unified composition in subdued relief' and one which, with its Ionic centre, set the tone for one of central London's most distinguished squares. Today

it includes the beautiful home, at no. 6, of the Georgian Group, a lobbying organisation that campaigns to preserve and maintain that portion of Britain's built environment dating from around 1700 to 1837. It was founded in 1937 by Lord Derwent and the travel writer Robert Byron expressly to 'rescue from demolition squares, terraces and individual buildings of beauty and importance'.

No fewer than five blue plaques (two of them at the same address) bear witness to the square's popularity, particularly among London's literary elite. At different times no. 29 was home to George Bernard Shaw and Virginia Woolf, the latter leasing the house with her brother Adrian and making much of their modest tripe suppers but nevertheless employing a number of servants and wishing to decorate the house with 'bright green carpets' and antique furniture. After five years the square proved too noisy for the budding writer, however, and complaining about the tradesmen's vehicles that 'grind rough music beneath my window' Virginia decamped to quieter Bloomsbury and Mecklenburgh Square. In the previous century the 3rd Marquess of Salisbury had had no such concerns – although he too was attempting to make a living by his pen whilst living at no. 21 in the 1850s – and at no. 7 a fourth plaque commemorates Sir Charles Eastlake (1793–1865). Eastlake was the first director of the new National Gallery and an influential secretary of the Fine Arts Commission. He assisted Prince Albert in the interior decoration of the fire-ravaged Palace of Westminster.

As it happens Queen Victoria's famously industrious consort was well known to the tenant at no. 9 as well, and it was through Albert's patronage that August Wilhelm von Hofmann (1818–92) was able to secure a

Fitzroy Square

professorship and the post of founding director at London's new Royal College of Chemistry in 1845. An early authority on synthetic dyes (including those still known as 'Hofmann violets') the professor regrettably left Fitzrovia for Germany in the 1860s and is now credited with laying down the foundations of that country's resounding expertise in the field of chemical dyes.

Fitzroy Street

The northern extension of Charlotte Street, Fitzroy Street is another thoroughfare of two halves. The houses on the western side running into Fitzroy Square are still largely intact and unspoiled, proof still of the Georgians' respect for elegance and careful proportions. Those on the opposite side, however, have been swept away, presumably as part of the familiar if regrettable post-war drive for higher-density housing, and replaced by a large, five-storey residential block of sandy-coloured brick.

Travelling south the redevelopment has been even larger in scale but more imaginative, in particular at the British headquarters of Arup at no.8, which includes a public exhibition space as well as extensive office accommodation for this large engineering and design multinational. Designed by Sheppard Robson, the exterior comprises a patchwork or mosaic of large glass panels – clear, translucent and opaque – which serve to regulate both solar gain and heat loss. The technology makes this one of the most environmentally sustainable developments in central London. Inside the building an elegant, self-supporting spiral staircase rises through a central atrium, while extensive use of recycled materials and excellent provision for those staff choosing to cycle to work emphasises the self-professed green credentials of the £40-million building.

Across the street the side return of another of the company's premises, known as Arup Fitzrovia Phase I in Howland Street, is distinguished by broad horizontal bands in emerald green and an extraordinary, insect-like pod above street level. Also green, with ten crab-like aluminium legs – they are actually ducts feeding back into the building – this has been likened to a giant bug or dust mite busily clambering up the façade of this contemporary-looking office development. By far the most obvious feature of Arup's 125,000 square foot London headquarters – nicknamed 'the hub' – it is actually designed to enable air to move more efficiently through the building. Formed from the conversion of two older buildings, the lower ceiling height reportedly ruled out the use of advanced under-floor heating and ventilation. Instead the Sheppard Robson team specified a complex system of air-handling ducts and solar-shading louvers. This seemingly advanced technology, which is surprisingly long-established in that London's Crystal Palace (1851) and the Galleria Vittorio Emanuele II in Milan (1877) employed something similar, in both cases subterranean air-cooling chambers and opening roof lights to regulate indoor temperatures. Opinion is nevertheless divided about the overall aesthetics of Arup's singular green creation, although one suspects that few passersby realise they are looking at a refurbishment of two otherwise deeply uninteresting 1960s blocks.

At no. 56, a blue plaque commemorates the street's most distinguished former resident, Captain Matthew Flinders RN (1774–1814), the navigator and surveyor who mapped the coastline of a vast territory in the southern hemisphere. This he christened Australia, and returning to London a relatively poor man he leased the house in Fitzroy Street for £100 per annum before settling down to write a fascinating account of his travels. A year later, *A Voyage to Terra Australis* was handed to his publisher just one day before the explorer's death at the age of forty. Today, on the continent that Flinders charted, more than a hundred places and geographical features still commemorate his name – and in Britain his likeness has appeared on a postage stamp.

Foley Street

In the mid-to-late 1700s when the street was laid out Thomas Foley, 2nd Baron Foley (1742–93) was a politician with an estate near Malvern and the unfortunate nickname of 'Lord Balloon' as a consequence of his intemperate diet. He kept a house in London, on land owned by his cousin Edward Harley, and when the latter developed a portion of his London estate he chose to take Foley's name for this part.

Today the architecture is a mostly pleasant jumble of styles, much of it Victorian, and once again one finds a cluster of artists among its former residents. These include Sir Edwin Landseer who lived at no. 33 until his mid-twenties, a precocious talent who submitted his first painting for consideration by the Royal Academy aged just twelve. No. 37 was home to Johann Heinrich Füssli (1741–1825), whom as Henry Fuseli became a leading colourist and art instructor.

Renowned for his paintings of the supernatural (which were to inspire the young William Blake) he counted Constable among his pupils and indeed Landseer.

Grafton Way

Formerly Grafton Street and together with Grafton Mews (which is entered via an archway adjacent to the Grafton Arms) clearly built on land once owned by the FitzRoys. Where it joins Fitzroy Square considerable redevelopment has robbed it of any charm, although towards the far end, particularly once one has crossed Whitfield Street, a number of nineteenth-century houses survive although most have shop fronts or are now offices.

No. 58 is of special note, as it has two blue plaques commemorating individuals born in Caracas. The first of these, Francisco de Miranda (1750–1816), saw in the American War of Independence a model for his own country to expel their Spanish overlords just as the colonials had overthrown the British.

The bid was successful, but the end was achieved only after de Miranda had been thrown into a Spanish gaol where he eventually died. The other plaque is to the revolutionary poet Andrés Bello (1781–1865) who stayed as a guest of de Miranda. It is tempting to wonder why, after celebrating the American success in throwing off the British yoke, either of them should have chosen to make London their home. At Pensacola and in the Bahamas, de Miranda even fought against the British, yet both married English women (Bello two of them) on whom they fathered seventeen children.

Great Portland Street

What was at first John Street was subsequently renamed after the Portland Estate it crosses, a substantial chunk of property originally in the possession of the aforementioned Edward Harley, Earl of Oxford and Mortimer before passing by marriage to the Dukes of Portland. When the 5th Duke died in 1879 without issue (a formidable eccentric,

Great Portland Street station

William John Cavendish Cavendish-Scott-Bentinck had miles of tunnels dug beneath his Nottinghamshire estate but never married) it came into the possession of the Howard de Walden family. They own it still, approximately 110 acres of the West End.

The Tube station on an island at its northern extremity is perhaps its single most interesting building, the street itself having suffered no fewer than twenty-eight direct hits during air-raids in the 1940s and numberless attempts at redevelopment. Prior to the unification of a clutch of privately owned lines to create the London Underground we know today, the station formed part of the world's first subterranean railway. This was the original Metropolitan Railway, which, opening for business in 1863, ran from Paddington to the City through shallow, arcaded, 'cut-and-cover' tunnels. Its early origins explain why the distinctive cream-tiled and columned façade differs so markedly from the more usual station types, created by Leslie Green (see Bloomsbury) and Charles Holden.

Howland Street

In 1695 Wriothesley Russell, the future 2nd Duke of Bedford, married the heiress of John Howland, a wealthy landowner with much property in what is now south London. Plans were soon advanced to develop part of this potentially valuable inheritance, and included the creation of what was called the Howland Great Dock. The forerunner of the vast complex of the Surrey Commercial Docks (which remained in commission until the late twentieth century) this was one of the foundation stones of the Russell fortune, hence the commemoration here of Howland's name.

In the street today by far the most outstanding building – in every sense – is one that has changed its name several times over the last forty years but which remains even so one of the most immediately identifiable in the whole of Britain. Originally (and still to many) the Post Office Tower, it was forged in the very core of Prime Minister Harold Wilson's so-called 'white-hot technological revolution' and was from the start conceived as something special and highly distinctive. Designed by the aptly named Eric Bedford (1909–2001) to soar above the noise and pollution of central London, it had a very specific function, namely to provide a support structure for the many dishes and aerials required to beam high frequency or microwave radio, telephone and television signals out over the raised edges of the London basin and across the country.

BT Tower, Howland Street

Incredibly, even now, virtually every picture on British television screens passes through the Tower at some point, making it what is believed to be the world's largest video-switching platform. Positioned on a fairly conventional eight-storey office block, and cleverly engineered to sway nearly eight inches from the vertical in high winds, the Tower is known to shrink by a full nine inches in the depths of a British winter. In fact Bedford's 580-foot-high design, with its 39-foot mast and slender 54-foot diameter, is less of a building than a hollow concrete column. This is clad in steel and green glass, thereby giving the appearance of a cloud-piercing, circular office block although none of the lower floors actually contains any offices. Interestingly, such a disguise was considered unnecessary for similar telecommunication towers erected elsewhere around the country. The 498-foot tower in Birmingham for example, which is also by Bedford, was left in its raw concrete state and still looks brutal.

In London, however, Bedford's solution worked extremely well and still does, although the ruse was dismissed by some of his contemporaries as clumsy and as dishonest by a few rival architects who espoused a purer, more function-driven approach to building design. However, the public loved the tower, still have great affection for it and do not seem to mind that for all its height and dominance the enigmatic structure contained little beyond two observation decks near the top, a cocktail bar and a once famous, and famously expensive, revolving restaurant.

Housed in a 30-ton section, which turns through 360 degrees every twenty-two minutes, giving it a speed of approximately six feet a minute, the restaurant and bar have unfortunately been closed to the public since 1971, when the building was attacked by Irish terrorists. A blast occurred in the early hours of 31 October, when a bomb concealed in one of the lavatories on the thirty-third floor blew a hole in the foot-thick wall, damaging cars and other buildings more than four hundred yards away. A call was subsequently received from a man claiming that the IRA's Kilburn unit was responsible. Fortunately, no-one was injured in the attack but the building was closed to the public shortly thereafter. Today it is accessible only to guests and employees of BT, for whom the view out over the West End and beyond remains as breathtaking as ever.

Margaret Street

An unexpected ecclesiastical cloister in an otherwise perfectly ordinary street of shops and offices, William Butterfield's Gothic Revival church of All Saints occupies a small and very constrained site. It is hemmed in on three sides, but nevertheless opens out into a wonderful courtyard complete with an arched entrance from the street and striking decorative railings. Providing accommodation not just for worshippers but also for a choir school and the resident priest, the compact Grade I-listed complex has been described as an 'immensely skilful piece of architectural organisation and gamesmanship,' a place as showy as it is clever and costly. The richly patterned brickwork conceals an interior of the 1850s that is colourful and decidedly High Church (the tiling alone cost £1,100) and, soaring above the courtyard, the 227-foot spire is taller than Westminster Abbey. According to John Betjeman, an enthusiastic advocate of Victorian design, 'it was here . . . that the revolution in architecture began'.

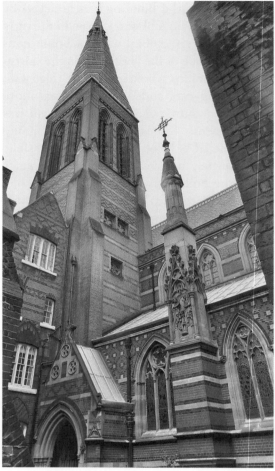

All Saints Church, Margaret Street

At no. 84 a Grade II building that formerly housed a training establishment for Anglican clergy, the London Fo Guang Shan Temple contains what is almost certainly Britain's largest collection of Buddhas.

Mortimer Street

Another street long dominated by the immense block of the Middlesex Hospital, Mortimer Street is today largely commercial and as unlikely a setting for a royal residence as one is likely to find anywhere in central London. Nonetheless in 1809 the house at no. 32 (no longer standing) was home to the jolly Duke of Clarence, who subsequently ascended the throne as William IV at the record-breaking age of 64. Among his nautically inclined neighbours was Admiral Lord St Vincent at no. 34, Nelson's patron and the victor of the 1797 sea battle from which he drew his title. In the early-twentieth century, no. 97 was leased by the stylish short-story writer Saki, otherwise Hector Hugh Munro (1870–1916). Serving with the twenty-second battalion, Royal Fusiliers, he was killed by a German sniper on the western front at Beaumont-Hamel.

Newman Street

In the mid-eighteenth century, Quendon Hall near Saffron Walden in Essex was called Newman Hall, the property of one William Berners (1710–83) on whose London estate Newman Street was laid out in 1746. (With its wonderful Upstairs Pie Room, the tiny Newman Arms in nearby Rathbone Street marks the same connection.) Nothing from Berners's era survives, but, once again, the street was to attract a number of successful artists over the following century, including sculptors Thomas Banks, James Bacon and William Behnes (at nos. 5, 17 and 31 respectively) and two presidents of the Royal Academy in Luke Fildes (no. 72) and Benjamin West (no. 14), whom we met in Cleveland Street.

Today the most remarkable building is the headquarters of the television production company, Talkback, at nos. 20–21. Created by the architectural practice Buschow Henley in 2001, the project involved the remodelling of two six-storey blocks dating from a century earlier and an open courtyard. The

Talkback Building, Newman Street

architects designed a new linking structure with basement studios and a first-floor 'garden', their imaginative use of materials such as zinc and galvanised steel providing a striking contrast with the old brickwork, and the whole set off by a campanile (actually a lift tower) clad in Douglas fir boards.

Two small alleyways lead off the street: Berners Mews, which is of course named after the original ground landlord; and Newman Passage at the rear of the Talkback building, the latter famously provided the setting for the opening scenes of director Michael Powell's 1960 creepy classic *Peeping*

Tom. This was based on a screenplay by wartime cryptographer Leo Marks, son of the antiquarian bookseller made famous by another classic of the period, *84 Charing Cross Road* by Helene Hanff. It included what is thought to be the first nude scene in British mainstream cinema.

Percy Street

Laid out on land owned by Francis and William Goodge (hence nearby Goodge Street) Percy Street was another developed by William Franks. As with nearby Percy Passage the name may be a reference to a coffee house of this name (which stood on the corner with Rathbone Place, and was frequented by James Boswell) but more likely the link is to Sir Hugh Smithson. Smithson changed his name to Percy on marrying into the aristocracy, and in 1766 was made Duke of Northumberland. An early and important patron of the great Venetian painter Canaletto, he fathered an illegitimate son, the chemist and mineralogist James Smithson, FRS (c.1765–1829), who became the founding donor of the Smithsonian Institution in Washington, now the world's largest museum complex. (This despite not setting foot on American soil prior to his burial there, some seventy-five years after his death.)

Though largely redeveloped in recent decades, particularly on the north side, the street contains an attractive mix of Victorian and late-Georgian buildings, mostly now business premises although many of the older houses have been converted into both shops and offices with some sensitivity. A high proportion are Grade II listed, unusually for this part of town, with a number worthy of note including nos. 4, 5–9 (which still have their original attached railings) 15–18, 28–30 (more railings) and 32–37.

The street was well known to George Orwell, who patronised a Greek restaurant at no. 13 for its moussaka, which his friend and correspondent Arthur Koestler refused to touch. In the 1940s he befriended Sonia Brownell, Cyril Connolly's assistant on *Horizon* who rented a flat above no. 18. In 1949, a few weeks before his death from tuberculosis, the pair married. Neither warrants a blue plaque here, but two adjoining properties have them in memory of an actor and a now largely forgotten poet. Charles Laughton (1899–1962) lived at no. 15 with his actress wife Elsa Lanchester, the original 1935 *Bride of Frankenstein*. Laughton, of course, made his name the same year as Captain Bligh in *Mutiny on the Bounty*, and when their combined salaries made it possible the two moved 'because an Indian restaurant had opened underneath and the smell of garlic and curry . . . was getting stronger'. They lived for a while in Surrey and then the US, remaining together until Laughton's death, although he was almost exclusively homosexual.

Making his name with a cycle of poems celebrating marital love, Coventry Patmore (1823–1896) lived next door at no. 14 but never recovered from the premature death of his wife Emily in 1862. He had begun the cycle ahead of this personal cataclysm, calling it *The Angel in the House* and only concluded it two years later before travelling to Italy and being received into the Church of Rome. On remarrying the same year, he quit Percy Street for the Sussex countryside.

Rathbone Place

The Percy name resurfaces again in Rathbone Place, an archway beneath the Wheatsheaf pub leading into Percy Mews. The Rathbone in question is Thomas Rathbone, who developed this portion of William Berners's property in the 1720s although curiously he is not thought to have had any business connection with the adjacent Rathbone Street. The pub, and indeed the former Black Horse where two immense wrought-iron lamps now grace a gourmet burger restaurant, are the real pleasures of this long, straight street. Otherwise, on its way down to Oxford Street, it presents a fairly unrelenting vista of offices and office conversions. There are occasional points of interest, such as the coloured brickwork and more imaginative fenestration above the shop at no. 9, but the grotesque post-office

The Wheatsheaf, Rathbone Place

building at nos. 35–50 is the sort of design which none but a public body would expect to get passed by the planning authorities. It blights the street entirely.

Rathbone Street

Smaller in scale, slightly removed from the traffic and architecturally far nicer, Rathbone Street is best viewed looking south from the Duke of York tavern, one of several pubs that spill out onto the narrow, mixed-use street. Nos. 29–35 is the only real behemoth, a large office block, but it is low rise and well finished in brick. Towards the lower end more of the original streetscape has been preserved, with businesses slotted in behind old shop fronts and into converted houses and warehouses. No. 15, occupied like so many in this part of London by a media agency, is particularly attractive.

Tottenham Court Road

On the western side of Tottenham Court Road the sole building of any real interest is the sombre brick bulk of the American Church in London, at no. 79a, on the site of the old Whitefield's Methodist Tabernacle. This had its origins in the mid-1750s when it was established by the preacher, George Whitefield (1714–70), who despite being a man of the cloth was actually a pro-slavery campaigner. The Tabernacle's popularity was such that by 1760 an extension to the original building was needed to accommodate a staggering eight thousand worshippers. Despite a somewhat uncomplimentary nickname – 'Whitefield's soul-trap' – it nevertheless caught the imagination of many educated admirers, including Horace Walpole and the philosopher David Hume. White-

The American Church, Tottenham Court Road

field himself travelled widely to preach – including to communities across the Atlantic and in the Netherlands and Gibraltar – and on his death John Wesley came here to read the sermon, which he later repeated at a sister tabernacle in Moorfields.

On at least two occasions Whitefield's chapel was badly damaged by fire and then in 1945, on Palm Sunday, in what is thought to have been the last such attack on London, a German V2 rocket laid waste to the entire building. It was then rebuilt in the form we see today, initially as a memorial chapel with the burial ground re-landscaped as a small public park. The building was subsequently rededicated as the American Church, and for the past thirty years its congregation has run a soup kitchen in the grounds for the local poor, homeless and elderly.

Whitfield Street

Renamed after the aforementioned Methodist preacher George Whitefield (note the slight difference in spelling), Whitfield Street was formerly in three parts: John Street from Windmill Street to Howland Street; Upper John Street from Howland Street to Maple Street; Hertford Street once it ran into the Fitzroy estate. Much of the west side was destroyed by enemy action in the 1940s, with only a few survivors such as no. 79, which is of plain brick with a mansard roof behind a simple parapet. Others of this type have been extended with an additional storey or altered to provide retail accommodation, although the survival of minor period details (such as railings) means that the overall impression is still attractive.

At the junction with Maple Street the Fitzroy chapel once stood, built by Reverend Anthony Bromley, who leased the site from Lord Southampton in 1777. Dedicated in 1788 the chapel was a simple brick structure, rectangular in plan and surrounded by railings, with the entrance front on Maple Street distinguished by a bold pediment crowned by a small bell-cote or tower. The upper story was lit by three circular-headed windows with three arched doorways, the centre one of which was framed a neat quartet of pilasters. Among the regular preachers was the noted wit, Reverend Sydney Smith – the evening preacher at the Foundling Hospital in Bloomsbury – and Benjamin West decorated the chapel with paintings of Moses and Christ. In 1863 the chapel was made a parish church, as the Church of St Saviour but this was destroyed in an air-raid in early 1945.

For many years Whitfield Street was also home to the Literary and Scientific Institution, which occupied a site at no. 23 almost opposite Scala Street. It was here in a spacious galleried hall that the Chartists met on 15 April 1848 before their massed gathering on Kennington Common. The building was later converted and used for somewhat less serious purposes, including shows by magicians and illusionists, and, later still, as a dancing academy.

Windmill Street

More than forty entries under 'Windmill' in the index of the *London A-to-Z* bear witness to the locations of many such structures, which would once have stood in what are now solidly urban areas to serve the ballooning population of London. Today just seven survive – that at Brixton being by far the closest to the centre – and it is to be supposed that this one on Windmill Street, almost certainly part of the aforementioned manor of Tottenham Hall, must have disappeared by the mid-part of the eighteenth century.

In the 1720s, on what was then a farm track, building plots were leased to the Goodge brothers, the street being more or less completed over the next fifty years. Resident at that time would have been the painter and engraver Henry Morland (1716–97) who lived at 36. Like his son George he enjoyed great success, but the pair fell on hard times and the son was twice gaoled for debt. Sandwiched between the Fitzroy Tavern at one end and the glassy twelve-storey block of MetBuilding London at the other there is nothing of the period left standing, although a number of later terraced houses have been tastefully converted into shops and showrooms with accommodation above.

BLOOMSBURY

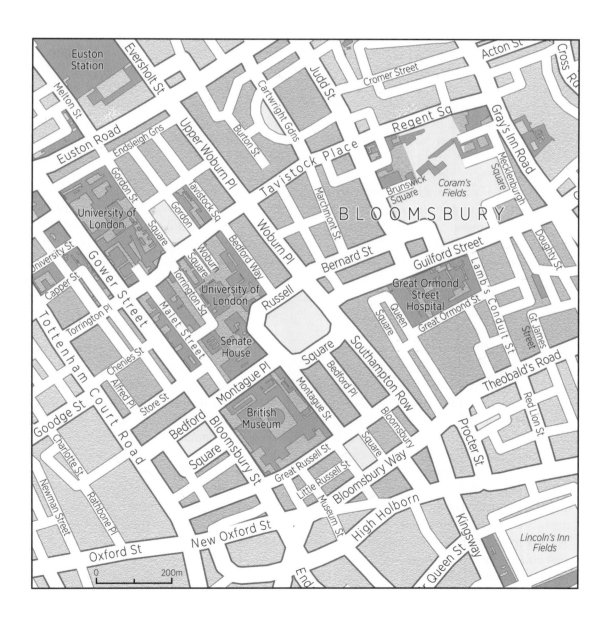

If such a vast, scattered and diverse city as London can be said to have a cultural and university quarter then Bloomsbury comes closest. The name of the area is derived from Blémont in France by way of a Norman, William de Blemond, who held the local bury or manor in the early thirteenth century. Within a hundred years ownership of the land had passed to the Crown and towards the end of the fourteenth century to Carthusian monks, who occupied the House of the Salutation of the Mother of God here. This priory, more commonly known as the London Charterhouse, had been founded for the Carthusians in 1370 by Sir Walter de Manny on thirteen acres of land lying between Smithfield and the old city walls.

A number of its ancient buildings still stand but in 1537 the foundation and its endowments were seized by Henry VIII (as part of the Dissolution of the Monasteries) and its possessions at 'Blemondsberi' subsequently granted to his Lord Chancellor, Thomas Wriothesley, 1st Earl of Southampton (1505–50). In 1661 his descendant, the 4th Earl, was responsible for the construction on this land of what was, in all likelihood, London's first formal square. This was laid out in front of his new mansion, Southampton House, but neither lasted more than 150 years: the house occupied what is now the north side of Bloomsbury Square and Russell Square was later laid out on part of the gardens.

In fact by this time Bloomsbury had passed out of the Wriothesley family – the 4th earl had married three times but produced no sons – and into the possession of the Russells following the marriage of Southampton's widowed daughter to the son and heir of the 5th Earl of Bedford. Lord William Russell did not live to enjoy this substantial inheritance, however, because in 1683 he was executed for his part in the Rye House Plot to kill Charles II. Fortunately for the family the Russells were rehabilitated two decades later when the ageing 5th Earl was made 1st Duke of Bedford by William III; and it is to the Russells that one must look to understand the further development of Bloomsbury through the seventeenth and eighteenth century.

The work undertaken by them was executed on a reasonably large scale but – if only compared to the encompassing and more unified vision of the Grosvenors in Belgravia – it proceeded in a relatively piecemeal manner. In 1730 Wriothesley Russell, 3rd Duke of Bedford, had built Bloomsbury Market; in the 1770s the widow of the 4th Duke (acting as regent during her son's minority) was laying out Gower Street and Bedford Square; and by 1800 Francis Russell, the 5th Duke, having decided he did not any longer wish to live in the area, had pulled down Southampton House (by this time renamed Bedford House) and was contemplating the construction of a new Russell Square on the site of its gardens.

Development continued until the turn of the twentieth century, lacking some of the rigour and symmetry of Belgravia but with a similar degree of control being exercised by the landowning family. This last factor meant the finished result – exceptionally handsome squares, broad, uniform streets (many of which were still gated until the 1890s) and various mews to service both – made for a largely coherent neighbourhood. The growth of the railway in the nineteenth century had seen London expand greatly in this direction, but present-day maps show how well the area has survived, the street pattern having changed very little over the centuries although a number of valuable terraces and buildings have been lost.

Compared to some other parts of London the area is nevertheless not easily defined around the margins, although today it is generally agreed that the area centred on what John Evelyn once described as 'a little towne' is bounded by Tottenham Court Road to the west and Gray's Inn Road to the east, and sandwiched between Euston Road in the north and Bloomsbury Way and Theobald's Row in the south. (Beyond this Bedford Row, for example, has no connection with the Russells but instead commemorates a seventeenth century Lord Mayor of London with strong connections to the shire town of that name.) Much of Bloomsbury is still residential too, despite losing 'tone' as long ago as the mid-nineteenth century when it was definitely being regarded as respectable rather than fashionable. Already by then the big institutions were beginning to take over, with the British Museum occupying the old Duke of Montagu's house in Great Russell Street from 1759 (see panel) and a century later the University of London beginning its remorseless consumption of more and more space. The effect of this in the short term was to attract scholars, doctors, writers and academics to the area, but longer term to compromise the smartly residential character of Bloomsbury to the point where students are now thought to make up approximately 30 per cent of the local population.

Inevitably much of Bloomsbury was also to be lost to offices and other commercial developments, part of a 'savaging' the *Illustrated London News* described, in 1971, as 'an alternating history of suicide, murder and back to suicide in defiance of every tenet of good town planning, of pleasant living, and even of economic sense'. But actually, more

than forty years on, one is inclined to think the writer of that piece was being unnecessarily pessimistic. Pictures taken at the time showing Bloomsbury Square being excavated for an underground car park filled one with dread – and the Brunswick Centre still does – yet Bloomsbury in a very real sense has survived and there is enough of it left to guide other town planners now and in the future.

Most obviously, with that first square in front of Southampton House, its creators helped to establish a pattern of urban domestic life that was to be repeated elsewhere in London and one which, in truth, has yet to be improved upon. Like small and strangely rectilinear (but quite lovely) village greens surrounded by neat terraces of well-proportioned townhouses, some very large, others less so, the Bedfords' garden squares linked by well-ordered streets and well-placed churches and markets make a real community of this part of London, and one that somehow has endured.

Of course, few places that are this central can escape the noise and traffic, and Bloomsbury certainly does not. Even so, and despite the concerns of a previous generation, much of the historic fabric of the old Bedford Estate survives intact, and much of what we see today is still handsome and of outstanding quality. As harmonious and as attractive as anything Evelyn would have known, it is still possible to see and appreciate historic Bloomsbury as a single, cohesive work of architecture and town planning.

Alfred Place

Capped at either end by its matching North and South Crescents, Alfred Place was laid out by George Dance the Younger (1741–

1825), the fifth and youngest son of the architect George Dance the Elder, although like much of his work nothing original has survived here. The most interesting building on the street is by Colonel Richard Seifert (1910–2001) the most prolific architect in post-war London, whose achievements include Centre Point and the former National Westminster tower in the City. With its glossy black exterior and unusual fenestration, no. 19–22 is unusual and successful, and occupies the site of the lodgings where Gustav Mahler stayed during his first trip to London.

Like Alfred Place both crescents are now offices, much of North Crescent being obscured by a quite extraordinary wartime survivor that is now called the Eisenhower Centre (postal address Chenies Street). This is a relic of a government network of so-called deep-level shelters, eight of which were built, seven of them beneath Northern Line Tube stations. Each comprised a pair of parallel tunnels 1,200 feet in length and with the accommodation for eight thousand or so people spread over two levels. The four beneath Camden, Clapham North and South and Belsize Park stations were intended for civilian use during air-raids,

Eisenhower Centre, Alfred Place

while the other shelters were secret citadels providing emergency accommodation for the civil authorities and the US military in the event of attacks by V1 and V2 rockets. This particular one was fitted out as a secure headquarters for Dwight D. Eisenhower, the future US president, in his role as Supreme Allied Commander during the Second World War, and was used as his main command-and-control centre for all D-Day operations. On the other side of Tottenham Court Road (by the Whitfield Memorial church) is a ventilation shaft on which can be seen the scratchy remains of a painted sign: _____D Property _____trance strictly _____ohibited _____out authority.

19–22 Alfred Place

Bedford Place

Amidst the destruction by German aircraft and postwar planners, one of the area's better preserved streets is Bedford Place which links the two gardens in Bloomsbury Square and Russell Square. An attractive piece of urban landscaping, which is still intact on both sides, around 1800 it was nevertheless held up as an example of 'the poverty of design in speculative development' during one of Sir John Soane's Royal Academy lectures. Today however the

11 Bedford Place

surviving houses by James Burton are exemplars of the period, being perfectly proportioned if largely plain, and now mostly hotels. The house at no. 11 has a particularly attractive covered balcony on the first floor, and during his time as Superintendent of Vaccine Inoculation the eighteenth-century medical pioneer Edward Jenner lived at no. 15.

Bedford Square

Its name obvious and its status unique as the sole surviving intact Georgian square in Bloomsbury, work began on handsome Bedford Square in 1775, making this the first extension northwards of the Russells' London estate. (It was also the first place in London where building leases were employed as part of a new development, enabling speculative builders to profit but with the houses returning to the landlord at the end of ninety-nine years.) The buildings at nos. 1–38 and 40–54 are all Grade I* listed, meaning almost the entire square has this distinction, in addition to which this was the only one in Bloomsbury to retain its original railings when the 12th duke permitted those in the other properties to be salvaged in the 1940s to support the war effort.

The principal architect and personally responsible for the whole of the southern side was Thomas Leverton (1743–1824), a builder's son from Essex whose nephew, also Thomas, co-founded the Royal Institute of British Architects. At no. 1 he built for himself a house with an unusually elaborate door case and an oval staircase, but elsewhere in the square a quiet uniformity was and remains the order of the day. Accordingly each side of the square has at its centre a stuccoed house with Corinthian pilasters and porticoes (or a pair of stuccoed houses in the case of the north and south ranges) while the remainder are of plain but attractive brick, three bays wide, with wrought-iron balconies at first-floor level.

Bedford Square

The doorways to the brick houses are also standardised and reasonably uniform, with artificial Coade Stone dressings from Lambeth, bearded keystones and vermiculated rustication. Narrow windows either side of the fan-lit doors create a pleasing tripartite pattern, and while many of the external features came from pattern books rather than being designed by Leverton or one of his collaborators the overall effect is still highly impressive. So too is the central garden, which is very densely planted but unfortunately strictly private.

Once defiantly upper-middle class, the square ceased to be residential many years ago, and the proliferation of once-famous publishers that clustered around this part of Bloomsbury – including Jonathan Cape, Chatto & Windus and The Bodley Head – have also now gone. Appropriately Bloomsbury Publishing still occupies three houses, however, nos. 49–51, and the Yale University Press is at no. 47. Others houses have become specialist educational establishments, including nos. 33–39, which form part of the Architectural Association School of Architecture, and no. 16, which houses the prestigious Paul Mellon Centre for Studies in British Art.

No. 11 is part of Royal Holloway College, University of London, but for nearly fifteen years was home to the brilliant but highly eccentric scientist the Hon. Henry Cavendish (1731–1810). A Fellow of the Royal Society, and noted for discovering the chemical composition of water (and demonstrating the existence of hydrogen), Cavendish was the grandson of the 2nd Duke of Devonshire. He famously never spent more than five shillings on dinner despite inheriting more than £200 million at current values, and kept two vast houses in London despite the fact that he lived alone. One he set aside to conduct his experiments, the other was piled high with academic papers and journals, which he made available at no charge to his fellow researchers. Both were equipped with a complicated system of internal mailboxes and double doors in order to prevent anyone approaching him directly or talking to him (including his own servants). He never married, had the interior of the house painted entirely green, and on his death was found to be holding more bank stock than anyone else in England. Much of this was bequeathed to Lord George Cavendish, builder of the Burlington Arcade (see Mayfair).

The nineteenth century Lord Chancellor, Lord Eldon, lived at no. 6, one of the central stuccoed houses that came under attack from the mob during the Corn Law riots of 1815, and at no. 49 another blue plaque commemorates the Indian scholar Ram Mohun Roy (1772–1833) who lodged here towards the end of his life. The novelist Anthony Hope lived at no. 41, he is perhaps best known for his 1894 adventure *The Prisoner of Zenda*, and at no. 35 two plaques commemorate Thomas Wakley, the founder of the medical paper the *Lancet*, and the physician and philanthropist Thomas Hodgkin (1798–1866) from whom Hodgkin's Lymphoma gets its name. An anti-slave trader, Hodgkin died during a visit to Palestine to investigate and report on the plight of its oppressed Jewish population.

Bernard Street

First laid out in 1799 and named after Sir Thomas Bernard, governor and treasurer of the Foundling Hospital on part of whose estate the street was built. This famous establishment had been endowed fifty years earlier by a rich seafarer, Captain Thomas Coram, and at one time owned some fifty-six acres.

John Rocque's *Map of London* (1746) shows the hospital standing well to the north of London, a pleasantly rural spot sandwiched between Lambs Conduit Fields and the extension to Grays Inn Road, running up to the villages of Hampstead and Highgate. Though childless, Coram was appalled at the fate of the London poor, particularly the very youngest infants who were often left on street corners to die, and he determined to do something of practical value to alleviate their plight. His solution was the 'all-comers basket', a relic of which can be seen in the broad, white stone pillar by the entrance to Coram's Fields in Guilford Street. Erected when the hospital opened in 1742, the large niche was designed to contain a revolving device into which single mothers (keen to avoid legal entanglement or moral censure) could deposit their unwanted babies without giving away their identities. The babies would then be collected and looked after by staff on the other side of the wall, rather than being left (as the Captain put it) 'to die on dunghills'.

It was an inspired idea, but if anything proved far too successful. On the first day following its installation an incredible 117 babies were deposited, with literally hundreds more flooding in over the next few weeks. Thereafter it was decided to adopt a new means of dealing with what was evidently a massive problem for London generally. For a while a ballot was seen to work, but eventually new rules were instituted allowing, for example, only one baby per unmarried mother to be admitted. Even then they would be admitted only

when three criteria were met: the child was less than a year old; the mother had been deserted by its father; the mother had been of demonstrably good character before her fall.

Despite having a host of wealthy patrons and celebrated benefactors – including the composer George Frideric Handel who once raised £7,000 for the hospital with a single performance of his *Messiah* – the governors soon began selling off land to increase their income. The Bernard Street parcel was one of the first to go, after which development of this area continued apace until, in 1926, the entire institution was moved out of London. Initially the governors – including Sir Thomas – took a commendably responsible path, sincerely believing that by developing squares such as Brunswick and Mecklenburgh (see below) they could preserve for the hospital 'the advantages of its present open situation,' while at the same time raising rather than ruining its character 'as an Object of National Munificence'. Their architect and the Surveyor to the Hospital, Samuel Pepys Cockerell (1754–1827) was even more explicit, insisting that 'there shall be such principal features of attraction in the plan so as to comprise all classes down to houses of £25 per annum and that the stile of the buildings [sic] be as respectable as possible consistent with their situations'.

Simply put, Cockerell's proposition was for a high quality, mixed development, something that nearly two centuries years later the local MP called 'a text fit to be hung round the neck of every developer'. But looking at Bernard Street today it has to be said that those lofty ideals are not easy to discern. In particular, there are the harsh concrete terraces of the Brunswick Centre on one side, and on the other the broad expanse of one of Leslie Green's distinctive ox-blood-tiled Tube stations, which break up a modest but otherwise attractive run of late Georgian townhouses.

As ever the problem comes down to money: in 1745 the land owned by the hospital was valued at just over £60 an acre; two hundred years later what remained of it fetched closer to £180,000 an acre. Fortunately, at the end of the street a small portion has been saved, and, using funds raised by the press baron Viscount Rothermere, seven acres were set aside in 1926 for a children's playground. These now comprise the aforementioned Coram's Fields to which, uniquely for a London park, adults are admitted only if accompanied by children.

Bloomsbury Square

Originally conceived in the early 1660s to occupy the space immediately before the entrance court to the aforementioned Southampton House, the first Bloomsbury Square was very much the hub of Evelyn's 'little towne'. This was an impressively compact, self-contained suburb in which the square was surrounded by smaller homes and a myriad of shops for traders and artisans. Of this nothing now survives, the earliest houses in the present square being nos. 5–6 and 15–16, which, beneath some modifications, are mid-eighteenth century.

These survivors, on the more attractive north side, were built around 1800 by James Burton, shortly after the 5th Duke of Bedford had obtained the necessary permissions to develop this portion of his estate. This allowed him to pull down his great house and develop the site as he saw fit. The new gardens were designed by the ageing but brilliant Humphrey Repton (1752–1818) but as previously noted these were then torn up in the early 1970s in order to excavate a huge underground car park. An attempt has since been made to restore the gardens, with some

Liverpool & Victoria Friendly Society, Bloomsbury Square

success, and for many years these have been open to the public. Happily, and despite many of the buildings at one time being compulsorily purchased for an aborted plan to keep the British Library in Bloomsbury, the future of the square we now see seems reasonably secure.

The area is now all offices, however, and since the 1920s the whole of the east side has been dominated by a vast building for the Liverpool & Victoria Friendly Society. On the south side some important houses were lost to later development or substantial remodelling, including the Earl of Chesterfield's at no. 45. The west side has fared better and, whilst something of a jumble, is still attractive and looks well maintained. More than this it demonstrates what can be achieved by later redevelopment when buildings are replaced individually but with commercial buildings that are sympathetic to the original concept of a residential square.

Bloomsbury Street

Running from Bedford Square to the boundary of Bloomsbury on New Oxford Street, Bloomsbury Street on the east side provides a nice continuation of the Georgian square. Its houses are of a simpler and more modest design, and mostly lack the Coade Stone decorations and eye-catching pilasters seen on the square. On the corner with Great Russell Street the Radisson Blu Edwardian Hotel, red brick with stone dressings, is immense and perhaps too tall for the site but manages to avoid dominating the street or junction.

The building at no. 6 occupies the site of Sass's Academy, a private school founded by an artist of Latvian origins called Henry Sass (1788–1844) who was a great friend of

Turner's. His pupils included several who later became eminent Royal Academicians, including Charles West Cope, William Powell Frith and William Edward Frost. Other alumni achieved even greater eminence: namely the Pre-Raphaelite painters Sir John Millais, who went on to become president, and Dante Gabriel Rossetti. At this time Bloomsbury Street was still called Charlotte Street (after George III's consort) but should not be confused with the similarly named thoroughfare which crosses Fitzrovia.

Brunswick Square

Built on land owned by the Foundling Hospital (see Bernard Street, above) the square takes its name from Caroline of Brunswick-Wolfenbüttel, George IV's unhappy queen. In 1795 it represented a genuine attempt by S. P. Cockerell to provide attractive new developments that would benefit the area while raising revenue for the hospital and not compromising the environment in which the children were being raised and cared for.

Specifically Brunswick Square was intended to balance Mecklenburgh Square, but little of Cockerell's plan now survives and this square in particular has been very rudely treated. The culprit is the angular and awkwardly cantilevered Brunswick Centre, a mixed development of shops, restaurants, a cinema and nearly six hundred apartments, on which work first began in 1967. Designed by Patrick Hodgkinson, it was from the first ambitious and controversial – private buyers failed to come forward in sufficient numbers, forcing the borough council to take it on – and while the entire complex is now Grade II* listed many still consider it to

Brunswick Centre, Brunswick Square

be a classic 1960s concrete eyesore. Like many of its contemporaries, particularly those which fell into the public sector, maintenance is ongoing and expensive.

Burton Street

The aforementioned James Burton was a Scotsman (born Haliburton) who as a young man approached the governors of the Foundling Hospital in the hope of accumulating a fortune as a speculative developer working on its land. In this he was highly successful and in due course he was able build for himself a large villa in Tavistock Square (where the British Medical Association headquarters now stands) before moving to The Holme in Regents Park. This in turn was designed by his son Decimus and is still one of the grandest private houses in London.

Burton Street was intended to be more modest than the squares of Bloomsbury and it still is with the east side the best preserved. Here the accommodation is still largely Georgian, made up of plain but attractive houses of four storeys over a basement. All have stuccoed ground floors, while those to the south have attractive wrought-iron balconies on the floor above. Fewer survive

on the opposite side as this is largely occupied by the rear of BMA House, a building of red brick with stone dressings which was designed by Edwin Lutyens during his 'Wrenaissance' period. This was originally the London headquarters of the Theosophical Society, an organisation formed in 1875 in New York for the 'study and elucidation of Occultism, the Cabala etc'. The Society still exists but has been subject to many schisms and splits despite founding principles based on belief in a universal brotherhood of humanity without distinction of race, creed, sex, caste or colour.

Capper Street

A rare exercise for Bloomsbury in Art Moderne, Shropshire House at nos. 11–20 is perhaps the only reason to wander off

Shropshire House, Capper Street

Tottenham Court Road and into Capper Street. The little horseshoe that runs off it has none of the charm suggested by its name, Mortimer Market, but with its combination of curved corners and the small but bulbous balcony above the main entrance, the gleaming white façade and its heavily emphasised horizontal lines, this beautifully maintained office block still looks much as it must have done when it was completed in 1932.

Cartwright Gardens

Originally Burton Crescent after its building (see Burton Street above) this 1807 development was renamed after the political radical, reformer and former Royal Navy commander John Cartwright (1740–1824) who lived at no. 37 and is commemorated by a seated statue in the adjacent garden. Whilst the terrace opposite has been replaced by university halls of residence, both halves of the crescent have remained intact making this an unusually elegant run of townhouses. Any conversions (to flats or hotels) have been done sensitively, so that the effect of the attractive first-floor balcony work and stuccoed lower portions has not been lost or in any way spoiled.

Doughty Street

Forever associated with Charles Dickens, who paid £80 per annum for a three-year lease on no. 48, pleasantly leafy Doughty Street still largely comprises Grade II* listed Georgian houses (most of them built between 1790 and 1840) although the vast majority have since been converted into publishing and legal offices. Like many in Bloomsbury it was gated until the end of the nineteenth century, with uniformed porters manning barriers at either end and requiring tradesmen to make their deliveries on foot.

Cartwright Gardens

Dickens Museum, Doughty Street

No. 48 is now the Dickens Museum, but other notable residents included Vera Brittain and Winifred Holtby at no. 52, *The Spectator* which was founded here in 1828 and only quit no. 55 as recently as 2007, and the lawyer Sir Travers Humphreys (1867–1956). The latter's cases included those of Oscar Wilde, Hawley Harvey Crippen, the 'Brides in the Bath' murderer George Smith and John George Haigh, the 'Acid Bath killer'.

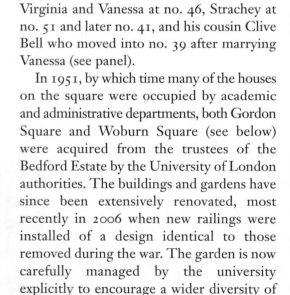

Tagore Statue, Gordon Square gardens

Gordon Square

Before departing for the swampy fields of Belgravia in the 1820s, Thomas Cubitt began building the houses around Gordon Square and they were completed around the time of his death in 1855. The 6th Duke of Bedford took a particular interest in the layout and planning of the gardens, naming the square after his second wife, Lady Georgiana Gordon, daughter of the 4th Duke of Gordon.

From 1910 onwards the square became the focus of the much celebrated Bloomsbury Group, a loose but intermingled and highly influential group of writers, artists and intellectuals who famously were said to 'live in squares but love in triangles'. Brought together by the ideas of the Cambridge

philosopher, G. E. Moore, and keen to pursue what he described as 'the pleasures of human intercourse and the enjoyment of beautiful objects,' they included Leonard and Virginia Woolf, Virginia's sister Vanessa, Duncan Grant, Clive Bell, Dora Carrington, Lytton Strachey, E. M. Forster and the economist, John Maynard Keynes. Several of them lived in Gordon Square including the young Virginia and Vanessa at no. 46, Strachey at no. 51 and later no. 41, and his cousin Clive Bell who moved into no. 39 after marrying Vanessa (see panel).

In 1951, by which time many of the houses on the square were occupied by academic and administrative departments, both Gordon Square and Woburn Square (see below) were acquired from the trustees of the Bedford Estate by the University of London authorities. The buildings and gardens have since been extensively renovated, most recently in 2006 when new railings were installed of a design identical to those removed during the war. The garden is now carefully managed by the university explicitly to encourage a wider diversity of wild and domestic plants.

Gordon Square

THE
BLOOMSBURY GROUP

Although its heyday was in the 1920s, the Bloomsbury Group and its radical ideas are still hugely influential today. A rarefied clique of privileged intellectuals its members rejected the Victorian emphasis on public virtue and fashioned new ways of thinking in a wide range of disciplines, including art, literature and economics. Some of the impetus for change undoubtedly stemmed from the lessening of the influence of Christianity, partly brought about by advances in science and technology, not least in the theories advanced by Darwin. As a result new questions on what constitutes a 'good' life were posed. The answer from Bloomsbury was to reject tradition and convention and focus instead on personal relationships, the life of the mind and aestheticism for its own sake. From this source sprang new social mores: pacifism, free love, feminism and an acceptance of homosexuality. The British establishment, of course, loathed Bloomsbury in all its forms.

If there is a date for the foundation of the Bloomsbury Group it s probably 1904. In that year the renowned literary critic and biographer, Sir Leslie Stephen, died and his family moved from Kensington to 46 Gordon Square. There were four Stephen siblings: Vanessa, Thoby, Virginia and Adrian. While all four made a real contribution to English culture it was the third-born child, Virginia, who would become the most celebrated. Her married name was Woolf.

The intellectual seeds of Bloomsbury had been sown five years before the move to Gordon Square. That was when Thoby Stephen went up to Trinity College, Cambridge and became part of a brilliant set of undergraduates that included Lytton Strachey, Leonard Woolf and Clive Bell. Three years later Strachey and Woolf joined the Apostles, a secretive, and highly select, society. Its other members included several who would later be highly influential in Bloomsbury circles, not least E. M. Forster. The Apostles, through their Saturday-evening philosophy symposiums, adumbrated many of the issues that would later occupy the Bloomsbury Group.

In Gordon Square, Vanessa Stephen (later Bell, as the wife of Clive Bell) set out to make Victorian domesticity a thing of the past: walls were painted white, Indian shawls thrown over furniture and photographs by her aunt, Julia Margaret Cameron, were everywhere. Perhaps more importantly the Stephen siblings entertained with a will, inviting Thoby's university friends to intellectual soirées. Their intellectual touchstone was the philosopher G. E. Moore, whose emphasis on the intrinsic worth of an action, as opposed to its consequences, became the bedrock of Bloomsbury thought. Lytton Strachey's work, especially *Eminent Victorians*, was also a profound influence in Bloomsbury circles. The book, a huge commercial success, broke new ground in the field of biography. In debunking his subjects – who included Florence Nightingale and General Gordon – and along with them Victorian morality, he anticipated the new critical freedom that the end of the First World War would unleash.

The Bloomsbury Group was also prominent in the visual arts, not least through the influence of Roger Fry. Assisted by Clive Bell, Fry did much to promote Post-Impressionist painters such as Cezanne, Matisse, Van Gogh and Picasso, a campaign that included two significant exhibitions at the Grafton galleries in London. Vanessa Bell was a talented artist whose willingness to experiment – inspired and encouraged by Fry – catapulted her to the forefront of the avant-garde. Through the Omega Workshops – another Bloomsbury creation – she became known for her interest in decoration, expressing herself on walls, screens and tables. This reached its apotheosis at Charleston, Bloomsbury's 'country house' in Sussex, which Bell was to make her permanent home. Scarcely a surface or piece of furniture was left untouched as Bell and her fellow members gave full vent to their imagination.

However, the brightest star in the Gordon Square firmament was Vanessa's younger sister, Virginia (who married Leonard Woolf in 1912). As one writer on the Bloomsbury Group observes, 'No other twentieth-century writer has been so thoroughly described, analysed, critiqued, satirised and appropriated as Virginia Woolf.' She did not want for ambition: her goal, no less, was to 'reform the novel' and thanks to the stream-of-consciousness technique she used in books like *Mrs Dalloway*, *To the Lighthouse* and *The Waves* she at least partly achieved that goal. Another literary form in which Woolf excelled was the essay and by the time of her death she had penned around four hundred such works, including many important peregrinations on feminism, pacifism and literary theory.

Some have questioned whether the many thousands of books and articles on Virginia Woolf would have seen the light of day had it not been for her troubled private life. Sexually abused by her half brother as a child she went on to have passionate affairs with members of both sexes, among them the novelist Vita Sackville-West. Her mental health was always, at best, fragile; she suffered from manic depression, an illness that saw her not only referred to psychiatrists but also confined in a variety of sanatoriums. After such a turbulent life it is not surprising that she took her own life: on 28 March 1941, at the age of fifty-nine she put a heavy stone in her pocket and drowned herself in the river Ouse.

Whatever the reasons might be for our continued fascination with this cultural coterie it shows no signs of abating. Film and television producers in particular have long been inspired by the Bloomsbury set and its exploits. The latest in the canon was *Life in Squares*, a major three-part series produced by the BBC and first broadcast in the summer of 2015. Described by one newspaper as the 'raciest costume drama ever seen' it focuses on the often tangled relationships of the Group and includes some of the most explicit sex scenes ever shown on a mainstream channel.

Gower Street

Its development largely the responsibility of Lady Gertrude Leveson Gower (1714–94), widow of the 4th Duke of Bedford, one of Gower Street's delights is the strange juxtaposition of the Classical main core of University College London and the Cruciform Building directly opposite. The Victorians generally were not keen on Georgian architecture, preferring the clash of styles that today gives London much of its character, and the Cruciform was conceived by Alfred Waterhouse (1830–1905). Originally constructed as part of University College Hospital (the university took this over in 1995) this immense and lively exercise in terracotta and red brick was the last building Waterhouse designed. Although its idiosyncratic layout badly disrupts the line of the street, its distinctive cross-shaped plan represents a typically Victorian attempt to maximise the light and air reaching the wards located on each floor. The external finish, equally practical, was selected to resist the heavy pollution of late-nineteenth-century London.

The same cannot be said of the white stone used for the building opposite, sadly, which is commonly referred to as the Octagon. It is characterised by the lofty dome above the main library and its beauti-fully proportioned ten-column Corinthian portico. It was designed by William Wilkins, architect of the National Gallery, Hailey-bury College for the East India Company and the elegant little Georgian Theatre Royal in Bury St Edmunds. The Octagon was completed in 1829 with the two compact, brick-built gate lodges and its north and south wings added some thirty years later. These were by the Scottish architect Thomas Hayter Lewis (1818–98), although Wilkins had proposed a similarly striking set piece for the site with shallower domes.

The choice of Grecian architecture here is of great significance as the University was expressly established as a non-denominational foundation. Its choice of architectural style served to emphasis this fact, clearly distancing the new institution from the Neo-Gothic traditionally favoured by the fellows of Oxford and Cambridge, whose colleges were at this time essentially tied to the established church. (The notable exception to this is in Cambridge is Downing College, which is also Grecian; but this is one of the newer colleges, founded in 1800, and in fact its two oldest chairs are demonstrably secular ones, in law and medicine.)

Particularly further south and also on the west side, Gower Street still boasts a number of large terrace houses of the late-eighteenth

Cruciform Building, Gower Street

University College London, Gower Street

century, mostly dating from around 1790. These the art critic John Ruskin found particularly offensive, although modern opinion has sensibly turned very much in favour of this sort of urbane and dignified Georgian style. Residents in Gower Street in the early years included Charles Darwin, who wrote part of *On the Origin of Species* here, George Dance the Younger, the Italian patriot Mazzini, Millais and, at a time when she could believe her house to be 'most effectually in the country,' the actress Mrs Siddons.

Elsewhere in the street, places of note include RADA, the Royal Academy of Dramatic Art. The Academy of Dramatic Art was founded in 1904 by the splendidly named Sir Herbert Beerbohm Tree, the leading actor-manager of the Edwardian era and renowned for his spectacular productions of Shakespeare. Its original home was His Majesty's Theatre in Haymarket but a year later it moved into two adjoining houses in Gower Street, at nos. 62–64. With a managing council that included the great playwrights Sir Arthur Wing Pinero and Sir James Barrie, and later encompassed Sir George Bernard Shaw and W. S. Gilbert, it was perhaps inevitable that the new institution rose quickly to its current eminence. Shaw's patronage was a real boon: he donated the royalties from his play *Pygmalion* to the Academy, enabling it to benefit from the huge success of *My Fair Lady*, the musical version of the work, which was adapted by Lerner and Loewe. In 1964 *My Fair Lady* became a multi-Oscar-winning film starring Rex Harrison and Audrey Hepburn. On his death in 1950 the reading of Shaw's will revealed that he had left one-third of the royalties from all of his literary works to RADA.

The Academy was granted a royal charter in 1920, and then, in 1921, a theatre was built in Malet Street, adjoining the Gower Street property. It was destroyed during the Second World War but was subsequently rebuilt, reopened in 1954 as the Vanbrugh and is now one of five theatres, plus a cinema, owned by the Academy. In 1927, a new, purpose-built building was put up to replace the adjoining houses (a project to which Shaw, with his usual generosity, donated £5,000).

The RADA alumni are, as one might expect, distinguished. In 1923 John (later Sir John) Gielgud studied for a year at the Academy, playing no less than seventeen parts, including two Hamlets. Gielgud would later become the president and first honorary fellow of RADA. Lord 'Dickie' Attenborough, a Leverhulme scholar at the Academy in 1941, became chairman in 1972. While a list of the great actors who have passed thought its portals would be several pages long, the names Sir Anthony Hopkins,

RADA, Gower Street

THE
UNIVERSITY OF LONDON

After Oxford and Cambridge England's third oldest university, London was first granted a royal charter in 1836. Although many of its constituent bodies are much older than this – University College and King's College, for example, were founded in the 1820s while the medical schools of St Bartholomew and St Thomas can trace their origins back to the twelfth century – the foundation date means that London was the last of the major European capitals to have a university. Established under the auspices of Lord Melbourne's administration, the bringing together of these bodies and the creation of others was done with the express purpose, somewhat quaintly described, 'of ascertaining by means of examination the persons who have acquired proficiency in Literature, Science and Art'. Its original governing body was suitably august, counting Michael Faraday among its members, as well as Dr Arnold, Rugby School's eminent headmaster, but University College was subsequently granted a new charter to once more become a separate institution.

From the earliest days of the new university, academic degrees were conferred regardless of a candidate's religious or social affiliations, a very important distinction because until the passage of the Universities Tests Act of 1871 the ancient seats of learning in Oxford and Cambridge were virtual closed shops for those outside the Anglican tradition. The University of London was also prominent in the field of women's rights: as long ago as 1880 the university became the first to award degrees to women. In 1838 the first examinations had attracted just twenty-three students but by the start of the Great War such progressive policies had helped make it the largest educational body anywhere in the country – with well over four thousand undergraduates – although for many years it was housed in a variety of buildings spread across the capital, something that disguised the scale of the establishment. It was only in the 1920s that Bloomsbury was chosen as its permanent home, and even then the students were to be displaced barely more than a decade later when Senate House and many of its other academic buildings were requisitioned by the government for the duration of the Second World War.

Following the war its expansion continued at a great pace, initially as part of the general expansion of university education and then in the 1980s when a number of amalgamations brought other institutions into the fold, including Royal Holloway College at Egham, Bedford College in Regent's Park and Queen Mary College at Mile End. Between times other significant bodies have joined, such as the Warburg Institute, Jews College and the Courtauld Institute of Art. Today it consists of eighteen self-governing colleges and ten specialist research institutes, including world-famous establishments like the London School of Economics and the London School of Hygiene and Tropical Medicine. As a result the student body is now thought to number in excess of 125,000, with an additional 35,000 students enrolled on its courses through distance learning. Such a total naturally dwarfs the total population of many well-known university towns and even cities, but even though many of the students are based in Bloomsbury the visitor is still left without the impression of proper campus, still less of a vast educational monolith. Most obviously this is because so many of its institutions and departments are housed in buildings separate from Charles Holden's towering Senate House, which still dominates much of the area. Examples of those which cluster in the immediate area include the School of Hygiene and Tropical Medicine, Birkbeck College, the Students' Union and the Institutes of Education and of Oriental and African Studies. Like Senate House, the more significant of them are described elsewhere in this chapter.

Peter O'Toole and Sir Roger Moore are known worldwide.

Gower Street is also where in 1808 Richard Trevithick demonstrated 'the first locomotive to draw passengers'. At that time a trip on the device he called the *Catch-Me-Who-Can* cost one shilling (5p) and on the site of Bonham Carter House at nos. 52–54 the first effective anaesthetic was administered to a patient, on 19 December 1846.

Great James Street

This is one of the area's lesser-known gems, with almost all of the original façades intact. That said, with a majority of the houses now converted to offer a mixture of office and residential accommodation the buildings behind have been almost entirely rebuilt. Popular with period film and television crews, the street still looks much as it must have done in 1720 when George Brownlow Doughty set out to develop the area with the help of James Burgess. The street is named after the latter, Doughty's own family connections being honoured by the names of Doughty Street, Doughty Mews, Brownlow Mews and so forth.

The street's most celebrated resident is Dorothy L. Sayers (1893–1957), the author

Great James Street

of numerous detective stories and the creator of Lord Peter Wimsey for whom she found accommodation at 110a Piccadilly (see Mayfair chapter). At no. 24, three 'small but very pretty rooms' she shared with numerous cats and an even greater population of mice, she wrote her first novel, *Whose Body?*, which introduced readers to Lord Peter, as well as *Clouds of Witness* and *Unnatural Death*. Marrying after the birth of an illegitimate child she moved out to rural Essex but kept the flat on for many years.

Great Ormond Street

Established in 1852 by Dr Charles West, Great Ormond Street Hospital for Sick Children – commonly just GOSH – like the street on which it stands takes its name from James Butler, 1st Duke of Ormonde (see Ormond Yard, St James's chapter) although the connection with this Royalist commander is not obvious.

Although it has now removed to Spital Square in East London, the presence here for nearly fifty years of the headquarters of the Society for the Protection of Ancient Buildings gives some indication of the street's quality. Several eighteenth-century houses are still standing, such as no. 41, which has an elaborate segmented pediment above the door and handsome painted, fluted Ionic columns. Elsewhere in the street, mostly on the south side, and opposite the sprawling hospital buildings, are a number of other interesting door cases and some attractive Georgian brickwork. On the same side of the street little Barbon Close suggests that the speculative Restoration-era builder and developer Dr Nicholas Barbon was active here, and indeed nos. 55 and 57 are thought to be by him.

Great Ormond Street Hospital

The institution that became Great Ormond Street Hospital started life as the Hospital for Sick Children. It was initially very modest, with just ten beds squeezed into no. 49 Great Ormond Street before the acquisition of no. 48 enabled it to spread into the adjoining gardens and entirely new premises designed by E. M. Barry were ready for use by 1877. Running costs were funded entirely from private sources, including subscriptions, donations and the proceeds of fundraising events. The annual festival dinner was a particularly lucrative source of income – accounting for around half of the hospital's revenues – and the impressive range of speakers included Oscar Wilde, Charles Dickens and members of the royal family. The majority of the doctors and surgeons who worked there did so without being remunerated, alongside paid work in their own practices.

Within fifteen years the hospital's capacity had further increased to nearly 250 beds, and following several generous bequests – including a gift of the *Peter Pan* royalties by the author J. M. (later Sir James) Barrie – work on the present building began in 1933. Expansion has continued ever since, one major extension in 1990 requiring Barry's St Christopher's chapel to be physically uprooted and moved more than sixty feet from its original position. The style of its richly coloured Franco-Italianate interior is now deeply unfashionable but well worth a visit.

West's initial vision for his hospital was to care for the children of the poor, work that would be complemented by clinical research in paediatrics and by the training of paediatric nurses and it is these noble principles that guide the work of this great institution today. It has come a long way since 1852 and it is estimated that there were in excess of two hundred thousand patient visits in 2012. GOSH is recognised internationally not only as a centre of excellence in treating child illness but also as a world-class facility for research and training. At the time of writing Great Ormond Street Hospital is being comprehensively redeveloped in a programme with four phases that will take until 2025 to complete. A particular priority has been to replace the cramped and out-of-date wards, most of which were built in the 1930s, and as well as providing children with modern facilities, such as playrooms and computers, there will also be accommodation for their parents.

While still prominently labelled the London Homoeopathic Hospital, the red brick and terracotta building at no. 60 is now the Royal London Hospital for Integrated Medicine and offers a range of complementary services as part of the NHS. It was originally established in Golden Square, Soho in 1849, by F. H. F. Quin (1799–1878) who is widely regarded as this country's first homeopathic physician. According to expectation he was denounced by the medical profession as a quack, and blackballed by the members of the Athenaeum; but despite being unable to cure his own asthma, Quin was lauded by London society, both socially and professionally.

Great Russell Street

Measuring six-and-a-half-feet by thirteen, and surveying more than ten thousand acres, John Rocque's mighty 1747 *Plan of the Cities of London and Westminster and the Borough of Southwark* shows Bedford House and Montagu House occupying almost the entire northern side of Great Russell Street with their gardens stretching away to the empty countryside behind.

Today the sites of these two buildings are occupied by the British Museum, an even more striking structure and with its more than thirteen million artefacts one of the world's great storehouses of human history and culture. Its earliest origins lie in a bequest from the scientist and physician Sir Hans Sloane (1660–1753), a sometime resident of nos. 3 and 4 Bloomsbury Place, who suggested to the authorities that after his death his very considerable cabinet of curiosities be acquired by the nation for the sum of £20,000. Though high the price represented a substantial discount on the collection's probable value (it had reportedly cost Sir Hans around £50,000 to put together) and with the bequest settled a new British Museum opened in 1759 on the present site, which was then occupied by the Duke of Montagu's old home. This too had been acquired and restored for the nation, at a cost of a further £23,123, although initial consideration had been given to housing the collections at Buckingham House (overlooking St James's Park, and not yet the royal palace it was to become) until this was ruled out on the grounds that its relatively remote location so much further west of London proper rendered it unsuitable.

To pay for all this a public lottery was instigated, and eventually raised in excess of £300,000, a quite astounding sum for this period, with the public generously permitted to visit but only in very carefully controlled numbers and for no more than three hours a day. In fact, all applications to visit had to be made in writing to the museum, with tickets issued at the rate of just ten per hour and groups of visitors ordered to stay together. It was not until 1879 that members of the public were allowed simply to turn up and enter, or to wander around at liberty enjoying what in a very real sense they had paid for.

The collections from the first were hugely impressive, comprising approximately forty thousand printed books and seven thousand manuscripts, together with many thousands of natural-history specimens, including more than three hundred volumes of dried plants, and many prints, drawings and antiquities from Egypt, Greece, Rome, the Far East and the Americas. To these were added two superb libraries, collected by Sir Robert Cotton and the Harley Earls of Oxford, and a third, the magnificent Royal Library, containing more than 10,500 volumes collected over many years by successive sovereigns from Henry VIII to Charles II. (It is also significant that the Royal Library was entitled to receive a copy of every book registered in the City at Stationers' Hall, which is to say one of every work published in the United Kingdom.)

In all subject areas the collections owned by this new 'universal museum' were to expand at a great pace, helped to a great degree over the next two centuries by more bequests, by plunder – for example the famous Rosetta Stone came by way of the defeated Napoleon Bonaparte – and by the rapid expansion of the British Empire. The latter brought with it a marked enthusiasm for collecting and classification, a development that followed the deployment overseas of thousands of military and administrative professionals. Among the most significant bequests included one in 1805 of a superb collection of classical sculpture – the collection of museum trustee Charles Townley which had hitherto been displayed at his house at 14 Queen Anne's Gate (see Westminster chapter) – and play scripts donated by the actor David Garrick.

With thousands of exotic specimens arriving from the likes of Captain Cook, the East India Company and Sir Joseph Banks, coins and other treasures from the Bank of England and precious Asian artefacts from Sir Stamford Raffles in Singapore, pressure on the available space meant that many items were soon being sent to subsidiary institutions. The first of these was the British Museum (Natural History) in South Kensington, but the growth of the core collection meant that very soon consideration had also to be given to developing the home site here in Bloomsbury.

Following the gift to the nation in 1822

British Museum, Great Russell Street

of yet more royal bounty in the form of the King's Library, comprising some sixty-five thousand volumes and nearly twenty thousand pamphlets, maps, charts and topographical drawings belonging to George III, Sir Robert Smirke was commissioned to produce a set of drawings for a much larger establishment than the old Montagu House. This was intended primarily 'for the reception of the Royal Library, and a Picture Gallery over it,' and was to take the form of a large quadrangle fronted by an open courtyard. As such it included much of what visitors would recognise today, including the famous Greek Revival façade facing onto Great Russell Street, its forty-four immense Ionic columns (referencing the Temple of Athena Polias at Priene) and in the pediment above the principal entrance Sir Richard Westmacott's figures depicting *The Progress of Civilisation*.

Once Sir Robert's plans were accepted what remained of the old Montagu House was demolished and work on the museum building as we know it now at last began. Building on such a massive scale, however, meant the project was to take many years to complete, and it was 1852 before the main forecourt was formally opened. Even then, such was the pace at which the collections were growing that new works were already in hand to create a number of additional buildings and galleries on the site and to infill many of the planned voids. The most notable of these was Sydney Smirke's circular Reading Room, which opened five years later. A conspicuously elegant structure – and at the time the second broadest dome in the world – Smirke's design was also an acknowledgement that his brother's vast empty quadrangle was an extravagance the museum authorities could no longer justify. As more and more artefacts continued to pour in from both official and private donors, yet another new wing, the White Wing on Montague Street, opened in 1884.

By the final years of the Victorian century, the premises were again found wanting, and, in 1895 using government money, the museum's trustees purchased dozens of private houses in Great Russell Street, Montague Street, Montague Place, Bedford Square and Bloomsbury Street. These they planned to demolish in order to clear a space for several new wings, and work began on the first in 1906, a new northern wing, although a lack of funds curtailed other developments. Instead new mezzanine floors and book stacks were squeezed in wherever possible to accommodate the unceasing flow of new acquisitions and many of the houses were allowed to remain standing. Private benefactors such as the art dealer Sir Joseph Duveen also provided the money for specific projects, such as a bespoke gallery that was completed in 1938 for the celebrated Elgin sculptures (better known as the Elgin Marbles) from the Parthenon frieze.

Not all of these 'side projects' reached fruition, however, including one somewhat curious scheme proposed by a reader of the journal *The Athenaeum* who proposed build-

ing new wings either side of the main block – one classical, one Gothic – to house what he called a British Walhalla [sic]. 'Grouping with, though detached from, the main building' this would contain the memorial busts of individuals who had distinguished themselves in the fields of Art, Science and Letters. A 1942 plan also ran into trouble when its promoters suggested demolishing scores of shops and houses in and around Museum Street in order to create a monumental vista running up from New Oxford Street.

In 1972, however, an important Act of Parliament succeeded in establishing a new British Library and with a demand for an additional 1.25 miles of shelving every year it was decided to establish this on a completely new site outside of Bloomsbury. This took until 1998 to accomplish but successfully liberated vast new areas for visitors and exhibits alike, including most obviously the splendid Queen Elizabeth II Great Court and a new gallery in the north wing. Designed by Norman Foster & Partners, and a technical tour de force, at two acres and a cost of £100 million, the Great Court is now the largest covered square in Europe and one of the most exciting public spaces in London.

Viewed from within or from above, the highlight is its elegant and mathematically highly complex roof structure, which one is tempted to describe as wonderfully light and airy although in reality it weighs a very substantial 793 tonnes. The illusion depends on thin steel supports and more than 3,300 individual panes of glass, each one a different size and shape to its neighbours, the effect of which, particularly in bright sunshine, is quite spectacular.

Much of this latest round of expansion was funded by the Sainsbury family but it is unlikely to be the last. Despite now covering almost a million square feet in total (and with more than two miles of exhibition space) the British Museum still finds itself unable to display more than 1 per cent of its collections at any one time, an astonishing thought for anyone who has spent time, energy and shoe leather trying to take it all in.

It would be impossible to list even the highlights in this temple of culture but mention must be made of the treasures from the Classical world and from Egypt. The aforesaid Elgin Marbles ('marbles' is a general term used to denote stone objects such as sculptures, inscriptions and architectural features) were removed from the Parthenon between 1802 and 1812 by Thomas Bruce, the 7th Earl of Elgin, and British ambassador to the Ottoman court in Istanbul. Elgin's actions have long been a source of controversy, and were so even at the time, with Lord Byron among the protestors. Perhaps understandably, the government in Athens has consistently campaigned for Britain to return the works to Greece, without success.

Those who argue that the artefacts should remain in London point out that Elgin had the permission of the Ottoman Empire, of which Greece was then a part, to remove them. They also note that these precious works had been damaged both by military action and by vandals and that Britain would be the best place to preserve them. Nor can Elgin's motives be questioned: he paid for the dismantling and shipping costs – and at £70,000 this was a colossal sum for the time – and then refused lucrative offers to sell them, including one from Napoleon Bonaparte. In fact he insisted that he would only part with the works in the public interest, and so, in 1816, Parliament agreed to acquire them, paying Elgin £35,000, just half of the sum he had expended on the project.

The Rosetta Stone – an artefact from ancient Egypt, part of a world-class collection from that country – dates from the reign of Ptolemy V. The inscription carved into the granodiorite stele is a decree by a council of priests from 196 BC, affirming the royal cult of Ptolemy, who was then thirteen. The decree is written in three different languages: hieroglyphic, Demotic and Greek. For this reason it is invaluable to our understanding of Egyptian language and culture. The Rosetta Stone was unearthed by Napoleon Bonaparte's soldiers in 1799, but, following the defeat of the French armies in North Africa, it became the property of the British government in 1801 and was first exhibited in the British Museum a year later. The Egyptian government would like the Rosetta Stone to be returned but given that it is the most-viewed exhibit in the British Museum this seems unlikely.

There is also much to admire from these shores in the British Museum. The Sutton Hoo collection is one of the most important Anglo Saxon resources in the world. In 1939 the amateur archaeologist Basil Brown was excavating on the Sutton Hoo estate in Suffolk when he uncovered a seventh-century ship that had been used to bury a person of noble, or more probably royal, blood. The ship, a full thirty yards long, was filled with period artefacts: these included richly decorated swords and buckles, dishes, spoons, gold coins and, perhaps the most impressive, a ceremonial helmet. From the other end of Britain there are the Lewis chessmen, discovered by a farmer, Malcolm Macleod, in a dry-stone chamber on the island of that name during the nineteenth century. The chess pieces are made of walrus ivory and whale teeth and are notable for the elaborate style in which they are carved and for the curious facial expressions of the kings, queens, bishops and knights. Dating from the twelfth century, most historians believe they are of Norwegian origin: Norway ruled the Outer Hebrides at that time and the chessmen may have been in transit from Scandinavia to Dublin (another Norwegian fiefdom) when the owner was, for whatever reason, disturbed and decided to conceal them.

Back outside the British Museum, a number of official blue plaques (and bronze ones erected by the Bloomsbury Estate) serve as a reminder that this was once a primarily residential street. Those commemorated include the writer and *Punch* cartoonist George du Maurier (1834–96) who paid 25 shillings a week for a second-floor flat at no. 91 with a studio behind the shop on the ground floor for an extra 10 shillings (50p). Another noted illustrator lived at no. 46, Randolph Caldecott (1846–86) who also drew for *Punch* and the *Illustrated London News*. Whilst living at this address he produced the drawings for *The House That Jack Built*, and his ghost is said to haunt the building.

Finally, no. 77 is the former home of Thomas Henry Wyatt (1807–80), a member of the great architectural dynasty. He trained under Phillip Hardwick (see Belgravia) and worked alongside him on a number of London projects including Euston Station and Goldsmiths' Hall. Today T. H. Wyatt is most highly regarded for his rural churches and country houses, but he also designed houses in Kensingston Palace Gardens, and in Mayfair on Park Lane and Berkeley Street.

Guilford Street

Another street built on land owned by the Foundling Hospital, and named after Frederick North, 2nd Earl of Guilford, who as

Foundling Hospital, Guilford Street

prime minister from 1770–82 was commonly known by the courtesy title Lord North. Once again the builder was James Burton, working to a plan of Cockerell's which included markedly smarter houses at the west end than at the east although the difference between these was mostly in scale rather than style. Only a few of these very late eighteenth houses have survived on the northern side, including nos. 71–73, now linked as an hotel, with their ten attached Doric columns rising through the first and second storeys.

The south side has been entirely redeveloped, the curious President Hotel replacing Baltimore House in which Frederick

71–73 Guilford Street

Calvert, 6th Baron Baltimore (1731–71) was accused of abducting and raping a young milliner called Sarah Woodcock. The trial caused a sensation in eighteenth century London – as the technical owner of the British colony of Maryland, Calvert was not only titled but also immensely rich – and, although he was eventually acquitted, his reputation never recovered. He died in Naples aged just thirty-nine, an outcast if not officially an exile. His son Henry took over the proprietorship of the colonial territory (on which, curiously, neither man was ever to set foot) but he was dispossessed after a few years by the momentous events of 1776.

Towards the eastern end of the street can be seen the pillar which once contained Captain Coram's 'all-comers basket' (see Bernard Street, above) and in Guilford Place the statue of a kneeling water-bearer. This commemorates a local benefactor called William Lamb or Lambe, a liveryman of the Clothworkers' Company in the City who in 1577 contributed a sum of money for 120 pails to be distributed to poor women of the parish. This enabled them to collect water from a nearby tributary of the Fleet River, the name of Lamb's Conduit Street marking this act of philanthropy and the pump he provided ('the property of the City of London . . . erected for the benefit of the Publick') although the latter has long since disappeared.

Lamb's Conduit Street

Affecting the air of one of central London's small self-contained village streets, Lamb's Conduit Street retains an impressive number of small independent retailers, mostly upmarket and well accommodated in the late-eighteenth-century buildings that line

The Lamb pub, Lamb's Conduit Street

the course of what in Elizabethan times was a small but important tributary of the Fleet. Among the beautifully restored buildings is the Lamb, a Grade II*-listed pub, which is visibly late-Victorian although the first tavern on the site was built around 1729. Its interior is particularly good, one of the very few in the country to retain the etched and frosted glass 'snob screens', which were once a popular feature and designed so that drinkers could keep their identity hidden from the publican and other customers. Another rare survivor is the pub's Polyphon, a primitive precursor to the gramophone or jukebox, a coin-operated device that plays large metal discs studded with picks like a large musical box.

Little Russell Street

The great church of St George's Bloomsbury was designed by Nicholas Hawksmoor, the sixth and final London church by this leading light of the English Baroque. It was completed in 1731 after the rejection of competing designs from Sir John Vanbrugh and James Gibbs, and erected on the 'ploughyard', a surprisingly small plot of land for such an important commission.

St George's, Little Russell Street

church of St-Giles-in-the-Fields they had to pass through the Rookery. This notorious criminal slum was depicted by Hogarth in 1751 as part of his great work *Gin Lane* (and visited by Charles Dickens a century later) and occupied a site close to where Centre Point stands today.

The design of St George's is also to be placed among the most unusual anywhere in the capital, its extraordinary stepped tower inspired by Pliny the Elder's description of the famous Mausoleum at Halicarnassus, and the portico based on that of the Temple of Bacchus in Baalbek (Lebanon). The combined effect of such scholarship was described (in 1876) as having produced 'the most pretentious and ugliest edifice in the metropolis,' but the church is now regarded as one of Hawksmoor's genuine masterpieces, and justifiably so.

On two occasions it has been expensively restored, the first time in 1870 by G. E. Street, who worked mostly on the interior, and then again in the early years of this century when substantially more than £8 million was spent on improving the fabric following generous grants from an American benefactor and the Heritage Lottery Fund. The spire is topped by a statue of King George I shown in Roman dress, and originally had figures of bellicose lions and unicorns at its base (symbolising his suppression of the First Jacobite Rising) although these fell into disrepair and were removed while Street was improving the interior. A gift of a brewer, the statue is the only one of King George in London – revenge perhaps on a king who spent so much of his reign in Germany – and can be seen in the background of the aforementioned Hogarth engraving. It was ridiculed at the time, but now wears its years well.

This had been acquired from the Russell family for a very substantial £1,000, somewhat at variance with the church and metropolitan authorities' insistence that any new buildings created in accordance with the 1711 Commissioners for the Fifty New Churches Act exclude smaller sites 'where the same will not admit the church to be placed East and West'.

Despite these constraints the church is both large and magnificent, taking a decade and a half to complete and costing in excess of £31,000, which was more than three times the architect's original estimate. Its creation was welcomed by parishioners who had long complained that in order to reach their local

Malet Street

Like the adjacent Malet Place, the street takes its name from Sir Edward Baldwin Malet (1837–1908) the English diplomat and Egyptian Consul-General whose daughter married the 9th Duke of Bedford. Formerly known as Keppel Mews North it is now almost entirely faculty buildings of the university, and entirely dominated by the impressive bulk of Senate House (see panel).

Mecklenburgh Square

Just as S. P. Cockerell named the first of two symmetrical squares designed to face each other after George IV's Caroline of Brunswick-Wolfenbüttel the second was intended in 1790 to commemorate her mother in law, Charlotte of Mecklenburg-Strelitz, Queen Consort to George III. The architect soon after resigned following a quarrel with the governing body of the Foundling Hospital, which owned and controlled the land he was developing. He was quickly replaced by a pupil, Joseph Kay, who took over the design of both the buildings around the square and its two acres of central garden, which took place over the next fifteen years.

Kay's square sadly sustained very heavy damage during the Second World War, including no. 37, which was briefly home to Virginia Woolf but now forms part of Goodenough College, a residential centre for postgraduate students. Other houses have survived along the north and east ranges, however, and these are now Grade II*-listed. These include the apartments of Byron Court at nos. 26–34, which, dating from 1808, feature an impressive eleven-bay centre portion with giant Ionic columns. The stuccoed building incorporates the former headquarters of the Women's Trade Union League and the National Anti-Sweating League, two organisations that campaigned against low wages and poor working conditions in the early years of the twentieth century. A plaque at no. 44 records the residency here of the American poet Hilda Doolittle (1886–1961) – 'H. D.' – who was married to Richard Aldington, the Great War poet and biographer of T. E. Lawrence.

Mecklenburgh Square was also briefly once home to the author Dorothy L. Sayers. At the time she was so poor that she was forced to dispense with curtains in order to buy food, and only later would her writing provide her with the £70 a year required for a move to more upmarket accommodation in Great James Street.

Museum Street

Predating the existence of the British Museum by as much as four hundred years, Museum Street was a rural backwater called Peter Street before being renamed. (The attractive Museum Tavern on the corner with Great Russell Street was similarly once known as the Dog and Duck, at a time when the fields to the back of Bedford House and Montagu House were popular with wildfowlers.) The older name is thought to refer to a local factory making saltpetre, a compound of potassium and nitrogen, with a long history of use in fertilisers, food preservatives and gunpowder. Now mostly Victorian, and with some unusual decorative shop fronts, for a short while it was also known as Queen Street during a period of gentrification.

SENATE HOUSE

Very much the centre piece of the University of London, and by far the most visible landmark regardless of the direction from which one approaches Bloomsbury, this nineteen-storey white behemoth was the second skyscraper to be built in London (after 55 Broadway, SW1). For more than two decades it was the capital's tallest building at 210 feet. As it happens both buildings were designed by Charles Holden (see Covent Garden and the Strand), this particular commission coming his way after he beat more than a dozen rivals in a rigorous selection process culminating in a black-tie dinner at the Athenaeum. His design was nevertheless a slightly rude interloper in an area of leafy squares and Georgian terraces – a 'disastrous cenotaph' some called it – but the King and Queen were in favour of it, and construction started in 1932. The site selected for this was large plot of land the University authorities had acquired from the Bedford Estate nearly a decade earlier for £525,000.

Holden's scheme in fact called for two massive towers, which he expected to cost £3 million to build and take up to thirty years to complete. One of his chief supporters was the University's principal, Sir Edwin Dellar, but he died in a bizarre accident during a guided tour of the site, when a builder's handcart struck him after falling from a great height. After that Holden's scheme never was completed, the University choosing to move into the building in 1937 and somehow never getting around to starting work on the second tower. Holden also intended his building to last for five hundred years, eschewing the newly fashionable steel frames that he said he didn't trust, and instead making the granite and Portland stone load bearing. (In fact there is steel within the tower, as this is used to support the very considerable weight of more than two million academic books and journals.) The stone was also chosen so that rainwater falling on it 'would wash its own face', but like most buildings in London it has proved susceptible to staining.

Whilst now taken very much for granted the building was far from universally popular. Employed here during its wartime role as the headquarters of the Ministry of Information (and working alongside Graham Greene, John Betjeman and Dylan Thomas) George Orwell found the place so depressing he used it as the model for the fictional Ministry of Truth in his dystopian epic *1984*, and the architectural critic Sir John Summerson felt its 'melancholy air' conveyed the idea that there was little joy to be had from learning. Indeed even now its design is occasionally described as Stalinist (or likened to the Constructivist architecture of the old Soviet Union) which

Trafalgar Square, with the National Gallery (*left and centre*) and St Martin-in-the Fields (*right*)

Piccadilly Circus, with its central statue of Eros

This page: Horse Guards Parade (*above*), the Foreign and Commonwealth Office (*below*).

Facing page: Bridgewater House, Cleveland Row (*above*), St James's Palace (*below*)

The squares of the West End. *This page*: Bedford Square (*above*) and Berkeley Square (*below*).
Facing page: Bloomsbury Square (*above*) and Eaton Square (*below*)

This page: The Nelson Column, Trafalgar Square (*above*) Constitution Arch, Hyde Park Corner (*below*)

Facing page: The Supreme Court of the United Kingdom (*above*) in Broad Sanctuary. The Royal Courts of Justice, Strand (*below*)

The Palace of Westminster seen from the Thames, the masterwork of its creators Sir Charles Barry and Augustus Welby Pugin

This page: The Ritz, Piccadilly (*above*) and Claridge's, Brook Street (*below*).

Facing page: Liberty, Great Marlborough Street (*above*), Fortnum and Mason, Piccadilly (*below*)

This page: Asprey, Bond Street (*above*), The Reform Club, with the Travellers' Club to its left, Pall Mall (*below*)

Facing page: London clubs: White's, St James's Street (*above*) with the Garrick, Garrick Street (*below*)

Entertainment capital: Shaftesbury Avenue (*above*) with the Odeon, Leicester Square (*below*)

Facing page: Cubitt's compact and beautifully detailed Woburn Walk, London's first pedestrian precinct (*above*). The delightful Queen's Chapel, by Inigo Jones, Marlborough Road (*below*)

Westminster Abbey, arguably the most important building in Britain and a focus of national consciousness.

is somewhat ironic given that the British fascist leader (and former Labour Party minister) Sir Oswald Mosley let it be known in the 1930s that he planned to relocate Parliament here in the unlikely event of his taking power.

In fact Mosley may not have been the building's only extreme right-wing fan. In August 1940, when the course of the war was such that Germany could allow herself to think she might be emerge the winner, an official SS minute noted that, 'ever since the Battle of Trafalgar, the Nelson Column has represented for England a symbol of British Naval might and world domination. It would be an impressive way of under-lining the German victory if the Nelson Column were to be transferred to Berlin.' Certainly Hitler is known to have had some sort of 'shopping list' detailing cultural and other artefacts he wished to acquire, and more recently it has been suggested he had plans to use Senate House as his headquarters for the north of Europe. The evidence for this is admittedly sketchy, although the fact that such a prominent and gleaming white landmark managed to emerge from six years of war more or less unscathed could be explained if German aircrews were warned not to attack it in the first place.

Queen Square

Laid out between 1708 and 1720, the eponymous queen of the square is Queen Anne
although no houses from the time of her
reign survive (and the lead statue in the
central garden is almost certainly of George
III's wife, Queen Charlotte.) The slender
rectangular shape may follow the outline of
an old reservoir on the site, built to serve
Greyfriar's in the City, the religious foundation established by four Franciscan friars in
Newgate Street as early as 1224. Nothing of
the reservoir now remains, although at the
southern end of the square there is an old
iron water pump marked 'Unfit for Drinking'. (Similarly, until as recently as 1910, a
trapdoor in the garden of no. 20 revealed a
dank, winding passage nicknamed the
Devil's Chimney. This led to a medieval well
that supplied water to another ancient City
institution, Christ's Hospital.)

Former residents include the philosopher
Jeremy Bentham, Jerome K. Jerome and
Francis Willis, the Lincolnshire physician
who treated George III during the early
stages of his madness. The aforementioned
house at no. 20 was home to Louisa Twining
(1820–1912), the Victorian philanthropist
who spent a lifetime working to alleviate the
conditions of the London poor, particularly

Queen Charlotte, Queen Square

St George the Martyr, Queen Square

women. At the time of its demolition in 1960 the house had been converted into Imperial Ladies Turkish Baths.

During the First World War an estimated one thousand lives were saved when a German Zeppelin was brought down in the square, but it is no longer residential and following the example of Dr Willis many of the replacement buildings now have medical connections. The Ospedalo Italiano was established here in 1884 and remained in the square until 1990 when the premises were taken over by Great Ormond Street Hospital. Elsewhere on the square can be found the National Hospital for Neurology and Neurosurgery (which is part of the Royal London Hospital for Integrated Medicine) the former Institute for Public Health and the Institutes of Neurology and Cognitive Neuroscience.

Like the square itself the church of St George the Martyr has undergone many changes. Originally constructed as a chapel-of-ease in 1706, it was consecrated in 1723 and then radically altered in the 1860s by the Gothic Revivalist S. S. Teulon. The bell tower is also nineteenth century, and in 1956 St George's was the setting for the marriage of Ted Hughes and Sylvia Plath. Before leaving the square there is one more reminder of tragic Queen Anne, the adjacent Gloucester Street taking its name from William, Duke of Gloucester, who at just eleven years old was to be the longest surviving of her seventeen children.

Russell Square

London's second largest square after Lincoln's Inn Fields, Russell Square was extensively re-landscaped in the early 2000s better to reflect the original Humphrey Repton layout of two hundred years earlier. The name of course refers to the ground landlords, and the large bronze by Richard Westmacott on the southern side is of Francis Russell, 5th Duke of Bedford. The gardens are public. With one side a major

Russell Square gardens

thoroughfare the square is neither secluded nor any longer original, although on the west side several James Burton houses survive. There are other survivors on the north and south side, although these have been much altered, and the east range is entirely gone. The site is now largely occupied by the immense late-Victorian Hotel Russell with its extravagant French-Gothic façade, a master class in nineteenth-century brick and *thé-au-lait* terracotta by Charles Fitzroy Doll. The designer of the dining room on the RMS *Titanic*, the architect commissioned a series of sculptures of British queens – nicknamed Fitzroy's Dolls – by H. C. Fehr, the sculptor of the figures on the front of Middlesex Guildhall (now the Supreme Court) in Parliament Square.

In a pattern that will by now be familiar, many of the surviving houses on the square are occupied by university departments, including the institutes of Advanced Legal Studies at no. 17, Germanic and Romance Studies at no. 19 and Commonwealth Studies at no. 28. However, when the square was residential it was popular with lawyers, writers and artists. In 1818 the legal reformer Sir Samuel Romilly killed himself at no. 21 after losing his wife and in 1832 Lord Tenterden died at no. 28 having presided over the trial of the Cato Street traitors. His neighbour at no. 50 was Lord Chief Justice Denman, who was responsible for acquitting the 7th Earl of Cardigan on a charge of attempted murder. Cardigan had even boasted about shooting someone in an illegal duel but was nevertheless found to be innocent on a technicality, because his opponent's name had been wrongly entered into the court records.

Southampton Row

This is a busy thoroughfare, with a character entirely in keeping with its official designation as the A4200, and is the link between Russell Square and Kingsway. Today the bulk of the traffic is conventional, but for many years trams ran beneath the roadway. Part of the old tunnel can be seen beneath large grilles set into the central reservation, and nearby the old Theobalds Road tram station is still intact but sadly not open to the public. The same grilles also guard the entrance to another of the tunnel's more recent occupants, the Greater London Council's centre for flood control, which somewhat curiously was built underground.

For a while Vincent Van Gogh, was employed here as an art dealer (in the 1870s he was living at Kennington Oval) and other famous residents have included the sculptor Robert William Sievier (1794–1865) and the conductor Sir John Barbirolli who was born in a house here in 1899 on a site now occupied by the Bloomsbury Park Hotel.

Southampton Row was also home to two important London institutions, the first of which is Central Saint Martins College of Arts and Design (or, more often, Central Saint Martin or just CSM). Now a constituent part of the University of the Arts London, this was formed as recently as 1989 with the merger of the Central School of Art and Design (founded 1896) and the even more venerable Saint Martins School of Art, which had been established in 1854. In 1896 the Central School's guiding light had been the architect William Richard Lethaby (1857–1931) a far-seeing pioneer whose work influenced many in Britain as well as the founding fathers of Germany's Bauhaus movement. Lethaby's recognition of the importance of practical teaching in art and design led him to employ, among others,

Edward Johnston (1872–1944) who today is regarded as very much the father of British calligraphy.

A failed medic, and largely self-taught, Johnston's work can still be seen across literally the whole of London, his best and most significant creation being the clear and beautifully proportioned typeface he conceived specifically for use by London Underground. Still recognised as having 'the bold simplicity of the authentic lettering of the finest periods,' but nevertheless giving the firm impression of 'belonging unmistak-

Spink coin dealers, Southampton Row

ably to the twentieth century,' this timeless classic is one of the unsung icons of London, a reminder of an era when the Tube was not only at the leading edge of what we now call corporate branding but also quite literally the envy of metropolitan authorities around the world.

The other venerable establishment, at no. 69, is the coin, stamp and medal dealers Spink. The company, still a world leader, can trace its origins at least back to 1666 when the premises of John Spink, then a goldsmith and pawnbroker based in Lombard Street, narrowly escaped destruction when the Great Fire swept through the old walled city.

Architecturally, Southampton Row has little to offer, although running diagonally with the point where it meets Kingsway and Bloomsbury Way, Sicilian Avenue is a pretty little exercise in small-scale planning. A street of shops and cafés with a screen of columns at either end, it is paved with marble from the Mediterranean island from which it takes its name and was laid out in 1905 by W. S. Wortley.

Former Central School of Art & Design, Southampton Row

Tavistock Place

An unexpected Bloomsbury gem, the delightful Mary Ward House at nos. 5–7 was the inspiration of the novelist and social reformer Mrs Humphrey Ward (1851–1920). One of London's finest Arts and Crafts buildings, it was designed by Arnold Dunbar Smith and Cecil Claude Brewer and in 1909 was the site of an historic debate on women's suffrage between Mrs Ward in her role as president of the Anti-Suffrage League. It was also the first building in England with classrooms specifically designed for children with disabilities, and is now an attractive venue for parties and business meetings.

Mary Ward House, Tavistock Place

Tavistock Square

With many squares and terraces in Bloomsbury lost to neglect, bomb-damage, the university and greed, only the west side façade of Thomas Cubitt's Tavistock Square has survived. Much of the remainder had disappeared as recently as 1938, by which time Tavistock House – now the British Medical Association headquarters – had been completed by Edwin Lutyens, as previously described (see Burton Street). While by no means an unattractive design, its creation necessitated the destruction of

the house in which Charles Dickens started *Great Expectations* and completed several other important works including *Bleak House*, *Hard Times*, *Little Dorrit* and *A Tale of Two Cities*.

In the central garden is Fredda Brilliant's seated bronze of Mahatma Gandhi, a 1994 monument to conscientious objectors, and a tree planted in memory of the victims of Hiroshima. More recently the square was the scene of quite hideous carnage, when thirteen passengers on a no. 30 bus were killed by a suicide bomber in July 2005.

British Medical Association HQ, Tavistock Square

Gandhi statue, Tavistock Square

Torrington Square

Originally known as the Field of Forty Foot-steps – in 1680 two brothers are said to have died after fighting a duel over a shared lover – Torrington Square is now a square in name only. A truncated terrace of just six houses built over a former archery ground around 1805, the remainder has been swept away by the expansion of London University. On one of the survivors, no. 30, there is an elaborate bronze plaque, surely the only one in London commemorating a 'poetess'. It was erected by the trustees of the Bedford Estate immediately before the Great War, the writer in question being Christina Rossetti (1830–94), the sister of the painter Dante Gabriel Rossetti. She lived and died in this building and was the model for her brother's *The Girlhood of Mary Virgin*, the first work ever to be signed 'PRB' for the Pre-Raphaelite Brotherhood.

Rossetti plaque, 30 Torrington Square

In 1950 the scientist and intellectual J. D. Bernal leased a top-floor flat at no. 22, and found himself playing host to Pablo Picasso when the latter was travelling to the Soviet-sponsored World Peace Congress in Sheffield. (Both were, at one time, communists.) During his stay Picasso created a mural in the flat, which was subsequently removed and sold to the Wellcome Trust Collection.

Looking at the square today the overwhelming feeling is one of regret, due almost entirely to its wholesale destruction by the university authorities. That said the remodelling by Robert Myers, who created a piazza as part of the 2005 extension to Birkbeck College, represents a huge improvement on its earlier treatment making it a worthy winner of the 2006 Landscape Institute Award.

Tottenham Court Road

Marking the western boundary of Bloomsbury, this busy central London artery takes its name from a thirteenth-century property owner William de Tottenhall. Variously known as Totten, Totham and Totting Hall, the name 'Tottenham Court' most likely dates from the time of a ninety-nine-year lease on much of the property, which was granted by Queen Elizabeth.

In the centuries following the area became a popular place for Londoners looking for entertainment, and in the mid-nineteenth century it was still sufficiently rural for the owner of a local farm (Cappers) to insist that provision be made for forty cows in the lease for the sale of some land and stables in 1840. The buyer was the son of the late John Harris Heal – a feather dresser and furniture maker, late of Rathbone Place – and more than 170 years

Heal's, Tottenham Court Road

later Heal & Son still occupy the same site at no. 196. The present building is by Sir Edward Maufe, architect of Guildford Cathedral, the Air Forces Memorial at Runnymede and of the Second World War extension to the Tower Hill Memorial in the City, which Lutyens built to the memory of the many thousands of seamen and fishermen who lost their lives during the two great twentieth-century conflicts.

Until 1922 the southern end of Tottenham Court Road was also home to the Horse Shoe brewery, site of the Great Beer Flood of 1814. Over many years in late-Georgian London brewers had competed with each other to build larger and larger tuns or barrels, and when Henry Meux commissioned the largest one yet for the Horse Shoe the finished article was twenty-two-feet high, and nearly three times as

wide. Said to hold more than a million pints, and large enough to seat two hundred guests at a celebratory dinner, it weighed more than a thousand tons. The vast wooden staves were held in place by giant iron hoops, each of which weighed five hundred pounds.

On 16 October 1814 a great misfortune occurred when one of these cracked and gave way, doing so with such a loud report that the resulting explosion was heard five miles away. A jet of beer shot out and with sufficient force to penetrate the neighboring tun, which itself promptly failed. A great flood of beer quickly formed a tidal wave, which pushed its way into the street, washing away several neighbouring buildings and sending pedestrians sprawling in the gutter where many drank their fill of the contaminated liquid. In all nine people died, but scores more were injured, many of them after becoming intoxicated and falling over or being hurt in the riots which followed a rumour that free beer was being given away. The brewers were eventually hauled into court, but found not guilty after the jury declared the incident to have been an act of God. Incredibly the directors were able to obtain a refund of the duty it had paid on the beer after a successful appeal to Parliament.

Following the brewery's closure in the 1920s the Dominion Theatre was built on the site, its largely period Art Deco interior playing host to musicals, rock concerts and a number of Royal Variety Performances.

Woburn Square

Taking its name from the ducal seat at Woburn Abbey in Bedfordshire, Woburn Square was built in the late 1820s, a smart residential enclave designed by James Sim. Completed in 1847 the houses were narrower and so less imposing than those in the adjacent Gordon Square but nevertheless attractive. The house at no. 15 still retains its Georgian wrought-iron arch over the entrance, a rare survivor complete with its original link-snuffer from the days when the better off would pay so-called link boys to run ahead of them lighting the path with a torch or link. These would be extinguished upon arrival, whereupon the boy would take off in search of another customer.

Despite Sim's general lack of recognition, Woburn was long regarded as one of London's nicest small squares, at least until its acquisition along with other parts of the Bedford Estate by the university in 1951. Amidst strong opposition much of the square was shortly afterwards demolished, including Lewis Vulliamy's Christ Church of 1831. This was done to make way for Sir Denys Lasdun's brutal Institute of Education, also an unattractive extension for the School of African and Oriental Studies, and Charles Holden's Warburg Institute building. (Among the houses demolished to make way for the latter was the home of Charles Fowler, architect of the market buildings in the Piazza at Covent Garden, and another with a charming relief panel depicting the Muses.)

Enthusiasts for Lasdun's work point out that several houses in the square and on nearby Bedford Way had already been destroyed or badly damaged by the Luftwaffe. But numerically more of them were swept away deliberately to clear space for the new buildings – at least 1,500 residents were forced out in this way – and indeed many would have been but for the objections voiced not least from within the university. After more than 150 years Woburn Square was nevertheless to be ruined, and like much of Bloomsbury effectively suffocated by buildings constructed on a much larger scale. Perhaps the best that can be said is that its example was to prove something of a turning point in the struggle against the large-scale redevelopment that characterised much of the 1960s and 1970s.

In defiance of Lasdun's plans and protestations several Georgian houses with their simple fenestration and wrought-iron first-floor balconies were hastily spot-listed and saved from obliteration. The lucky survivors include a short terrace on the eastern side which, ironically, now forms part of the Institute of Education. Since then, and as at Gordon Square, the renovation by the university of the gardens has included the installation of new railings. Its small summerhouse has also been restored, and the nearby 1999 sculpture called *The Green Man*

Institute of Education, Woburn Square

by Lydia Kapinska was inspired by the writings of Virginia Woolf. More significantly the surrounding area, in almost its entirety, has been designated a conservation area.

Woburn Walk

In marked contrast to the present day, little if any thought was given to retail displays or presentation in shop windows until at least the 1750s. Nor until that time were shops rarely anything but tiny and dark with the goods and merchandise piled high and kept largely inaccessible behind the counter. Windows were typically small, being used either as a simple serving hatch or to advertise what sort of wares were on offer by placing a single, unchanging example of something suitable in a prominent place.

In fact it was not until the Regency period that any serious consideration was given to the design of individual shops, or indeed to the notion of a street dedicated purely to the pleasures of shopping. The change, when it came, was led by the designers of the few fashionable covered walkways which appeared in the West End, including Samuel Ware's Burlington Arcade on Piccadilly (see Mayfair) and the Royal Opera Arcade built by Nash and Repton as part of their redevelopment of the King's Opera House in St James's.

Woburn Walk

One attractive alternative to this route, however, was this one offered by Thomas Cubitt in 1822, although his achievement has tended to be overlooked. Prominently employed on the Duke of Bedford's estate, where he was responsible for Woburn Place, Endsleigh Street, and much of Gordon and Tavistock Squares, what Cubitt created in Woburn Buildings (as it was then called) might nevertheless be termed London's first pedestrian precinct, if not its first purpose-built shopping street.

Today, with its beautiful monochromatic bow-fronted buildings, the attractive pedestrianised street at the northern end of Bloomsbury seems rather more like a film set than a piece of real London and certainly more so than its later, southern cousin at Sicilian Avenue. Nevertheless it formed an important part of Cubitt's master plan for what had hitherto been pasture and fields: somewhere for the better class of retailer to meet the needs of the aspiring middle classes who were now flocking onto the Duke's increasingly popular estate.

Nearly two centuries on, not much has changed. Tucked away from the noise of Woburn Place and the Euston Road, Woburn Walk still feels pleasantly exclusive with a diverse range of tenants selling books and prints, food and antiques. At no. 5 a plaque marks the lodgings of the poet and dramatist W. B. Yeats (1865–1939) who lived here from 1895–1919. Somewhat less well known is his neighbour in the house opposite, Dorothy Miller Richardson (1873–1957), who in her four-volume, semi-autobiographical series *Pilgrimage* is credited with pioneering the stream-of-consciousness novel. A 'flagged alley,' she called Woburn Walk in 1905, describing it as 'a simply terrible place to live'.

SOHO

With a reputation the world over as a place for those inevitable bedfellows entertainment and sleaze, the very name Soho continues to conjure up images of London that are at once exciting and slightly dangerous. Fashionable but never smart, expensive but often still quite seedy, Soho is so deeply cosmopolitan (and has been for centuries) that more than anywhere in London foreign tongues have frequently seemed to outnumber the native one. But out of this veritable Babel has come something unique and wonderful. Successive waves of immigration have created in Soho a vibrant and lively area quite unlike anywhere else in the capital. Better than any other part of the West End it exemplifies London's status as a world city, its theatres, bars and restaurants pulling in Londoners as well as trippers and tourists although, deep down, even those who think they are locals know they can never really claim it as their own.

For historians the name is associated with one of the great lost houses of London, although in truth not much is known about the Duke of Monmouth's mansion on Soho Square beyond its staggering proportions and the fact that – after being implicated in treason – its creator lived barely long enough to enjoy it. Nothing remains of it today, but, clearly, with a frontage of 76 feet on the south side of what was then King Square and a depth of 280 feet, Soho House was conceived on a truly palatial scale, with its extensive stabling and coach houses occupying much of the east side of Frith Street. By 1685, however, barely three years after work on its construction had begun, His Grace had been beheaded. His crime was attempting to unseat his Catholic uncle, James II, the executioner Jack Ketch reportedly requiring several blows with the axe,

and then a knife, to complete the job. With the family declining rapidly thereafter his widow was eventually able to sell her leasehold to a city merchant, and after substantial remodelling it was leased to the French and then the Russian ambassador. By 1773 its demolition was well underway, however, and very quickly all trace of Monmouth's mighty edifice had disappeared.

At the Battle of Sedgemoor in 1685, commonly held to be the last proper pitched battle on English soil, the doomed nobleman's password and rallying call had been a hunting cry of 'so-ho', and more than three hundred years later this is often said to be the origin for the name of this part of central London. In fact the term was already in use before this date, for example when an area known as Kemp's or Soho Fields was leased by Charles II and his mother to Henry Jermyn, 1st Earl of St Albans. The connection is not entirely false, however, as the area had previously been formed part of a convenient hunting ground for the court when it was centred on Whitehall Palace.

Lord Jermyn, as we have seen, was to make his name and fortune as the developer of St James's, by far the most exclusive and most successful of the seventeenth-century suburbs, but socially and architecturally Soho was never to reach such heights. Apart from other considerations its reputation is popularly imagined never quite to have recovered from the grisly fate of the would-be usurper. Certainly with the aristocracy relatively quick to abandon Soho as they migrated further west from the historic core of the city, their townhouses were soon appropriated by commercial interests, converted to taverns, or divided into low workshops and slums. No. 20 Soho Square, for example, once home to Cromwell's daughter

Mary and subsequently to the Duke of Argyll, became first a 'genteel' hotel, and then a tavern. It was eventually incorporated into a pickle- and condiment-bottling plant owned by Crosse & Blackwell, before finally being torn down.

Soho as we know it today, the area so accurately described by London author Russ Willey as a 'zone of continuous commotion', falls within the area bounded by Regent Street, Oxford Street and the Charing Cross Road and extends down to the south to take in Leicester Square and the surrounding streets. As with other parts of central London much of its history can still be read in the familiar street names: Richard Frith, a successful bricklayer, was one of the pioneering developers who leased land from Lord St Albans; and Greek Street just one of several corners of the neighbourhood settled by Greek Christians and later French Huguenots.

In fact the vibrant character of Soho has often been determined by immigrants and others seeking refuge. The House of St Barnabas-in-Soho (see Greek Street, below) was established as a safe haven for the homeless, but many of those seeking sanctuary came from much further afield. The French for example arrived in large numbers after fleeing persecution in their own country, in particular following Louis XIV's 1685 revocation of the Edict of Nantes. (Decades later, in 1739, William Maitland in his *The History of London from its foundation by the Romans to the Present Time* noted on a visit that it was still 'an easy matter for a Stranger to imagine himself in France'.)

The fact that the streets hereabouts have more than their fair share of cafés, bars and restaurants is also a reflection of Soho's long and cosmopolitan history. For example, following the failed uprisings across the Continent in 1848 droves of disappointed radicals flooded into London from France, Germany, Poland and the collapsing Hungarian Empire. Many of them opened cafés and restaurants to serve their own countrymen the food they missed, others worked in these places cooking and serving, and in the process introduced the variety of different cuisines for which Soho is still known. The novelist John Galsworthy described the result as 'untidy, full of Greeks, Ishmaelites, Italians, tomatoes, restaurants, organs [and] coloured stuffs' – but modern Londoners love it that way, and the fact that in their wake have come the Chinese and other south Asian peoples, whose colourful influence still predominates.

According to contemporary accounts the atmosphere in the mid-nineteenth century was already bohemian as well as highly cosmopolitan, but seedy too, although this probably represented business as usual in an area where, as early as 1641, a 'lewd woman' had been bound over to keep the peace. The fact that Anna Clerke was charged merely with 'threteninge to burn the houses of Soho,' suggests her lewdness was taken as a given, although Soho's reputation as London's premier red-light district really took hold three centuries later in the years following the Second World War. By far the biggest period of growth was the mid-1960s when striptease clubs, clip joints, peepshows and the like began to squeeze out many more legitimate businesses and eventually to threaten the very existence of Soho as we know it now.

Fortunately things have improved markedly since, thanks in large part to lobbying by the Soho Society and new legislation requiring premises associated with the sex industry to be licensed. The results have not been hard to discern: property values have risen steeply, along with the population, and the area has lost its earlier threatening demeanour. According to one estimate the number of sex-related enterprises declined by more than 80 per cent between 1981 and 1991, and certainly Soho now feels very different both day and night. People visit mostly for the food and the atmosphere, which still distinguish the neighbourhood from anywhere else in London. The school serving the local population is also thriving, and in mosoho – the Museum of Soho – the neighbourhood now has a repository for documents and artefacts pertaining to its fascinating history.

Admittedly over the years not everyone has found the place welcoming and, during his family's residency in Frith Street, Leopold Mozart (Wolfgang's father) complained about the place and the population, describing greed and godlessness in what he considered to be an expensive culinary wasteland. In particular he recoiled from Londoners' habit of 'guzzling solidified fat' – beef dripping, presumably – and must have regretted returning to the city from their previous lodgings in the relatively rural calm of what is now Ebury Street in Belgravia.

Archer Street

In 1675 this was Arch Street and later Orchard Street when it was described as 'broad, but of no great Account'. By the 1740s it had acquired its present name although at that point it was still a cul-de-sac with only a narrow foot passage connecting it to Rupert Street. The accommodation was always modest, the last seventeenth-century survivors a pair of small, cottage-like buildings, which until their demolition in 1912 looked decidedly more market town than capital city with simple brick fronts, large windows and hipped roofs. Latterly occupied by a firm of upholsterers they were replaced by the vaguely Georgian offices of the Orchestral Association. Designed by Charles Holden and with a draped figure of Euterpe (the muse of lyrical poetry) above the first-floor window these are now occupied by a public-relations consultancy.

In fact it is this change from residential to light industrial to commercial that characterises the entire street, with much of the southern side occupied by the rear entrances of three theatres – the Apollo, Lyric and Windmill – but with a few interesting buildings opposite. These include Archers Chambers at no. 9, which provided working class or artisan accommodation in the 1880s behind a simple but attractive rusticated entrance arch. The incised and faceted brick segmental arches above the windows, narrow stringcourses of nail-head ornament and a bracketed main cornice are typical of the sort of detailing that Victorians sometimes used to lift even the most workaday buildings. It has since been taken over by the Soho Housing Association.

Berwick Street

James Fitzjames, 1st Duke of Berwick, was the illegitimate son of James II, after whom was named a 'pretty handsome strait street' in which John Strype's 1720 *Survey of the Cities of London and Westminster* found 'new well built houses much inhabited by French where they have a church'. Sadly, L'Eglise du Quarré has not survived, nor the nearby L'Ancienne Patente – another place of worship – although there are a number of eighteenth-century houses still standing.

Berwick Street market

These include nos. 26, 31–32, 46–48, 50–52, 69–71 and 79–81, all of them very much beneficiaries of Soho's turnaround in fortune, with most now beautifully restored and the street (whilst by no means smart) providing a pleasing mix of office and residential accommodation with the inevitable addition of cafés and pubs. Some of the latter are particularly well established: the site of the Green Man, for example, has been a licensed premises since the reign of George II.

Berwick Street market too is also of ancient origins, today's stallholders inheriting pitches which originally casual – the market began as early eighteenth century shopkeepers informally spilled out onto the street – were formalised as long ago as the 1890s. At that time the area was largely slums, and like residents in other parts of Soho the locals more than once succumbed to cholera. The market today is busy and mixed, mostly selling fruit and vegetables and operating every day except Sundays.

Broadwick Street

A relatively recent coinage, until 1936 this ancient street was in two halves with Broad Street to the west and Edward Street to the east (see Wardour Street). Development began as early as 1686, initially as a fashionable place to live although by 1750 the decline in its fortunes was evident and the street was largely occupied by tradesmen, shopkeepers and craftsmen. A number of houses from this period have survived, including nos. 60–74 on one side and 51–67 on the opposite side. Although each has been much altered since, these brick houses with stuccoed ground floors are still very handsome.

In one of them (now no. 54) Charles Bridgeman lived, from 1723 until his death fifteen years later. A pioneering landscape designer, the first to adopt a more naturalistic and less rigid approach to landscaping, he abandoned what Horace Walpole called the 'square precision of the foregoing age' and in this way foreshadowed William Kent and Lancelot 'Capability' Brown. Surviving works of his include Rousham House in Oxfordshire, Claremont, Stowe, Wimpole Hall and Cliveden. Alexander Pope thought his creations 'work to wonder at' and as royal gardener to Queen Anne he was also responsible for the gardens at Windsor, Kensington Palace, Hampton Court Palace, St James's Park and Hyde Park.

The artist William Blake was born in a house on the corner of Broadwick Street and Marshall Street, but in fact the most significant building in the street today is the John Snow public house at no. 39, which commemorates the physician responsible for identifying the water-borne nature of cholera. This followed his enquiry into a lethal outbreak of the disease in 1854. Over the course of three days, 127 people living on or near Broad Street died and with only a dozen households escaping without a fatality Snow managed to trace the infection to a water pump in the street. There is now a replica of this outside the pub, Snow having discovered that the original pump had been pumping water from a well situated just three feet from a cesspit brimming with faecal bacteria. Correctly identifying that the survivors were in the main brewery workers who did not drink from the pump, he had the pump chained or the handle removed (accounts differ). Unfortunately, this was still not enough to prevent a staggering 616 residents succumbing before the epidemic abated. The pub, formerly known as the Newcastle-Upon-Tyne, was renamed in the 1950s in his honour.

In this most mixed of streets Broadwick House at no. 33 provides what is perhaps the strongest contrast to this slice of history, occupying an island site and designed by the

Dr Snow's water pump, Broadwick Street

Broadwick House, Broadwick Street

Richard Rogers Partnership in 1996 to provide mixed office and restaurant accommodation. An uncompromisingly modern design with a double-height studio located beneath a sweeping arched roof, the addition of a glazed lift tower provides an echo of Lloyds of London and the Pompidou Centre while its vast floor-to-ceiling windows give the workforce within the best views in this part of London.

Carlisle Street

Standing on the corner with Soho Square, until its destruction on 11 May 1941 by German bombers, a property known as Carlisle House provides another snapshot of Soho's declining fortunes. A handsome house of 1687, the 2nd Earl of Carlisle's spacious five-bay brick house sat beneath a large triangular pediment with a lavish plasterwork interior. It was clearly grand, although the attribution to Christopher Wren is almost certainly incorrect. Among its more noteworthy occupants was the 3rd Earl's idiotic wife, Lady Anne de Vere Capell (1675–1752) who attempted to pass through London, and indeed through most of her life, without once speaking to anyone she regarded as her social inferior.

After its sale by the Carlisle family the house was taken over by Domenico Angelo Malevolti (1716–1802), the great swordsman, who taught that fencing was the ideal activity for promoting health, poise and grace, and in the process helped to make it a sport. He wrote the standard work on fencing, entitled *L' cole des Armes* (The School of Fencing, published in 1763), a book that is still highly influential today. His pupils included David Garrick, Richard Brinsley Sheridan and members of the royal family. The painters George Stubbs and Sir Joshua Reynolds were also frequent visitors, and Malevolti, who was also a great horseman, later built a riding school at the rear, whilst charging a substantial fee of one hundred guineas a year for boarders wishing to learn the arts of arms and manners. In common with other large houses in the area, however, Carlisle House was destined soon to be divided and subdivided as Soho's social prestige declined. By the 1780s the tenants included small tradesmen, a wood carver, an art restorer and several artists with a Masonic lodge meeting regularly in what had been the ballroom. Dickens is said to have modelled the lodgings of Dr Manette in *A Tale of Two Cities* on the house, although this cannot be confirmed.

Later still Carlisle House became a home for medical and clerical students, a furniture warehouse and then offices for the new British Board of Film Censors before its destruction by the Luftwaffe. In 1938 the building was still being described as 'one of the most valuable survivals of old Soho' but three years later, on a clear night with a full moon, three occupants died in the German attack and the house was left in ruins. Since then it has not infrequently been confused with another Carlisle House that stood on the opposite side of the square. (This too was owned by the Earls of Carlisle and is described in the section below on Soho Square.) Elsewhere, Carlisle Street today contains a number of modest if attractive buildings, but none is original and the sole blue plaque in the street – to John Christopher Smith 'Handel's Friend and Secretary' at no. 6 – is not official and the dates given are not certain.

Carnaby Street

Until London's first boutique opened here in 1957, Carnaby Street was just another old, but uninteresting, and rather run down west-end thoroughfare. A market existed here as long ago as 1830, having supplanted the local, largely Huguenot, community, and in his 1845 novel *Sybil*, Benjamin Disraeli describes 'a carcass-butcher famous in Carnaby-market'. A typical tenant would have been the 'ironmonger and oilman' who occupied a spectacularly dingy shop at nos. 37–39 until the 1940s, and for a long time the street's only real claim to fame was that the firm of Inderwick & Co at no. 45 was reportedly the first shop in England to sell Meerschaum pipes. (The fashion quickly caught on and at the start of the nineteenth

Carnaby Street

century John Inderwick even purchased a small quarry in the Crimea to ensure a ready supply of suitably high quality clay.)

All that changed in 1957 when Glaswegian John Stephen (1934–2004) opened a shop called His Clothes, his second, as the first (in Beak Street) had burned down. He was a former employee of Moss Bros, where he had learnt traditional tailoring, but, while still in his early twenties he took the plunge and decided to start his own business. Selling trendy new Levi jeans at five guineas a pair, Stephen chose Carnaby Street because it was cheap but close enough to smarter Regent Street to catch some passing trade. Others soon followed suit, including a number of equally modish rivals such as I Was Lord Kitchener's Valet, Cecil Gee, Lord John and Mr Fish, all keen to capture younger customers who were desperate for the emerging Mod and hippy styles. Soon Stephen's clothes were being worn by the Beatles as well as by members of the Kinks,

Small Faces and Rolling Stones, and their fans, determined to avoid dressing like their parents, rushed to buy the same styles as their idols. Thanks to his uncanny ability to catch the Sixties *zeitgeist*, Stephen became perhaps the most influential fashion entrepreneur in Britain, catering to the counterculture and making it acceptable for men to dress flamboyantly. Stephen himself dressed reasonably conservatively, but had loud music blaring out of his doorways and racks of pink velvet jackets, hipsters and bright, floral shirts to tempt buyers in. Soon he had more than fifteen shops in this street alone, selling what the *Daily Telegraph* rather dismissively described as 'mini-kilts for men, elephant-cord low slung trousers and androgynous flared velvet double-breasted jackets hung alongside kaftans'. He was more than just a shopkeeper, being responsible for many eye-catching and innovative designs. Perhaps inevitably, he was dubbed the 'King of Carnaby Street' by the press.

A relentless self-publicist who shipped his Rolls-Royce across the Atlantic on trips to America (he owned his first Roller at the age of twenty, prompting one bemused policeman to enquire if it belonged to his father), Stephen soon became synonymous with Swinging London. Liberace played in one of his shops, Petula Clark filmed one of her television shows in another, and, on 15 April 1966, *Time* magazine in the US sealed the deal by declaring in its cover feature that 'perhaps nothing illustrates the new swinging London better than narrow, three-block-long Carnaby Street, which is crammed with a cluster of the "gear" boutiques where the girls and boys buy each other clothing'. In short, Carnaby Street had arrived and nearly half a century on people still come from across the world simply to see what the fuss was all about. Among the most famous in London, the name is nevertheless still mysterious and commemorates the curious sounding Karnaby House, the nearby residence of a successful bricklayer. Today, however, the street itself has little of interest architecturally although houses close by at 17 Newburgh Street, 10–12 Ganton Street and 7–8 Kingly Street do still give a good impression of how Carnaby Street might have looked in the 1720s.

Dean Street

Its name uncertain – there is no obvious connection to any ecclesiastical authority, although nearby Old Compton Street's Henry Compton was a seventeenth century Dean of the Chapel Royal – Dean Street was laid out in the 1680s. Initially fashionable it soon acquired its own small community of French refugees although some titled residents remained including the 7th Earl of Abercorn and the 2nd Earl Bathurst who served as Lord Chancellor from 1771–8.

The demolition, at the time of writing, of an entire block at the Oxford Street end (part of the ongoing £15 billion Crossrail project) is just the latest in a series of redevelopments. These have resulted in the messily varied architecture of modern-day Dean Street, a street where sadly none of the original houses remains, although there are some good eighteenth-century survivors. Among the oldest are nos. 67–68, dating from 1732, no. 69 which is also early Georgian (and now a private club and hotel) and the bow-fronted shop at no. 88 of around 1790. In July 2009, no. 76 – widely regarded as having had one of the best early Georgian interiors in London – was gutted by fire. The impact was particularly great as the

grade II listed building contained some of the best-preserved early eighteenth-century townhouse murals anywhere in the country, naval scenes shown in great detail, as well as many of its original fixtures and fittings.

Other houses of the period have long since disappeared, but not always without trace: the site of no. 75, for example, was previously occupied by a fine townhouse of 1730 components of which, when demolished, were removed to North America and displayed at the Art Institute of Chicago. Several painted panels in the house were attributed to William Hogarth on the grounds that the house was lived in by his artist father-in-law Sir James Thornhill, but unfortunately neither man had a connection to the house making the attribution unlikely. Because of this a protracted battle was lost to prevent its demolition in 1919 – a move the *Times* described as 'inexcusable vandalism' and a very poor outcome for the first attempt ever in this country to preserve a building under the Ancient Monuments Act of 1913.

Across the street the premises of the long established Quo Vadis restaurant in an earlier incarnation provided lodgings for a passionate but personally shambolic young Karl Marx in the 1850s. Moving here from 64 Dean Street, the place was described by one of his visitors as being in 'one of the worst, therefore one of the cheapest, quarters of London'. Marx lived here with his wife and maid in 'two evil rooms,' fathering children on both of them, and the plaque was unveiled in 1967 by the then chairman of the Marx Memorial Library in Clerkenwell. Other notable residents of the street included Hester Thrale in the 1760s (see Mayfair chapter) and the architect Thomas Hardwick. The latter was George III's clerk of works at Hampton Court and the restorer of St Bartholomew-the-Less in the City, St Paul's Covent Garden and Wren's church of St James's on Piccadilly. The Groucho Club is at no. 45.

A substantial majority of the more recent buildings are not of especial interest, although the Soho Theatre of 1996–2000 is both stylish and interesting for being a relatively low-cost project. The architects, the late Richard Paxton and his partner Heidi Locher, took a site occupied by the West End Great Synagogue, a spacious but undistinguished seven-storey block. This was stripped out and completely transformed with a two-hundred-seat performing space at first- and second-floor level, a bar and restaurant accessible

Soho Theatre, Dean Street

from the street, and above the rehearsal rooms and other ancillary areas three floors of apartments. The exterior is clean, glassy and exceptionally well lit after dark – the idea is to be transparent and therefore inviting to passers-by – with the cost of operations effectively underwritten by the returns from the residential part of the development. Cool and airy, and with a concentration on new writing, comedy and cabaret the auditorium itself is deliberately stark but very intimate and so speaks volumes about the organisation's stated desire to break the mould of conventional West End theatres. The site is also thought to be where Mozart gave his first London performance, although the precise location of the recital is by no means certain. Nelson is known to have spent his last night in London at no. 33, however, studying his charts at what was then Walker's Hotel before setting sail for Trafalgar and his appointment with a French marksman from the Téméraire class, seventy-four-gun *Redoubtable*.

More recently the street enjoyed some notoriety when it emerged that the Golden Lion pub – at no. 51, on the corner with Romilly Street – had been a favourite of the serial killer Dennis Nilsen. A pub of this name has been on the site for at least 250 years, and starting in the 1970s this former Army chef and trainee police constable used it to meet new victims, whilst managing to kill and conceal more of them than would seem plausible in a city the size and sophistication of London. Of course it might just be that the precise opposite is true – that such crimes and concealment could happen only here – Nilsen carefully preying on vulnerable, lonely drifters, the sort of casual dropouts whom big cities attract and swallow up whole. Their bodies he buried

Golden Lion pub, Romilly Street/Dean Street

French House, Dean Street

beneath a suburban garden and the floor-boards of a rented north London flat, the truth coming to light only after a fellow tenant called in a plumbing company to unblock a drain, which turned out to be clogged with human remains. On being arrested the homosexual Nilsen – seeming relieved by his arrested – confessed to police that he had murdered 'fifteen or sixteen' young men. He wasn't sure, and, chillingly, some twenty years after being apprehended, the identities of at least seven are still unknown, a depressing reflection on the chaotic and disconnected lives the individuals in question must have led during their time hanging around these streets.

Finally, at no. 49, is the French House, for most of its life the York Minster pub until finally adopting its nickname as its official title in 1984. Its first owner was a German national named Schmidt who was deported at the start of the Great War when the licence was taken over by a Belgian who was running the Restaurant Européen next door. Under Victor Berlemont and his son Gaston (who was born in the pub in 1914 and remained here until his retirement in 1989) the establishment thrived. It is popularly said to be where de Gaulle wrote *À tous les Français*, his celebrated speech rallying the French people ahead of the formation of the Free French Forces. More certain is that Brendan Behan wrote much of *The Quare Fellow* on the premises and that Dylan Thomas misplaced the manuscript of *Under Milk Wood* while drinking in here. (It was subsequently found under his chair.)

Other regulars included the hard-drinking members of the Soho artistic and literary sets, including Francis Bacon, Lucien Freud, Daniel Farson, Frank Auerbach and Augustus John. Another habitué, composer Pierre Labric, claimed to have ridden his bicycle down the Eiffel Tower, and Lord Beaverbrook visited frequently with a succession of 'nieces'. With such a clientele it is inevitable that a number of legends have grown up around the place, including a claim that it sells more Ricard than anywhere else in Britain. Similarly the change of name to the French House is said to have been a direct result of the devastating 1984 fire at York when M. Berlemont received many cheques and other donations clearly meant for restoring the great Gothic Minster. On forwarding these to the church authorities (so it is said) Gaston Berlemont learned that they had regularly been receiving his deliveries of claret – and so the name was promptly changed. Famously, it is the only pub in London to serve beer by the *demi-pint* only, except on April Fool's Day when it is possible to order a full pint.

Many of the French House's customers would also have been regulars at the Colony Room, a raffish, members-only drinking club for the artistic and literary elite. In the days when pubs closed for the afternoon, it became a regular haunt for notables such as Louis MacNeice, Charles Laughton, E. M. Forster and of course Bacon and Thomas. Accessed by a flight of dingy stairs at no. 41, it was known to its older clientele as Muriel's, after the original proprietor, Muriel Belcher, who opened for business in 1948.

Reflecting the character of its members the decor was eccentric, even bizarre: a small, bright-green room with leopard-skin barstools, mottled mirrors and plastic tropical plants. Muriel Belcher was as much a character as her famous clientele, being described by one observer as a 'theatrical, Portuguese Jewish lesbian' of Welsh extraction, with a mouth fouler than a navvy and as 'camp as Christmas'. She was much loved by the members, especially Francis Bacon, who painted her portrait three times. The ultimate Bohemian retreat – an oasis of drink and conviviality while conventional members of society were at work – the Colony Room was able to thrive, thanks in large part to Muriel's uncanny ability to create a free-and-easy atmosphere. Its relaxed ambience proved fatal for some and a recent book on the Colony Room lists a number of suicides and alcoholic episodes: the most gruesome concerns Nina Hamnett, the writer and artist and so-called Queen of Bohemia, who, after a drunken escapade, threw herself out of a window and was impaled on the railings below. After Muriel Belcher's death in 1979 the club went slowly downhill, closing its doors for good in 2008 after a string of problems with the lease and other legal disputes.

Denmark Street

Immortalised as London's own Tin Pan Alley – and the nearest equivalent Britain has to the quite extraordinary concentration of talent found in New York's Brill Building – today this narrow seventeenth-century cut-through enjoys a reputation as one of the birthplaces of British popular music, although once again the first artists to colonise the area were painters rather than performers. Of these by far the most significant was Johann Zoffany (1733–1810) who lived at no. 9 before his success made it possible for him to move into a splendid riverside house at Strand-on-the-Green in Chiswick. However, it was the arrival of music publishers and music agents – many of whom are still here – in the second half of the twentieth century that put Denmark Street on the map. Songwriters and performers quickly followed and many of them made the first significant advances of their careers in the numerous basement rehearsal rooms and studios.

Architecturally it has little to offer, but seemingly every building has a tale to tell or a famous name attached to it. The Rolling Stones cut their first long player at Regent Sound Studios (at no. 4), playing catch-up with The Beatles, with the inelegantly titled collection, *England's Newest Hit Makers*. Others who recorded here included Jimi Hendrix and Donovan, whilst a young Reg Dwight briefly worked as an office boy at Mills Music (at no. 20) before emerging as Elton John and taking the world by storm. The street made an appearance in his semi-autobiographical album, *Captain Fantastic and the Brown Dirt Cowboy*, and in countless articles about him and many others which were to be published in the *New Musical Express* (at no. 5) and *Melody Maker* (at no. 19). The latter folded in 2000; its small ads having helped many a budding musician find the ideal band mates.

Badfinger, an early signing to the Beatles' Apple label, rented a rehearsal room at no. 6, which was later taken over by the Sex Pistols. Between times, in 1988, a promotional video for the Moody Blues showed a man walking into one of the many musical-instrument shops on the street. Acting as the most obvious magnet for established artists as well

Music shop, Denmark Street

as those just starting out, these outlets were patronised by the likes of George Harrison, Thin Lizzy's Phil Lynott, and scores of keyboard players, both amateur and professional, keen to kit themselves out at Argent's (no. 19) founded by Rod Argent of 1960s group The Zombies.

Frith Street

Listed as Thrift Street on John Rocque's map of 1746, Frith Street takes its name from a wealthy builder, Richard Frith, who was listed as a rate-paying resident of a house on the east side as early as 1684. The street's origins are slightly earlier than this, with the first houses appearing in the late 1670s – just three of them, on what was then described, with a certain inevitability, as New Street. Its popularity grew fast: by the time Frith was listed as a resident the street had eighteen houses occupied. There were twenty-one within another year and by 1691 the development was more or less complete. Once again the first occupants were fashionable and frequently titled, and lease-holders at this time included Sir William Waldegrave, physician to Queen Mary of Modena, the 1st Viscount Teviot, the 3rd Earl of Bellomont and the widow of the 1st Duke of Wharton. Professionals were also well represented, with later residents including Peter Gillier, violinist to the Chapel Royal, John Hinchliffe, the headmaster of Westminster School (and later a bishop) and Dr John Snow of cholera fame.

Here too, newer arrivals were to include a number of artists and also immigrants with the number of Continental names appearing in rates books rising sharply from around 1790, although the proportion of French still remained lower than in some of the surrounding streets. Within half a century the familiar pattern had emerged of houses being broken up and subdivided, and by 1850 many were in the hands of retailers and tradesmen including several engravers, tailors and dressmakers, and a couple of goldsmiths or watchmakers. In view of Soho's later reputation it is also interesting to notice the arrival, in 1869, of the area's first 'advertising contractor'.

John Constable was living in Frith Street, around 1810, so too Peter Vandyke, John Francis Rigaud, the miniaturists Henry Edridge and Anthony Stewart, and the Royal drawing master J. A. Gresse. Sadly, in such cases it is not possible to be precise about occupants of individual houses – of these artists, none of them warrants a blue plaque here; nor indeed does the young Mozart at no. 21 – and in any case genuine survivors in Frith Street are relatively thin on the ground. The house at no. 6, for example, certainly looks the part although the façade is an inexact if attractive copy of the 1718 original, and the 'Gothic' shop front at no. 15 – once a bookbinder, now a burger restaurant – is very pretty but no earlier than 1815. Of nos. 51–52, with their once splendid fanlights and rococo cast ironwork, nothing remains.

Among the best and most complete of the survivors, no. 5 dates from the 1730s and is a plain but evidently very fine house. Now the only one still standing of a small terrace of four it would once have been typical of a street which the chronicler of London John Strype described as being 'graced with good buildings well inhabited'. Comprising four storeys above a basement, with a purple-red brick front three bays wide, it is nicely detailed with a stone door case and recessed box frames although not all such features are original. Now an art gallery, no. 60 is almost certainly older still, and was originally let to a Lady Butler and then Colonel Beaumont, who enjoyed a reputation as a lethally effective duellist. A few other eighteenth-century houses remain, but decades of redevelopment and remodeling mean that many are not identifiable as such from the street.

As well as artists the street was popular with writers, and, on the aforementioned no. 6, a blue plaque confirms it as the final lodgings of the essayist William Hazlitt (1778–1830), after whom the hotel which now occupies this and adjacent buildings is named. Hazlitt's early inclinations were towards painting (the artist John Hazlitt was his brother) but befriending the likes of Wordsworth, Coleridge and the Lambs he started writing for newspapers and periodicals and enjoyed some success. He published his first collection of essays, *The Round Table*, in 1817, but, dogged by ill health and bad luck – including the unfortunately timed bankruptcy of his publisher – he was arrested for debt at least once. Claiming with his last breath to have nevertheless enjoyed 'a very happy life,' he died in a back room of this building with very little to his name. Even then it was to be some months before his great work, *The Life of Napoleon Buonaparte*, was finally able to be published in its entirety.

A well-connected but struggling writer, Hazlitt is in a sense the definitive Soho character of his age but somewhat more unexpected is a second plaque erected in the street in the early 1950s to the late John Logie Baird (1888–1946). In November 1924, Baird had taken the decision to rent a couple of attic rooms above no. 22, and it was here that he set out to test his ideas about the transmission of moving images. A little over a year later, working away in this cramped, eyrie-like laboratory in January 1926, the Glasgow-educated engineer was able successfully to transmit a moving image of his 20-year-old office boy, William Edward Taynton. Keen to publicise his invention as quickly as possible, Baird was famously rebuffed by the news editor of the *Daily Express*, who described him as 'a lunatic who . . . says he's got a machine for seeing by wireless' and ordered staff members to eject Baird from the building. Fortunately, using what he called the Televisor, Baird was subsequently able to prove to the satisfaction of a witness from the *Times* that it worked, that it was indeed possible to 'transmit and reproduce instantly the details of movement, and such things as the play of expression on the face'. According to the reporter the results were 'faint and often blurred' but within a year the world's first television sets were on sale at Selfridges. A year after that the inventor was able to beam moving images in colour across the Atlantic, and by 1929 the system was undergoing trials at the British Broadcasting Corporation although in the end the organisation opted to use a rival system. Taynton's name is perhaps less well-known than one might suppose, as the world's first television celebrity, but he returned to Frith Street in 1951 when, for the cameras, John Logie Baird's plaque was installed and unveiled above what is now Bar Italia.

Established in 1949 by Lou and Caterina Polledri, Bar Italia is one of the area's oldest coffee bars and in the Soho way has thus become something of a landmark. So too no. 47, the home of Ronnie Scott's eponymous jazz club, which was established in the 1950s by saxophonists Ronnie Scott and Pete King before moving to Frith Street in 1965.

Showcasing everyone from American jazz greats, such as Ella Fitzgerald and Count Basie, to rockers Jeff Beck and Jimi Hendrix, the club's pre-eminence remains unrivalled and whilst the loss of its co-founder in 1996 was an exceptionally heavy blow – as master of ceremonies his idiosyncratic mid-set repartee was an intrinsic part of the club's unique appeal – Ronnie Scott's continues to thrive under new management.

Finally, and rather charmingly, until the summer of 1985 the premises at no. 26 were home to a Welsh dairy, owned by the Pugh family of Ceredigion, inheritors of a long tradition of Welshmen keeping cows in this part of London and supplying residents with fresh milk. For a long time the proprietor had been R. J. Pugh, an air-raid-precaution (ARP) warden during the war, whose daughter Jean later recalled measuring out pints of milk from a large vat and cutting and patting butter from a forty-pound block. The company archives are now held at mosoho – the Museum of Soho – together with a variety of implements such as a traditional three-legged, wooden milking stool, milk bottles and caps, and a supply of greaseproof paper used to wrap the pats of fresh butter.

Gerrard Street

Originally Gerard Street after the seventeenth-century ground landlord Charles Gerard, 4th Baron Gerard (1634–67) of Gerards Bromley in Staffordshire. Until the early 1660s the area formed part of the Military Ground, some three acres or so leased for training by one of the several bands of volunteer soldiers that were formed during the reign of James I. Once their lease was terminated the area was developed by Nicholas Barbon (see Bloomsbury) with some of the early houses being sufficiently grand to attract tenants such as the future 1st Duke of Devonshire, the 4th Earl of Manchester, the 5th Baron Wharton and the 1st Earl of Scarborough. As it happens, these four noblemen successively occupied the very same address although there is some evidence to suggest that the house at no. 9 was by no means typical of the rest of the street and that most of Gerrard Street at that time comprised somewhat more modest quarters. In any event, by the time of the house's demolition in 1732, Gerrard Street is known to have had rather more taverns than toffs, and many more artists and writers than there had once been aristocrats. These included John Dryden, James Boswell and Edmund Burke, while architects John Crunden and James Gibbs are also known to have lodged in the street at some point during their careers.

The most celebrated of the taverns, the Turk's Head, survived until the 1890s and in the 1760s had provided the original meeting place of The Club. Founded by Sir Joshua Reynolds and Dr Johnson, this prestigious and exclusive dining society famously black-balled Winston Churchill and at least two Lord Chancellors. Described in recent times as 'the Establishment at play' and as secretive as it is exclusive – membership is thought not to exceed fifty – it still exists and meets privately for dinner and conversation one Tuesday a month at Brooks's in St James's Street.

It goes without saying that the modern Gerrard Street could not provide a stronger contrast with the place Johnson and Reynolds would have known (nor indeed with the atmosphere at Brooks's) and today it is very much the heart of London's China-town. The transformation began in the 1950s when falling rents in this part of town coincided with the post-war escalation in immigration from what was then the British colony of Hong Kong. Finding their traditional destinations in Limehouse and Poplar still badly devastated from wartime bombing, a new Chinese community sprang up in Soho with scores of new arrivals choosing to open food shops and restaurants to serve both their own people and adventurous visitors to the neighbourhood. By 1970 the Chinese were very much in the majority, and following the later pedestrianisation of the street Westminster City Council formally recognised this. More explicitly Chinese features started springing up, such as the Oriental gateway, red-gold street furniture, a pagoda and a large stone lion. In addition, the familiar black, white and red City of Westminster street signs were altered to include Chinese as well as Roman characters.

Colourful and crowded, modern Gerrard Street is certainly an adornment to the area, and as a huge tourist draw it is an important contributor to the local economy, with an estimated eighty to ninety Asian restaurants located in the immediate vicinity. That said, the success of Chinatown has tended to

Gerrard Street

overwhelm aspects of its earlier history, and today it is easy to forget that Gerrard Street also provided the original home for Ronnie Scott's jazz club at no. 39, for the studios of Harrison Marks, the pioneering blue-movie director, and for the Linnean Society (the world's oldest active biological society), which, from 1805–21, occupied a mid-eighteenth-century building at no. 9.

The author and statesman Edmund Burke (1729–97) also lived here, in a house approximately where no. 37 is today, and in the 1920s the notorious 43 Club was operating from the basement of what is traditionally assumed to have been John Dryden's house. (In fact while a plaque in his memory is affixed to no. 43 it is now thought that he lived at no. 44.) More commonly just 'The 43', the unlicensed club occupied a damp, dark cellar and was run by an incorrigible night owl called Kate Meyrick. In 1920 she was fined £25 for running what the court described as 'a sink of iniquity' although the clientele was known to include the Prince of Wales and many of his circle. Outwardly perfectly respectable (she was a doctor's wife from Brighton) Mrs Meyrick had eight children and insisted she was running the club simply to meet their school fees. However, she was eventually gaoled five times for repeat offences, and again in 1926 on a more serious charge of attempting to bribe a police officer. During one of many court appearances the prosecuting counsel described her as 'the most inveterate law-breaker with regard to licensing matters that the police have ever dealt with in the metropolis'. For Soho, even then, that must have been quite a claim.

Glasshouse Street

Once almost certainly less appealing than is apparent today, the name refers to the process of obtaining potassium nitrate for commercial glassmaking, a craft that is known to have been practised here in the seventeenth century. The preferred means of obtaining the substance was to 'shoote the Night Stuffe and Boyle for Salt Peter', in other words to extract saltpetre from domestic effluence, which, euphemistically known as night soil, was collected for this purpose each morning from the surrounding houses. The name 'Glasshouse' first appears in official documents in 1678, the street being shortly afterwards described as only 'meanly built'.

Today much of one side is occupied by the rear of the Regent Palace Hotel, a triangular extravaganza for J. Lyons & Co. In architectural terms it is most noticeable for the finish of Burmantoft's 'Marmo', a kind of faïence or glazed terracotta. When it opened in 1915 with 1,028 bedrooms it was said to be the largest hotel in Europe. Lined with marble the entrance vestibule opened into a circular lounge beneath a shallow dome, while another much larger dome sheltered the Rotunda Court and Louis XVI restaurant. Unfortunately, it was almost immediately requisitioned, and then again during the Second World War when it was damaged by enemy action. Thereafter, despite its early promise and some tremendous Art Deco interiors, it was never to be counted among London's truly great hotels.

Golden Square

Briefly one of the most fashionable and prestigious addresses in Soho, in the early eighteenth century Golden Square included among its residents the Duchess of Cleveland, late mistress to Charles II, the future Duke of Chandos (see St James's Square) and the 1st Viscount Bolingbroke, a favourite of Queen Anne. By the time John Strype documented it for his *Survey* of 1720, the aristocrats had moved on, however, although he still found it 'a very handsome place, railed round and gravelled with many very good houses'. Several of these were subsequently leased by foreign diplomats and legations, including representatives from Russia, Portugal and – in an age before Italian and German reunification – the states of Bavaria, Brunswick and Genoa.

Today not much of the grandeur survives. The central gardens were dug out to build an air-raid shelter during the Second World War, and houses once occupied by the likes of painters Angelica Kauffman (1741–1807) and Martin Archer Shee, President of the Royal Academy (1769–1850) and William IV's great love Mrs Jordan have long since been replaced by offices. In fact just four eighteenth-century houses remain, at nos. 11, 21, and less good at nos. 23 and 24. For much of the twentieth century many of the offices were connected to the textile industries, particularly those concerned with wool production and processing, which at one point occupied all but four of the buildings on the square. Latterly these have been replaced by film companies, by the advertising giant M & C Saatchi and various allied trades.

Great Marlborough Street

According to one eighteenth-century visitor, surpassing 'anything that is called a street in the magnificence of its buildings and gardens,' the name comes from the celebrated English

soldier and statesman John Churchill, 1st Duke of Marlborough. Today with the possible exception of nos. 47–48 (which though modified are eighteenth century) there is little today which is reminiscent of the days when it was 'inhabited by all prime quality'. Since the middle of the nineteenth century Great Marlborough Street has been largely commercial.

At the Regent Street end it is dominated by one of the most joyful buildings in central London, which is the great timbered range of Liberty, one of the most distinctive shops in London. Nikolaus Pevsner loathed it, describing various aspects of this most exuberant exercise in Stockbroker Tudor as 'wrong', 'wrong' and 'wrongest of all,' and objecting to the artificiality of its basic concept and the admittedly clumsy contrast it makes with the classical façade of the store's main block on Regent Street. Today one is inclined to be more forgiving, however. Not just because time has been kind to the design of architects E. S. Hall and E. T. Hall but also because the two of them worked hard to create something of value, which even now is by far the most interesting building on this side of the street. The timbers for the linking bridge over Kingly Street, for example, came from two genuine Royal Navy men o' war: HMS *Hindustan*, which was launched in 1824, just as Nash was completing his Regent Street scheme; and HMS *Impregnable*, which, in 1865, was said to be the largest wooden vessel afloat. Similarly, each roof tile was handmade, the leaded windows really are leaded and the wood throughout, whatever its provenance, was all correctly mortised and tenoned and is held together by proper wooden pegs.

The shop, in other words, was conceived to represent everything that Arthur Lasenby

Liberty stood for, as one of the champions of England's pioneering and largely admirable Arts & Crafts Society. It was designed around three light wells that were the main focus of the building, and, because Liberty wanted to create the feeling that you were walking around your own home when you came into his shop, each of these wells was surrounded by smaller rooms to exude a homely feel. As for the clash of styles on the façades it was scarcely his fault, but rather one forced on him by a requirement to accommodate the conflicting demands of a retailer (who needed large windows to display his wares) and the more conservative aims of the Crown Commissioners' planning office. Sadly, Arthur Liberty died in 1917, seven years before his magnificent emporium was completed. Today however, Liberty, his life's work, is still one of the great shopping

Palladium House, Great Marlborough Street

destinations, selling clothing, furniture and fabrics that reflect not only today's cutting-edge fashions but also design classics. The store attracts around five million visitors a year and such is its lustre that it was the subject of a Channel 4 fly-on-the-wall documentary series, *Making Liberty*, in December 2013.

On the other side of the street the severely rectilinear Palladium House is now a restaurant on the ground floor with apartments above. Pevsner disliked this too: its uncompromising, polished, black-granite façade reminded him of a cinema organ. It is the work of the American Art Deco architects Raymond Hood and Gordon Jeeves, who completed the building in 1929 (when it was known as Ideal House) for the National Radiator Company of New York. At first glance the effect is almost too dark, brutal and dominating, but on closer examination the building springs to life through a series of vibrant enamel friezes on the top-storey cornice with its bright yellow,

Liberty, Great Marlborough Street

orange, green and gold detailing. These mirror the original company colours. It is admittedly curious, and emphatically transatlantic, but to have just one example of such an uncompromising but suave style in London must surely be good.

Great Windmill Street

A windmill still stood here until the early 1700s, although development was already quite advanced by that stage, having begun in the 1670s. Much of the early work was clearly of poor quality, and even now the street is something of a jumble with little of note beyond the premises of the Soho Parish School – the only one in the neighbourhood – and at the top end the St James's Tavern. Both are Victorian, although the latter occupies the site of the old Catherine Wheel Tavern, which opened during the reign of George III.

The Windmill Theatre was established here in 1910, initially as a cinema, and famously 'never closed' (or 'we never clothed', as one wag had it) during the Second World War, except from 6–14 September 1939, when all West End theatres were required to do so. An authentic case of necessity being the mother of invention, early failure as a cinema – as the Palais de Luxe, it was too small to compete with its rivals – saw the Windmill reborn as a theatre when the owner, Laura Henderson – an elderly, bored, but wealthy, widow – gave the manager free rein to try something new. That manager, Vivian Van Damm, spotted an opportunity in the staging of *tableaux vivants*, a series of decidedly risqué performances in which the law permitted girls to appear on stage naked or nearly naked providing they did not move around. Starting in 1933 with the French-themed Revudeville, the theatre found itself with a runaway success on its hands. Clearly modelled on the success of the Folies Bergère and Moulin Rouge in Paris it was soon packed out for the shows, which ran from after lunchtime until eleven at night.

The management had to keep on the right side of the Lord Chamberlain, whose office was charged with the censorship of live performances, and the steps taken to cover the girls' modesty seem quaint compared to our own permissive age. While male and female performers danced and sang one girl would stand stock still, naked except for a strategically placed feather or scarf that was designed to conceal even the slightest hint of pubic hair. Despite the relatively innocent pleasures to be had in the Windmill – always nude, never rude, as the saying went – men were desperate to sample its delights, queuing from early in the morning for a seat. Those in the front six rows, just under the footlights, were well placed to ogle, and almost touch, the girls and when they vacated their seats there was an almighty scramble from those in the rows behind them to take their places. This rather unseemly process was known as the 'Windmill steeplechase' and such was their enthusiasm that the bolts on the seats had to be tightened up on a daily basis by theatre workmen.

Van Damm remained at the helm until 1960, when control passed to his daughter. The theatre closed in the mid-1960s and was rebuilt, once again, as a cinema before being acquired by the successful publisher and Soho landowner Paul Raymond. Raymond revived its saucy reputation by restaging nude revues, and by reinventing the Windmill as the permanent home of the hugely successful La Vie en Rose show bar and later of Paramount City. Today it is a private club – complete with table dancers, lap dancers and private booths – and its reputation as one of the loci of 'naughty' Soho is secure. But Van Damm – who was often referred to by the amusing nickname 'VD' – was an energetic and successful entrepreneur who achieved far more than simply spotting a useful loophole in Britain's strangely restrictive laws. As an authentic West End impresario his legacy includes helping to launch a number of hugely successful comic talents, including the likes of Harry Secombe, Tony Hancock and Barry Cryer, all of whom appeared on the bill at the Windmill in the early days of their careers. A splendid 2005 film, *Mrs Henderson Presents*, starring Dame Judi Dench and Bob Hoskins and directed by the late Stephen Frears, charts the relationship of the eponymous owner and her trusty lieutenant Van Damm.

Greek Street

Going by the bucolic sounding name of Hog Lane at a time when Soho was still fields, Greek Street was developed from the 1670s by Richard Frith and others and may have taken its new title from an Orthodox church being planned in what is now Charing Cross Road. This would have served the growing Greek community but in the 1930s the site was acquired for the construction of St Martin's School of Art. (Some inscribed stonework from the church has survived however. Salvaged during the demolition, it can be seen at the Cathedral of Aghia Sophia in Moscow Road in Bayswater.)

The street has always provided a mixture of residential and commercial accommodation, and even in the earliest days (when historian John Strype described it as 'well built and inhabited') two earls – Fingall and Anglesey – and any number of minor peers and professional men would have rubbed shoulders with the denizens of the many taverns, coffee houses and workshops that lined the street. None of this now remains, so that the highly decorative Pillars of Hercules at no. 7, for example, is an Edwardian structure although a tavern of this name is known to have occupied the site since at least 1733. (This, too, was described by Charles Dickens in his novel *A Tale of Two Cities*.) The Coach and Horses at no. 29 has an even longer history, dating back another decade at least, although the present building is from the mid-nineteenth century. Much of its celebrity today relies on it having provided the setting, in 1989, for Keith Waterhouse's popular play *Jeffrey Bernard is Unwell*, and for Norman Balon, its former licensee, who took great pride in being known as 'London's rudest landlord'. The otherwise undistinguished west-end boozer is also the venue for fortnightly lunches hosted by the satirical magazine *Private Eye*.

Until his move to St James's Square, nos. 12–13 – once among the largest houses in the street – provided warehousing and showroom space for the ambitious firm owned by Josiah Wedgwood, who paid £200 per annum for a twenty-one-year lease. (When the celebrated dinner service he created for Empress Catherine of Russia went on display, it occupied five rooms over two floors.) And at no. 17 the vast windows belong to an attractive, wooden, nineteenth-century shop front; a rare survivor of the period, which replaced a musical-instrument museum that occupied this site at the time of the French Revolution.

Architecturally, however, the chief glory of the street is neither of these but rather no. 1 with its twin obelisks, the aforementioned House of St Barnabas-in-Soho. A large, plain but handsome building dating from around 1740, it was completed for the Beckford family, which built a vast fortune in the Jamaican slave and sugar trades before leasing the site from the Duke of Portland. In contrast to the exterior the house has several very richly carved and plastered rooms, this work carried out for William Beckford who was twice Lord Mayor of London (1762 and 1769) and evidently of such quality that it effectively doubled the rateable value of the property. As a consequence 1 Greek Street is now regarded as having some of the finest rococo work of the period surviving in the whole of London.

In a pattern by now familiar, however, Soho's pronounced social decline saw the likes of Beckford moving out of the area almost as quickly as they had moved in, and by 1811 the property was in the hands of the Westminster Commissioners of Sewers. This was soon renamed the Metropolitan Board of Works, and it thrived under the renowned, and highly innovative, civil engineer Sir Joseph Bazalgette. Half a century

1 Greek Street

later, finding it surplus to requirements, the Board sold the property to the House of Charity, an organisation dedicated to the care and resettlement of the homeless, which had been founded in 1846 and is still in occupation of the Grade I listed building today. Providing relief to 'as many destitute cases as possible', and attempting to encourage 'a Christian effect' among the poor it sought to help, the charity from the first expected those who came through its doors regularly to worship. A chapel was built at the rear, which still exists and can be visited, while in an attempt to boost the charity's revenues the house and surprisingly leafy garden has more recently been reinvented as one of Soho's more popular venues for parties and events.

Although neither warrants an official Blue Plaque, past residents of Greek Street include Giovanni Giacomo Casanova (1725–98), Italy's great adventurer and lover who is thought to have lodged at no. 47 for a guinea a week, and Thomas de Quincey (1785–1859). Long before he achieved fame for his *Confessions of an English Opium Eater*, the latter – much troubled psychologically – absconded from school in Manchester and after a period spent living as a tramp arrived in London where he took a room in a house with a suitably 'unhappy countenance of gloom and unsocial fitness'.

Much of Greek Street, especially in a damp London winter, has that same countenance, not helped at one end by the long, blind side-wall of the Prince Edward Theatre. But among the many bars and restaurants there are at least two of great repute, including the long established L'Escargot at no. 48. This was established in the 1920s, and was said to be the first restaurant in England to serve fresh snails, which were raised in the basement. In its heyday, under the watchful eye of its forceful manager Elena Salvoni, it enjoyed the patronage of Diana, Princess of Wales, as well as her two brothers-in-law, princes Andrew and Edward.

Trained in Budapest in the 1930s, the Swiss-Welsh restaurateur Victor Sassie opened another restaurant here, the Gay Hussar at no. 2, in the 1950s. His signed-book-and-picture-lined dining rooms and the distinctive cherry-red façade proved particularly popular amongst the political left, and for years regular diners included Aneurin Bevan, Barbara Castle, Ian Mikardo and Michael Foot, as well as literary figures such as T. S. Eliot and the archaeologist Sir Mortimer Wheeler. That said, by far the most fashionable address in Greek Street today is almost certainly no. 40, the premises of the Soho House club, although from the street there is little to see of it bar a narrow door, which remains locked to all but members and their guests.

Leicester Square

Like Covent Garden once the property of the convent or abbey of St Peter at Westminster, Leicester Square was laid out by the diplomat Robert Sidney, 2nd Earl of

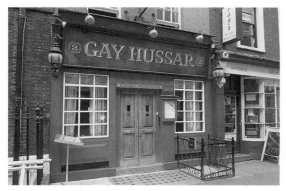

Gay Hussar, Greek Street

Leicester (1595–1677). Work began in 1670 after the Earl had obtained a licence to build three ranges of large houses, the fourth side of the square being taken by an even larger and more splendidly decorated house he had built for himself forty years earlier. This, Leicester House, survived in some form until 1792 when Lisle Street was built over the site. The square was intended very specifically to profit the Earl and his descendants, a large-scale speculative venture for the 'benefit of the family, the advancement of revenue and the decency of the place before Leicester House'. To this end the Earl aimed high, choosing Pall Mall as the model for his houses, refusing to allow tradesmen leases or permission to open for business within the square and as a consequence quickly acquiring an enviable roster of tenants including the earls of Ailesbury, Deloraine, Rockingham, Scarsdale, Sunderland and Westmorland.

For a while Leicester House itself was let to Frederick, Prince of Wales (who predeceased his father George II) but by 1782 Sidney's heir had decided to allow the first of a succession of tradesmen onto the square. He retired to Penshurst, the family seat in Kent, and the fate of the great house and indeed of the square was sealed. Gradually hemmed in by inferior buildings Leicester House was eventually let to the owners of the Holophusikon – essentially a museum of curiosities, and for a while highly popular – while that formerly occupied by Lord Rockingham fell so low as to be used as a brothel.

Today Leicester Square is entirely commercial, and with no trace whatever of the most interesting of its former residents, including William Hogarth, Sir Joshua Reynolds, the architect 'Athenian' Stuart and the eighteenth-century Scottish surgeon and anatomist John Hunter whose astonishing collection of physiological specimens and medical curiosities can still be seen at the Royal College of Surgeons' Hunterian Museum in Lincoln's Inn Fields. In 1907 a plaque in memory of Hunter was affixed to what was then no. 31, but in 1931 his seventeenth-century house was knocked down and rebuilt as offices and the present building on the site dates from as recently as 1999. It should be noted, however, that the first two named above lived in the square whilst at the very peak of their careers. Hogarth for example completed some of his most famous works – including *Marriage A-la-Mode* and *A Rake's Progress* as well as *Beer Street* and *Gin Lane* – whilst living at no. 30, a property he occupied for more than thirty years. The founder and first president of the Royal Academy, Reynolds lived for slightly longer at no. 47, taking the house on in 1760 and remaining there until his death in 1792. During that time he expensively extended the property to include a large picture gallery, somewhere appropriately grand to display many of his own works at a time when his income was said to be £6,000 a year. (This is comfortably in excess of what the Russells were at that time receiving in rents for half a year from their market at Covent Garden.) The house is also thought to be where he and Dr Johnson hatched their plans for The Club (see Gerrard Street, above).

As it happens the aforementioned collection of Dr Hunter and the splendidly named Holophusikon were to prove trailblazers for Leicester Square, and they were followed in due course by the National Museum of Mechanical Arts, the Royal Panopticon of Science and Art, and James Wyld's Great Globe, a sphere sixty feet high containing a representation of the surface of the earth, which visitors were invited to study from a four-storey gallery at its centre. There was also a museum in which famous paintings were represented in tapestry, and several somewhat less reputable displays of the unusual such as the spectacle of Mary Tofts who arrived from Surrey claiming to be able to give birth to rabbits.

Today of course visitors still arrive here expecting to see something new and unusual, Leicester Square having become very much the heart of London's theatre land and in particular *the* venue for Britain's most important cinematic premières. Whilst around the country most of the old picture houses have been subdivided into multiplexes, or simply driven out of business by newer ones, London still boasts the largest screen and the most spacious auditorium – with seating for nearly 1,700 filmgoers – in the Odeon Leicester Square. Its glassily dark bulk and *moderne* tower dominates the east side of the square, its only possible rival (in terms of size) being the Empire on the northern side, which seats 1,330. Facing it the Odeon West End can seat only a thousand patrons for individual performances, these divided between two separate auditoria, but like the Empire it too frequently hosts premieres, albeit slightly smaller ones. From outside however most of the buildings are deeply mediocre, and sadly none has an interior to rival those in outlying areas, such as the gloriously Moorish Odeon Cinema in Ealing, Brixton's Astoria with its art deco foyer and extraordinary Mediterranean auditorium, or the mock-medieval splendour of the Granada in Tooting. That said – and, unlike this splendid trio, respectively now a church, a concert venue and a bingo hall – they are at least still showing movies.

Odeon, Leicester Square

Lexington Street

Close-packed and narrow, Lexington Street even now suggests a very different Soho, a down-to-earth commercial one with many of the office buildings converted from Edwardian and even Victorian warehouses. More than a few of these have attractive, decorated entrances despite the utilitarian nature of the accommodation they once provided. Robert Sutton, 2nd Lord Lexington (1662–1723) was an English diplomat and a gentleman of the horse to Princess Anne of Denmark before she succeeded William III in March 1702. He inherited much of the land on which the street was built, although until well into the nineteenth century Lexington Street was known as Little Windmill Street at the southern end and Cambridge Street at the other.

Today, mostly towards Broadwick Street, a very few converted early nineteenth-century houses remain and the car park at no. 2 was one of the earliest in the country to connect the floors with a rising ramp. As it happens Soho was something of a pioneer in this field with Britain's first ever multi-storey car park opening for business in May 1901 just off Piccadilly Circus. At a time when cars were a very considerable rarity even among the London rich, the entrance on Denman Street gave on to what was then the world's largest car park with seven storeys and an hydraulic lift capable of raising a three-ton vehicle.

Old Compton Street

Combining in one place God and Mammon, Soho's first real retail street took its name from the Honourable Henry Compton, Bishop of London from 1675 to 1713. By 1720 the few remaining residents were largely French Protestants, and by 1800 all the remaining houses had acquired shop fronts and were open for business or had been converted to taverns and small workshops. None of the survivors are especially distinguished, although the stucco facades of nos. 40–42 and 50 still appear mid-nineteenth century above ground-floor level.

Soho's French population grew again following the suppression of the Paris Commune in 1871, and both Arthur Rimbaud and Paul Verlaine were known to frequent taverns in Old Compton Street, giving impromptu recitals at a bar at no. 5 as other poets (most famously Dylan Thomas) were to do in the twentieth century. For a while the street was also home to George Wombwell (1777–1850), an energetic and highly entrepreneurial shoe- and boot-

RUINED CHURCH OF ST ANNE, SOHO

On 24 September 1940 a German bomber all but destroyed a famous Soho landmark, leaving standing only fragments of walls and the idiosyncratic tower of a church that had been consecrated by Bishop Henry Compton as early as 1686 (see Old Compton Street). The design has been attributed to both Sir Christopher Wren and William Talman, and may indeed be the work of both men working together or in succession, although the tower is an early nineteenth-century addition by Samuel Pepys Cockerell (1754–1827) who was active at this time in Bloomsbury working on behalf of the Foundling Hospital.

Prior to its destruction (and that of the rectory at 58 Dean Street) the church was conspicuously grand, eighty-feet long and more than sixty wide, and the chapel of St James's Palace provided an organ for it in 1699. On perceiving 'an Inclination to come to this Church' the young George II was a worshipper here when Prince of Wales, and had his son Prince William Henry, Duke of Gloucester and Edinburgh baptised in the church. In 1725 it was also the setting for the marriage of Edward Harley, 3rd Earl of Oxford and Mortimer. St Anne's was an equally fashionable place to be buried and by 1851 the church authorities were claiming to have carried out nearly fourteen thousand interments in the course of twenty years, or more than a dozen a week. Because of this the graveyard had to be artificially raised more than six feet above street level in order to accommodate the bodies, hence its position today.

Memorials to those interred here include one with an epitaph by Horace Walpole to the eighteenth century King Theodore of Corsica – actually a German, and more of an adventurer than a legitimate sovereign – and another for the essayist William Hazlitt. In 1853 the ground was finally closed to new burials in favour of the new London necropolis in Surrey, and afterwards redesignated as a public garden. One notable exception to this was the novelist and former churchwarden Dorothy L. Sayers, whose ashes were buried in a brick chamber beneath Cockerell's tower in 1957.

The survival of the church's tower (*facing page*) at least leaves Soho with one of its more extraordinary buildings, a distinctive yellow brick monolith below a lofty Portland stone bell chamber. This is topped by a slightly bulbous lead and copper 'spire' with immense circular portholes and four vast clock faces looking out over the surrounding streets. The old burial ground has also survived, at least in part, and today as gardens provide a pleasant place for local shop and office workers to meet and relax as well as being a focus of the local residential community.

maker who established a number of travelling menageries. Wombwell successfully bred many of his own animals, including Britain's first captive lion, and is buried under a carved representation of the beast in Highgate cemetery. (Unfortunately, many of the animals he imported from the tropics quickly died on being exposed to the British climate, but, undeterred, Wombwell cheerfully put their corpses on display instead and curious Londoners could pay to poke at their remains.)

The aforementioned Prince Edward Theatre opened in 1930, the proprietor favouring a vaguely Italian and rather heavy *palazzo* style in exceptionally sombre dark-brown brick. In recent years it has enjoyed considerable financial success, as the home of a number of such long running shows as *Evita*, *Mamma Mia* and *Jersey Boys*. Its earlier history had rather more ups and downs, however, and at various times the building operated as a cinema, a club for servicemen and a 'cabaret restaurant'. The latter, somewhat confusingly called the London Casino, advertised itself as the most sumptuous such establishment anywhere in the world. Dinner and dancing to an orchestra cost 15s. 6d. per head during the week and 17s. 6.d on Saturdays (or just under 90p). Prior to this it was The Emporium, a vast drapery that enjoyed royal patronage until its reputation began slipping in the 1920s.

From 1956, Old Compton Street was also home to the famous 2 I's Coffee Bar. The owners at no. 59 were brothers called Irani, whom no one remembers now, but after being taken over by a pair of Australian wrestlers it reinvented itself as the birthplace of British rock. The stage in the basement launched the careers of Tommy Steele, Adam Faith and Gary Glitter, as well as Cliff Richard and Hank Marvin of the Shadows. The club finally closed in 1970, however, afterwards becoming a bar and restaurant.

In recent decades Old Compton Street has been given a new lease of life by London's gay community, members of which now own and run many of its shops and bars. In 1999 one of these, the Admiral Duncan at no. 34 – named after the victor of the Battle of Camperdown against the Dutch in 1797 – was the scene of three deaths and massive physical devastation when a nail bomb exploded in the pub after being planted there by a far-right extremist.

Piccadilly Circus

An integral part of Nash's great Regent Street scheme, Piccadilly Circus was an elegant solution to the problem of dealing with a staggered crossroads until it was reduced to a meaningless jumble of converging streets by the driving through of Shaftesbury Avenue in the mid-1880s. Today the vast illuminated advertisements on the Soho side of the Circus are one of the iconic sights of London, as prominent as those in New York's Times Square if slightly less elaborate. When these electric hoardings first appeared, however – in 1910, for Schweppes and Bovril – they were considered grossly offensive by many who saw them. Fortunately, Crown leases on the remainder of the Circus prevented the contagion spreading, and today, if they are no longer to be considered an eyesore, it is probably only because one has become used to them being there. (They could in a sense also be regarded as Soho's revenge on Nash, the developer having cheerfully demolished some seven hundred of its dwellings as part of his plans, most of them occupied by

Piccadilly Circus

'mechanics and the trading part of the community' and therefore, presumably, not due any especial consideration.)

Today the Circus's most interesting building lies beneath it, namely the underground station created by Charles Holden and Stanley Heaps in the late 1920s. For Holden in particular the work represented a major departure as – uniquely at this time – both the concourse and the booking hall were to be entirely below ground. The commission was completely to redesign the station serving what had been the old Baker Street & Waterloo and the Great Northern, Piccadilly & Brompton railways, a uniquely complex interchange and a major logistical challenge. Recognising that at street level the original circular outline of the Circus was gone, Holden and Heaps hoped to reflect the grandeur, form and importance of Nash's original vision with a large, sweeping ellipse down below. Of course closing the junction for months was out of the

question, and the vast buildings above with their massive, multi-storey basements severely restricted the options open to the two men. It is fortunate that they were permitted temporarily to relocate the Shaftesbury Memorial Fountain (also known as Eros) to Victoria Embankment Gardens, and so could sink a wide shaft from which to explore and untangle the immense and hitherto unmapped mess of sewers, water and gas mains, and electrical and hydraulic conduits which lay beneath. This job done, a massive excavation was then required, the spacious new 155-by-144-foot concourse calling for the removal of more than fifty thousand tons of London clay and the importation of six thousand tons of cement, a vast quantity of precast iron segments and in excess of a million bricks. Holden also chose to face almost every available surface in luxurious marble, and beneath the unusual coffered ceiling to use bronze framing for all the window surrounds and display stands. In all, the project took three years to complete, and cost many tens of millions of pounds at current values. However, when the station opened in 1928, a reporter from the *Illustrated London News* unhesitatingly declared it to be 'the best in the world' while another writer described its transformation 'by modern architecture and modern art into a scene that would make the perfect setting for the finale of an opera'.

Above ground, sadly, there is nothing to match the station. The gold-tiled interior of the Criterion Bar and Restaurant is striking but its Second Empire façade looks grimy and commonplace. And while the theatre of the same name is unusual in that (like the station) it was one of the first to be built fully under the ground, the experiment nearly ended in disaster and in the early years the proprietors were forced to pump in air during the performances to prevent both cast and audience from suffocating. On the corner between Piccadilly and Regent Street the former Swan and Edgar department store is an undistinguished exercise in late-period Edwardian by Sir Edward Blomfield, and facing down Lower Regent Street even Ernest Newton's County Fire Office (1924) somehow fails without the great sweeping triumphal route and serried columns that Nash envisaged as he worked his way north from Carlton House to Regents Park.

The monument now universally known as *Eros* continues to provide a focal point on an area of the Circus pedestrianised in the 1990s. It consists of a statue of Eros, sitting atop a pedestal and fountain, and, for many, it is quite simply *the* symbol of London. One suspects that most people assume the sculpture to be of Cupid, but in fact Eros (or, more properly, Anteros) was a fairly minor Greek deity and the statue of him was the first in London to be cast in aluminium instead of bronze. *Eros* was conceived as a monument to the politician, philanthropist and social reformer, Anthony Ashley Cooper, 7th Earl of Shaftesbury (1801–85), hence its official title of the Shaftesbury Memorial Fountain.

Shaftesbury's position on the political spectrum is hard to pin down: elected as MP for Dorchester in 1830, he was a lifelong Tory who opposed extending the vote to the working classes and spoke against the re-introduction of Roman Catholic institutions. However, in his mid-thirties his always strong Christian beliefs moved in an evangelical direction and he became convinced that Christ's second coming was imminent. Galvanised by his these much more fundamentalist beliefs, in particular the thought of

being held accountable by his maker, he now saw it as his mission to reform national life and in particular to help those less fortunate than himself. Shaftesbury threw himself into a wide range of causes, many of which, thanks to his drive and determination, achieved their aims: the abolition of child chimney-sweeping; the improvement of slum housing; better conditions for agricultural workers; provision for destitute children; and his most passionately pursued policy, the proposal to limit the number of hours that children and young people could work in factories to ten hours.

At his death in 1885, there were widespread expressions of grief at the loss of the man who had become known as the 'poor man's earl' and within a year a statue to him had been unveiled in Westminster Abbey. That was followed by the establishment of a committee to erect a memorial in a more public place, for which purpose Piccadilly Circus was chosen. Given Shaftesbury's deeply held beliefs it is doubtful if he would have approved of the monument erected in his name: when it was unveiled in 1893, it caused quite a stir due to its nakedness. Then the sculptor, Alfred Gilbert, refused to attend the opening ceremony, which was led by the 1st Duke of Westminster, probably a result of his constant arguments with the memorial committee about the design, scope and positioning of the piece. These controversies did nothing to damage either the affection Londoners feel for *Eros* or the esteem in which the British people hold Shaftesbury. Indeed the inscription on the fountain comes from the pen of William Ewart Gladstone, the Grand Old Man of British politics and prime minister of this country on four occasions, and as a Liberal technically an opponent of Shaftesbury, the

Tory scion. In 1939, shortly after the outbreak of war, *Eros* was removed to the comparative safety of Egham, in Surrey for the duration. In 1947, after being returned from Surrey, the figure was carefully positioned in order to honour Gilbert's original intention that the archer's arrow be aligned towards Wimborne St Giles, his lordship's seat in Dorset. (Note too that the bow is also directed slightly downwards, ensuring that the *shaft* is *buried*.)

Shaftesbury Avenue

Named in memory of the aforementioned Earl of Shaftesbury, the avenue was conceived by Sir Joseph Bazalgette and Lewis Vulliamy, a pupil of Sir Robert Smirke's. The plan was to alleviate traffic congestion without affecting the existing street pattern of Soho, doing this by widening a couple of existing roads where major new routes might have achieved rather more. (This was definitely done for reasons of economy, rather than to avoid disrupting the lives and livelihoods of those living and working in the neighbourhood.) The new route involved the destruction of many slum properties but their replacements were mostly unremarkable, and today the only buildings of any real note on the streets are theatres. These are the Apollo, the Gielgud, the Lyric, the Palace (which fronts onto Cambridge Circus) the Queen's, the Saville and the Shaftesbury. All of them are situated on the north side of the street and constructed within a few years of the street being opened (1886) except for the Saville which was completed in 1931.

The Apollo was technically the first Edwardian theatre in London, having opened just four weeks after the death of Queen Victoria. The smallest of these theatres, seating just 775, it was built mostly to stage musicals. The Gielgud, formerly the Globe, opened in 1906 and was renamed in 1994 both to honour Sir John – who first appeared here in 1939 in *The Importance of Being Earnest*, which he also directed – and to avoid confusion with Sam Wanamaker's superb recreation across the river in Southwark of Shakespeare's 'wooden O'. (This nickname is derived from its structure and approximate shape when viewed from above.)

Completed in 1888 the Lyric is said to have been built using the profits from just one show, *Dorothy*, a comic opera that had a phenomenally successful run at the Prince of Wales Theatre. It is now owned by Lord Lloyd Webber's Really Useful Group, as indeed is the Palace Theatre. Originally the Royal English Opera House, this multi-tiered extravaganza was designed for Richard D'Oyly Carte by T. E Collcutt, architect of his Savoy Hotel and theatre. Despite a seating capacity of 1,400 and a succession of long runs starting with Sir Arthur Sullivan's *Ivanhoe* in 1891 it frequently struggled to break even.

With its lavish Louis XVI interior, the auditorium of the Queen's Theatre provides the strongest possible contrast with its somewhat stark plate-glass-and-brick façade, the latter a blunt 1950s replacement for the original façade, which was all but destroyed in the Blitz. Prior to this the theatre hosted popular afternoon dances, so called Tango Teas costing two shillings and sixpence, having struggled like so many before and since to make it as a theatre. Its neighbour, indeed, is currently a cinema although the Saville for a short while was managed by Brian Epstein, the 'fifth Beatle'.

Finally, at no. 210, the Shaftesbury was first known as the New Prince's Theatre, and then simply the Prince's before being renamed the Shaftesbury to replace a theatre of that name that was lost in the war. It has hosted everything from Gilbert and Sullivan to more risqué choices such as Diaghilev and *Hair*, and in 1997 was home for one season to the company of the Royal Opera House while the latter underwent a massive programme of redevelopment.

Soho Square

Intended, as might be expected, as the centrepiece of that portion of Soho Fields that was granted by Charles II and Henrietta Maria to Lord St Albans, a complicated series of leases and assignments meant that much of the actual development devolved to a developer called Gregory King who began work on what was to be called King Square in the 1680s. In addition to Monmouth House, which dominated the southern side, his builders and others constructed a total of forty houses, most of them conspicuously fine and several particularly so such as Fauconberg House at no. 20 and Carlisle House.

The fate of either of these can be allowed to speak for the history of the square. Fauconberg House, for example, was designed for the earl of that name, and by 1753 was occupied by Arthur Onslow, Speaker of the House of Commons for a record thirty-three years. On his retirement from Parliament he moved to Bloomsbury, selling the house to the 4th Duke of Argyll before, in the 1770s, it was remodelled by Robert Adam who created an imposing seven-bay façade with rusticated ground floor and a giant order of pilasters. This was done for a rich lawyer and plantation owner with a fortune based in Grenada, that is

Charles II, Soho Square

someone a step or two down socially, and the decline was to continue from there. Before the turn of the century the house was converted to a hotel, then taken over by a musical instrument maker and finally – as we have seen – by Messrs Crosse & Blackwell. Photographed in 1908 the house still looked solid if decidedly unloved, and by 1924 its site had been cleared for offices.

Carlisle House did not survive even this long, however, and fared rather worse. Occupying a large plot on the southern corner of the square, it was built for Edward Howard, the short-lived 2nd Earl of Carlisle (1646–92) who occupied it from 1685. The 4th Earl disposed of the house in the 1750s, and following a period when it was used by envoys of the King of Naples and the Dutch government the property was then rented to a soprano and noted courtesan on whom Casanova believed he had fathered a daughter.

Teresa Cornelys remodelled the house as a fashionable set of assembly rooms, a place of leisure she described as a 'Temple of Festivity' and where, on payment of a ticket, guests could enjoy gambling, dancing and masquerades. Fanny Burney praised 'the magnificence of the rooms [and] the splendour of the illuminations and embellishments' and Horace Walpole suggested that it was not unknown for the Commons to adjourn early in order that members could attend. But unfortunately the lady's ambition routinely exceeded her revenues, the entertainments at Carlisle House became increasingly tawdry, and, by October 1772, Mrs Cornelys was declared a bankrupt and confined at the King's Bench prison in Southwark. She eventually died in another debtors' gaol, the Fleet, by which time Carlisle House had been seized by her creditors (one of whom was the cabinet maker Thomas Chippendale of St Martin's Lane).

The Neapolitan envoy had consecrated a chapel on the site during his tenure of Carlisle House and, following its demolition in 1791, the vacant plot was given over to a larger religious institution, St Patrick's Roman Catholic Church. This was replaced a century later by the fine red brick Italianate building we see today, still dedicated to St Patrick and numbered 21a, and of Carlisle House nothing now remains bar its mention in many memoirs of the period. It can also claim one of London's more unusual firsts, in that roller skates were first worn during one of the popular masques held at the house. Unfortunately their inventor, the Belgian horologist Jean-Joseph Merlin (1735–1803) sadly misjudged the size of the ballroom whilst attempting to skate whilst playing the violin. Crashing into a large mirror at one end, he was seriously injured.

As for the remainder of the houses, those John Strype described in 1720 as 'very good . . . especially the East and South, which are well inhabited by Nobility and Gentry' most were gone within half a century, and their inhabitants replaced by the middling classes, professional men on the whole, and a number of foreign legations from Europe, Russia and Scandinavia. The wealthy botanist and president of the Royal Society Sir Joseph Banks (1743–1820) remained at no. 32 for more than forty years, but as a residential square Soho's days were numbered. Mid-Victorian London witnessed the arrival of music and book publishers, including a couple of imprints that are still current in Routledge (at no. 36) and A & C Black at nos. 4–6, and Sir Joseph's house with its curious but attractive tiered Venetian windows finally came down in 1937. The replacement

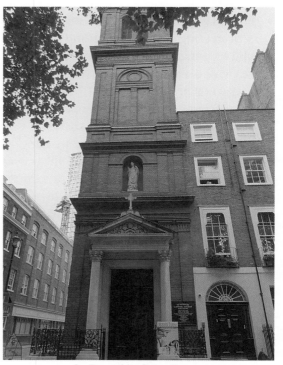

St Patrick's, Soho Square

building is now occupied by Twentieth Century Fox.

In fact the character of the square had been much changed by the construction of the Hospital for Women in 1852 and the aforementioned development by Crosse & Blackwell. Though both have now gone the appearance in the square of these much larger, taller and more obviously commercial buildings effectively opened the gates to others and today the results are there to be seen. Admittedly a few of the newer buildings are slender enough to maintain something of the square's old and diverse character, but with the exception of no. 10 – which actually comprises two Frith-era houses – and no. 15, almost certainly the only house on the square where the original layout can still be read, nothing in Soho Square would be familiar to Mrs Cornelys and her clients.

Sadly, this includes the central gardens too. As late as 1839 the square was described as 'presenting a very pleasing and somewhat rural appearance, having in the centre a large area within a handsome iron railing, enclosing several trees and shrubs,' but at least what remains today is well-tended and well used as one of the few open spaces in this part of the capital. Like those working in Lower Grosvenor Gardens (see Belgravia) the gardeners also have one of central London's nicest little potting sheds, a tiny half-timbered octagon thought to have been designed in the 1880s by S. J. Thacker. The building formed part of an important scheme of improvements, the costs for which (£200) were borne by the square's residents who unfortunately afterwards refused to admit the public to the gardens. The bill included the removal of a wooden arbour and a carved stone statue of Charles II in armour, the work of William III's sculptor-in-ordinary,

Caius Gabriel Cibber, a Dane. In a state of some disrepair, and badly corroded by the London air, this was removed to the garden of Royal Academician Frederick Goodall at Harrow Weald. It has since been returned, however, largely thanks to the efforts of the widow of the librettist W. S. Gilbert.

The statue is sometimes mistakenly assumed to represent the unfortunate 1st Duke of Monmouth, and originally stood on a pedestal, 'enriched with fruit and flowers [with] on the four sides of the base figures representing the four chief rivers of the kingdom – Thames, Severn, Tyne, and Humber'. Also included were figures of an old man and a naked virgin ('only nets wrapped about her') reposing on a fish, and out of whose mouth flowed a stream of water. Presumably eighteenth century, the fountain disappeared at the same time as the statue and its whereabouts are not known.

Wardour Street

Long associated with the offices and studios of various film-production and film-distribution companies, Wardour Street takes its name from Edward Wardour MP a seventeenth century Clerk of the Pells who owned land alongside a path known as Colmanhedge Lane (sometimes just Hedge Lane) running down to the King's Mews in what is now Trafalgar Square. The name Wardour Street seems first to have appeared in 1689, by which time development was underway but to no great plan and in a fairly haphazard manner. For a short time, a portion of the new thoroughfare was known as Prince's Street, named like Rupert Street in honour of Prince Rupert – the Royalist general and nephew of Charles I – but despite this handsome moniker the accommodation was never fine and by the early 1700s most had been rebuilt or remodelled. The new buildings were occupied by furniture makers and dealers, most of them producing goods manifestly inferior to those associated with Thomas Sheraton (1751–1806). Sheraton was one of the so-called 'big three' of eighteenth-century furniture design (along with Thomas Chippendale and George Hepplewhite) and lived at no. 163 towards the end of his career, and later no. 98, but latterly the term 'Wardour Street' came to be used to describe antique furniture that was not only unfashionable but also bogus.

Sadly the architecture of Wardour Street was rarely much better, and it seems that even when an architect of some quality was employed here the results were not good. William Burges (1827–81), for example, drug-addicted, destined to die young and physically so unprepossessing that even friends called him ugly, is nevertheless to be counted among the greatest of Victorian architect-designers although his personal brand of romantic medievalism was very much at odds with many of his peers. At both Cardiff Castle and the thirteenth century Castell Coch he worked to very good effect for the 3rd Marquess of Bute, and Evelyn Waugh's Burges-designed washstand was one of the great novelist's most prized possessions. (Waugh it was who observed how it is that the British appreciate their cultural heritage only after it is gone.) But in Wardour Street in 1864, Burges appears to have been very much out of his depth when asked to design for St Anne's Court a set of model dwellings and to no-one's real surprise this grim structure was torn down less than a hundred years later.

There are, nevertheless, some buildings of merit: for example, nos. 103–109, its bold stone façade and immense glazed arch the work of Detmar Blow (1867–1939) following his dismissal as the 2nd Duke of Westminster's estate manager. There is, in addition, nos. 152–160, designed for the music publishers Novello and Company in 1906, Pevsner calling the result 'an original piece of scholarly adaptation of period elements,' based, he says, on a 'Hanseatic town hall'. At ground level an attractive arcade of arches on Ionic columns, happily it is still in the music business as the headquarters of the long established Chappell of Bond Street, which recently celebrated its bicentenary.

Albeit commercial rather than residential, some of the street's losses have been grievous. For example until the 1920s, on the corner of Wardour Street and Old Compton Street, the premises of 'W. Hairsine, Chemist' had an exceptionally elegant Regency shop front with a pair of matching façades. Each had a large, shallow bow window facing onto the street, with between them an immense carriage lamp slung over the door at the corner. More recently, in September 2006, the BBC announced the possible loss of another well-known building, following the

142 Wardour Street

closure of 'one of London's oldest pubs' despite a campaign that involved more than five thousand supporters. The pub in question was the famous Intrepid Fox at no. 99.

Named after Charles James Fox, rather than the quarry of those early hunters in Soho Fields, it later became a popular stop on the rock-and-roll tourist map of London. Among the regulars mentioned in the BBC's coverage were Hawkwind and Motörhead singer Lemmy and the late Svengali of the Sex Pistols, Malcolm McLaren. According to some authorities it is the place where Mick Jagger persuaded Ronnie Wood to ditch the Faces in favour of the Rolling Stones – hard to imagine Mick in a pub these days – its popularity among musicians due in part to its proximity to the once popular Marquee Club at no. 90, which, regrettably, is also now defunct.

During the Blitz, which largely destroyed

The Intrepid Fox, Wardour Street

St Anne's church (see panel above), this part of London was struck by another killer, in the form of Gordon Frederick Cummins. In less than a week the so-called Blackout Ripper attacked six women, killing four of them. Cummins relied on the activities of the Luftwaffe to provide him with the opportunity, and indeed the fact that he is not better known is also because of the war. The rationing of newsprint, and a very rapid trial, meant that the 28-year-old serviceman was already dangling from a rope at HMP Wandsworth before most Londoners even realised what was going on.

His first attack, or at least the first for which he is generally held to be responsible, took place in Montagu Place on 9 February 1942, when he strangled his first victim before stealing £80 from her handbag. When he struck again it was in Wardour Street, cornering a prostitute called Evelyn Oatey in her flat at no. 153. The following night he killed another prostitute, this time north of Oxford Street, and the following day a fourth body was found at 187 Sussex Gardens, W2. Once again the victim was a prostitute known to the police, and once again she had been strangled and mutilated.

The final attack took place just off Piccadilly Circus, but Cummins made off down Haymarket after being disturbed by a delivery boy. Police were quickly on his trail – he had dropped his gas mask, the case of which had printed on it 525987, his RAF service number – and he was apprehended near Paddington railway station. Hauled up before a judge at the Old Bailey, the expected death sentence was handed down after a trial lasting little more than an hour. Cummins had no previous convictions.

COVENT GARDEN
& STRAND

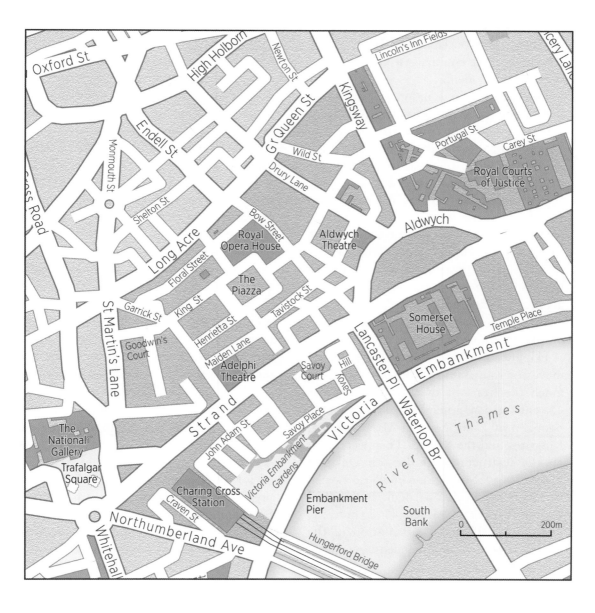

Oxford St

High Holborn

Newton St

Lincoln's Inn Fields

Kingsway

Gr Queen St

Endell St

Monmouth St

Cross Road

Wild St

Drury Lane

Portugal St

Carey St

Shelton St

Royal Courts
of Justice

Long Acre

Floral Street

Bow Street

Royal
Opera House

Aldwych
Theatre

Aldwych

St Martin's Lane

Garrick St

King St

The
Piazza

Tavistock St

Somerset
House

Temple Place

Henrietta St

Goodwin's
Court

Maiden Lane

Adelphi
Theatre

Savoy
Court

Hill

Savoy

Lancaster Pl

Embankment

The
National
Gallery

Trafalgar
Square

Strand

John Adam St

Savoy Place

Victoria

Waterloo Br

Thames

Victoria Embankment
Gardens

River

Craven St

Charing Cross
Station

Embankment
Pier

South
Bank

0   200m

Northumberland Ave

Hungerford Bridge

Whitehall

Strong emotions were aroused in the 1970s when the old Covent Garden market was swept into the dustbin of history. This change occurred almost exactly three centuries after its stallholders had first started supplying fruit and vegetables to the people of London. In medieval times this historic part of London had been a garden belonging to the convent or abbey of St Peter at Westminster, and very few of those who knew the area well had any faith that its bland successor at Nine Elms in Vauxhall – while the largest market of its kind anywhere in the country – would provide a suitable replacement.

For visitors and Londoners alike there had long been a kind of magic to Covent Garden, something to do with its central location and of course the robustly Georgian market buildings, which, unexpectedly, were still utterly functional and looked so elegant. Also the contrast – perhaps best seen in *My Fair Lady* – between the top hats and tails emerging from a late performance at the Royal Opera House just as the market traders and their customers were beginning yet another long and arduous day. It was the glamour of stage and society coming face to face with genuine cockneys and their barrows of fruit and vegetables.

Happily, although the market itself has moved on those same buildings are still very much the heart of the area we know as Covent Garden, a neighbourhood roughly bounded by Long Acre, St Martin's Lane, Kingsway and the Strand. They were built on the instructions of the 6th Duke of Bedford (1766–1839), one of whose Russell forebears had been a particularly favoured Garter Knight. Granted land here by Henry VIII after the Dissolution of the Monasteries, he was subsequently made 1st Earl of Bedford.

At the time of the grant much of the land was just pasture and market gardens, but, in 1586, Bedford's descendant the 3rd Earl had decided to build a house for himself on a portion of it known as Friars Pyes. With its entrance on the Strand, Bedford House was conspicuously large with a 100-foot frontage, a huge courtyard onto the Strand and very extensive gardens to the rear. Its development was somewhat random, with new ranges being added as needed, and in the thirty years from 1643–73 the number of hearths (counted for tax purposes) nearly tripled from twenty-three to sixty. The family stayed in occupation until around 1700 at which point – with the family now raised to ducal status – it was decided to move to a house elsewhere on their London estate at Bloomsbury.

Back in 1670, the 5th Earl had obtained a royal charter permitting him to hold a fruit, flower and herb market on the land behind Bedford House, an area which the family had already begun developing some fifty years earlier. This market expanded rapidly, and within five or six years more than twenty shops had been constructed along the back wall of the gardens. Approximately fifty further stalls were erected when the old house was abandoned and pulled down; its site quickly cleared for development and on which Southampton Street, Tavistock Street and Tavistock Row were laid out around 1706–10. (In the normal practice for the times the names of these were far from incidental, the Duke's heir being the Marquess of Tavistock and the old Lord High Treasurer Thomas Wriothesley, 4th Earl of Southampton, one of his kinsmen.)

By 1750 the whole area was alive with market traders, gambling dens and coffee houses, and had become a popular haunt for artists and actors. Some flavour of the times can also be gauged from such publications as *Harris's List of Covent Garden Ladies*, which, from 1757, was considered the 'essential guide and accessory for any serious gentleman of pleasure'. In other words Covent Garden was never to recover socially from the departure of the Duke. As the migration westwards of the richer middle and upper classes continued the market expanded still further, overwhelming the residential character of the old convent garden as hawkers and others moved in to sell goods of all sorts and dubious quality from often entirely illegal pitches.

It was still technically ducal property, however, and over the coming decades the Russell family lawyers complained repeatedly to the authorities that the market now wholly lacked 'that systematic arrangement, neatness and accommodation which tends obviously to facilitate and increase public convenience'. Because of this moves were soon afoot to regularise matters, to restore the estate's control over traders and to raise revenues from them. Accordingly, in 1828, a new bill was introduced in Parliament, and once this was accepted construction began on a number of handsome new market buildings designed by Charles Fowler. These are described below in the entry for the Piazza.

From this point until the Great War the market – and with it much of the surrounding area – remained under the family's ownership and its control, with as many as a thousand market porters being paid and supervised by twelve officials employed by the Bedford Estate and assisted where necessary by officers on retention from the Metropolitan Police. Several times the incumbent 9th Duke attempted to sell his

interests in it to the Metropolitan Board of Works and even the City of London Corporation, but his offer was not taken up. Eventually, a sale was arranged on behalf of Herbrand, the 11th Duke, who put the bulk of the money received into bonds issued by the Tsarist regime in Russia. Unfortunately for him, worth more than £100 million at current values, these were immediately wiped out by the Bolshevik revolution.

With the market's removal to its present riverside location in Vauxhall in 1974 the area was given a new lease of life following a thorough renovation of the old market buildings by Greater London Council. Most of the latter were converted to shops and bars, with offices above, and the adjacent flower market was remodelled for the London Transport museum. Additional market stalls were established in the early-twentieth-century Jubilee market hall making the whole area a huge draw for tourists.

Much of what they come for is naturally still centred on the Piazza, the street performers and pavement cafés, the most visible manifestations of what is rightly considered a rare triumph of urban conservation. At the eastern end the London Transport museum is also hugely popular, located in part of the old market, an original Victorian iron-and-glass building, after being moved here in 1980 from its former premises at the Duke of Northumberland's Syon Park on the western outskirts of London. The collections were first assembled by London General Omnibus Company, which began to preserve old buses in the early decades of the twentieth century. Its exhibits now include trams, trolleybuses and trains, as well as buses and many artefacts, and exhibits related to their operation and marketing.

As for the Russells, while in no way matching the great survivor that is the Duke of Westminster's Grosvenor Estate (see Mayfair, Belgravia), they still own around twenty acres of the nearly three hundred they held a century ago in central London. Today that property is mostly to be found in Bloomsbury, but many streets and addresses in and around Covent Garden still bear family names or names related to the present Duke's subsidiary titles and his rural estates and manors in Bedfordshire and Devon.

Adelphi

London having grown organically over the centuries (which is to say haphazardly) successful large-scale planning schemes such as Belgravia and Bloomsbury are very much the exception, and the sad fate of the Adam brothers' imposing riverside development is rather more typical. In 1768 the four – John, Robert, James and William – took a ninety-nine-year lease on a substantial plot of run-down land between the river and the Strand for which they agreed to pay the Duke of St Albans £1,200 per annum. Once on site they set about building a quay, and several storeys of warehousing, in extensive vaults set back from the river. This was to be called the Adelphi, from the Greek *adelphoi* meaning 'brothers', and in style it was modelled in part on Diocletian's palace at Split. Relying on cheap labour from their native Scotland (for a while pipers were employed to keep the workforce happy) the Adam siblings planned a series of streets above their warehouses, two running parallel to the river and two running perpendicular to it. The centrepiece of their development was to be the Royal Terrace: eleven four-storey, stuccoed-and-pilastered houses overlooking this stretch of the Thames with high-quality interiors decorated by the likes of Angelica Kauffman and G. B. Cipriani.

The brothers, however, quickly ran into difficulties. The Corporation of the City of London had initially attempted to block the development by claiming it owned all rights to the riverbed. There was also a severe funding shortfall, partly because the government of the day declined to rent the massive vaults beneath the development for fear that these would flood at high tide and destroy the gunpowder and munitions that were to be stored here. In addition, the brothers found it hard to let such large and prestigious properties, which were considered too far from the newly fashionable West End to attract the right class of tenant. The brothers were not without influence, however, and a special Act of Parliament was passed in 1773 allowing them to rescue their scheme by holding a lottery. The following year 4,370 tickets were offered and sold at Jonathan's Coffee House in Change Alley. The tickets cost £50 each, and when finished the forty-one-bay development looked highly impressive especially when viewed from the river.

With an attractive centre and the façade closed by the projecting terraces in nearby Robert Street and Adam Street, the crisply neo-classical design and decorated pilasters of the eleven main houses attracted a number of artistically inclined tenants to the development, including actor David Garrick, the poet Thomas Hood, J. M. Barrie and Thomas Hardy. But unfortunately the construction of the Victoria Embankment in 1870 cut the warehouses off from the river, and after falling into disuse these rapidly became a dismal haunt where 'the most abandoned characters pass the night, nestling on foul straw'. Thereafter the decline of the streets above was perhaps inevitable, and within two years the exterior of the Royal Terrace was crudely cemented over and the decorative ironwork removed. In 1936 the whole was finally torn down and replaced by the office block we see today, which is also called the Adelphi but has little else in common with the original development. Now just fragments of the latter survive including 7 Adam Street (next door to Sir Richard Arkwright's old home) 1–3 Robert Street and 4–6 John Adam Street, which stand alongside the pretty headquarters building of the Royal Society for the Encouragement of Arts, Manufactures and Commerce (more commonly just the Royal Society of Arts or RSA). Some of the vaulting can also be seen from Lower Robert Street, but by no means enough of it to provide a fair impression of the brothers' ambitious, but short-lived, scheme.

However, the most significant fragment is the aforementioned RSA building. Located at 8 John Adam Street, it was designed by the Adam Brothers in 1774, and has a façade that encompasses three wide bays and Ionoic columns. The interior includes the magnificent Great Room, designed originally for members' debates and notable for a sequence of paintings by Irish artist James Barry, *The Progress of Human Knowledge and Culture*. The title alone speaks volumes for the mission of the RSA, a body established in 1754 (and granted a royal charter in 1847) to 'embolden enterprise, enlarge science, refine art, improve our manufacturers and extend our commerce'. The aim was above all to alleviate poverty and secure full employment, and so the focus of the society has always been on the practical rather than

7 Adam Street, Adelphi

Royal Society of Arts, Adelphi

just the underlying philosophical or theoretical principles.

The RSA has sponsored or initiated many notable events, including the Great Exhibition of 1851 of the Works of Industry of all Nations, a celebration of modern technology and design, which was held in the Crystal Palace in Hyde Park, a massive glass structure designed by Joseph Paxton. Opened by Queen Victoria on 1 May 1851 – the concept had been enthusiastically supported by Prince Albert – the Great Exhibition attracted six million visitors and much of the profit it generated, £186,000, was used to fund the museums of South Kensington. Today the RSA carries on the good work of its eighteenth-century founders, funding valuable research in many areas, including technology, design, education and entrepreneurship. With a royal patron and more than 27,000 fellows around the world, winners of its prestigious Albert Medal have included the likes of Michael Faraday, Sir Henry Bessemer, Lord Kelvin and Louis Pasteur. Stephen Hawking and Nelson Mandela have been among its more recent recipients.

In hindsight, the Adelphi must be considered one of London's most grievous architectural losses, and, of the brothers, it is Robert whose reputation has burned brightest as an interior designer and furniture designer as well as one of the fathers of British Neoclassicism.

Aldwych

A large crescent created in 1905 to link the newly widened Strand with Kingsway, the name dates back to Saxon times when this area – then known as 'Aldwic' or the old settlement – was granted to the local Danish population. Its three principal buildings came slightly later, all of them monumental: Australia House was completed in 1918; Bush House, where construction began in 1923 and rumbled on for a dozen years; and India House, which was built in 1928–30. Of these the first is an unusual exercise (for London) in Beaux Arts, the work of Alexander M. Mackenzie and Alexander G. Mackenzie. It was designed to incorporate the recently completed old Victoria State Building into a new High Commission following the establishment of the Commonwealth of Australia as a dominion of the British Empire.

With Ashoka columns outside and a black granite entrance, India House was to serve a similar function for that part of the subcon-

Australia House, Aldwych

Bush House, Aldwych

tinent, the architect Sir Herbert Baker (who built much of New Delhi) including in the design various Indian motifs and stylistic details intended to recall the great Rajput and Mughal dynasties. Inside the use of red sandstone and perforated *jaali* screens for balustrades – the latter carved in India by craftsmen sent to Rome for instruction – are complemented by large-scale murals by a number of Indian artists.

By comparison with these two, as the home until 12 July 2012 of the world's largest international broadcaster, the BBC

World Service, Bush House should be British to the core. But here too, behind the slightly bombastic Portland stone façade, one finds quite the opposite. Reputedly the most expensive building in the world when it was finally completed at a cost of more than £2 million (and the first in London to have a self-service canteen) it was designed by one American, Harvey Wiley Corbett, and owned by another, the industrialist Irving T. Bush (1869–1948).

Bush had intended it to be a trade centre – entering through its immense Corinthian columns one found an interior lavishly equipped with marble corridors lined with expensive shop fronts – but it failed in this role, and, following the Wall Street Crash of 1929 and its global ramifications, the owners found life difficult. Eventually, in 1941, the building was leased to the BBC for its European (later to be World) Service, that department having been bombed out of its studios in Oxford Street. From then on, and for more than seventy years, the sound of 'Lillibulero' was beamed across the world, the World Service signature tune based on an Irish jig said to be by Purcell.

With the BBC as tenant, Bush House played a central role in British broadcasting, and, indeed, in wider British life: during the Second World War, General de Gaulle sent out daily messages of support to his compatriots in the Resistance, helping to keep up French morale during the dark days of the German occupation; Henry Kissinger was interviewed for the news programme *Outlook* on American foreign policy; Paul McCartney made a live broadcast on the BBC's Russian service. Some of the employees were equally distinguished: George Orwell worked here and when he was writing his dystopian novel, *1984*, is said by some to have had the idea for Room 101 from his environs. One employee, however, did not have such a happy time: one day in September 1978, at the height of the Cold War, Georgi Markov, a broadcaster with the Bulgarian service, came back from lunch, after being stabbed in the leg by a poisoned umbrella. He died a few days later. Markov, an acclaimed novelist and playwright who had defected to the West, was very critical of the communist government in Bulgaria and it is thought that the regime in Sofia had him killed, using the KGB's expertise in assassination techniques. Despite extensive and ongoing enquiries by Scotland Yard, carried out after the fall of the Iron Curtain, no one has ever been charged with Markov's murder. Bush House was briefly owned by the Church in Wales (the Episcopal church of the Principality), but was recently sold to a Japanese corporation, which owns it at the time of writing.

Another American, William Waldorf Astor built and owned the nearby Waldorf Hotel. With its French pavilion roofs and elegant Palm Court it too was designed by Alexander M. Mackenzie, a strange choice of style and perhaps of architect as well for such a keen Anglophile as Astor (who was eventually naturalised and raised to the peerage). The nearby Novello Theatre enjoys the distinction of having been bombed in both world wars, and as the Strand it housed a record-breaking run for a farce with that classic of the genre *No Sex Please, We're British*, penned by Alistair Foot and Anthony Marriott. Ivor Novello, the great actor, writer and composer, after whom the theatre is named, lived in a flat above the premises for thirty years.

Also worthy of note is the Aldwych Theatre, built as the second of a pair of

The Aldwych, home of British farce

theatres with the Strand, both buildings the work of Australian-born architect W. G. R. Sprague, a protégé of the great theatre designer Frank Matcham. The Aldwych opened its doors in 1905 and is perhaps best known for the eponymous Aldwych farces, which ran almost continuously from 1925–33, and include classics of the genre like *A Cuckoo in the Nest* and *Rookery Nook*. Written by 'house dramatist' Ben Travers (1886–1980), the Aldwych farces are notable for their inventive plots and meticulous construction and took full advantage of a highly talented acting team that included actor-manager Tom Walls (always the hero),

Ralph Lynn (hero's friend), Robertson Hare (henpecked husband), Winifred Shotter (heroine) and Mary Brough (nubile woman). Travers, a great influence on modern playwrights such as Joe Orton, worked to a ripe old age and his last play *The Bed Before Yesterday* was staged in 1975 when he was eighty-nine.

The tired façade of the disused Aldwych underground station gives on to one of around forty so-called ghost stations in the capital, many of which can be identified at street level, or in some cases glimpsed from passing trains, the platforms now deserted and the advertising posters peeling from dirt-streaked walls. Aldwych was a stop on the Piccadilly line until it closed in 1994, the closure due to low passenger numbers and the high cost of replacing its ancient lifts. It is said to be haunted, and several 'fluffers' who used to clean the station after hours claim to have disturbed the ghost of an actress once employed at the Royal Strand Theatre, which formerly occupied the site. Now available for hire it is frequently used as a film set, and its appearances include scenes from *Battle of Britain* (1969), *Patriot Games* (1992) and *Atonement* (2007). The name also surfaced in a Lara Croft *Tomb Raider* computer game, although the digital version was quite different to the actual station.

Bow Street

Laid out in the shape of a bow in the mid-seventeenth century, Bow Street was subsequently extended beyond Long Acre and down to the Strand. For half a century or more it was respectable and largely residential but the first Covent Garden Theatre opened here in 1732, to be followed by as many as eight taverns and eventually a number of brothels. Its most celebrated building is the magistrates court, now closed but established as long ago as 1740 under the control of a former army officer. His replacement was Henry Fielding, novelist and magistrate, who with his blind half-brother John, founded a small corps of highly mobile 'thief-takers' charged with augmenting the somewhat patchy efforts of the old watchmen and parochial constables who at that time represented the law in London. Nicknamed the Bow Street Runners, the corps survived the creation of the Metropolitan Police in 1829 by ten years but was then broken up.

The present building dates from 1881. It was designed by Sir John Taylor, in what Pevnser describes as a 'gravely Palladian' style; one presumably intended to underline the gravity of its mission. Now Grade II

Magistrates Court, Bow Street

listed, and costing £38,400 at the time of its construction, it housed four courts. In one of these in 1895 Oscar Wilde was charged with gross indecency, and peace campaigner Bertrand Russell OM, 3rd Earl Russell, also found himself in the dock here following a lively demonstration outside the Soviet embassy in 1961.

Diagonally opposite, the Royal Opera House replaced a theatre built by Edward Shepherd (see Mayfair, St James's), which was said to be the most luxurious in London. Designed by Edward Middleton Barry in 1858, and incorporating elements of the earlier buildings on this site, the replacement building was used as a government store in the Great War and a dancehall from 1939–45, but, with those two exceptions, has otherwise focused very much on ballet and opera. Its two resident companies were incorporated by royal charter to become the Royal Ballet (in 1956) and the Royal Opera (1968) and for their supporters the view up to the portico, with its six giant Corinthian columns, is one of the most spectacular in this part of London. Either side are statues of Melpomene and Thalia – respectively the muses of singing and comedy – by John Charles Felix Rossi (1762–1839) and above these a frieze by John Flaxman showing Tragedy and Comedy. The effect is striking but for many this same building – whilst

Royal Opera House, Bow Street

noticeably less opulent or monumental than Milan's La Scala or the Paris Opera – remains little more than a byword for poor management and enormous subsidies spent unwisely on what critics claim are likely to remain minority art forms.

Whatever one's view of the principle of subsidy for these traditionally upper-middle-class pursuits, there can be no doubting the place of both the Royal Opera and the Royal Ballet as world-class purveyors of their respective arts. While several of its musical directors inclined towards the development of a strong ensemble company, a host of internationally renowned guest singers have appeared in operatic productions, including Maria Callas, Elisabeth Schwarzkopf, Placido Domingo and Cecilia Bartoli. Conductors from the wider musical world are frequently invited: Claudio Abbado, Sir Simon Rattle and Sir John Eliot Gardiner among them.

The opera company has also enjoyed huge successes with guest producers like Franco Zeffirelli, whose work encompassed a 1959 *Lucia di Lammermoor* that made Joan Sutherland an international star, and a legendary staging of *Tosca* in 1964, with Callas and Tito Gobbi. However, much of the credit for the Covent Garden-based company's acceptance as one of the world's most eminent can be traced to the distinguished tenure as musical director of Georg Solti from 1961–71. Solti was responsible for many innovations in repertoire and performing style, foremost among them his new productions of operas by Richard Strauss, most of which he directed himself. It is fitting that it was during this period that the company became the Royal Opera.

The Royal Ballet's history can be traced to Dame Ninette de Valois, a dancer, choreographer and impresario. She formed the Vic-Wells ballet in 1931, a small company that originally performed at the Old Vic and the Sadler's Wells Theatre. To train new dancers de Valois also set up the Vic-Wells Ballet School. In 1946 the company transferred to the Royal Opera House, premiering a new full-length production of *Sleeping Beauty* in that year, which marked the reopening of the theatre after the war. It was to recognise twenty-five years in existence, that the company was granted a royal charter in 1956. The Royal Ballet has been fortunate in its directors: not only de Valois, but also Frederick Ashton, assistant director from 1952 and who took the reins when she retired in 1963.

Ashton's work is said to embody the 'English' style of ballet, nuanced and lyrical rather than dramatic. It was his collaboration with Margot Fonteyn – the prima ballerina at Royal Ballet for several decades – that led to the so-called golden age of British ballet. With the resident company – and sometimes with the participation of guest artists like Rudolf Nureyev – Ashton and Fonteyn created a stream of memorable works, not least *Giselle* (1962), which was received with twenty-three curtain calls. Today Royal Ballet is Britain's largest ballet company and the wide range of productions includes works from the classic repertoire as well as those conceived by modern choreographers.

To the left of the ROH, the rebuilt Floral Hall, with its huge barrel-vaulted roof, forms part of the substantial 1997 improvement scheme, and such was its scope that the main house had to be closed for two-and-a-half years. At a cost of well over £200 million the works included new theatre and studio spaces, better lighting and changing rooms, and what purports to be the longest bar in

London. More interesting is the imaginative bridge twisting high above Floral Street to link the building with the Royal Ballet School at no. 46. It was designed by Wilkinson Eyre and won a Solutia Design Award in 2004.

Craven Street

More Bloomsbury in feel than Strand, the former Spur Alley is named after the Craven family, ground landlords when the street was built around 1730. While no single house is of special interest to the architectural aficionado, the combined effect of many in a terrace is attractive and gives a good impression of a prosperous street of this period. In fact the left-hand side (looking down to the river) comprises the longest run of eighteenth-century houses in this part of the capital. Nos. 25–42 are particularly nice, as are nos. 11–15 opposite, although much of the right-hand side of the street has been ruined by insensitive redevelopment.

A number of plaques commemorate famous residents, including the German-Jewish poet Heinrich Heine who complained about the fog, coal-smoke and poets whilst living at no. 32, the architect Henry Flitcroft at no. 33 and Herman Melville at no. 25. Grinling Gibbons was another, although the most significant is perhaps Benjamin Franklin, the American scientist and statesman. No. 36 (originally no. 7 and now a museum) is the only one of his many homes still left standing.

Beyond Charing Cross Station (which since 1865 has occupied the site behind this terrace) some seven acres of ground were granted in 1624 to George Villiers, 1st Duke of Buckingham. He built the magnificent watergate, which still survives, marooned

Craven Street

and melancholy in Embankment Gardens (see below) and spent a fortune on a house that in October 1626 the French ambassador described as 'the most richly fitted up than any other I saw'. Following his murder two years later, his heirs used it only intermittently.

In 1672, with speculators making offers for the potentially valuable site and finding himself very heavily mortgaged, the 2nd Duke gave permission for the land to be developed. As well as receiving £30,000, the 2nd Duke – also George – insisted that the new streets all pay due respect to every syllable of his name and title. Today as a result we have Buckingham Street, Villiers Street and Duke Street, which is now part of John Adam Street. More recently someone with authority, but with neither a sense of history nor of humour, has insisted that George Street and the delightful-sounding Of Alley both be renamed.

Drury Lane

For many years little more than slums, Drury Lane was substantially improved when Aldwych and Kingsway were driven up from the Strand in the early 1900s. A century on its most notable building is the Theatre Royal Drury Lane, so-called although its main entrance is round the corner on Catherine Street. It has a good claim to be the oldest theatre of the forty or so in this part of London, and architecturally it is certainly the finest. However, the West End has not always been the home of London theatre: for years entertainments tended to be offered only in London's outlying districts, so that the first playhouse appeared in Shoreditch in 1576 with others such as the Rose (and of course Shakespeare's 'wooden O', the Globe) appearing along Bankside in Southwark, where the powerful writ of the City of London did not reach.

For London's theatrical classes a move across the river to the West End, and to the kind of horseshoe-shaped auditorium and proscenium arch we recognise today, did not come until the Restoration in 1660. As little as two years later the pleasure-loving Charles II granted a patent to Thomas Killigrew and his company (known as The King's Servants) for a new theatre on Drury Lane. Technically, the servants formed part of the royal household, so wore a livery of gold and scarlet. They were based in the first, seven-hundred-seat Theatre Royal, constructed on the site of an old riding yard,

Theatre Royal, Drury Lane

and the place where the King reputedly first saw the 15-year-old Nell Gwynn. The original Theatre Royal was small by modern standards, being approximately the size of the present-day stage. Unfortunately, it burned down a decade later, after which Wren designed a replacement twice as large and in which – it was reported – a performance of *The Merchant of Venice* so moved George II that he was unable to sleep either during it or for some time thereafter.

No doubt greatly assisted by royal patronage, the Theatre Royal was able to attract the leading lights of the day in both acting and production. The great David Garrick was actor-manager for twenty-nine years from 1747 and his many reforms and innovations revolutionised not only acting but also theatrical practice. Garrick retired in 1776 and when he died, just three years later, he was buried in Westminster Abbey, in Poet's Corner, the first actor to be accorded this honour. The new manager of the Theatre Royal was a no-less distinguished figure: the eminent playwright, Richard Brinsley Sheridan, whose best-known play, *The School for Scandal*, received its first performance here in 1777.

Sheridan oversaw the demolition of the ageing building and its replacement by a 3,600-seat auditorium, which opened in 1794. However, it too burned down and so much of what we see today is the work of Benjamin Wyatt. Wyatt's 1812 design was funded by the brewer Samuel Whitbread (the chairman of the organising committee was none other than Lord Byron) and modelled on the elegant neo-classical Grand Theatre at Bordeaux. The porch on paired square Doric pillars is a later addition, as is the long Ionic colonnade on Russell Street with its cast-iron columns, but even this work was completed by 1831 and subsequent alterations have happily been restricted mostly to the interior. The theatre is said to be haunted by the ghost of the clown Grimaldi, who has been known to kick actors on the backside if they turn in a particularly poor performance. (Others insist that the Grimaldi connection is bogus. They take the view that the ghost is that of an unknown man, whose corpse was found bricked up behind a wall in 1840 with a knife between the ribs.)

The Theatre Royal continued to mount many theatrical landmarks. In the late nineteenth century, and early-twentieth, it became well-known for its spectacular productions; these included *Ben Hur*, complete with chariot races, the Battle of Rorke's Drift in *Youth* and a train crash in *The Whip*. In 1931 Noel Coward had a major success with *Cavalcade*, whose four-hundred-strong cast included the young John Mills as well as lavish set pieces portraying the Relief of Mafeking and Queen Victoria's funeral. Drury Lane, as it is often known, also staged many of actor-singer-composer Ivor Novello's major triumphs of the 1930s, such as *Glamorous Night*, *Careless Rapture* and *The Dancing Years*.

In the post-war years, a number of American musicals made London debuts in Drury Lane, among them massive hits by Rodgers and Hammerstein, such as *Oklahoma!* (1946), *South Pacific* (1951) and *The King and I* (1953). More recently, the Theatre Royal has enjoyed another run of musical successes, including *Billy* (based on Billy Liar by Keith Waterhouse) *A Chorus Line* and the hugely popular *Miss Saigon*, which was staged from 1989 until 1999 and holds the record for the highest number of performances at the venue with 4,263. The small theatre opposite is the Duchess, an unconvincing exercise in faux Tudor-Gothic, and indeed the interior too is somewhat un-showy, with its best feature a pair of bas reliefs (one either side of the stage) showing draped figures holding the masks of tragedy and comedy.

Embankment Gardens

Now stranded 150 yards inland and separated from the river by this small park, and a queue of traffic at least four cars deep, the old watergate to the Duke of Buckingham's York House perfectly illustrates the scale of Sir Joseph Bazalgette's achievement. When Charles Dickens lived nearby at 15 Buckingham Street (in a building previously occupied by Tsar Peter the Great and the aforementioned Henry Fielding) the Thames would have lapped up against the base of the gate, which formed a ceremonial entrance to the Duke's domain. By confining the river within a series of great embankments – Victoria, Albert and Chelsea – Bazalgette created more than fifty acres of new land, of which the gardens form just a small part. Beneath the surface he provided space for service pipes, badly needed new sewers, wide tunnels for what was to become the District and Circle lines, and for a pioneering pneumatic railway to run underneath the river although sadly this last feature was never built.

Today the watergate is the last surviving relic of a whole series of riverside palaces that belonged to the rich and influential. Ideally situated between commerce and the Crown, between the twin cities of London and Westminster, these included John of Gaunt's Savoy Palace, Durham House (which for a time was home to Simon de Montfort) and numerous 'inns' for the pow-

York House watergate, Embankment Gardens

Lamb and Flag side entrance, Floral Street

erful abbots of Tewkesbury, Faversham and Winchcombe. The clerics were in time followed by noblemen such as Buckingham, the inns gradually evolving into extensive and impressive private properties.

The watergate, now nearly four hundred years old, is still something of a mystery, its maker known (the aptly named Nicholas Stone, who built tombs and funerary monuments) but its designer still not confirmed. For a while it was assumed to be the great Inigo Jones but a more likely candidate is Sir Balthazar Gerbier, who was employed by the Duke, and is said to have modelled it on the Fontaine de Medicis in the Luxembourg Gardens in Paris. Highlighting the Villiers arms and motto – *Fidei coticula crux*, (the touchstone of Faith is the cross) the anchors on the carved lions' shields symbolise the Duke's service to the Crown as Lord High Admiral and Warden of the Cinque Ports.

Floral Street

The name clearly derived from the nearby market, Floral Street was formerly Hart Street after the White Hart, which stood in Long Acre in the seventeenth century with its yard backing onto this narrow thorough-

fare. In 1881 a report for the landlord, the 7th Duke of Bedford, confirmed that the street was mostly warehousing, of which no. 24 is an excellent example. The three-storey building dates from around twenty years earlier and was designed by a local architect C. G. Searle in an attractive if obviously industrial style with a formal pattern of metal-casement windows with stone sills set in a plain face of stock brickwork. Wider windows at each end have iron lintel-plates supported by slender Doric colonnettes of cast iron, a Victorian structure but with a positively Georgian sense of detail and proportion. In 1860 the same architect was charged with remodelling the attractive brick-built Parish Schools at the southeastern end, which is now a restaurant.

On the other side, a narrow alleyway towards Garrick Street leads to the Lamb and Flag at no. 33 Rose Street, a seven-

Lamb and Flag, Floral Street

teenth-century public house with a later façade. The interior is characterised by old varnish and creaking joists, pleasantly blackened panelled walls and bare floorboards, and has an ambience that positively reeks of old pewter mugs, serving girls and navy press gangs. It is where, in 1679, the Poet Laureate, John Dryden, was attacked and beaten after writing scurrilous lines about the Duchess of Portsmouth, Charles II's mistress.

Garrick Street

London has older clubs, much grander clubs and more exclusive clubs, but the name of none is as famous as the Garrick's and no other club has lobbied to change the name of the street on which it stands – and succeeded. Founded in 1831 by a group of literary gentlemen under the patronage of the Duke of Sussex, the King's brother, the club originally met at Probatt's Family Hotel before moving to what was then still called New King Street and had hitherto been slums. Named after actor-manager David Garrick (see Drury Lane above), it was intended as 'a society in which actors and men of education and refinement might meet on equal terms'. Committed to stimulating debate and a lively atmosphere, the original committee stipulated that, in order to attract the right kind of member, 'it would be better that ten unobjectionable men should be excluded than one terrible bore should be admitted'. It is a principle to which the club cleaves to this day.

The Garrick's celebrity today depends very much on the high profile of the members – which in an age when none but the grander actors can afford the subscription is drawn largely from the media and the law – and their willingness to sport the club's salmon-and-cucumber tie. The latter is distinctive, if slightly bilious, but the clubhouse is undeniably handsome: a large and Italianate *palazzo* worthy of Pall Mall and as such somewhat unexpected this far to the east. It was designed by Frederick Marrable and completed in 1864 and inside its theatrical heritage is still much in evidence. Besides paintings by Zoffany of David Garrick and C. F. Reinhold, the library is full of historic playbills and theatrical biographies. The club table is also slightly narrower than at other clubs in order, it is said, that the more sociable members can hear each other without leaning forward. The narrow design might not always be a good thing: Dickens and Thackeray, both of whom were members, had a famous stand-up row in the coffee room – the club still has the table at which the verbal fisticuffs took place – after which each refused to acknowledge the other for more than fifteen years.

Few of its 1,300 members now are as voluble or as distinguished, but with so many loose-tongued lawyers and journalists among them the Garrick is frequently written about in newspaper gossip columns and so appears less mysterious than its older rivals in St James's. By far the most embarrassing example of this was during the 1987 debate on the book *Spycatcher* (written by the former MI5 officer, Peter Wright) when the counsel for the defence claimed to have gathered useful intelligence about the prosecution's tactics by listening to the Attorney-General, Lord Havers, discussing his plan of attack whilst standing at the club urinals.

In fact the club has rarely been a stranger to controversy. The splendidly named Lord de Roos, for example, was once sacked for cheating at cards, a journalist John Foster (whom a fellow member described as a 'low scribbler without an atom of talent and totally unsuited to the society of gentlemen') came close to meeting a similar fate after publishing details of a private dinner in his newspaper and at least one member has been forced to tender his resignation after being accused by a housemaid of stealing the soap.

On the corner with King Street is an attractive mid-nineteenth century building by Arthur Allom who designed the first grandstands at Lord's Cricket Ground in the 1860s. Now a restaurant, it was built in a fashionable *palazzo* style for the auctioneers Debenham Storr & Sons. Behind it, on Rose Street, another attractive Victorian survivor is the rear entrance to the Westminster Fire Office at no. 34

Goodwin's Court

Approached from New Row or St Martin's Lane, and easy to miss, this narrow alley dates back to the 1690s although tiny shop fronts on the south side (the bowed windows of which give it such charm) are all eighteenth century. Intimate rather than impressive, and seemingly ramshackle despite being in very good order, they provide a very good impression of another Covent Garden, one far less grand or planned than the nearby piazza, which, as we shall see, was in its day a radical departure from the norm and as such an authentic innovation for London.

By comparison Goodwin's Court seems positively Dickensian, although with their blackened timbers, worn steps, comically bulging windows and bowed walls, what were once mostly tailor's shops predate the great man by well over a century. With the entrance from St Martin's Lane consisting of no more than a doorway off the street, with a couple of steps down, it is all too easy to miss (the other end of this charming thoroughfare is just as quaint, being a narrow passage). But once found there is plenty to see in Goodwin Court, from working gas lamps outside no. 1 and an attractive clock face over the archway out onto Bedfordbury. There are also a number of old metal plates

Goodwin's Court

or 'fire-marks' affixed to the buildings. These date from a time when householders had to rely on privately funded groups of watermen and fire-fighters who at the height of a blaze would have looked for these plates (which indicated which buildings were insured against fire) and concentrate on saving them rather than any adjacent properties with no such cover. The system worked until the establishment of a central fire brigade, and presumably helps explain the survival of Goodwin's Court into the twenty-first century.

Great Queen Street

For years a feature of Great Queen Street was a statue of Charles I's queen, Henrietta Maria, although records show that the street was actually named for her mother-in-law, Anne of Denmark. In 1640 the street was completed and mostly residential, although the oldest surviving buildings are of the early eighteenth century. These can be seen at nos. 27–29 and nos. 33–35, while slightly later survivors include nos. 4, 6, 36 and 37.

Today the street is dominated by the extraordinary Freemasons' Hall, designed in a lavish art deco style as the ceremonial and administrative headquarters of the United Grand Lodge of England. In common with many of the grander buildings associated with Masonry here and abroad the columns either side of the main entrance appear *distyle in antis*, meaning a pair set between walls to form a porch. This is thought to be a subtle way of alluding to the lost Temple of Solomon, although it is a common enough feature in many non-Masonic Graeco-Roman buildings too. The hall was built in memory of those English Masons who did not survive the Great War, and is

actually the third building on a site that the Masons have occupied since at least 1775. Its official opening in 1933 was conducted by the Grand Master, HRH the Duke of Connaught, Queen Victoria's last surviving son. With its lofty proportions and corner site it is more than a little reminiscent of Sir Edwin Cooper's Port of London Authority building on Tower Hill. Both are vast edifices, in this case containing a Grand Temple that can seat more than 1,500 people as well as a score of lodge rooms, an extensive library and a museum of Masonry. (The building is open to the public.)

It is nevertheless regrettable that nothing of the original Freemasons' Hall survives, as it included work by Philip Hardwick and Sir John Soane. Of the second, by F. P. Cockerell, a portion of the façade has survived, however, and is incorporated into the New Connaught Rooms at nos. 61–65.

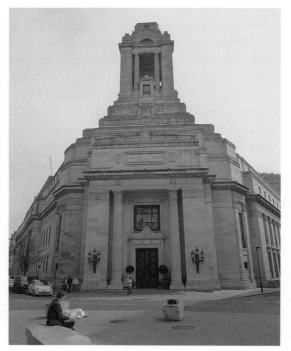

Freemasons' Hall, Great Queen Street

Almost certainly London's largest permanent banqueting hall, with a capacity of more than 2,500, this was built in 1905 on the site of the former Freemason's Tavern in which, in 1863, the Football Association held its inaugural gathering to formulate the rules of the game.

Henrietta Street

The area now covered by Henrietta Street, King Street and Bedford Street would once have contained some of the finest townhouses in the capital, the first of these having been laid out as early as 1631. Sadly none survives – the street was almost entirely rebuilt in the eighteenth century – although something of the atmosphere survives, at least when the crowds have gone home. For a while the street's very future seemed uncertain, with concerns that much of it would be swept away in the redevelopment following the market's removal. Fortunately commonsense prevailed and today it is possible to identify a number of eighteenth-century houses, including nos. 3–10 although they have slightly later stucco fronts. Dating from the 1730s, nos. 7 and 8 are particularly handsome, a matched pair with smoothly rusticated ground floors, outstanding door cases and Ionic columns.

King Street

Contemporaneous with Henrietta Street – the king in question is Henrietta's husband, Charles I – King Street was once smartly residential with some of the seventeenth-century houses the first in the capital to have doors of imported mahogany. At various times it has been home to Thomas Arne (the composer of 'Rule, Britannia!'), the afore-

mentioned dramatist Thomas Killigrew, David Garrick and Admiral James Russell, Earl of Orford. Once again only one of the original houses remains: Arne's at no. 31, although even this had a new façade built in 1860. The south side is largely nineteenth century, but the opposing side has a number of buildings of interest.

With Roman Doric columns and some nice classical detailing, no. 27 is the old Westminster Fire Office (see Garrick Street). It was originally an eighteenth-century house but was twice modified in the nineteenth century, when no. 28 was built to match it and the two joined together. No. 32 is also of this period, although this is harder to read at ground floor level which is now a shop front. More successful is no. 35 – what Pevsner calls 'a four-storeyed Italian *palazzo* in the High Roman Renaissance style' – a building of 1866 with a powerfully rusticated ground floor and elegant fenestration above. Next door to this no. 36 is as early as 1715, and no. 37, while half a century younger, is even more interesting: the intriguing and complex brick façade is thought to be the work of James Paine (1717–89), the Palladian architect who built several bridges over the Thames in Surrey and worked to good effect at Chatsworth and Kedleston Hall.

Kingsway

The last of the metropolitan improvements to Victorian London was also one of the largest. The development of Kingsway and Aldwych cost the extraordinary sum of £5 million, and in the end took so long to complete that, when finally finished, the Queen was dead and it was named for her son, Edward VII.

The chief aim of the new road scheme

Imperial Buildings, Kingsway

was to improve traffic flow from north to south – Drury Lane and Chancery Lane were too old and narrow – but it also gave planners the opportunity to sweep away more than twenty acres of slums in narrow courts and alleys. Deciding how to proceed took more than sixty years, but in 1892 plans were finalised for a new, 100-foot wide route linking the Strand to Holborn with – running beneath it – an innovative tram subway down to the Embankment. (Abandoned after the last tram, E/3-1904, was towed away to Charlton and destroyed, this route

can still be seen through locked gates and grilles in Southampton Row.)

With the British Empire at its Edwardian peak the buildings lining the road were conceived almost without exception to be uniformly large and impressive, most being designed by the West End firm of Trehearne and Norman. Their names give an indication of the intended effect: Imperial House, Regent House, Windsor House, York House, Alexandra House, Victory House, Princes House and Africa House. With its stone face, and heavy with columns, the last of these (also the last to be built) is typical, but not particularly distinguished, although elsewhere in Kingsway the eagle-eyed will spot some unexpectedly nice details such as the mermen on Kingsway House and an angel on Aviation House. The view towards Aldwych and the apsidal entrance to Bush House is also good.

Sadly, having survived the Gordon Riots the old Sardinian Chapel was swept away in the slum clearances needed to clear a route for the road. The oldest of London's embassy chapels (founded in 1648), this formed part of the Sardinian ambassador's residence in Lincoln's Inn Fields and was where Fanny Burney married General Darblay in 1793 (see Mayfair).

Maiden Lane

Prior to the seventeenth century a track ran this way, a noisy alley behind the Bull Inn on the Strand and reportedly named after a statue of the Virgin Mary, which stood at one end. Development began in the 1630s, but for more than two hundred years it was a cul-de-sac with a narrow footpath through to Southampton Street. Residents at this time included the exiled historian and philosopher François-Marie Arouet – better known by his pen name Voltaire – who lived at the White Wig Inn in 1727 and J. M. W. Turner, who was born above a barber's shop at no. 21 in 1775.

The road was only driven through to Southampton Street in order to enable Queen Victoria's carriage to drop her at what is now the stage door to the Adelphi Theatre on the Strand. This entrance was formerly the royal entrance, as evidenced by the arms above the door, to a theatre that was the first in London to have a mechanically sinking stage. Today the plaque next to the door records the murder here in 1897 of William Terriss, who was stabbed three times by a jealous fellow actor. Admitting the crime his assailant, Richard Prince, was declared insane and remained in Broadmoor until 1937.

The site of the old White Wig Inn, Voltaire's former digs, is now occupied by the rear of the Vaudeville Theatre with its large elegant window. An establishment originally built for three actor-owners – Messrs James, Montague and Thorne (nicknamed the Jew, the Gent and the Gentile) – this was where Henry Irving launched his career. Next door and discreet to the point of invisibility the Catholic church of Corpus Christi was designed in 1873 by F. H. Pownell and was the first church in England to be dedicated to the Blessed Sacrament since the Reformation.

Across the street at no. 35 is Rules, the oldest restaurant in London. It has had an uninterrupted run on this same site since 1798, Thomas Rule's establishment first attracting attention for its 'porter, pies and oysters' – most of which are still on the menu today, together with its speciality, seasonal game. Deeply traditional, although

Rules restaurant, Maiden Lane

recently the dress code has been abandoned to favour tourists, the restaurant for a long time had a special door through which Edward VII could enter unobserved when entertaining Lillie Langtry. Other regulars included Dickens, H. G. Wells and Graham Greene.

The Piazza

What has been called London's first successful model of high-style town planning, the 4th Earl of Bedford's highly original piazza, with its noble church and portico and elegantly arcaded blocks of townhouses, was conceived by Inigo Jones (1573–1652). As such it was the capital's first planned residential square, and today this lively and largely open area forms the heart of the area we know as Covent Garden. After inheriting the titles and estates of his cousin in 1627, the 34-year-old Earl had managed to obtain a licence to demolish the poor quality buildings that had clustered around this site and to construct in their place 'a distinguished Ornament', meaning specifically 'houses and buildings fit for the habitations of gentlemen and men of ability'. The permission to do this provided the impetus for what was, in effect, the first attempt in London to create an explicitly elite enclave. Commercially, in 1631, it was also a highly acute move, one designed to take full advantage of the flight of the rich and aspiring classes whose members were being driven west both by a degree of snobbery (in particular the urge to distance themselves from tradesmen) and by the deteriorating environment of a dramatically overcrowded City of London.

The permission cost Lord Bedford £2,000 but fortunately for him he had married a rich heiress, the daughter of Giles Brydges, Baron Chandos (hence Brydges Place and Chandos Street to the west). He was persuaded – required, really – to use Inigo Jones as his chief architect, who, as Surveyor General, was by no means the cheapest choice. In a bid to keep costs under control Bedford agreed that there would an arcade

or colonnade on only two sides of the square with a church at one end and the boundary wall of his own house making up the fourth, southern, side. Knowing this the oft-cited story is believable, that for the new church the Earl insisted on something simple – 'not much better than a barn' – prompting Jones to promise him, albeit at a cost of £5,000, 'the handsomest barn in England'. And St Paul's is certainly that: the building we see today actually a complete but entirely faithful rebuild (after a fire in 1795) but still one of the most outstanding structures in the whole of London. Now famously the 'actor's church', among the memorials are ones to Ellen Terry, Charlie Chaplin, Noël Coward, Gracie Fields, Boris Karloff, Ivor Novello and Edith Evans.

Plain and majestic, visually powerful and highly original, the view of St Paul's that is most commonly seen – of the east end – is actually the rear of the church. (The entrance is in a small garden best entered via one of two passageways off King Street and Henrietta Street.) Jones used the plain and sturdy Tuscan order to make of its huge projecting eaves a really imposing portico, a striking feature that dominates the busy Piazza even now as well as providing what

St Paul's, Covent Garden

Market buildings, Covent Garden piazza

amounts almost to a stage for the street performers who gather here each day. Elsewhere in the square the same Continental influence was evident, the symmetry and design of the façades clearly borrowing from the Palazzo Thiene in Vicenza, while the square itself had more than a few echoes of the Place Royale (now the Place des Vosges) in Paris.

In Bedford's day the aforementioned arcade was a full twenty-two-feet high and the covered walkway almost as wide, the latter a wholly sensible innovation given London's climate but one only very rarely repeated. At Greenwich and Whitehall, Jones had used stone – his client, the sovereign, usefully held the Manor of Portland – but here he worked in brick, creating uniform facades behind which the homes of Bedford's wealthy tenants had their own subtle variations. The houses around the square were all extremely spacious, however, with thirty-foot frontages, coach houses and stabling to the rear, modern 'shuttynge windows' and fifty-foot elevations with an additional eleven feet made up of a pitched roof. Residents of the new square also enjoyed the right to walk beneath the portico of the church, and – crucially – to insist on the removal of anyone therein who caused a nuisance.

Unfortunately, this elegant idyll was not to last: the dual commercial/residential function of the arcade failed to catch on in this country and within forty years the daily presence of the 5th Earl's market meant that socially the area was visibly in decline. Soon the colonnade and houses along the north and east sides began to deteriorate, and the richer residents resumed their westward journey. In due course, sadly, everything Jones built was to be swept away: the south-east side in 1769, the remainder by 1890. His basic concept was to survive – and the space itself, of course – along with some stylistic features he introduced such as giant pilasters running through two storeys. In the north-west corner in 1879, an attempt was also made by Henry Clutton to reproduce the overall effect of Jones's work with his Bedford Chambers.

In the square itself the market buildings are also still highly impressive, their expert restoration a key factor in the area's entirely successful regeneration. These were designed in two parts: the central buildings of around 1830 by Charles Fowler; the aforementioned Floral Hall – perhaps inspired by the Great Exhibition – by E. M. Barry. Fowler's work pays its dues to Jones's splendid church, with a bold but plain exterior of Tuscan granite columns, some as many as three deep, and an entrance at the western end positioned to align with the door of St Paul's. Its central axis is roofed in glass, beneath which are dozens of small but beautifully proportioned shop fronts, mostly still original though the lettering has been redone. Either side of this, two large areas are also protected by glass, each roof supported on iron shafts with slender iron arches. Taken as a whole, positioned in the centre of the great square, it is one of London's most successful compositions: handsome, functional, and delightful.

St Martin's Lane

Around 1610 five acres of land were granted to Robert Cecil, 1st Earl of Salisbury, whose family are still seated at Hatfield House in Hertfordshire. He immediately began development of what was at first called West Church Lane, creating a fashionable residential street with large houses on the west side and tradesmen opposite. Until the construction of Trafalgar Square (on the sloping site of the old King's Mews) the road ran into the Strand.

No. 31 with its large, arched window, and distinctive keystone to the window surrounds, is the oldest surviving building in the street. Otherwise nothing remains of the seventeenth century – including the residences of Sir Joshua Reynolds, Sir James Thornill and Louis-François Roubiliac – nor indeed of the extensive workshops of Thomas Chippendale, father and son. An official London County Council plaque at no. 61 records the latter's sixty-year occupation. No. 62 is the only eighteenth-century survivor in the street, a number of others having been demolished as recently as 1964 to be replaced by offices and a cinema.

There are however a number of attractive public houses, including the Angel and Crown at no. 58 and the extraordinary Green Man & French Horn at no. 54, with its four matching wrought-iron balconettes on the third and fourth floors. The finest however is the Salisbury at no. 90, a particularly well-preserved Victorian public house of 1852. Like a much larger version of the Red Lion in Duke of York Street (see St James's) it displays the same attention to detail in its cut, bevelled and frosted glass, the 'Lincrusta' ceiling and delightful bronzed art nouveau light fittings comprising leaves, flowers and female figures. The derivation of the name is logical, an earlier pub on the site having been called the Coach and Horses and later the Ben Caunt's Head after the celebrated bare-knuckle boxer of that name who in the 1840s owned and ran the pub.

When completed in 1903 the Noel Coward Theatre was called the New Theatre, possibly as it stood opposite the entrance to New Row. It was renamed in the early 1970s after the theatrical director Sir Bronson Albery – son of the original founder, a drunk who died of cirrhosis of the liver – and then again in 2006. In contrast to its classical exterior it has a lively rococo interior that was home to both the Old Vic and Sadler's Wells when these were bombed in the 1940s. The Duke of York's was similarly renamed in 1895 (in honour of the future George V) having previously been known as the Trafalgar Square when it opened three years earlier. In 1904, two days after Christmas, the theatre was the setting for the debut performance of J. M. Barrie's *Peter Pan*.

By far the most striking theatre in St Martin's Lane, however, is Frank Matcham's mighty London Coliseum, which has towered over the southern end since it opened

Coliseum, St Martin's Lane

as the 'people's palace of entertainment' (meaning a music hall) and known at the time for its vibrant Edwardian interior. The largest venue in London at that time, since 1904 the most distinctive feature of this floridly baroque building has been the globe, although for many years the owners were required by the local authority to disable the mechanism that enabled it to revolve. The stage was still permitted to do so, however, and was the first of its kind in London's theatre land.

With a huge seating capacity of nearly 2,400, the Coliseum has been the home of the English National Opera since 1968. As well as the largest proscenium arch in the capital, at fifty-five-feet wide and thirty-four-feet high, a recent remodelling means it now has a rooftop bar affording wonderful views over Trafalgar Square. ENO was formerly known as Sadler's Wells Opera and displaced a 'cinerama' which had been here for many years. With offerings that are intended to be more accessible than the Royal Opera House, performances are given in English and ticket prices are appreciably lower. The stage is immense at 80-feet wide, with a throw of more 115 feet to the back of the balcony, giving scope for productions that are both spectacular and hugely popular.

Savoy Court

Most famously the only road in London on which motorists must drive on the right – although in fact there is another, by Hammersmith bus station – Savoy Court is now the principal entrance to the Savoy Hotel. There is another on the river side, but the main entrance was originally on Savoy Hill (see below). The hotel was commissioned by the great theatrical impresario,

Richard D'Oyly Carte, in 1889. It was located next to his Savoy Theatre, which had been built eight years earlier to stage the increasingly popular light operas of Gilbert and Sullivan. As *The Times* reported in 1881, 'This is the first time that it has been attempted to light any public building entirely by electricity. What is being done is an experiment, and may succeed or fail.' By all accounts it succeeded so the new hotel naturally followed suit, while introducing a host of other notable advances including six hydraulic-electric ascending rooms (or lifts) and what at the time was an unusually high ratio of baths to bedrooms, with seventy of the former for its five hundred guests.

The hotel's architect was Thomas Collcutt (1840–1924), who also built the Palace Theatre at Cambridge Circus and in South Kensington the vast Imperial Institute (of which only the splendid near-300-foot campanile now survives as London's tallest and most covert folly). Whilst as a building the Savoy does not look particularly outstanding, it was designed to compete with the best in America. The first manager was César Ritz (appointed in 1889), its first chef Auguste Escoffier and behind the innovative Doulton tile exterior the luxurious Arts and Crafts interior was fitted out with William

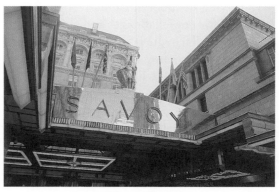

Savoy Hotel, Savoy Court

Morris wallpapers and ceramics by William De Morgan. Its most recognisable feature, the gleaming metallic awning, came somewhat later, in 1929, and was the work of Sir Howard Robertson. Such was the immense prestige of the Savoy in the early days that the house orchestra was briefly led by Richard Strauss – composer of operatic standards like *Der Rosenkavalier* and *Salome* – while he was a guest in the hotel. Similarly, a dishwasher employed in the kitchens was so inspired by the quality of the guests and their spending power that he returned home to Italy and established a luxury goods firm to profit from what he had learned during his time in London. His name was Guccio Gucci.

Thanks to Ritz's dynamic leadership and flair for promotion, the Savoy had quickly become a great success, attracting the rich and the famous not just from Britain but also the rest of the world. At the same time Escoffier – the 'king of chefs and the chef of kings' – had revolutionised London dining by hiring leading French chefs and introducing classic haute cuisine. There was also an important social development: under Ritz and Escoffier, eating out, which until then had been a largely a male preserve, became commonplace for women, who flocked to after-theatre suppers in the Savoy's dining rooms.

Having conquered London society, Ritz looked for new challenges and alongside his job in the Savoy he began to develop hotels on the Continent. Inevitably, the Savoy's takings declined, which led to an acrimonious parting of the ways between the D'Oyly Carte Company and its manager and head chef. Ritz and Escoffier left in 1898, and legal proceedings were started to recover monies the Savoy alleged that its celebrated employees had embezzled. It did César Ritz's reputation little harm and he went on to found many more luxury establishments, including of course the eponymous Ritz Hotel in Piccadilly.

For César Ritz nothing was too much trouble for his guests, a principle adhered to throughout the history of the Savoy. Besides its position overlooking the river, much of the hotel's popularity among the rich depends not just on the approach to luxury – its nearest rival had only four baths, the Dorchester just one for forty bedrooms – but also its commitment to providing whatever its guests desired. Examples of this included allowing the Maharaja of Patiala to take over an entire floor of the Savoy when he and his entourage turned up in 1925. (According to the gossip columns of the time the potentate occupied thirty-five luxury suites and wore special underpants costing more than £200 a pair.)

Twenty years earlier the management had gone even further, flooding the courtyard of the hotel for the American millionaire George A. Kessler, who entertained two dozen guests on a giant, flower-laden gondola floating in the middle. With the courtyard painted to resemble Venice, a giant birthday cake arrived on the back of an elephant as the great tenor Enrico Caruso sang 'Happy Birthday' but unfortunately the occasion was marred slightly by a quantity of dead swans that had been killed off by a toxic blue dye introduced into the hotel's temporary lagoon.

Today it is hard to imagine such a request being made, or indeed granted; but the Savoy's management still tries to satisfy even the strangest request, and for many years has kept a large figure of a cat on hand, known as Kaspar, which in the event of thirteen superstitious friends sitting down to eat is given its own table setting to ward off any bad luck.

Determined to providing the very best standards of service and accommodation to its guests, the Savoy closed its doors in 2007 for the first time in its 118-year history. The reason for the closure was to allow for the complete refurbishment of the hotel in a £100-million project lasting fifteen months. However, by the time it was officially reopened by the Prince of Wales in 2010 the work had taken nearly three years at a cost of £220 million.

Savoy Hill

By virtue of her descent from John of Gaunt, the sovereign, as Duke of Lancaster (never Duchess) owns some 18,200 hectares. This land is quite separate from the Crown Estate and is spread mostly across the Midlands and north-east England. However, a very small part of the Duchy is in central London, and is a relic of the Savoy Palace, which was given by Queen Eleanor to her son Edmund, Earl of Lancaster in the mid-thirteenth century.

The palace disappeared long ago – it was largely destroyed in the Peasants' Revolt of 1381 – but this portion of the estate survives and includes the ground beneath Charing Cross Station and the Charing Cross Hotel, Thomas Collcutt's Savoy Hotel and the adjacent theatre. Also, on Savoy Hill, there is the Queen's Chapel of the Savoy, which dates back to 1510 and once formed part of the Hospital of St John, an establishment for the poor that once stood here. This small and unexpectedly rough stone church became, in 1890, the first place of worship in England to be lit by electricity, and as the personal property of the sovereign remains exempt from Episcopal interference and lies outside the jurisdiction of the church

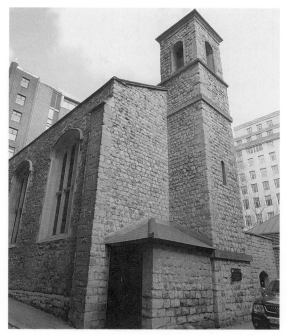

Queen's Chapel of the Savoy, Savoy Hill

authorities. Perhaps to underscore this, the choir traditionally sings its own version of the national anthem: 'God Save our Gracious Queen, Long live our Noble Duke, God Save the Queen'.

Strand

Long enough to link Westminster and the City and conspicuously broad, as the name suggests the old riverside route (from the Old English *strond*, meaning edge) the road known as Strand is now entirely commercial although this stretch of the north shore of the river was grandly residential as long ago as the twelfth century. Illustrations of the time show just how grand, with a procession of immense palaces and inns belonging to various noblemen, courtiers and senior clerics, among them the bishops of Norwich and Carlisle, and the Count of Savoy. A

Wenceslaus Hollar drawing gives a flavour of the place in 1830, with Durham, Worcester and Salisbury Houses lined up along the river and showing the architectural progression from the first (thirteenth century, and more or less a castle) through the Elizabethan gable-jumble of Worcester to the quasi-Renaissance style of the last. In their day these were very much the greatest houses in London – in particular the aforementioned Savoy Palace and Somerset House – the best of them self-contained semi-urban estates that were occupied by important individuals with strong connections to the cities of both London and Westminster, but who were rich enough to escape living cheek-by-jowl in either of them.

As early as the 1500s there were calls for the road to be paved, the original surface being considered 'full of pits and sloughs, very perilous and noisome,' and the Strand as we know it began to take shape. Within another hundred years, the palaces had disappeared, however, some replaced by more modest houses for well-to-do merchants, and the remainder by shops, small traders and low taverns that did little but hasten its decline.

Albeit briefly a little of the prestige it had lost was restored by the construction in 1608 of the New Exchange or 'Britain's Burse'. Built on the site of Durham House, this was a 'place of great resort and trade for the nobility and gentry,' and for a few brief years it was a fashionable place to shop. Today, sadly, it is lost beneath the buildings at nos. 54–64, so perhaps the nearest to it that we can see is along the street at no. 216, home since 1706 of Thomas Twining, the celebrated tea merchant, which claims to be the longest established ratepayer in Westminster. (The firm's logo, created in 1787, is similarly thought to be the world's oldest in continuous use.)

The creation by the Victorians of the embankment cut off the Strand from the river, since when its development has been piecemeal. As a result one finds none of the uniformity that once characterised parts of John Nash's Regent Street, although the length and width of the street would suggest some grandeur. That said, the only attempt to remodel what Disraeli insisted was 'perhaps the finest street in Europe' was indeed made by Nash in the 1830s. Today the creamy stucco of his West Strand Improvements, and the distinctive, diagonally placed 'pepper-pots', are the most obviously impressive feature of the Strand as a whole, although much of what we see –

St-Mary-le-Strand

including the lofty glazed Coutts' Bank at no. 440 – is actually a 1970s recreation by Sir Frederick Gibberd.

There are even so a number of notable buildings scattered along its three-quarter-mile length. By far the most ancient are the two churches, of St Clement Danes and St Mary's-the-Strand, both now on island sites as a consequence of road-widening schemes. The first of these survived the Great Fire of London in 1666 but was later pronounced unsafe and rebuilt in a Baroque style by Sir Christopher Wren. The name is a reference to a Danish settlement thought to have existed in this part of London in the ninth century (see Aldwych) although the evidence for this is slight. Today it is closely associated with the Royal Air Force, as that service's central church, having had the interior destroyed by its German opposite numbers in May 1941. Today many of the most striking memorials have a military connection, and outside are two statues of important wartime leaders, Sir Arthur 'Bomber' Harris and Lord (Hugh) Dowding.

Immediately north of Somerset House (see panel) the second church is St-Mary-le-Strand, whose history has been one of demolition and near-demolition. The original church was knocked down to clear the site for Somerset House, the parishioners resorting to the Savoy Chapel from 1549 onwards when Edward Seymour, 1st Duke of Somerset, reneged on his promise to build them a replacement (and used the stone from their old church for his new palace). In fact they had to wait until 1711 and an Act of Parliament, which created the Commission for Building Fifty New Churches. Construction duly began three years later, architect James Gibbs budgeting £16,000 for his first public building, which was consecrated in 1723.

Twice in recent years the spectre of demolition has stalked St-Mary-le-Strand, the London County Council launching the first attempt (whilst widening the street) before being forced to reconsider. On that occasion only the churchyard was lost, and the graves removed to Brookwood cemetery in Surrey. The second attempt came courtesy of the Luftwaffe, whose bombers caused massive damage to the surrounding streets in the early 1940s, although the church sustained blast damage rather than a direct hit. In 1809, by which time traffic noise was already being considered a problem, its elaborate

'Bomber' Harris statue, Strand

SOMERSET HOUSE

Lost for years to the Inland Revenue, which shamelessly squandered one of the capital's most unexpected and exuberant open spaces by using it as a car park, Somerset House offers spectacular views up and down the river and takes its name from the Strand palace of the sixteenth century Dukes of Somerset. The present building stands on the site of what had been England's first Renaissance palace, built in part using stone salvaged from the demolition of the cloisters of the pre-Great Fire St Paul's but demolished in 1775 by which time it was reportedly highly dilapidated. Its replacement is primarily the work of the Swedish-born Scottish architect Sir William Chambers (1723–96). As Comptroller of the Office of Works he sought, in the name of greater efficiency, to accommodate in one unified structure various government offices, the Navy Board and three centres of scholarship in the Royal Academy of Arts, the Royal Society and the Society of Antiquaries. From the first then this new Somerset House was to be institutional, and constructed on a truly vast scale.

Perhaps inevitably, given that it was public money being spent, there were lengthy debates in Parliament about whether the new buildings should display splendour or economy, convenience rather than ornament. Unexpectedly, the debates mostly came down on the side of splendour, Sir William being instructed to produce 'an ornament to the Metropolis and a monument of the taste and elegance of His Majesty's Reign'. Such a thing is hard to imagine in the present climate but it paid off, because Somerset House is without doubt one of the finest eighteenth-century structures in Britain, even if the original 1775 estimate of £135,700 had spiralled to £462,323 in 1801 when the building work was completed.

Access to the Thames was important because the King's barge-master was also to be accommodated at Somerset House, and of course officers attached to the Navy Board needed to be able to disembark here when travelling up from the docks and depots at Deptford and Greenwich. Living quarters were also required, not just for the chiefs of staff but also on a smaller scale for their many cooks, housekeepers, secretaries and so on. Sir William's solution was to build what was in effect a series of linked townhouses arranged around a quadrangle, with the whole covering more than six acres. Each government department or learned body would then be granted a vertical slice of six

storeys through the terrace, although in the event Sir William did not live to see its completion and James Wyatt was left to carry on and finish the job in 1801.

To maintain the correct scale on such a complex site, two floors of each townhouse were below ground level, wherein – according to one critic – 'the clerks of the nation in these damp, black and comfortless recesses . . . grope about like moles, immersed in Tartarean gloom, where they stamp, sign, examine, indite, doze, and swear'. Others described the finished building as 'a frightful thing' and one that 'exposed to general derision the bad taste of the King, the Government, and the country'. In their defence Chambers and Wyatt might have highlighted the challenges they faced when it came to developing the site, as this included the steep slope down to the river, highly unstable ground and the need to make the most of the lengthy river frontage. Today one is also mindful of the radical changes that have been made in the years since, particularly when increasing congestion – in terms of both traffic and waste disposal – necessitated the building of Sir Joseph Bazalgette's Victoria Embankment, which, whilst necessary and expertly constructed, made a mockery of Sir William's carefully considered elevations and removed the building from its river.

Worse was to come, however, and, during the long years of civil-service occupation, mezzanine floors were carelessly introduced and much of the original joinery removed on health-and-safety grounds. A high proportion of the building was also left empty, and for nearly twenty years, before commonsense prevailed and the civil servants moved on. Today, following a massive programme of restoration, the building, its river terrace and its peerless central courtyard, have been returned to use and together now comprise one of the most majestic and imaginative cultural venues in the capital.

The first real move in this direction came in 1990 when the Courtauld Institute of Art, a college of the University of London, moved into some of the vacated area. The Institute was joined by the celebrated Courtauld Gallery in 1998, the latter taking over, most appropriately, the Fine Rooms: that is the portion of Somerset House originally designed to accommodate the Royal Academy. The Gallery houses works from the Middle Ages to the twentieth century, but is perhaps best known for its splendid collection of Impressionist and Post-Impressionist paintings, as well as outstanding temporary exhibitions.

The Somerset House Trust was formed around the same time, with the aim of developing the House and the open spaces around it for the public. The process was assisted by the forceful and fortuitous intervention of Lord Rothschild, which paved the way for the arrival of new collections of art. So far these have include the superb collection of gold, silver and precious Roman and Florentine mosaics amassed by London-born Sir Arthur Gilbert (1913–2001), the successful property-developer son of poor Polish-Jewish immigrants. Comprising more than eight hundred items, the collection includes pieces created for Louis XV, Napoleon Bonaparte and Catherine the Great. Said to be worth in excess of £75 million in 2001, the entire collection was left to the nation by the previously quiet and unknown collector and funds are being provided by the Heritage Lottery Fund to build a museum to house Gilbert's legacy. Elsewhere in the complex the Hermitage Rooms stages exhibitions of artefacts on loan from St Petersburg's State Hermitage museum, and concerts and film shows regularly take place in the vast central courtyard. In addition, the upper levels of the building have been let to a wide array of cultural and artistic organisations, including the National Youth Orchestra and the Royal Society of Literature.

baroque interior provided the setting for the marriage of Elizabeth Barrow and John Dickens, parents of Charles.

On the north side, the television age has made G. E. Street's Royal Courts of Justice complex one of the most familiar buildings in this part of London. Occupying a huge site of more than eight acres, its construction in 1866–8 required the destruction of entire streets, courtyards and alleyways – more than 30 of them – and the demolition of nearly 350 private dwellings and 60 commercial premises. In their place arose a massive structure, one built around twenty-four courtyards, and comprising more than a thousand rooms in all, and with an estimated 35 million bricks concealed behind the gleaming decorative white stone of its façade.

None of this came cheap. The site cost more than £1.4 million (despite the fact that much of it was slums), building costs for the Gothic structure rose swiftly from £700,000 to more than £820,000 and the final toll included the premature death of Street, who is said to have been overcome by his exertions. The results are impressive, however, with a vast central hall – seventy-five-metres long, nearly twenty-five-metres high – and immense Gothic arches and doorways leading off to the courts, of which there were nineteen although extensions have lifted the total to around sixty. There is also a museum on site, containing examples of court dress, while the colourful stain glass depicting the heraldic achievements of past Lord Chancellors and Keepers of the Privy Seal. In Pevsner's considered opinion, the total effect of Street's creation is 'the greatest secular monument of the Gothic Revival in London after the Houses of Parliament'.

Clearing the site for all this had required the wholesale eviction of an incredible 4,125 inhabitants, residents of what must have been an area of positively medieval over-crowding and squalor, and doubtless one the authorities were glad to see gone. Today

Royal Courts of Justice, Strand

nothing of this remains, although across the street two adjoining houses – standing at the meeting place of Fleet Street and the Strand, the very place where the cities of London and Westminster collide – give one some small idea of this older London.

The original intention in creating the Royal Courts of Justice had been to centralise those superior courts handling civil cases, although more recently criminal trials have been held here to alleviate the considerable pressure on the Central Criminal Court (meaning the Old Bailey in the City). Whilst the Old Bailey remains perhaps the better known of the two buildings the workload is greater at the Royal Courts, and arguably in real terms more significant to the typical citizen of this country. The buildings house the Court of Appeal of England and Wales, which deals with both civil and criminal appeals, and the High Court of Justice of England and Wales, which deals with higher-level civil matters. Perhaps surprisingly, the court buildings are also available to hire, for a wide range of activities ranging from weddings to bar mitzvahs and corporate events.

Until 2003, nos. 229–230 were the premises of a famous if undistinguished club for lawyers and journalists. Called the Wig & Pen, and for years the most tangible evidence of those longstanding ties binding the fourth estate and the profession of law, its former home is a unique and extraordinary building: one half is by far the oldest building in the Strand and the only one to predate the Great Fire of London in 1666. It is thought to date from as early as 1625, and with its overhanging first and second floors is said to have been built on Roman ruins although the evidence for this is not at all clear. The other half is rather more recent, early eighteenth century, but with its

unusual canted bay window it is just as picturesque. Together the pair provides a wonderful contrast in both style and scale to the vast Victorian Gothic complex opposite.

The Embassy of Zimbabwe at no. 429 was originally built for the British Medical Association in 1907–8. It was designed by the young Charles Holden (1875–1960), later to be celebrated for his outstanding work for the new London Underground and for a number of more sensitive commissions undertaken on behalf of the Imperial War Graves Commission following a wartime commission in the Royal Engineers.

His building on the Strand featured a series of sculptures plotting the advance of science and the Ages of Man. These were by the then little-known Jacob Epstein and became something of a cause célèbre when straight-laced Londoners objected in no uncertain terms to his series of nude sculptures. These were eventually modified, although it is possible that certain specifically masculine portions of stonework (one of which reportedly snapped off and hit the pavement) might have been cut back for health-and-safety reasons as much as for reasons of prudishness or aesthetics.

Interestingly the furore had still not died down twenty years later and Holden and Epstein ran into similar problems with a couple of figures called *Night* and *Day*, which formed part of 55 Broadway, the headquarters of London Transport above St James's Park station. With the press enthusiastically fanning the flames of public outrage – Epstein was accused of obscenity, bestiality, pederasty and even cannibalism – the boss of London Transport felt obliged to tender his resignation.

On the south side the so-called Strand Campus of King's College occupies a prominent site next to Somerset House. As well as a couple of brutal 1970s concrete structures the campus includes the lengthy façade of Sir Robert Smirke's Grade I-listed King's Building of 1831, and the college chapel in a contrasting Norman-Byzantine Gothic style, which was remodelled thirty years later by Sir George Gilbert Scott. As recently as 2010 the east wing of Somerset House was incorporated into the college for use by the School of Law, and still on campus by walking through an arched entrance at no. 33 Surrey Street a so-called Roman bath or plunge-pool can be glimpsed through a window. Its provenance is by no means certain, but it is evidently ancient and is now in the care of the National Trust (and signposted accordingly).

One final landmark is the celebrated Simpson's-in-the-Strand at no. 100, originally called the Grand Cigar Divan and a popular haunt of Victorian chess aficionados. Its origins have been traced to 1818, although the first premises became a victim of one of the aforementioned street-widening schemes. It was eventually rebuilt by T. E. Collcutt (see Savoy Court), reopened in 1904 and today is a splendidly maintained Edwardian gem. An attractive plaque on the nearby Coal Hole at no. 91 records a connection with colliers working on the Thames in the early years of the nineteenth century when coal still powered the city and was a major cargo on the river. This semi-subterranean tavern was also the meeting place of the Wolf Club, established in 1826 by the popular actor Edmund Kean as a late-supper club. Its membership was said to comprise henpecked husbands who, amongst many other things, were forbidden by their wives to whistle or sing in the bath.

Simpson's-in-the-Strand

Villiers Street

With much of one side taken up by the towering bulk of the Charing Cross Hotel, in 1864 one of the first buildings in the country to be faced with artificial or reconstituted stone, Villiers Street takes its name from the aforementioned George Villiers, 2nd Duke of Buckingham. It was built in the 1670s on the site of the latter's York House by the physician and land speculator Dr Nicholas Barbon (1640–98), one of the more successful and prolific developers of the Restoration period.

Almost the entire west side of the street was unfortunately cleared to make room for Charing Cross Station and the hotel, the latter at first a significant addition to the London skyline by E. M. Barry with its rich Renaissance detailing, ornate window surrounds or aediculae and mansard roofs. The artificial stone was manufactured by Mark Blanchard, who completed his apprenticeship with Mrs Coade in Lambeth, but unfortunately the finished effect has been spoiled by twentieth-century additions. These include two new storeys, and today it sits uneasily with the recreation of the thirteenth century Eleanour Cross (also by Barry) in the front courtyard.

Among the buildings swept away were the lodgings of the writers Richard Steele and John Evelyn, but at no. 43 is the (much renovated) building where Rudyard Kipling lived in three rooms above a sausage shop in the late 1890s. In *Something of Myself*, a memoir, he describes 'small rooms, not over-clean or well-kept,' and how the 'Charing Cross Trains rumbled through my dreams on one side, the boom of the Strand on the other'. From his window he could see 'through the fanlight of Gatti's Music-Hall entrance, across the street, almost to its stage'. With the decline of music halls generally Gatti's eventually became a cinema, and then a fire station during the Second World War. It is now a conference centre.

Today the most evocative building in Villiers Street is Gordon's Wine Bar at no. 47, thought to be London's oldest. Mostly below street level and largely unchanged since Arthur Gordon first opened for business in 1890, the old wooden walls are covered in historical newspaper cuttings and memorabilia and there is a terrace to the rear. The building originally provided warehousing for a firm of seed merchants but the embanking of the Thames in 1870 reduced their usefulness and prompted Minier & Fair to move on. By a happy coincidence it is still owned by a Mrs Gordon, although she is no relation to the founder.

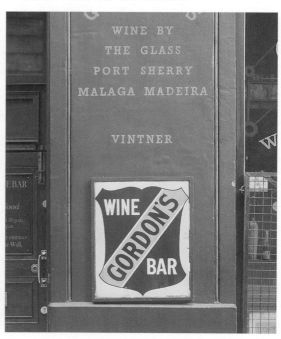

Charing Cross Station, Villiers Street

Gordon's, Villiers Street

WESTMINSTER & WHITEHALL

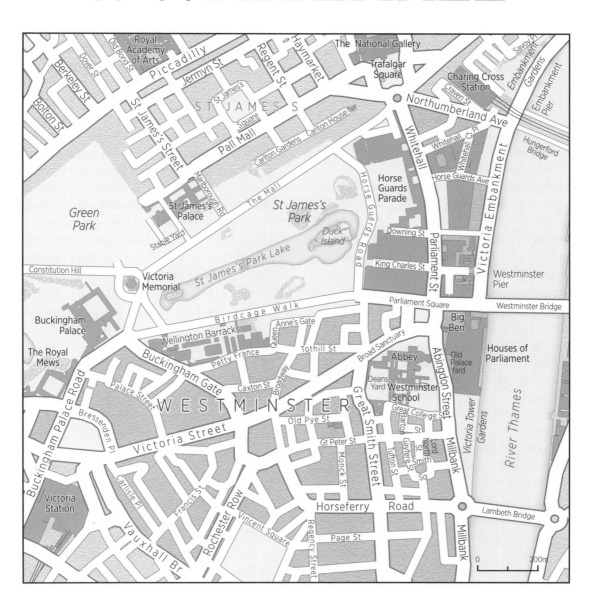

The identity of this area was once quite literally the west minster, a geographical reference to the monastic abbey church of St. Peter's, which lay to the west of the City of London and was thus to be distinguished from the east minster: that is, St Paul's. Historically, the small but uniquely important settlement that grew up around the powerful religious foundation fell within the old county of Middlesex and is therefore not to be confused with the more recently created City of Westminster. Since its creation in 1965 this large and typically diverse London borough, an administrative entity incorporating much of Marylebone and Paddington, has extended as far north as Kilburn and the fringes of suburbia and so lies well beyond the remit of this book.

That first monastic foundation was built around the year 785 on Thorney, otherwise the eyot or island of thorns, and stood on what was possibly the site of a pagan temple dating back to the second century AD. The island was at this time an unprepossessing and low-lying prominence on a bend in the river, and at low tide it would have been possible to walk across to it from Lambeth. Its precise extent is even now not clear, however, although one 1831 account describes its boundaries as approximating to the locations of the eighteenth century Chelsea Waterworks, the Grosvenor Canal and the ornamental water in St James's Park. Choosing to live nearby, Edward the Confessor provided generous support for the foundation, and known for his piety in 1065 consecrated a new stone abbey on the site. Its pre-eminence and proximity to the Crown have rarely been questioned since that time, and quite aware of the powerful symbolism of the gesture William the Bastard took care to have himself crowned in

the Abbey on Christmas Day 1066. (Saxons were also banned from entering the building during the proceedings, to underline their new vassal status.) Over the next thousand years, the Abbey's status ensured that it remained the place of choice for coronations, and it was to become the final resting place of no fewer than eighteen monarchs.

For almost all of that time Westminster itself provided the seat of the monarchy, the Palace of Westminster being adopted as the official London residence of the Crown in the eleventh century and only surrendering this position in 1530 when Henry VIII acquired nearby York Place (from his former favourite Cardinal Wolsey) and renamed it Whitehall Palace. Westminster remained a royal palace in name, but from this point it provided London and the country with a seat of government and justice, the institutions we know as parliament having emerged from the thirteenth century onwards from the king's council. Colonising the abandoned palace as the sovereign and court moved on, Westminster was thereafter used by the two Houses of Parliament and by the various royal law courts. As the seat of both Crown and government, Westminster naturally proved to be an irresistible magnet for those keen to serve or engage with either institution, and grew rapidly. At the same time this physical separation of royalty, civil administration and justice from the commercial hub of London was to have far reaching and enduring impacts on the development of the capital as a whole with London growing to accommodate its swelling population but commercial interests remaining largely within the old City walls.

Of course business was being transacted in Westminster too, and among the early traders listed as residents one finds William Caxton working as a dealer in Continental luxury goods. As a sometime governor of the Company of Merchant Adventurers of London, and trading 'at the sign of the Red Pale,' he observed printers during his travels to Cologne and famously came home to produce the first printed document in England: a religious indulgence dated December 1476. Alongside Sir Walter Ralegh, he is buried in the churchyard of St Margaret's Westminster.

As the presence of a printer might suggest to the modern reader, Westminster by this time would have been quite as noisy, busy, filthy and unhealthy as any other town in England, indeed unhealthier than many thanks to its position on a marshy and sometimes pestilential stretch of the river. Today nothing could be farther from the truth, with this very specific part of the borough now boasting one of the highest life expectancies anywhere in the country. (This evidently declines as one travels east, one recent health study indicating that, travelling along the Jubilee Line to Canning Town, one loses the equivalent of one year of life per stop.)

Crime was also rife in Westminster's early days, in large part due to the proximity of another of London's immense slum areas or rookeries (which stood where Victoria Street is now) and a number of other areas of chronic poverty, such as the rundown eighteenth-century terraces of Parker Street and Princes Street. This longstanding but particularly undesirable aspect of the local economy worsened during the sixteenth century, a time when many of those who made a slender living supplying goods to the court and its hangers-on resorted to criminal enterprises when the monarch left the

capital on one of the many interminable progresses around the country.

More than four hundred years later the names of Broad Sanctuary and Little Sanctuary allude to this, as indeed does a public house called the Sanctuary in Tothill Street, commemorating the ancient tradition of criminals and other fugitives finding refuge from the law in and around the Abbey. (Sharing similar origins, the name of Thieving Lane has sadly disappeared from maps of the area, although it is interesting to note that the buildings of Her Majesty's Treasury now occupy much of the same ground.)

Barton Street

Barton Street and its extension Cowley Street were built by Barton Booth (1681–1733) who left Westminster School for Trinity College, Cambridge before taking to the boards and enjoying a considerable reputation. He was twice married, the second time to a Drury Lane dancer. Hester Santlow was the mistress of the 1st Duke of Marlborough and is occasionally considered Britain's first ballerina. Booth's country house was at Cowley, hence the name, near to where he lies buried in Uxbridge. A number of houses in Barton Street – including nos. 1, 3–7 and 9–14 – are original, with one or two thoroughly convincing copies.

At the junction of the two streets lived Lord Reith, the first director general of the BBC. He broadcast news of the start of the General Strike in 1926 from his study at 6 Barton Street, but later abandoned the 'dirt and confinement' of London life for the countryside. Between the wars the architect Sir Herbert Baker (see Dean's Yard, below) kept an office at no. 14, and, in 1922, he

*House at junction of Barton Street
and Cowley Street*

agreed to sublet the attic to Lieutenant Colonel T. E. Lawrence, whom he knew from Oxford. Initially the man memorialised as Lawrence of Arabia found it 'a haven of peace,' and as such a much-needed release from a life characterised by the battle between his addiction to self-promotion and an almost pathological desire to be left alone.

It was during this period that he worked on the final draft of his memoir, *Seven Pillars of Wisdom*, a replacement for an earlier version of the 250,000-word document which he had lost at Reading railway station. Despite finding Sir Herbert's attic 'the best and freest place I ever lived,' Lawrence went on to buy a plot of land in Epping Forest. There he built himself a simple hut where he could swim in peace and read, resigning his commission and reinventing himself as 'Aircraftman Ross' after joining the ranks of the RAF. Soon afterwards he was reborn again as 'T. E. Shaw' of the Royal Tank Corps, but was quickly outed by the *Daily Express*, although it is hard not to suppose that in part at least this was what he had wished for.

Birdcage Walk

Forming part of the redevelopment of St James's Park from a hunting ground, the name refers to a royal menagerie and aviary created on this site for James I and expanded by Charles II. These are mentioned in the diaries of both Pepys and John Evelyn, nearby Storeys Gate taking its name from one Edward Storey who was the Keeper of the King's Birds in the 1660s. On 18 August 1661, Pepys recorded a visit here and how he saw 'a great variety of fowl which I never saw before,' an experience shared by many modern visitors to a park that is said (erroneously) to be home to every species of duck known to science. Evelyn's diary entry a few years later went into rather more detail, observing 'the extraordinary throat of ye Onocratylus, or Pelican . . . a melancholy waterfowl brought from Astracan by the Russian Ambassador,' and commenting on how 'diverting [it was] to see how he would toss up and turn a flat fish, plaice or flounder, to get it right into its gullet'.

Birds of another kind entirely were also present here in considerable numbers, namely those involved in a popular but brutal sport on which Londoners and others gambled for many years. The area was home to one of the capital's many cockfighting venues, its presence commemorated by a small Grade II* listed passageway called Cockpit Steps, which links Birdcage Walk and Old Queen Street. The pit itself was once the meeting place of a group characterised by one early nineteenth-century visitor as 'a collection of peers and pickpockets, grooms and gentlemen, *bon vivants* and bullies'. By this time, however, public opinion was turning against such activities, and in 1835 cockfighting was finally banned in England and Wales although it took

Cockpit Steps, Birdcage Walk

they belong to Queen Anne's Gate (q.v.) and Old Queen Street and hold their gardens on a special licence from the Royal Parks authority.

Notable exceptions to this are the Institution of Mechanical Engineers at no.1, which was founded by George Stephenson in Birmingham in the 1840s. It moved to London in 1899, into a new red brick and Portland stone building (by Basil Slade) which featured several notable innovations for the time. These included an electric ascending room or lift, an electric fan in the main lecture theatre, a single telephone and a 'Synchronome', which provided central control over all the clocks in the building. In 1943 the building accommodated those members of the Royal Electrical and Mechanical Engineers (REME) who were involved in planning the D-Day landings, and two years later Frank Whittle came here to unveil his new jet engine to the public.

By far the most prominent building, however, is the large complex of the Wellington Barracks at the western or palace end. This provides a London base for the five regiments of Foot Guards, the earliest structures on the site dating back to 1833.

another sixty years for people north of the border to follow suit.

Until 1828 Birdcage Walk itself was still a strictly private thoroughfare, reserved for the sovereign's family and successive Dukes of St Albans. This was by virtue of their position as England's hereditary grand falconers, the 12th Duke, Osborne de Vere Beauclerk, Earl of Burford, Baron Vere of Hanworth and of Heddington (1875–1964) famously choosing to boycott the 1953 coronation when he was refused permission to attend with a live falcon on his arm. (Palace officials tactfully suggested he wear a stuffed bird instead, but Obby as his friends called him declined and striking out for America was subsequently observed taking a Greyhound bus from coast to coast.)

Today most of the buildings on Birdcage Walk merely back onto it. Strictly speaking

Wellington Barracks, Birdcage Walk

These are by Sir John M. F. Smith and Philip Hardwick, but the barracks include many newer buildings as well such as a major block completed in 1985, a museum that is open to the public and the Guards' Chapel.

The latter was dedicated in 1963 and replaced one with a 'neat and imposing exterior, both chaste and elegant,' which was lost on 18 June 1944 following a direct hit by a German V1 bomb. The attack happened at eleven o'clock during the morning service, killing 121 military and civilian worshippers and seriously injuring another 141, although the news of casualties was suppressed at the time. With masonry ten-feet deep in parts, the altar somehow remained undamaged and candles placed upon it were said to have stayed alight. Very few inside emerged unscathed, however, possibly only the Bishop of Maidstone who was conducting the service and was sheltered by a Byzantine apse that resisted collapse. Among the dead was a royal favourite, Lord Edward Hay, commanding officer of the Grenadiers and heir presumptive to the Marquessate of Tweeddale.

Broad Sanctuary

The stretch of road running from Parliament Square into Victoria Street, and sandwiched between the Abbey and Middlesex Guildhall. The name commemorates the Sanctuary Tower which until its demolition in 1776 stood on the site of the Guildhall. In John Strype's *Survey* it appears as 'a very handsome broad and open Place, adjoining to St Margaret's churchyard, from whence it is severed by a Wall, and hath the Prospect of the Abbey'. Today it is dominated by the angular Queen Elizabeth II Conference Centre, which occupies the site of the old

Supreme Court, Broad Sanctuary

Westminster Hospital and whose aggressively modern style seems unfortunate in such a prominent and historic location.

In Strype's words a place 'formerly of more Note than at present,' fugitives arriving in Broad Sanctuary and the aforementioned tower would have expected to be protected from the authorities by the sacred character of the Abbey. However, in practice, this ancient tradition was more honoured in the breach than the observance. In Richard II's time a judge was dragged away to the gallows, in 1440 the Duchess of Exeter was denied sanctuary entirely after being accused of witchcraft, and in 1483 the young Richard, Duke of York was surrendered by his mother and then murdered at the Tower of London with his brother, Edward V. During the reign of Elizabeth the privileges of sanctuary were severely curtailed – by this time only debtors were eligible – and James I abolished even this right two years before his death in 1625.

Now expensively refurbished to house the Supreme Court of the United Kingdom and the Judicial Committee of the Privy Council, the aforementioned Middlesex Guildhall or Sessions House was completed in 1913. During the eighteenth and nineteenth centuries these so-called sessions had been held in a building by Thomas Rogers on Clerkenwell Green, and with officials wielding more power than those in ordinary magistrates courts this new building occasionally served as a supplementary court to the Old Bailey.

It was designed using ornamental Gothic forms by J. S. Gibson and today displays a profusion of carved allegorical figures and heraldic symbols by Henry Charles Fehr (see Russell Square). By 1965, however, it had lost its original function following the abolition of Middlesex and with it the county council and the associated sessions. Thereafter the building continued to be used for a while by the Greater London Quarter Sessions, and later still as a Crown Court.

Now repurposed once again the exterior of the Grade II* listed building has remained unaltered but unfortunately the remodelling of the building to meet the needs of the Supreme Court has involved the removal of many important interior features. This was something conservation lobbyists fought hard against, but lost; most obviously they objected on the self-evident grounds that 'no other owner [but the state] would be allowed to strip out interiors of this quality on the basis of a vague promise to display a few key pieces in the basement'.

Broadway

The Old Star pub at no. 66 has long been a popular watering hole for members of MI6 (see Queen Anne's Gate) but, as Pevsner was quick to observe, 'Broadway architecturally means no. 55'. The address was the headquarters of what is now Transport for London, Charles Holden's design being in a very real sense London's first and oldest skyscraper.

Arguably none but Holden would have attempted to design such a building, nor did others at that time have the very considerable technical expertise needed to pull it off. At 175-foot tall, and with a cruciform ground plan of more than 31,000 square feet, in 1929 this conspicuous monument in steel, bronze, granite and marble (and nearly 80,000 cubic feet of Portland stone) was unlike anything London had seen before and it is still a quite remarkable piece of work.

55 Broadway, by Charles Holden

Indeed it is so tall that it breached the existing London County Council fire regulations, which were so inflexible that for more than a decade the bright, sunny offices in the central tower (being beyond the reach of ladders) were simply deemed too high to be safe. It must nevertheless be considered a success, both structurally and aesthetically. The cross-shaped plan made for bright, well-ventilated offices and pleasantly short corridors; at the same time eight dramatic carved reliefs at sixth-floor level (and the use of Portland stone) defused any accusations that the architect was simply following in the wake of America.

That said Holden's creation was not without its detractors, many of whom objected to the use of avant-garde artists to create the friezes. The latter include Eric Gill, Henry Moore and Jacob Epstein (see Covent Garden and Strand). Of these, once again, it was the last-named who caused the most upset, with particular objections being voiced about the physical attributes of two of his figures, called *Night and Day*. More than three-quarters of a century later it is tempting to wonder what all the fuss was about – you need binoculars to see anything – but at the time the outrage was such that one group of protesters attempted to conceal the offending items by throwing globs of tar from the ground while an anonymous businessman offered to pay to have Epstein's figures removed.

Eventually, with the *Daily Mirror, Express, Manchester Guardian, Times* and *Telegraph* all whipping up a frenzy in their editorials, and the boss of London Transport offering to resign, the sculptor reluctantly agreed to reduce the dimensions of one key piece of stonework. Holden himself was not censored, but promised not to commission any

Epstein sculpture, Broadway

more work from Epstein, although the two of them had been working together since at least 1912 when they had collaborated on Oscar Wilde's tomb in Paris.

Buckingham Gate

Linking Buckingham Palace Road and Birdcage Walk before turning south to intersect with Victoria Street, Buckingham Gate still contains a handful of eighteenth-century houses including one particularly early one at no. 16. Completed in 1706, it is thought to be the work of William Winde (1645–1722) who turned to architecture when his military career ended, switching from fortifications to private commissions and gaining a reputation as one of the leading English country-house architects of his day. His portfolio of works includes Belton House in Lincolnshire for the Brownlow family, Combe Abbey in Warwickshire for the Earl of Craven, and the 2nd Duke of Buckingham's Cliveden House. For the latter he also designed Buckingham House at the far end of Buckingham Gate, although this has subsequently been entirely subsumed into Buckingham Palace.

At no. 10 we find the offices of the Duchy of Cornwall, designed by Sir James Pennethorne, who included the feather motif of the Prince of Wales on the columns between the railings. In existence since Saxon times, the Duchy belongs to the Prince of Wales personally and remains his private possession until the moment he accedes to the throne when it passes to his heir. As the name suggests it is based principally in the west country but in London includes around 1,500 properties south of the river in Kennington where the Black Prince, Edward of Woodstock (1330–76) had his palace.

When Edward was created Duke of Cornwall at the age of seven it was the first appearance of a ducal title in the English hierarchy. Today the Duchy comprises some 128,000 acres in nine counties, together with 230 potentially valuable miles of foreshore, 14,000 acres of 'fundus' or riverbed, and 40 acres of inner London.

The latter includes the Oval cricket ground and some of Lambeth's most attractive buildings, these being traditional in style, small in scale, but perfectly proportioned. Providing not just attractive housing for the people of London but also a very persuasive lesson in how to rebuild small, urban communities, these could be said to fit perfectly with the philosophies of the present Prince of Wales and to exemplify his popular, well-argued support for the sort of architecture designed to give charm and character to a city. In the Prince's own words the best of the Duchy's London estate – areas such as Courtney Square and Denny Street – comprises 'civilised architecture employing the simplest of means. . . . Not of the finest materials, nor richly decorated, nor on a grand scale. [It] works because of its proportions and straightforward detailing.'

Back in Buckingham Gate, St James's Court, the immense hotel and restaurant complex at nos. 45–51, was completed in

Fleur de Lys, Buckingham Gate

St James's Court, Buckingham Gate

BUCKINGHAM PALACE

With the present edifice fashioned around the core of the Duke of Buckingham's old town house, Buckingham Palace (at that time Buckingham House) was added to the royal portfolio of properties only in 1761 when it was acquired by George III. Not until the accession of Victoria in 1837 did a British head of state move here permanently, and even now Buckingham Palace is only the sovereign's actual residence with the official residence still across the park in St James's.

Over more than two-hundred-and-fifty years it has been modified in many stages and very extensively, John Nash, Edward Blore, Thomas Cubitt, and most recently Sir Aston Webb being among those who have worked to refashion the original core. Between them they have built such considerable extensions that it is no longer even faintly recognisable as the ducal home it once was. Some of the modifications are quite surprising too, such as the conversion before the Second World War of a small pavilion at the rear to accommodate an indoor swimming pool for the two princesses, Elizabeth and Margaret.

George III bought Buckingham House from Charles Sheffield, illegitimate son of the Duke of Buckingham, for £21,000. The main reason for the purchase was to secure a domestic idyll for his beloved queen, Charlotte, away from the pressures of court. The arrangement clearly suited the uxorious monarch: she was delivered of fourteen of their fifteen children in what soon became known as the Queen's House. George spent a good deal of money on alterations, most of which were rather haphazard, and in consequence was much criticised, with one commentator describing them as 'a mere jumble of patchwork'.

George III's descent into madness led to a regency being established in 1811. This was under the eldest son, the future George IV, and remained in force until the king's death in 1820. Unfortunately, the new king was dissolute and distinctly less than dutiful, and was thought to have secretly (and illegally) married a widow. (That Mrs Fitzherbert was six years his senior and a Roman Catholic only made matters worse.) He was also extravagant, running up huge debts thanks to his mania for gambling and his propensity for favouring female friends with expensive jewellery. His spendthrift nature extended to property – he was largely responsible for the spectacular Royal Pavilion in Brighton, designed by his friend John Nash – and a few years into his reign he decided that he needed a residence the equal of any crowned head in the world.

The plan was to demolish the Queen's House and to replace it with a fine new palace by Nash. When the politicians baulked at the latest example of his extravagance, the Prince instead renamed his grand designs 'renovations' and was then able to inveigle the huge sum of £252,000 from Parliament to pay for the work. (The final cost was closer to £1 million).

Unfortunately, the ageing Nash came up with a scheme that pleased virtually no one and his design was excoriated for an exterior of 'general feebleness and triviality'. If there were any saving graces, they came in the shape of the many elegant apartments and also the imposing Marble Arch that led into the forecourt. (The Marble Arch was later moved to its current site north of Hyde Park.) But in the event this was of little moment as George IV was never to live in his grand palace: on 26 June 1830, in Windsor Castle, he died of a stomach haemorrhage and was barely mourned by his subjects.

The new king, William IV, younger brother of his predecessor, hated Buckingham Palace, as it had become known by the early 1830s. Although Nash's scheme was in the process of being completed by a new architect, Edward Blore, William proposed it as a new home for the legislature when the Houses of Parliament burned down in 1834. 'Mind, I mean Buckingham Palace as a permanent gift – mind that,' he told the politicians, who did not take him up on the offer. Although William later famously changed his mind and declared he was desperate to move into Buckingham Palace he was in such a weak state by the time work was completed in 1837 that he was never able to call it home. He died a month later, meaning that the first monarch officially to live there was Queen Victoria.

Victoria and Albert's main concern about Buckingham Palace was that it was too small for their rapidly growing family, which came to encompass nine children, forty grand-children and dozens of great-grandchildren. Blore's 1847 solution was a new east front across the courtyard, and modifications to Nash's north and south ranges. Few admired the result, however, and it fell to Webb – whilst positioning the Queen Victoria Memorial and building Admiralty Arch – to reface the entrance front in an inoffensive neo-classical style and to have done it in time for the coronation of George V. Including the now world-famous balcony, he completed the task within three months, an astonishing achieve-ment by any measure. Today few would hold up Buckingham Palace as one of London's finest architectural features – typically Edwardian, Webb's hasty work has been likened to a provincial bank – but it remains an authentically global icon before which many hundreds of thousands assemble each year to be photographed.

As a consequence of Blore's extensions, Victoria was frequently to complain that the distances involved in moving from one wing to another made living here 'so fatiguing', while her son Edward VII described the finished result as a sepulchre that he found no more comfortable than 'the Highland Barn of a Thousand Draughts' (as he called Bal-moral). Equally disparaging, George V likened it to a grand hotel, George VI to 'an ice box' while his elder brother, Edward VIII, was still complaining about its 'dank, musty smell' long after he had been reduced to a duke and exiled to France.

To no-one's surprise the present sovereign does not express an opinion about it either way, although it has long been noted that at the first opportunity she and Prince Philip leave for Windsor Castle. In a sense any negative feelings are perhaps hardly surprising: with more than 828,000 square feet of floor space – included among its 775 rooms are

240 bedrooms and 78 bathrooms – Buckingham Palace is in no sense a family home. Nearly a hundred rooms are offices, and clearly much of the vast machinery required to run a modern constitutional monarchy operates from within this singular building.

There is nevertheless much to admire about the palace's interior. The grand hall with its marble columns and nymphs opens out into the magnificent grand staircase in Carrara marble, exquisitely lit by Nash's glass dome. Prominent among the state apartments are the Green Drawing Room, the scarlet-and-gold Throne Room with its frieze depicting the Wars of the Roses and the 155-foot Picture Gallery with its array of old masters. The Queen hosts state banquets in the Ballroom, which is also the venue for her subjects to have honours conferred on them. Art lovers can view paintings from the royal collection in the Queen's Gallery, located on the south side of the palace. This is a quite extraordinary treasure chest that draws on a collection of seven thousand pieces, several times larger than the collection owned by the National Gallery.

For many years, this place has also been the most important focal point for celebrations in the country, a very real symbol of the monarchy, the capital and Great Britain as a whole. This clearly is why no-one cares that it is not an architectural masterpiece or indeed even regarded as such by anyone who knows it. Winston Churchill appeared with the royal family on Aston Webb's balcony to greet the crowds celebrating VE Day on 8 May 1945; decades later people came from all over the world to see Prince William and Kate Middleton kiss on the very same spot; and few of us are immune to the sight of the Battle of Britain Memorial Flight swooping low over the Mall with the sound of their Merlin engines breaking through the imperial strains of Sir Edward Elgar.

In the final analysis there is only one observation left to make, which is that in ways large and ways small Buckingham Palace has played – and continues to play – a key role in Britain's national consciousness. For this reason if no other, one might thus paraphrase a historian from English Heritage and ask: who should care that what visitors to the capital are looking at is no more than a mongrel of early-nineteenth and early-twentieth-century elements carelessly assembled around an early-eighteenth-century core? With such a building as this, the answer is surely no-one.

1899 to a design by Charles James Chirney Pawley, its red-brick and white stone bands highlighted by exceptionally elaborate hammered-ironwork and fancy corbelling. 'Ostentatious in materials and colour' according to Pevsner, it originally comprised eight proximate blocks of serviced apartments, the best of them overlooking an internal courtyard which is even more showy than the street façade, with jade and primrose-coloured faience decoration, blue columns and colourful friezes featuring Shakespearean characters. H. G. Wells nevertheless chose to live at no. 52, and at other times the street was home to William Gladstone (who lived briefly at no. 20) and the poet Wilfred Scawen Blunt whose blue plaque is at no. 15. The latter, an inveterate womaniser, also kept a flat by Victoria Station for his not infrequent trysts.

Caxton Street

Named for the pioneer printer, Caxton Street has two buildings of particular note in the former Blewcoat School – now a National Trust shop – and the nineteenth century Caxton Hall, which in recent years has been converted into apartments.

With its idiosyncratic spelling and an air of being slightly marooned among the office blocks, the Blewcoat School is not to be confused with the Bluecoat School, the popular name for the sixteenth century Christ's Hospital, which relocated from the City to Sussex and is still thriving. Instead this much smaller establishment was founded in the year of the Glorious Revolution to teach fifty poor children of the parish of St Margaret's to 'read, write, cast accounts and the catechism'. The present building dates from 1709, and was endowed by a local

Blewcoat School, Caxton Street

brewer called William Greene. By this time there were more than fifty charity schools spread across the City of London and Westminster and this one remained in use as a school for the next 230 years before in 1939 being taken over by the army for the duration of the war. The figure of a charity boy still stands above the door, although from 1713–1876 the school also educated girls.

Designed in a French medieval chateau style by William Lee and F. J. Smith in the 1870s, Caxton Hall was for many decades the register office of choice for celebrity marriages. These included those of Peter Sellers, Elizabeth Taylor and Ingrid Bergman, and musicians Yehudi Menuhin, George Harrison, Ringo Starr, Adam Faith and Mick Jagger. Not unnaturally, this aspect has tended to overshadow its arguably more historic role as an important place for protest and lobby groups to gather, somewhere close to Parliament where rallies could terminate and public meetings assemble to promote diverse political and social aims. Key meetings in the distinctive red-brick-and-pink-sandstone hall included several organised by members of the suffragette movement, and, in the 1940s, press conferences on behalf of the wartime

Ministry of Information. In 1907 leading suffragette Christabel Pankhurst and seventy others were taken from Caxton Hall into custody, and more than fifty of them were eventually confined in Holloway prison. (In this connection a nearby memorial commemorates 'the courage and perseverance of those men and women who, in the long struggle for votes for women, selflessly braved derision, opposition and ostracism'.)

In March 1940 the hall was similarly used to host a conference held under the auspices of the East India Association and the Royal Central Asian Society. During the proceedings one of the speakers, Sir Michael O'Dwyer, a former Lieutenant Governor of the Punjab, was assassinated by a fanatical supporter of the Indian independence movement. Shaheed Udham Singh had waited nearly twenty-one years for his revenge, after witnessing the so-called Amritsar Massacre in the gardens of Jallianwala Bagh. The 1919 atrocity, in which as many as a thousand people lost their lives with hundreds more injured, had been ordered by Reginald Dyer, a brigadier general in the British Army, and for a long time it was supposed Singh had confused the two men. However, the existence of a cable from O'Dwyer to Dyer congratulating him on preventing a revolution implicated the writer and seems to have sealed his fate. Despite an enquiry finding no evidence of such a revolution, Shaheed Udham Singh was hanged at Pentonville Gaol on 31 July 1940.

Constitution Hill

Popularly supposed to be where Charles II liked to take his morning constitutional (for which there is no evidence) the slight gradient of the hill separates the gardens of Buckingham Palace from Green Park and was the scene of several attempts on the life of Queen Victoria. The first failed regicide was perpetrated by an unemployed 18-year-old Londoner called Edward Oxford. On 10 June 1840 the Queen was out for her daily carriage drive with her beloved Prince Albert. When she passed Mr Oxford, he cocked his pistol and fired two shots in her direction, both of which missed. There was quite a crowd on Constitution Hill that day and they mobbed the hapless Oxford, shouting 'Kill him, Kill him!' Although he was charged with high treason – which, of course, brought with it the threat of being sent to the gallows – Oxford was delighted by the attention his nefarious act had attracted. At his trial he was found guilty but insane and sentenced to life in a mental hospital. The last attempt on Victoria's life here took place in 1849 and it is interesting to note that none of the perpetrators hanged for it.

Just a year later, in June 1850, the former prime minister, Sir Robert Peel, was thrown from his horse here and died of his injuries three days later. Peel had been out for his normal early-evening ride on a new horse, one that had a reputation for bucking. After signing the visitors' book at Buckingham Palace, the great statesman set off for home in Whitehall Gardens. However, when he came across friends, who were also on horseback, his less-than-reliable mount threw him, tripped and landed on Peel's prostrate body, breaking many of his bones in the process. Despite receiving the best medical attention available, he died an agonising death on 2 July 1850. His passing dismayed the many hundreds who had gathered outside his house, desperate for information on his condition, and millions more up and down the country. Peel had been prime minister in 1846, the year in which the Corn Laws were repealed, a measure he saw as essential despite the bitter opposition of many in the Tory party, which of course he led. Forced to resign a short time thereafter, many saw Peel's actions as the ultimate example of principle before political expediency.

The road has never been built upon, but there is a notable memorial of recent construction. Completed in 2002 and inaugurated by the Queen in November of that year, it commemorates the more than five million African and Asian subjects of the Empire who served alongside Allied forces in two world wars. Largely of Portland stone, Indian granite and bronze it names only holders of the Victoria Cross and George Cross, but lists India, Pakistan, Bangladesh, Sri Lanka, Africa, the Caribbean and Nepal as the territories from which invaluable support twice came during Europe's hour of need. Taking the form of a gateway, it is used to close the road to wheeled traffic on Sundays and public holidays.

Dean's Yard

Hidden from view this surprisingly large private courtyard is best entered through the neo-gothic archway forming part of a stone-faced office building on The Sanctuary designed in 1854 by Sir George Gilbert Scott. Unauthorised vehicles may not enter the yard, but pedestrians may do so either through the archway or via a small passage running off Great College Street. The lawned quadrangle comprises in part those surviving portions of the former monastery precincts that are not occupied by the Abbey. It is known simply as 'Green' by the

Church House, Dean's Yard

pupils of Westminster School (see separate entry) who reserve a supposedly ancient right to play football here. Unusually for London, the space itself is larger now than in previous centuries, following the demolition of the old monastic granary which for many years served as a dormitory for the school's Queen's Scholars and occupied the southern end.

Stone from the granary still underpins Church House, which occupies the whole of the south side and part of Great Smith Street, a 1930s structure designed by Sir Herbert Baker and opened by George VI. With its large Great Circular Hall and immense statue of Christ (by Charles Wheeler) the administrative headquarters of the Church of England provided a new home for both the House of Commons and the House of Lords following the wartime

Westminster School, Dean's Yard

Westminster Abbey behind Dean's Yard

bombing of the Palace of Westminster. Church House was itself struck in 1940, resulting in the deaths of six people.

On the east side is the entrance to Little Dean's Yard and Westminster School, while on the west is the Westminster Abbey Choir School and a number of small residential properties. The latter command predictably high prices on the rare occasions they come up for sale. Among the Yard's former residents can be identified Henry Purcell who died here and is buried close to the organ in the adjacent Abbey, the eighteenth-century Scottish feminist poet and author Charlotte Lennox, and the bookseller Edmund Curll (c. 1675–1747), who grew rich through a policy of publishing anything that would sell, including pornography and scandalous tittle-tattle.

In 1679, a group of King's Scholars famously killed a man in Dean's Yard, reportedly a bailiff who is thought to have entered the school in order to pursue the impecunious mistress of one of their number. Incredibly, Dr Busby – the school's headmaster for some fifty-five years – sought and managed to obtain a royal pardon for the boys, the grounds for his appeal being that the man had breached the sanctuary of the Abbey despite (as previously noted) this having long since been abolished. The document, signed by Charles II, is still in the possession of the school.

Downing Street

Coming from an entirely respectable Suffolk family (his mother was Lucy Winthrop of Groton, whose brother John was the founder and first governor of Massachusetts)

WESTMINSTER SCHOOL

With buildings dating back more than nine hundred years, and at one time fees of just a shilling a day for boarders, Westminster School's ancient origins lie with the early medieval establishment for the training of clerks attached to the pre-Conquest Benedictine Abbey. One of the earliest known documents associated with the school is the royal charter of 785 AD, which makes reference to buildings in 'the terrible place which is called Westminster'. None survives of that antiquity, however, although the number of ancient structures crammed into what is really quite a small site still offers a uniquely rich and rewarding part of the Abbey precincts for the casual explorer.

The room known as School, for example, dates back to the eleventh century, when it would have formed part of the old monastic dormitory. From 1602 for nearly three hundred years this same building housed the entire school population for lessons, the older and younger boys being separated by no more than a curtain slung from an iron bar down the middle of the room. The bar is still there, incidentally, and each Shrove Tuesday a pancake is hurled over it after which the students compete to grab and hold onto it. The lucky winner used to receive a guinea from the Dean, a substantial prize, but these days an iTunes voucher seems more likely.

College Hall Cloisters, now the refectory, is relatively modern and in 1376 would have been the abbot's state dining hall, and Ashburnham House newer still, Pevsner identifying it as the best example in the capital 'of a progressive and stately mid seventeenth century house'. The curious shape indicates that it was built onto the side of an existing structure, and indeed part of the red-brick façade (by John Webb, son-in-law of Inigo Jones) conceals a fourteenth-century rubble wall, a surprising feature in a building of this period and prestige.

The dormitory block known as College is also worthy of note, originally drafted by Wren, a former pupil, but executed by Lord Burlington. Completed in 1730, as a replacement for an old dormitory block that was housed in a medieval granary, it is modelled on Palladio's study of the Roman baths at Agrippa and his own cloister at San Georgio Maggiore. Unfortunately, it was badly damaged in the Second World War and with the original ground floor colonnade of fifteen bays now glazed rather than open, it looks somewhat less remarkable than must once have been the case.

Sir George Downing (1632–89) was a soldier, spymaster and turncoat described by Pepys as a 'perfidious rogue'. Whatever the truth he was certainly shrewd enough somehow to serve both Cromwell and Charles II and to gain a baronetcy whilst doing so. After a spell in the Tower of London, he managed to manoeuvre himself into a position where he could both afford and obtain a valuable parcel of land adjacent to Whitehall, land on which had once stood a brewery owned by the Abbots of Abingdon. In the 1680s Sir George built 'foure greate houses . . . fronting St James Parke west and east' in a position John Strype described forty years later as 'a pretty open place especially at the upper end . . . fit for persons of honour and quality'.

Today just three houses are extant (the south side was redeveloped as government offices in 1868) these being numbered 10, 11 and 12 and all now interconnected. Of these the most famous is, of course, no. 10: indeed with its much-photographed front door it is among the two or three best known addresses in the world. However, it was originally no. 5 and comprised two houses.

Until the 1730s the lease was held by a Mr Chicken, the office of the First Lord of the Treasury (as the earliest prime ministers were known) at that time conferring no special benefit on the holder with respect to living accommodation. Most being rich men preferred to stay in their own homes, Sir Robert Walpole abandoning his much larger house in St James's Square only at the request of George II. He did so on the understanding that the house would not be a gift to him personally but instead would 'be & remain for the use & habitation of the first Commissioner of his Majestys Treasury [sic].' Mr Chicken and his neighbour Mr

Scroop were accordingly moved on, and, after the two houses were expensively adapted to their new role, no. 10 became the official residence of the British prime minister. Extremely modest by the standards of the White House or the Elysee Palace, it has not always proved a popular choice however.

Tony Blair famously chose to live next door, while Harold Wilson only pretended to live in Downing Street and after being photographed pipe in hand going through the famous doorway would nip back to his own home in Lord North Street (q.v.) and light a large cigar. As long ago as the 1880s Lord Salisbury similarly preferred to commute from Hatfield House in Hertfordshire rather than make his home in Downing Street, and the only prime minister to die there was Henry Campbell-Bannerman in 1908, his wife having already labelled the place the 'house of doom'.

Fortunately, others felt differently, such as William Pitt the Younger who reportedly liked the place and missed it when he left office. More recently Baroness Thatcher described to the author of the house's unofficial biography 'how much I wish that the public . . . could share with me the feeling of Britain's historic greatness which pervades every nook and cranny of this complicated and meandering old building'. All prime ministers, she insisted, 'are intensely aware that, as tenants and stewards of number 10 Downing Street, they have in their charge one of the most precious jewels in the nation's heritage'. As the centre of government it has inevitably been a target for enemies of the state: despite the elaborate security measures, IRA terrorists were still able to set off a bomb there in 1991. It was planted in the garden of no. 10 and just a few

Downing Street

Security gate, Downing Street

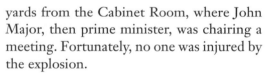

yards from the Cabinet Room, where John Major, then prime minister, was chairing a meeting. Fortunately, no one was injured by the explosion.

The interior of no. 10 has many highlights. The Cabinet Room is arguably the most important apartment in the land, the location for weekly Cabinet meetings, chaired by the prime minister of the day. For obvious reasons the room is soundproofed, allowing ministers to engage in vigorous debate without being overheard. It was enlarged in 1796 by knocking a wall down and inserting two pairs of magnificent Corinthian columns to carry the extra span. The grand staircase, in the centre of the house, is one of the best-known parts of the house. Installed in the 1730s at the behest of Walpole, the walls that surround it are adorned by portraits of every prime minis-

ter in British history. The elegant State Dining Room was designed by one of Britain's finest architects, Sir John Soane, in 1827 and also functions as the venue for the prime minister's regular press conferences. Other apartments worthy of note include the Study, the Terracotta Room and the White Drawing Room.

Next door, no. 11 serves as the official residence of the Chancellor of the Exchequer. It too has a number of fine rooms, not least the State Dining Room, which was also designed by Soane.

Gayfere Street

Quiet but extremely conveniently located (and eternally popular with those Members of Parliament who can afford to live in the locality) Gayfere Street was laid out in the

Cast-iron grilles, Gayfere Street

*South wall Westminster Abbey,
Great College Street*

1720s and with its often quite modest, two-storey terraces now forms part of the conservation area centred on Smith Square. In 1990 it was from a private house in Gayfere Street that supporters of Mr John Major launched the campaign to secure for him the leadership of the Conservative Party.

Some of the yellow-stock brick houses are now divided into apartments and have not been listed; others are post-war, neo-Georgian. Nevertheless the street as a whole still gives a very good impression of the eighteenth century; and in common with many of these smaller streets in the immediate vicinity several houses still have the original iron boot scrapes set into walls and cast-iron grilles where their front light wells are set beneath the pavement. Period coal-hole covers are also still quite common in this part of Westminster, many produced locally by 'A. Smellie' of Rochester Row, as are the scratchy remains of several black-and-white signs that were stencilled onto the brickwork in the 1940s directing residents to air-raid shelters.

Great College Street

Developed in 1722, Great College Street follows the course of a southern tributary of the Tyburn stream and is still dominated along nearly the whole of one side by the long southern wall of the Abbey precinct, an authentic medieval relic, with attractive arched gateways. Nos. 16–19 are Grade II* listed, and again one finds a good selection of decorative ironwork, much of it nineteenth century, on the south side of the street. Many far older discoveries have been made here too, however, including part of a Roman structure, a second-century Roman statue and evidence of a thirteenth-century corner tower and a medieval ditch. Around 1900 the same site yielded a seventeenth-century bellarmine or 'witch-bottle', still corked and containing old pins and rusty nails thought to have been used for some arcane magic rituals.

Great Peter Street

Originally a narrow footpath from St Peter's Abbey running behind the several acres of vine gardens utilised by the monks along Millbank, development of Great Peter Street began in the 1620s and today the road extends as far as Horseferry Road.

On the north side, in St Matthew's church, can be detected the hands of two great Victorian architects. The church was built around 1850 to a design by Sir George Gilbert Scott, with colourful stained glass and embellishments by some of the leading ecclesiastical designers of the day, including George Frederick Bodley and Charles

St Matthew's church, Great Peter Street

North House, Great Peter Street

Eames Kempe. The Lady Chapel was completed forty years later, the work of the Aberdonian, Sir Ninian Comper, one of the last great Gothic Revivalists.

Unfortunately, St Matthew's was gutted by fire in 1977, and only rededicated seven years later after a major programme of restoration, but the chapel is now recognised as one of Comper's finest early works. St Matthew's owes its origin to William Buckland, Oxford's first professor of geology, who famously claimed – and was frequently to demonstrate – that he could tell where he

was in the country simply by tasting the local topsoil. A distinguished geologist who fathered an even more distinguished (and equally eccentric) naturalist, he spent the last eleven years of his life as Dean of Westminster. During that time his wife found herself deeply disturbed by the social conditions evident in the shadow of the great church, an area known as the Devil's Acre, which was flanked on all sides by disreputable taverns, brothels and the like. To alleviate the problems that resulted she persuaded the Dean to build a new church in the parish, together with a parish school and other amenities, and St Matthew's is the result.

On the opposite side of the street are two interesting Grade II* listed buildings, North House and Gayfere House, both of the early

Gayfere House, Great Peter Street

1930s. Designed by Oliver Hill (1887–1968) their Queen Anne style, with construction materials of red brick and Portland stone, is typical of this area. The houses were conceived at a time the architect found himself gradually abandoning Arts and Crafts for Modernism as his career progressed. Barely two years later, he completed the Midland Hotel in Morecambe, a radical Streamline Moderne design that could not contrast more strongly with what he accomplished here, but his career was badly interrupted by the war and did not recover afterwards.

Horse Guards Parade

Horse Guards Parade is a display area that lies to one side of Horse Guards Road.

Horse Guards, viewed from Whitehall

Originally the old tilt or jousting yard of the Palace of Whitehall, London's principal parade ground was in use for this purpose until the reign of James I, when so-called Accession Day tilts combined elaborate theatrical elements with jousting, poetry and pageantry. Since then it has traditionally provided the backdrop for official displays and reviews, most obviously Trooping the Colour on the sovereign's official birthday and Beating Retreat. In 2012 it was used for activities forming part of the London Olympics.

The unashamedly martial character of the ground is exemplified by a number of bronze statues of British Empire heroes, including three field marshals – Lords Kitchener, Wolseley and Roberts – and a Turkish gun 'taken in Egypt by the British Army, 1801'. Similarly on Horse Guards Road stands Gilbert Ledward's large Great War memorial 'To the glory of God and in memory of the officers, warrant officers, non-commissioned officers and guardsmen of His Majesty's Regiments of Foot Guards'. Erected in 1926, it features representations of members of the Grenadier, Coldstream, Scots, Irish and Welsh regiments cast from German guns captured during the First World War. On the parade ground itself the Cadiz memorial – a French mortar mounted on a Chinese dragon – commemorates the raising of the siege of that city in 1812 by Wellington's forces. Almost exactly forty years later the funeral procession for the Iron Duke formed up here.

For many years, some five hundred civil servants were given the right to park on the parade ground (the so-called 'Great Perk' for senior grades) and many of them fought hard to prevent the right being overturned. However, since 1997, vehicles have been

Cadiz Memorial, Horse Guards Parade

barred, and now only the monarch is still permitted to drive through the central archway of Horse Guards without special permission being first sought and obtained. Guarded during the day by two mounted troopers, conceivably the most photographed individuals in London on any given day, the arch is technically the formal entrance to St James's Palace. Historically anyone else permitted to drive through the arch was identified by an ivory token provided for this purpose.

Happily the vast empty space left by the departing civil servants allows visitors a glorious uninterrupted view from the park of the buildings that surround it, including Horse Guards itself, which replaced an earlier Carolingian building. The present, exceptionally elegant, Grade I-listed Palladian structure was built between 1751–3 by John Vardy to a design by the late William Kent. Until 1906 it housed the offices of the commander-in-chief of the home forces and his successor the Chief of the General Staff. Today it is the headquarters of two army commands, the London District and the Household Cavalry. Seen from the park – with the London Eye and the towers and domes of Whitehall Court behind it – the early evening silhouette of Horse Guards forms part of the most magical skyline in the capital.

In the north-west corner is one of London's most recognisable but most mysterious

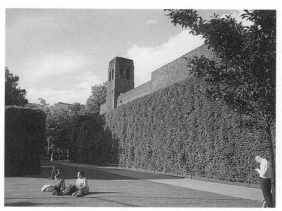

Admiralty Citadel, Horse Guards Parade

Churchill War Rooms, Horse Guards Parade

buildings, the Admiralty Citadel. This was constructed in 1940–1 as one of several bomb-proof operations centres in and around London, secure beneath a twenty-foot concrete roof and with foundations extending at least thirty feet underground. Linked by tunnels to several government buildings on Whitehall (and according to rumour Buckingham Palace) it was also fitted with gun loops so that *in extremis* it could provide a last bastion or redoubt in the event of a German invasion.

In an early volume of his bestselling *The Second World War*, Sir Winston Churchill describes it as that 'vast monstrosity which weighs upon the Horse Guards Parade' and – always a great enthusiast for underground hideouts – he wryly observes that 'the demolition of [its] twenty-foot-thick steel and concrete walls will be a problem for future generations when we reach a safe world'.

In this he was proved right and today, in much the same way that the Home Counties are still scarred by the gaunt husks of disused pillboxes, the relative indestructibility of the Citadel has allowed this unique if unlovely building to survive long beyond the war that gave it meaning. Encouraging

Russian vine to colonise the exterior has helped to some degree, and as the stone frigate HMS *St Vincent* it has continued to be of value to the Ministry of Defence although its precise use is not known.

The Churchill (formerly the Cabinet) War Rooms have their entrance on Horse Guards Road but run under Whitehall, where they are described.

Lord North Street

A precious survivor in that it is an almost complete street of the 1720s, Lord North Street was originally 'North Street' as it exited Smith Square in that direction. It was subsequently renamed after Frederick North, 2nd Earl of Guilford (1732–92) who was known by the courtesy title of Lord North for most of his political career. Only North House, which is dated 1930 and by Oliver Hill, is not original. Like other streets in the small grid around Smith Square, Lord North Street has long been popular with politicians, including Brendan Bracken, Walter Elliot and the disgraced Jonathan Aitken. As previously noted, the Labour prime minister Harold Wilson so much

Lord North Street houses

Jewel Tower, Old Palace Yard

preferred it that he used to return here from Downing Street when the television crews had finished for the day, and continued to do so even whilst believing it was bugged by MI5. The street also provided the last home of Sibyl Colefax, the *salonnière* and co-founder with John Fowler of the eponymous Brook Street, Mayfair interior decorators. Lady Colefax died at no. 19 in 1950.

Old Palace Yard

Of which not much remains beyond a pair of semi-detached houses, now offices, by John Vardy. It was however the execution site for Ralegh and for Guy Fawkes and several of his co-conspirators. Today the chief point of interest is perhaps an analemmatic sundial, designed by Quentin Newark as a gift from Parliament to mark the golden jubilee in 2002 of HM Queen Elizabeth II.

Distinctive granite paving and gas lanterns define the extent of the yard, which technically is still part of the Palace of Westminster. Vardy's two houses clearly masquerade as an eighteenth-century Palladian country house, particularly as the pair now stands in quite splendid isolation with Parliament to one side and on the other the so-called Jewel Tower of Edward III. Built around 1365 to house his treasures, but correctly termed the King's Privy Wardrobe, the latter is one of only two buildings from the medieval palace to have survived the fire of 1834. It features a wonderful fourteenth-century ribbed vault, and overlooks College Green where television news crews traditionally congregate to interview politicians and political commentators.

PALACE OF WESTMINSTER

On 22 October 1834, the old Palace of Westminster burned to the ground. A rambling, somewhat makeshift clustering of buildings that had grown haphazardly around the part-Norman Westminster Hall, what had been the centre of government for more than three centuries had fallen victim to a couple of careless workmen, who, keen to get home, had overstocked a wood-burning stove. The great building that replaced it, the House of Commons at one end and the House of Lords at the other, is thus less ancient than many visitors to Parliament suppose.

The confusion is understandable, and arises in part as a consequence of the ancient ceremonials performed within its walls and in part from the authorities' decision to accept only Gothic or Elizabethan designs from the ninety-seven architects who competed to build a replacement and win a £1,500 'premium'. In the event a mere half

dozen of those submitted to the selection committees looked Elizabethan, and today the creation of Charles Barry and the depressive and volatile Augustus Welby Northmore Pugin is to be counted among the finest and most famous neo-Gothic buildings anywhere in the world.

As a leading classicist, cautious and practical, Barry would ordinarily have favoured an Italian style and so placed a good deal of responsibility on the 23-year-old Pugin, the son of a French artist father whose job it was to make architectural drawings of medieval buildings such as Lincoln Cathedral. It was while travelling with his father that Pugin became inspired by the Gothic style, a process that would find its ultimate expression in the Palace of Westminster, his greatest creation. The quality of his ebullient, imaginative and largely self-invented Gothic Revival style had already been established at Scarisbrick Hall in Lancashire, and now, in London, Pugin claimed never to have 'worked so hard in my life for Mr Barry'. Shortly after completing the project he subsided into madness, collapsing and dying at just forty; but in the Perpendicular Gothic Palace of Westminster he has the finest possible monument, the happy result of an almost perfect partnership.

Very soon to be Sir Charles, Barry's contribution was typically hugely advanced for its day, his technical tour de force being the cast iron, brick and limestone-clad Elizabeth Tower on the northernmost corner, completed in 1858. Originally just the clock tower this British icon was renamed in June 2012 to honour Queen Elizabeth II, who was celebrating her Diamond Jubilee. The Elizabeth Tower's bellchamber houses the thirteen-ton bell universally known as Big Ben, as well as the great clock. The great clock chimes quarterly, while Big Ben bongs on the hour. According to one historian, Sir Robert Cooke, the Elizabeth Tower at Westminster 'has become the symbol of a nation and one of the most familiar landmarks in the world'. Cooke goes on to argue, with some justification, that the unit of great clock and bell 'is undoubtedly the most celebrated timepiece devised by modern man'. Maintenance apart, clock and bell rarely fall silent: they have only been stopped intentionally twice since the war, on both occasions for the funerals of prime ministers: Sir Winston Churchill in January 1965 and Baroness Thatcher in April 2013. Note also, at the other end of the Palace, the magnificent Victoria Tower, which soars to a height of 323 feet. The lower part is the royal entrance to Parliament and the Tower has eleven floors in all.

Despite Barry's undoubted flair, it is Pugin's work that most catches the eye, the beautiful, minutely detailed coloured drawings with which he impressed the selection committee being successfully translated into reality; hugely intricate detailing covering every aspect of the building's interior. Not just doors, walls and windows, but everything from locks to latches, floor tiles to fireplaces, woodcarvings, stained glass and furniture, was to be covered in Pugin's picturesque ornamentation.

At the heart of the building are the two debating chambers, but walking through such an immense building visitors to the Lords and Commons rarely fail to be struck by how small – and intimate – they are, perhaps forgetting how much more goes on there in addition to the great parliamentary setpiece of prime-minister's questions. For ceremonial purposes, for example, the Palace still retains its original style and status as a royal residence; more prosaically it houses the offices of literally hundreds of members, noble and otherwise, and battalions of functionaries and support staff. In fact, with nearly nine hundred feet of private river frontage, the building covers an extraordinary eight acres in all, and comprises more than 1,100 rooms, which are organised around a series of open courtyards.

Much of the original fabric was badly damaged in a series of eleven successful air raids carried out by the Germans in the 1940s, in particular the almost total destruction of the House of Commons on 10 May 1941. After the war Sir Giles Gilbert Scott was commissioned to rebuild, a process that took no less than five years. During the period of refurbishment MPs used the House of Lords, which had been made available by peers volunteering to decamp to the Robing Room. Scott was required to respect and retain the traditions of the old building so that, from a decorative standpoint, the building is still as impressive as it is extensive. Frescoes in the robing room by William Dyce, for example, retell the Arthurian legends, and, in the royal gallery, with its glorious Minton tiles, Nelson and Wellington are commemorated in works by Daniel Maclise, each one some sixty feet in length. Elsewhere in the building lavish mosaics depict the patron saints of the four countries of the United Kingdom, and in the corridors and lobbies – the antechambers where members congregate either side of debates – are life-size statues of leading statesmen and women. These include Gladstone, Lloyd George, Churchill and Lady Thatcher.

There are distinct differences between the two chambers. The House of Lords was built for the State Opening of Parliament, rather than as a venue for the day-to-day deliberations of the upper house. It is, in consequence, elaborately ornamented, and according to one commentator, 'the finest specimen of Gothic civil architecture in Europe; its arrangements and decorations perfect'. There is so much to admire in the Lords: the intricately carved wood; the perfectly proportioned stained-glass windows with their splendid representations of kings and queens; the statues of Magna Carta barons in their niches; the gold throne, with canopy, used by the sovereign for the state opening of Parliament every November. Proceedings in the Lords are overseen by the Lord Chancellor, who sits resplendent on the Woolsack, a large, wool-stuffed cushion covered in red cloth.

The House of Commons offers a contrast to the Lords, although not an unwelcome one. Scott's design for the post-war reconstruction of the chamber, although much criticised by his 1950s contemporaries for its plainness and functionality, is much admired today. Small in size – it has seats for only 427 of the 650 MPs – the House is divided into government benches on the west side, with the opposition parties facing them. This layout – unlike continental legislatures with concentric or semi-circular chambers designed to foster a spirit of consensus – contributes in no small measure to the famously adversarial nature of British politics, a tendency seen to best advantage at Prime Minister's Questions on a Wednesday afternoon.

The wartime damage to the Palace of Westminster was devastating: on the night of 10 May, the building is known to have taken at least a dozen hits with three lives lost. However, by happy chance what is arguably the most precious fragment survived: the ancient Westminster Hall, which, while neither as well known as 'Big Ben' nor as iconic, is the West End's oldest surviving interior. From an architectural standpoint it is also among the most impressive, with Norman foundations and lower walls, and the earliest hammer-beam roof in the country, supported by immense external buttresses and estimated to weigh around six-hundred tons. One of the most atmospheric buildings in the capital – much of the wood- and stonework dates back to the reign of Richard II – this long, lofty, cathedral-like space has witnessed some of the most momentous events in English history. With footsteps echoing on the stone floor – 240-feet long, and nearly 70-feet wide – it is hard not to feel the weight of this on first entering. In the past it has been the scene of jousting and banquets for Christmas and coronations (the last such feast being in 1953) but also of trials and torments of many famous historical figures.

Guy Fawkes was put on trial for his life in Westminster Hall and condemned to death, as was King Charles I before Cromwell had himself proclaimed Protector in the same building. More than three hundred years earlier it was in Westminster Hall that Edward II abdicated in favour of his 14-year-old son, and in his own rebuilt hall that Richard II was deposed by the Lords of Council so that Henry IV, incidentally the first English king to have two English parents, could be placed on the throne. More recently the bodies of Edward VII, George V, George VI and his widow Queen Elizabeth the Queen Mother were brought here to lie in state, their coffins marked at each corner by a silent honour guard. Also that of Sir Winston Churchill, the only commoner to be so honoured in the last hundred years.

Today it forms the entrance used by most members of the public visiting the Palace of Westminster – how many realise, one wonders, that a guided tour is available to anyone writing to his or her MP? – and it is hard to conceive of a more splendid approach to what the building's most famous biographer, the late James Pope-Hennessy, described with an engaging simplicity as 'this great and beautiful monument'.

Palace Street

Exiting Victoria Street and curving up towards the Royal Mews, Palace Street is a rich mix of office and residential buildings, less distinguished in appearance than the name and postcode might suggest, but not without interest.

From 1641 this area was dominated by industry, Watney's Stag Brewery eventually growing to take in more than six acres of production and storage facilities although by the 1930s it was definitely something of an industrial anomaly in such a central and otherwise reasonably prestigious area. The demolition and development of the site in 1959 (when the brewers removed to Mortlake) means that much of Palace Street was then taken up by large office developments and apartment blocks. More recent redevelopment of the 1960s Stag Place means that the effect is now not unattractive, but the loss of the tall boundary wall of the brewery is regrettable. The north side is far more interesting than these modern additions, however, and more attractive with a number of interesting survivors. These include simple, but solid, workers' homes (provided by the brewer) Westminster City School in mid-1870s Gothic brick and, on the corner

Palace Street – old

with Wilfred Street, a pleasant industrial building with attractive terracotta detailing. The Cask and Glass, on the same side of the street, is one of the smaller pubs in London, but deservedly popular.

Some Georgian townhouses have also survived, the best at nos. 25–31 being for the managers of the brewery, although many others in this and adjoining streets such as Stafford and Catherine Place are neo-Georgian or neo-Queen Anne but very nicely done. At 1 Buckingham Place, for example, the building is not authentically Georgian although the interior includes a number of genuine eighteenth-century fixtures and fittings. Now the headquarters of the Royal Warrant Association, it will be recognisable to fans of the cult 1960s television series from the opening credits of *The Prisoner*.

Palace Street – new

Until June 2002 Palace Street was home to the monolithic Westminster Theatre, depending on one's taste an enigmatic or sinister 1965 replacement for the eighteenth century Charlotte Chapel, which stood immediately north of the Phoenix tavern. As well as a working theatre the building was a memorial to the members of the Moral Re-Armament movement who gave their lives in the Second World War. After it was largely destroyed by fire a question mark hung over the site for many years, but a new 312-seat auditorium called the St James Theatre opened in 2012 and has been pulling in audiences.

Parliament Square

Too noisy both night and day ever fully to be enjoyed, the square overlooked by Westminster's palace and abbey was laid out by Charles Barry, who was keen to create a suitably stately approach and vista for his new Houses of Parliament. Formerly it had been a large area of slums and other mean dwellings, and today the only residents are statesmen cast in bronze, chiefly the greats of Imperial Britain – such as Palmerston, Disraeli, Canning and Peel – but also the South African Smuts and Abraham Lincoln. The most recent additions are Nelson Mandela and Winston Churchill, the latter lightly electrified to keep the pigeons off but with insufficient power to deter demonstrators who frequently gather here and have been known to tamper with the great man's likeness.

On the south side is St Margaret's, Westminster, the parish church of the House of Commons and where many MPs have chosen to marry or seen their children marry. The church traces its origins to a

Sir Winston Churchill, Parliament Square

group of Benedictine monks in the twelfth century (the Pope controversially attempted to remove it from the jurisdiction of the Bishop of London) although much of what we see today, including the tower, dates from the eighteenth century when the old church was refaced in Portland stone. The interior, however, still retains some rare Tudor elements, including some early sixteenth-century Flemish glass. This was a gift from Spain's Ferdinand and Isabella on the betrothal of Prince Arthur to their daughter Catherine of Aragon, but following the

Church of St Margaret, Westminster Abbey

Government offices in Great George Street, from Parliament Square

prince's death (and Catherine's hasty remarriage to Arthur's brother, the future Henry VIII) much of the glass was quietly removed to Waltham Abbey in Essex. Despite its immediate proximity to the Abbey, and the fact that the rector is traditionally a canon at the Abbey, St Margaret's has played a very full role in the history of this part of London. Charles II's mistress the Duchess

of Cleveland was baptised here (see St James's chapter), Pepys, Milton and Churchill were married here and Sir Walter Ralegh was buried here following his beheading nearby. The churchyard – which is now cleared and grassed – also contains the remains of many leading Parliamentarians who had originally been interred in Westminster Abbey before their bodies were removed on the orders of Charles II and buried here in an unmarked pit.

Petty France

With no known connection to the South Gloucestershire hamlet, the name Petty France is of obscure origin although the presence here of a community of French merchants in the sixteenth century has been suggested. The address itself is certainly an old one, the street being described in Hatton's *New View of London* (1708) as being 'a considerable street between Tathill Street, E., and James Street, W.'. Former residents include John Milton, Jeremy Bentham and John Cleland, who famously secured a government pension on the understanding that he would 'write nothing more of the same description,' as his scandalous *Fanny Hill*. Unfortunately, none of their houses has survived.

For readers of a certain age the address is synonymous with a last-minute queue for a new passport – the Passport Office relocated to Pimlico in 2001 – and today the street is still dominated by government buildings. Chief among these is the forbidding bulk of the Ministry of Justice at no. 102. Formerly known as 50 Queen Anne's Gate, when it was part of the Home Office, the fourteen-storey 1976 tower was designed by Fitzroy Robinson & Partners in association with Sir

Ministry of Justice, Petty France

Basil Spence. Nicknamed the Lubianka by those condemned to work within its walls (after the KGB headquarters) it replaced Queen Anne's Mansions, which had also been of fourteen storeys. The latter was described in an 1897 court circular as 'a stupendous pile which, for solidity, comfort and general convenience, sets all rivals at defiance' but its presence greatly upset Queen Victoria whose view of Parliament was ruined. (She may have had a point. For many years the complex with its technologically advanced hydraulic lifts was the tallest residential building in the world.) Past residents included Sir Edward Elgar, the colonialist and explorer Sir Henry Hamilton Johnson, and Frederick Quin (see Bloomsbury chapter) the pioneering homeopath who unable to cure his own asthma died here of complications in 1878.

Queen Anne's Gate

Very much a street of two halves, Queen Anne's Gate comprises the former Queen Square, laid out around 1704, and L-shaped Park Street, which was developed later that same century with a gateway in to St James's Park. Until 1873 the two were separated by a high wall, the position of which is now marked by the statue *Anna Regina* outside no. 15, thought to have occupied a plinth against a wall in Queen Square as early as 1708. Representing the late queen wearing the Collar and George of the Order of the Garter, and carrying the Orb and Sceptre, the figure is of high quality but the artist remains unknown.

Perhaps the most striking thing about the street itself is the unusually high proportion

Queen Anne, Queen Anne's Gate

of survivors among the attractive brown-brick terrace houses, several of which on both sides of the street have exceptionally richly carved door canopies, a final flourish of individuality and ornamentation before the Building Acts of 1707 and 1709 imposed a more rigid and uniform Georgian taste on London as a precaution against fire. These and others in the street also have carved keystones (in the form of heads) to the straight-headed windows, and particularly at the western, Queen Square end it can be said that London has nothing finer of the period.

Mostly of three storeys with stone bands, hipped roofs and dormer windows, and from three to five bays, several houses have been extended upwards although the original pattern can be seen in nos. 15, 17 and 26. The slightly jarring redbrick addition known as no. 34a – adjoining the premises of the St

Queen Anne's Gate

Stephen's Club – is more recent, early twentieth century, by Detmar Blow. So too is the building beyond the entrance to St James's Park, no. 36, which might have been designed entirely to disrupt the unity of this beautiful street. Curiously, given this, it was for a long time the headquarters of the National Trust, but was originally designed (in 1909) for the Anglo-American Oil Company.

Since *The Spectator*'s relocation from Doughty Street (see Bloomsbury chapter) the venerable political weekly has been based at no. 22, and, for many years, the house at no. 21 was occupied by officers of the Secret Intelligence Service, MI6. In the 1720s the house had been owned by trustees of the South Sea Company (of 'bubble' fame) but from 1909 until his death in 1923 it served as both home and office for Captain Sir George Mansfield Smith-Cumming, the first chief of MI6 and with his codename 'C' the model for author Ian Fleming's taciturn, pipe-smoking 'M'. It was during this period that a secret passageway was constructed between the house and the MI6 head-quarters building at 54 Broadway, although it is not known if this is still extant.

With his artificial leg and twelve siblings, Smith-Cumming was perhaps the street's most enigmatic resident, but by no means the most illustrious. Today this small enclave boasts half-a-dozen blue plaques, including the former foreign secretary, Sir Edward Grey, at no. 3, the eighteenth-century antiquarian and British Museum trustee Charles Townley at no. 14 and Lord Palmerston, who was born at no. 20. The house at no. 16 has two plaques, commemorating the abolitionist William Smith MP (who was Florence Nightingale's grandfather) and Admiral of the Fleet Lord Fisher OM, who on being elevated to the peerage chose as his motto the punning *Fear God and Dread Nought*.

Today's no. 28, which as 10 Queen Square was one of the first houses to be built, was for many years home to Viscount Haldane of Cloan, Secretary of State for War from 1905–12 and twice Lord Chancellor (once for the Liberal interest and then again for Labour). Haldane's house was remodelled by two leading twentieth-century architects, both of whom were neighbours. Sir Edwin Lutyens at no. 17 created a new library for the great man, and Sir Aston Webb at no. 19 subsequently returned the house to its eighteenth-century glory.

The Sanctuary

From the Sanctuary, at the west end of the Abbey, rises one of London's most photographed but least known memorials, Sir George Gilbert Scott's red granite Westminster Column. This was erected in 1881 in memory of those Westminster School old boys who fell in the 'Russian and Indian Wars AD 1854–1859' meaning in the Crimea and in the troubles following the 1857 Indian Mutiny. Surmounted by a depiction of St George dispatching the dragon, the figures beneath are by sculptor J. R. Clayton and represent Edward the Confessor and Henry III as the builders of Westminster Abbey, Queen Elizabeth (who re-founded Westminster School) and Queen Victoria who is shown facing down Victoria Street.

The column stands on the site of the former Gatehouse Prison, built around 1370 by the Abbey cellarer Walter de Warfield and only completely demolished in the nineteenth century, more than 450 years later. Its inmates over that time included Sir Walter

Dean's Yard entrance, Sanctuary

Westminster Column, Sanctuary

Ralegh, the night before his execution in Old Palace Yard, the seventeenth-century poet Richard Lovelace – who penned the line insisting that 'stone walls do not a prison make, nor iron bars a cage' – and Samuel Pepys. Today, however, the only building on the Sanctuary is a large Gothic structure by Gilbert Scott, the Bath-stone façade of which includes the gateway to Dean's Yard (see above).

Scott's Grade II* listed terrace of eight properties, owned by the Church Commissioners, has for many years accommodated the Vicar General's Office for marriage licences, and the Faculty Office, which has its origins in the sixteenth century Ecclesiastical Licences Act. This gave the Archbishop of Canterbury the authority to grant 'all maner licences, dispensacions, faculties, composicions, delegacies, rescriptes, instrumentes or wrytynges [that] have byn accustomed to be had at the see of Rome'. In the 1930s the building was also briefly the London headquarters of Sir Oswald Mosley's British Union of Fascists, their vaunted leader perhaps won over by Scott's more than usually Germanic mock-medieval style.

Smith Square

Developed in 1726 on behalf of the ground landlords, a family called Smith, this is the heart of one of London's most engaging and coherent conservation areas, although large-scale redevelopment on two sides means it is by no means the jewel.

On the north side a handful of eighteenth-century townhouses have survived, including nos. 8 and 9, which, once a single dwelling, were home to Sir Oswald Mosley during his marriage to Lady Cynthia Curzon, the younger daughter of the Indian Viceroy. Together with nos. 4–7 and no. 9 it is the best house in the square, nos. 1 and 2 being pastiches as are many on the west side of the square, which was flattened during the war. That said: no. 36, a Lutyens design of 1911, is also of interest. The detailing on the original houses is delightful, however, rusticated door cases, pilasters and decorative ironwork giving the dark brickwork a perfect lift.

The same cannot be said for many of the newer developments, which, besides any individual merits, serve mostly to dominate the square having usurped a role correctly belonging to the church of St John's in the centre. This is a large and audacious baroque design by Thomas Archer, a contemporary of Sir John Vanbrugh. Distinguished by its broken pediment, decorative triglyphs and radical, curved surfaces, this was the second of the fifty new churches to be built following the 1711 Act (see Covent Garden and Strand) and with its four semi-circular lantern towers also the most expensive. The church is known locally as 'Queen Anne's footstool', a popular but unsubstantiated tale suggesting that Her Majesty upended the relevant piece of furniture when the architect was canvassing opinions as to how his new church should look.

Costing well over £40,000, despite a number of specific economies such as cupolas on its towers where Archer had drawn pinnacles, it was gutted by fire just fourteen years after its consecration, and then again following a German air raid in 1941. In the 1960s the decision was taken to remodel the Grade I building as a concert hall – its acoustical qualities have proved to be excellent – and it has fulfilled that function ever since as well as being a popular venue for radio broadcasts. The exterior has

St John's, Smith Square

fortunately not been compromised by this change of use and is best viewed from Lord North Street. From such a vantage point one suspects that few now would agree with the sentiment expressed by Charles Dickens in *Our Mutual Friend*, in which the church is described as appearing to be 'some petrified monster, frightful and gigantic, on its back with its legs in the air'.

Given such a line one wonders what Dickens might have made of the square's other additions, some of which rise through a dozen storeys. The worst include the former Conservative Central Office (now the London base of the European Parliament and the European Commission, in a building which Pevsner and his co-author describe as 'exhausted neo-Georgian') and the grim block of Transport House on the corner of Dean Bradley Street. The latter was constructed as the headquarters of the old Transport & General Workers' Union. It was for many years Labour Party headquarters and entirely fails to respect both the scale of the square and its architecture.

Tothill Street

The name marks the location of Tothill Fields, a toot or tote hill being an old name for an area of high ground on which a signalling beacon could be erected.

The fields were an open area between the Abbey and Millbank, routinely used for pasturing cattle and kitchen gardens, but also for duelling and tournaments, parades and large-scale celebrations, such as that which followed the coronation in 1559. Plague pits were dug here in the 1660s, the dead joining the bodies of many hundreds of Royalist prisoners – mostly Scots – who had been interred following the Battle of Worcester in 1651. Despite these grisly associations the seventeenth century saw many large houses constructed overlooking the fields, in one of which (Lincoln House, now gone) was the Office of the Revels which was responsible for organising royal celebrations. One notable Master of the Revels, Sir Henry Herbert (1595–1673), served both Charles I and his son, Charles II, having somehow retained the post during the Interregnum.

The fields had disappeared almost entirely by the 1850s, by which time many smaller, less aristocratic houses had been thrown up together with the inevitable taverns, workshops and stalls operated by small traders. From 1818 until 1884 this was also the location of the Tothill Fields bridewell, a house of correction for the compulsory incarceration and employment of indolent paupers as well as of conventional criminals. Eventually, these functions were taken over by Millbank penitentiary and a stone gateway in Little Sanctuary is now the only visible remnant of the place.

Today the street is largely a mixture of retail premises and offices, the most interesting building being the monumental domed structure on the corner of Storeys Gate. This is Methodist Central Hall, a building that combines a church and exhibition space with a great hall able to accommodate more than 2,500 individuals. Created to mark the centenary of John Wesley's death, it was constructed between 1906 and 1911 on the site of the old Royal Aquarium, Music Hall and Imperial Theatre. From 1876 until 1903 this immense emporium of glass and stone had afforded Londoners the opportunity to wander amidst palm trees and 'tanks of curious sea creatures' whilst watching scantily clad women and 'genuine Zulus' performing dances and other entertainments. Notwithstanding its French renaissance styling, the building that replaced it was considered

hugely advanced for its day, the architect Edwin Alfred Rickards relying on a framework of reinforced concrete to support the dome which remains one of the largest of its type anywhere in the world. The intention, honouring the Methodist founder, was to create a sense of space similar to that experienced at meeting in the open air but with the protection and security of a roof. In 1946 the building hosted the inaugural meeting of the United Nations General Assembly, and speakers at the many political rallies held here have included Sir Winston Churchill and Mahatma Gandhi. In 1966 it was also chosen as a suitable place to display the World Cup – the tournament was being held in London that year – but the trophy promptly disappeared (see panel).

Methodist Central Hall, Tothill Street

HOW PICKLES THE DOG SAVED
THE WORLD CUP

As the nation looked forward to the 1966 World Cup, the first time it had been held in England, disaster struck. The iconic cup, known after the tournament's guiding light as the Jules Rimet trophy, had been on display at a 'Sports with Stamps' exhibition at Methodist Central Hall in Westminster. But thieves struck on Sunday, 20 March 1966, removing it from a glass cabinet despite the apparently heavy security and leaving the building undetected. Standing twelve inches high and weighing nine pounds, the trophy is made of solid gold and was insured for £30,000. The shockwaves reverberated around the world, with the Brazilian sports federation calling the theft 'sacrilege' and insisting that it would never have happened in their country because 'Even Brazilian thieves love football.'

The World Cup had arrived in England just ten weeks before the theft and was stored in a safe place pending the start of the tournament. It was only released for display on the specific written authority of Sir Stanley Rous, president of FIFA, and of course an Englishman. He insisted that the trophy had to be placed in a glass case and guarded night and day by a reputable security firm. However, on the Sunday, the guard whose job it was to stand next to the glass case had the day off and when the other four guards assigned to the room were either on a break or answering a call of nature, a thief, or thieves, got in the back door of Central Hall and stole the cup.

It was a nightmare scenario for not just the Football Association but also for Sir Stanley Rous and FIFA. Just three months to the finals of the biggest tournament on the planet and there would be no trophy for the winners. Scotland Yard swung into action, with the fabled Flying Squad, or 'Sweeney', being handed the task of recovering the stolen cup. Led by top detective chief inspector Len Buggy, the Sweeney made immediate contact with their underworld sources, hoping to find a scrap of evidence that would lead them to the light-fingered villain. A reward of £4,500 was offered for information leading to the recovery of the trophy, with

£3,000 being put up by the insurers, £1,000 by the National Sporting Club and £1,000 by Gillette Razors.

Len Buggy got the breakthrough he so desperately needed when a man calling himself Jackson made contact with the Football Association. His offer was short and to the point: pay me £15,000 in unmarked £1 and £5 notes and you can have the World Cup back, but if the ransom is not met it will be melted down and sold as scrap gold. What followed was nothing short of farcical: Len Buggy went out to meet Jackson but the thief spotted the police back-up team in a Transit van and tried to escape. Although Jackson was arrested – at which point the police discovered his real name was Edward Betchley – the World Cup was not in his possession.

The scene was now set for Pickles the heroic 4-year-old mongrel. Two days after the bungled ransom transaction, David Corbett, a Thames lighterman, left his flat in Norwood, south London to make a phone call and Pickles went with him. As they passed a parked car, Pickles strained at the leash, dragging his master towards the front wheel. There Corbett found a package, tightly bound up in old newspaper, which, when he opened it, revealed the solid-gold outlines of the Jules Rimet trophy. Sprinting back to the house, he shouted to his bemused wife: 'I've found the World Cup! I've found the World Cup!'

With the trophy now returned safely to a relieved Football Association, Pickles became a celebrity. His story knocked the impending general election off the front pages, and, after acquiring an agent, Corbett was able to charge his faithful pooch out at £60 a day for personal appearances. A few months later, master and dog were invited to the party for England's World Cup-winning team, where Messrs Moore, Charlton and co. welcomed them with open arms. Pickles later starred in a film – *The Spy with the Cold Nose* – appeared on a host of television programmes, including *Blue Peter* and *Magpie*, and was awarded a year's supply of dog food by Spiller's. His lucky owner, who received £3,000 as a reward, was able to buy a new house in Surrey. For his part, Edward Betchley ('Jackson') got two years in prison for demanding money with menaces.

Trafalgar Square

Britain was surprisingly slow to acknowledge one of its great heroes, the site of the King's Mews being renamed Trafalgar Square, after Nelson's famous victory, after more than thirty years had elapsed. The area had been used to house royal falcons since the late thirteenth century, from the reign of Richard II to that of Henry VIII. The latter transferred his horses here in 1537, after the royal stables burned down in what was to become Bloomsbury, but the name mews – referring to the shedding of a bird's plumage – remained in use. Later still the buildings provided barracks for Cromwell's men, and following their victory served as a prison for several thousand Cavaliers.

Following the Restoration, Wren had plans to rebuild the Mews on a massive scale, and William Kent began work on a block for

National Gallery, Trafalgar Square

George II on the north side of the square. However, after the purchase of Buckingham House in 1762 with new mews built behind it, this area was cleared on the orders of Nash as part of his remodelling of central London for the future George IV. As we saw in chapter two, it was of course his ill-fated Carlton House that was to provide some of the materials for the National Gallery – in particular the Corinthian columns from Henry Holland's portico – which dominates the whole of one side more as a consequence of its width than its design, which is slightly insipid.

Today the National Gallery has more than 2,300 works of art, ranging from the medieval to the modern, all of which are housed in a building by William Wilkins, architect of University College (see Bloomsbury). His design is one most locals and visitors now take for granted, but, with its undersized dome and slightly fussy turrets, it was something William IV thought 'a nasty little pokey hole' and which Thackeray – more engaged with the arts but equally scathing – likened to 'a little gin shop of a building'. The leading architectural historian Sir John Summerson managed to be no more complimentary, describing it as

Nelson Column, Trafalgar Square

looking 'like the clock and vases on a mantelpiece, only less useful'.

The National Gallery's origins lay in the acquisition in the 1820s of thirty-eight pictures owned by the émigré banker and collector, John Julius Angerstein. For some years these were shown at Angerstein's house at 100 Pall Mall, Wilkins completing his design only in 1831 for a building not completed until six years later. The collection continued to grow, E. M. Barry being commissioned to build a new wing in 1876, and Sir John Taylor more display rooms just a decade later. The creation of the Tate Gallery in 1897 enabled works by British artists to be siphoned off to a new riverside home, but five more galleries were created in 1911, with expansion continuing well into modern times with the Sainsbury Wing completed as recently as 1991.

The last named, a western extension, had a famously difficult genesis. In 1984 the original design for the new wing, which was to include commercial office space, was excoriated by the Prince of Wales as 'a monstrous carbuncle on the face of a much loved and elegant friend'. A new architectural competition was then promulgated, with the new structure to be used exclusively as a National Gallery extension. The winners, with their postmodern design, were Venturi, Rauch and Scott Brown. (Prince Charles, incidentally, gave his blessing to the new plans.) Following the completion of the Sainsbury Wing in 1991 work on a new east wing began to create yet more display space.

From the collection of 2,300 paintings around a thousand are on permanent display. The Sainsbury has the oldest works, ranging from the thirteenth to the fifteenth centuries, while the main building concentrates on the period from the sixteenth to the twentieth century. The quality on show is impressive, with almost every Old Master, from Vermeer to Velazquez and Raphael to Rembrandt, represented. The National Gallery is also particularly strong in the fields of Impressionism and Post-Impressionism, with works by the likes of Monet, Renoir, Cezanne and Van Gogh proving very popular with the public. Despite much of the collection of British art relocating to the Tate Gallery, there is still a host of fine paintings from this country. These include two of the best known in the history of British art: *The Hay Wain* by John Constable and *The Fighting Temeraire* by J. M. W. Turner.

The National Portrait Gallery sits just to the east of the National Gallery, with its entrance in St Martin's Place. Founded in 1856, thanks largely to the efforts of the 5th Earl of Stanhope, the NPG did not have a permanent home until the late 1890s, at which time the philanthropist William Henry Alexander provided substantial funding, allowing the building we see today on Trafalgar Square to be erected. The main block as Pevsner points out, is a 'Florentine Quattrocento palazzo' of 1890–5 by Ewan Christian with J. K. Colling. A western extension, the Duveen wing, dates from the 1930s, and the Ondaatje wing was completed in 2000.

In terms of the criteria for inclusion an important decision was taken by the National Portrait Gallery's founders: that the gallery was, firstly, to be about history and not about art, and, secondly, that it would concern itself with the status of the sitter and not with the artistic merits of the portrait. That is not to say there are no fine works to be found, with artists of the calibre of Holbein and Lucian Freud on display. However, with its ten thousand-plus portraits the National Portrait Gallery has fulfilled the original intentions of the founders by providing a comprehensive record of the great and the good. The range is impressive: royalty, writers, adventurers, engineers, businessmen, soldiers and scientists, all prominent in their fields, adorn the walls. Perhaps the best known piece is the only known portrait of William Shakespeare painted from life, in which he sports a pair of gold hooped earrings. Attributed to the painter John Taylor it was the first portrait acquired by the Gallery, having being donated by the Earl of Ellesmere in 1856. The NPG also owns a fine array of works either by, or depicting, members of the Bloomsbury Group (see Gordon Square, Bloomsbury).

Also situated to the east of the National Gallery is St Martin-in-the-Fields, a large church whose origins can be traced to a small chapel possibly created as somewhere for monks of St Peter's abbey to worship whilst working in their 'convent garden' behind (See Covent Garden chapter). The present building, by James Gibbs, dates from 1726 but the interior is largely Victorian and the work of Sir Arthur Blomfield.

Combining a portico similar to those of St George's Hanover Square (see Mayfair) and St George's Bloomsbury with a tall, Wren-like steeple the design proved hugely influential particularly in the United States of America, where many churches came to follow the same form. Specifically, the hexastyle design of the portico with its Corinthian columns and richly decorated pediment drew inspiration from the temple built in the first century AD by Marcus Vipsanius Agrippa at Nîmes in France. Inside two box pews underline the church's special status as the parish church of the Admiralty,

St Martin-in-the-Fields, Trafalgar Square

whose white ensign can be flown on state occasions, and of the sovereign as most of Buckingham Palace falls within its domain. The royal arms, shown in high relief or *alto-relievo* within the pediment, are a reminder that Charles II was christened at St Martin's.

Under no circumstances should the vast crypt be overlooked by visitors to the church. The roster of those buried here is especially impressive, and a long list of interments includes the King's lover Nell Gwyn, the artists Hogarth, Sir Joshua Reynolds and Louis-François Roubillac (also spelled Roubiliac), the architect James 'Athenian' Stuart, and, perhaps most surprisingly, Jack Sheppard, the notorious highwayman. He was hanged at Tyburn in 1724 before an estimated two hundred thousand bystanders, or approximately one-third of all Londoners.

Further round the square is South Africa

House, a 1930s design penned by Sir Herbert Baker who under the patronage of Lord Milner and Cecil Rhodes established himself as one of the dominant forces in colonial architecture between the wars. The sculptural adornments are by Coert Steynberg and Sir Charles Wheeler PRA, and for many years the building was the focus of vociferous anti-apartheid protests although it took the poll-tax rioters of 1990 actually to damage the building (fortunately not seriously).

The building's companion piece is Canada House opposite, a century older but with similar colonial associations. It was designed in the 1820s by the Greek Revivalist Sir Robert Smirke as conspicuously prestigious if overly grand premises for the now-defunct Union Club (1800–1949) and the Royal College of Physicians which remained here until 1964 when it relocated to Regents Park. With porticoes to the north and south and a third recessed one facing the square, the Bath-stone façades of its old home are beautifully proportioned although additional storeys have since dampened somewhat the impact of the Giant order of Ionic columns fronting the square.

The only other genuinely significant structure is Admiralty Arch, Aston Webb's busy but graceful Portland stone curve, which cleverly reconciles both the change in axis from Trafalgar Square to the Mall and the dissimilar environments of the square and park. Providing a ceremonial entrance onto Webb's new Mall and towards Buckingham Palace, the concept thus brilliantly transformed an area of architectural clutter into a magnificent new heart for the Imperial capital. Intended by Edward VII as a memorial to his mother Victoria, the scheme was completed in 1912 meaning that the King did not live long enough to see it himself, but the prominent Latin inscription nevertheless records that ANNO : DECIMO : EDWARDI : SEPTIMI : REGIS : VICTORIÆ : REGINÆ : CIVES : GRATISSIMI : MDCCCCX (In the tenth year of King Edward VII, to Queen Victoria, from most grateful citizens, 1910). It is, incidentally, London's largest and longest inscription. The sculptural figures on the arch representing 'Navigation' and 'Gunnery' are by the sculptor Thomas Brock, and in the northernmost arch between immense Corinthian columns is a small protrusion akin to a human nose. This is popularly said to be a good luck charm for mounted soldiers who rub it when passing through, recalling the Iron Duke's famously prominent proboscis, or tweak it thinking that it is Napoleon's nose. In fact it was put there as recently as 1997, one of more than forty installed on London landmarks as a protest by artist Rick Buckley against the increasing intrusion of what he saw as the 'Big Brother' society.

Finally, the Nelson Column, at 170 feet still the world's tallest Corinthian column, its design by William Railton (who won £200 for his trouble) the winner among more than 160 ideas submitted when looking for a way to honour Trafalgar's victor. Curiously these included a gigantic pyramid, a globe, an octagonal Gothic cenotaph, a statue not of Nelson but of William IV, and another column with Nelson at its base rather than its summit on the grounds that it would be inappropriate for a 'mere subject, however heroic, to look down on Royalty'.

The cost of the Dartmoor granite column, Nelson himself and Sir Edwin Landseer's splendid lions was met by public subscription, one of the most generous

Admiralty Arch, Trafalgar Square

subscribers being Queen Victoria (who donated £500) and the least a Mrs Beeby, who contributed 2s. 6d. (12.5p).

Thereafter the work was however very slow – the lions were still not in place more than sixty years after Nelson's death – and few now recall the name Edmund Baily, the man responsible for carving the sailor's likeness in Craigleith limestone. Standing on a capital made from melted guns of war, Nelson, shown three-times life-size, looks with his one good eye down Whitehall towards the Abbey. At the base of the column four bronze bas-reliefs cast from captured cannon show scenes from his service career. Describing the bombardment of

Copenhagen, his victories in the battles of the Nile and Cape St Vincent, and its final chapter at the hand of an unknown French sniper, they were affixed in 1867. Inevitably, with their look of resignation, Landseer's lions also have a tale to tell, the paws being modelled on those of a domestic cat because (it is said) the corpse of the beast the sculptor was using for reference had inconveniently decomposed.

Finally, there is Hubert le Sueur's 1638 statue of Charles I, carved during the King's lifetime and so the oldest object in the square. It happily survived Cromwell's depredations after being buried beneath a private garden, and was reinstated by

Charles II on a plinth widely said to have been designed by Wren and executed by Grinling Gibbons. Standing on the site of the original Charing Cross, the King's likeness therefore marks the point from which all distances from the capital are measured and can thus be said in a very real sense to be the centre of modern-day London. This part of Trafalgar Square is also where Daniel Defoe was pilloried in 1703 for libelling the government, during which ordeal he was pelted with nothing more than sweet-smelling flowers by a public that found itself in broad agreement with his claims.

Tufton Street

Richard Tufton (1640–84) sat as MP for Appleby before succeeding his brother as 5th Earl of Thanet when he lived in Tothill Street (q.v.). As Bowling Alley, the street already existed at that time, and was a popular venue for cockfights; but it was renamed in his honour sometime before 1680.

Its most famous resident, Thomas Blood, died in his house on the site of what is now nos. 1–19 Westminster Mansions. Blood, it may be recalled, stole the crown jewels but on being caught famously picked up a pension instead of being beheaded. Variously described as a colonel and a captain – in all likelihood he was neither – the Irishman was charming but something of a desperado. He switched sides more than once during the Civil War, but found himself on the wrong side when the dust had settled and the monarchy was restored.

Embarking on what the historian Christopher Hibbert memorably described as an 'extra-legal career spanning two decades,' the pinnacle was to be a crafty raid on the cupboard at the Tower of London where,

bizarrely, the royal regalia was stored. Their custodian was the feeble, 76-year-old Talbot Edwards, whom Blood befriended before beating him up and fleeing with the goods. In the event Blood got no further than Tower Wharf, demanding when caught that he see the King and insisting, 'it was a gallant attempt, however unsuccessful! It was for a Crown!' Charles agreed to meet him, and Blood emerged with land in Ireland worth £500 a year. The reason why has never been established, although quite possibility Charles had put him up to it, being at that time more in need of money than jewels.

Until its redevelopment in the 1930s the street was what one might term 'respectable working class'. The area's many handsome eighteenth-century houses had been subdivided into smaller dwellings, but pre-Great War photographs of the residents show them well shod and smartly dressed and the wonderful octagonal tracery in the windows of the Gothic school buildings still intact.

Victoria Street

Nearly forty years in the planning and completed in the 1880s, the creation of Victoria Street involved the destruction of a huge area of slums at the Broad Sanctuary end, the route itself conceived to be wide enough to accommodate conventional traffic as well as trams.

These had only recently been introduced by the eccentric and unsuccessful American presidential candidate George Train (1829–1904), and briefly ran from the Abbey out to Pimlico. With the notable exception of Westminster Cathedral the modern street is dominated by modern commercial and retail blocks although one happy survivor is the

Westminster Cathedral from Victoria Street

1903 before the building could be used. Even then the striking Byzantine design in red brick with Portland stone banding was still very much a work in progress. The wonderful off-centre 83-metre campanile was more or less finished – the cross on top now contains a small fragment of what believers hold to be the true cross – but much of the interior decoration was left to be completed over the following decades.

It is even so one of Westminster's real glories, dedicated to the precious blood of Our Lord Jesus Christ, and with the widest nave in England giving onto a rich interior decked out in mosaics and other decorations incorporating marble from more than a hundred different quarries around the world. Chief among these are eight immense columns of Turkish green marble and the fourteen Stations of the Cross, which were carved by Eric Gill during the Great War, a controversial artist whose unorthodox Catholic beliefs were nevertheless deeply held. The grand organ, unusually, has dual controls enabling it to be played from either end of the cathedral and in 1906 it was used for the first London performance of *The Dream of Gerontius* when its composer, Sir Edward Elgar, conducted the choir.

Despite its relative youth the cathedral includes a number of historic artefacts, including a near six-hundred-year-old statue of *Our Lady and Child* and the remains of St John Southworth, the seventeenth-century martyr. In the crypt below are buried four cardinals of Westminster, Wiseman in a tomb designed by the great Gothicist A. W. N. Pugin, with their red caps hung in display in accordance with tradition.

red-brick mass of Artillery Mansions (1895), one of the earliest apartment blocks in London. The Victoria Palace, now a theatre, was formerly an Edwardian music hall.

The Cathedral is actually in Francis Street but the best view is from Victoria Street across its huge open piazza. Its creation was first mooted in 1862 when substantial sums of money were donated by Roman Catholics in Britain and abroad in memory of the late Archbishop of Westminster, Cardinal Wiseman (1802–65). It was designed by John Francis Bentley, a recent convert to Roman Catholicism, on a site known as Bulinga Fen on which markets had long been held. This had been acquired by the congregation in 1884 but it took until

WESTMINSTER ABBEY

In a very real sense this is the building that gave life to the West End, and certainly the original beating heart of Westminster before the political establishment began to dominate the area. It may be as Pevsner insists 'the most French of all English Gothic churches' but Westminster Abbey is also arguably the most significant single building in English history. The Tower of London is perhaps its only possible rival in terms of the central role each has played in national life, and which, in the case of the Abbey, it continues to play after nearly a thousand years. Correctly termed the Collegiate Church of St Peter Westminster, and a royal peculiar meaning that the dean and chapter fall under the personal jurisdiction of the Crown rather than the Bishop of London, the Abbey as we have seen traces its origins to Saxon times. Of that early foundation nothing remains, indeed it is tradition rather than documented fact which points to Sebert, King of the East Saxons as its instigator and to 616 AD as the year of its first consecration.

More certain is that Edward the Confessor began to build an abbey here in stone following his accession in 1042, and that this was consecrated in 1065 shortly before his demise. A little over two hundred years later it was rededicated by Henry III after being rebuilt by Henry of Rheims, a French master mason, and in the fourteenth century a new nave was created by Henry Yevele. Yevele was the most successful and prolific master mason of the late medieval period and the individual who was responsible for Westminster Hall. Much of his work is what we see today, although the building has been refaced several times to compensate for the soft Reigate stone which was employed. In addition two more periods of construction have left their mark in the astonishing Henry VII chapel (of the sixteenth century) and Hawksmoor's 225-foot twin towers at the western end. The latter, whilst very much the newest part of the building (having been completed in 1745) are perhaps the Abbey's most distinctive and most recognisable external feature.

That said it is to view the interior that most visitors come, and even with the crowds – with a million visitors annually these are never anything but immense – it is a glorious and astonishing space to wander through. At 103 feet the nave is the highest of any Gothic cathedral in this country, the great square of the main cloister almost the identical measurement along each side, and is it not incredible to think that the chancel, transepts and crossing were already in place by 1260 together with several bays of the nave? The building was also as innovative as it was inspirational; the several radiating chapels at the eastern end the first in the country to form a *chevet*, the name for a curved ambulatory area behind the altar.

In such a place it may be iniquitous to trumpet one feature over another, but as the finest late-Perpendicular structure in the capital particular attention must be drawn to Henry VII's Lady Chapel. With its widely spaced piers supporting some breathtakingly elaborate and elegant fan vaulting, and huge areas of glass for its period, in 1545 this structural and aesthetic marvel was described as 'the wonder of the entire world'. Approached by a flight of steps and through finely wrought bronze gates displaying heraldic Tudor motifs, representations of ninety-five saints look down on the tombs of Henry and his queen (beneath which is buried James I) whilst around the perimeter are the stalls and emblems of successive generations of Knights of the Order of the Bath. The

chapel's exterior is equally impressive, the load-bearing buttresses folded, pierced, panelled and decorated to disguise the brilliant structural engineering that underlies their function.

Adjacent to the Lady Chapel is the sacred heart of the Abbey: the coronation chair and the shrine of Edward the Confessor (c. 1003–1066). The coronation chair was made to hold the fabled Stone of Scone (or Stone of Destiny as it is also known), which was placed underneath the seat. The Stone, used in the coronation of Scottish kings, was appropriated by Edward I in 1296 during one of the interminable wars between England and Scotland and it has since been used in the coronation of every English and British monarch since 1308, including that of Queen Elizabeth II in 1953. Indeed such is the symbolism attached to the coronation chair that Oliver Cromwell had himself proclaimed Lord Protector on it in the early 1650s, albeit in Westminster Hall.

In 1996, the by then unpopular government of John Major made a brief attempt to curry favour with the Scots by returning the Stone of Scone to Scotland and it now sits, somewhat out of place, in Edinburgh Castle. The gesture did Major's election prospects no good at all and in the 1997 election he lost almost every seat in Scotland. Close by is the shrine of Edward the Confessor. As the original feretory, or bier, was destroyed in the Reformation, what we see today is a wooden superstructure dating from the sixteenth century, along with the original thirteenth-century marble base.

As Westminster Abbey is the closest thing we have to a national pantheon – the burial place of kings and queens as well as of statesmen and soldiers, poets, writers and priests, and both heroes and villains – it is the hundreds of memorials that tend to detain visitors the longest. Since 1066 a majority of our sovereigns have been crowned here, and until George III in 1820 (who established a new tradition at St George's Chapel in Windsor Castle) more than two dozen crowned heads and consorts have been buried here too. Interments at St Paul's include hundreds of national eminences from Donne through Nelson and Wellington to Churchill, but here at Westminster history seeps through the stones in a way that even Wren's masterpiece cannot match – and the diversity of individuals buried here seems somehow greater and more engaging.

As many as three thousand people have been accorded the honour of an Abbey burial, and a staggering six hundred wall tablets and sculptures make up what is by far the finest collection of monuments anywhere in the country. Besides the inevitable squadrons of sovereigns and statesmen, the soldiers and grandees, that so many of these scores commemorate the likes of Dickens, Darwin and Handel as well more recently departed (such as Dame Peggy Ashcroft and W. H. Auden) perhaps explains their enduring appeal, and how it is that their study can become so absorbing as literally to eclipse the building of which they form a part.

Many of those buried in the Abbey, who are not of royal blood, lie in Poet's Corner in the south transept. The first to be buried here was Geoffrey Chaucer, in 1400, not because of his status as a poet but because he was an official at court. The tradition of burying great writers here, or alternatively of erecting a monument to them, developed only gradually. Although Edmund Spenser was buried in the Abbey in 1599 and Ben Jonson in 1637, the term Poet's Corner only became common currency in the mid-eighteenth century. The principle that it was to be considered the final resting place of the great and the good, from whichever field of endeavour, can be dated to the lavish funeral in 1727 of Isaac Newton, whose obsequies were attended by government ministers and the grandest aristocrats.

For all that, however, none comes even close to the Tomb of the Unknown Warrior at the western end of the nave, a place which remains uniquely sacred in an otherwise largely secular city and which for many visitors is still the focus of the place and its near-thousand-year history.

For this reason alone it is worth explaining how it came to be, the realisation of a concept at once simple and brilliant, and whose touching genius can be read in the way in which it has been copied so many times around the world. The idea came from a vicar in Kent, the Rev. David Railton MC, who had been serving on the Western Front as an army chaplain. In 1920 he wrote to the Dean of Westminster in 1920 suggesting an anonymous interment be made with due reverence 'amongst the kings'.

Fearful of reawakening buried sorrows the King himself reportedly found the notion distasteful, but the idea was taken up Lloyd George and an emotional upwelling from the public soon persuaded the authorities to take action. In November of that year four bodies recovered from the Western Front and draped with Union flags were removed to a chapel near Arras in France. One was selected at random by a senior British army officer, and placed in a simple pine coffin bearing the legend, *A British Warrior who fell in the Great War*. This was then transferred to an oak casket (the timber came from Hampton Court Palace) to which was attached a medieval crusader's sword chosen by George V personally from the royal collection. Before its departure for England, Marshal Foch saluted the casket as it was carried up the gangway of the destroyer HMS *Verdun* and escorted by six battleships the casket received a nineteen-gun field marshal's salute as it passed Dover Castle.

Once landed it was taken to Victoria Station, arriving at platform eight at 8.32 pm and remaining there for the night of 10 November. (A plaque nearby now records this fact.) On the morning of 11 November 1920, the casket was loaded onto a gun carriage of the Royal Horse Artillery and drawn by six horses through immense and silent crowds. As it passed Whitehall the new Cenotaph was formally unveiled by the King, the cortège then making its way to Westminster Abbey followed by His Majesty, the royal family and various government ministers. At the Abbey, where it was flanked by a guard of honour comprising one hundred recipients of the Victoria Cross, the coffin was then lowered into the grave together with soil from each of the main battlefields and beneath a cap of black Belgian marble.

Today it is the only tombstone in the Abbey on which one is forbidden to walk and bears the following inscription, composed by Bishop Ryle, Dean of Westminster, and engraved with brass melted down from wartime ordnance:

> BENEATH THIS STONE RESTS THE BODY
> OF A BRITISH WARRIOR
> UNKNOWN BY NAME OR RANK
> BROUGHT FROM FRANCE TO LIE AMONG
> THE MOST ILLUSTRIOUS OF THE LAND
> AND BURIED HERE ON ARMISTICE DAY
> 11 NOV: 1920, IN THE PRESENCE OF
> HIS MAJESTY KING GEORGE V
> HIS MINISTERS OF STATE
> THE CHIEFS OF HIS FORCES
> AND A VAST CONCOURSE OF THE NATION
> THUS ARE COMMEMORATED THE MANY
> MULTITUDES WHO DURING THE GREAT
> WAR OF 1914 – 1918 GAVE THE MOST THAT
> MAN CAN GIVE LIFE ITSELF
> FOR GOD
> FOR KING AND COUNTRY

FOR LOVED ONES HOME AND EMPIRE
FOR THE SACRED CAUSE OF JUSTICE AND
THE FREEDOM OF THE WORLD
THEY BURIED HIM AMONG THE KINGS BECAUSE HE
HAD DONE GOOD TOWARD GOD AND TOWARD
HIS HOUSE

Marrying the future King George VI on 26 April 1923, Lady Elizabeth Bowes-Lyon famously laid her bouquet at the tomb, a gesture since copied by every royal bride who has married in the Abbey. Conversely, when the Nazi ideologue Alfred Rosenberg laid a wreath here with a swastika during a diplomatic mission in 1933, an old soldier promptly picked it up and threw it into the Thames. On both occasions the sentiments aroused by the action were strong and sincere, the tomb embodying at a very fundamental level the sanctity and significance of this great building. The Abbey in turn symbolises so much of what visitors – from both Britain and abroad – hold to be important about Crown and country and the part which quite possibly any one of them could have played in the long history of these islands. Some of it will be mythic, some of it real yet still magical. There is something about Westminster Abbey that blurs the edges for us, and which, if only temporarily, makes the distinctions seem to disappear.

The Abbey has continued to play a crucial role in the life of the nation. On 6 September 1997, it was used for the funeral service of Diana, Princess of Wales, an event watched by more than two billion people around the world. As well as the huge displays of public emotion it engendered, there was a remarkable break with tradition. Prime Minister Tony Blair read emotively from St Paul, Elton John sang a rewritten version of his hit 'Candle in the Wind' ('Goodbye England's Rose', which became the biggest selling song of all time, with the proceeds going to charity) while the Princess's bereaved brother, Earl Spencer, gave a peroration that in the eyes of many observers appeared to criticise, albeit indirectly, the royal family. The speech was even more remarkable, given that it was delivered from the very spot in which the Queen had been crowned forty-five years earlier. Then in 2002, there was another landmark event: the Queen Mother's funeral was held in the Abbey, the first of a king or queen for more than two hundred years. Given that the Abbey has been designated for the funerals of both the Queen and the Duke of Edinburgh it is clear that Westminster Abbey is as important now as it has ever been.

Westminster Bridge

Whilst London Bridge, in some form, has been in existence since Roman times at least, the original Westminster Bridge was completed only in 1750. It was nevertheless the first of more than twenty bridges that now span the river between the City and Hampton Court. Now in its second incarnation – 'stretching across the water in splendid simplicity' – it is also the second oldest in central London.

The original bridge was built to a design of the Franco-Swiss engineer Charles Labelye and painted by Canaletto. It was torn down a century later, however, by which time subsiding and badly dilapidated it was replaced by Thomas Page's new seven-arch wrought-iron bridge. The Gothic detailing is by Sir Charles Barry, the architect of the Palace of Westminster, and the green colour references the leather of the benches in the nearby House of Commons just as the red of Lambeth Bridge echoes the red leather of the Lords.

At the Westminster end the statue of Boudicca and her daughters is by Thomas Thornycroft and having taken fifteen years

South Bank Lion, Westminster Bridge

to create – the Prince Consort lent several horses as models – it was not cast until fifteen years after his death, in 1902. Its companion at the far end, the celebrated South Bank Lion, is a Coade-stone giant that once stood atop the five storey main block of the Lion Brewery near Hungerford Bridge, on a site now occupied by the Royal Festival Hall. Created in May 1837 – the date is carved into one of his paws – and a Lambeth landmark until the brewery's demolition in 1949, at George VI's suggestion the splendid thirteen-ton creature was remounted at Waterloo Station and then in 1966 removed to his current site.

Whitehall

In common parlance a shorthand reference to the senior echelons of government and the civil service, Whitehall is also one of central London's longest streets, the parade

Boudicca, Westminster Bridge

of government offices at the Abbey end occupying land that was once covered by the rambling complex of ecclesiastical and then royal buildings we know as the Palace of Whitehall.

Acquired in his usual manner by Henry VIII, much of it from Wolsey and Westminster Abbey, the Palace was almost a town within a town, its diverse range of late-medieval buildings and courtyards enclosing gardens and orchards. The buildings themselves were mostly small scale and provided lodgings and offices not just for Henry and his family but also for courtiers and others whose clearly privileged existence was nevertheless balanced by the need to adhere to certain strict rules. Of particular note was the requirement that they should be 'loving together, of good unity and accord,' and all were warned not to let their 'grudging and rumbling' upset their notoriously testy neighbour. Henry died at Whitehall, on 28 January 1547.

At various times attempts were made to bring order to this extensive and unplanned community – a complex so large that it came to span the street – the best of these a proposal from Inigo Jones and John Webb who planned a new classical palace stretching from Charing Cross to Westminster and as far inland as St James's Park. In the end nothing came of this, however, and following a devastating fire in 1698 nothing remains but the Banqueting House and a few fragments underlying Downing Street and between the Ministry of Defence and the river (see below). After the fire the royal family chose to relocate to St James's Palace, and with courtiers gradually morphing into civil servants Whitehall was left to the political establishment and its ministries.

One of the few buildings at the Abbey end

Banqueting House, Whitehall

without any overt political function, the aforementioned Banqueting House is by far the finest building on the street. It was built in 1619–22 for the masques and more formal spectacles of the Court, and as one of the first Classical buildings in Britain – Jones was the pioneer in this country when it came to adopting the new style – it is also among the most important. In 1604 a previous banqueting house on the same site had hosted the first ever performance of *Othello*, and from 1724–1890 the present building served as the Chapel Royal despite never being formally consecrated. A new north entrance and stone staircase date from this period, and were installed by James Wyatt in 1809.

From the pavement the sophisticated use of Classical orders – inspired by Vicenza and refaced in 1829 by Sir John Soane – suggests an ornate but restrained two-storey building, something that effectively disguises the size and scale of the superb 55' x 55' x 110' double-cube space within. With its elaborate Venetian ceiling, designed to be seen from various vantage points (and painted by Peter-Paul Rubens for a fee of £3,000 and a knighthood) this is once again being used for exhibitions and other entertainments, but

Cabinet Office, Whitehall

Dover House, Whitehall

most famously in 1649 it was from this room that Charles I stepped (through an open window) onto a wooden scaffold and to his bravely borne death.

Occupying a prominent position in the middle of the Whitehall the Cenotaph – the word means 'empty tomb' – is Britain's principal national war memorial, conceived and created by Sir Edwin Lutyens immediately following the Great War. Initially it was built of timber and cloth until 1920 when the public made plain its need for something more permanent at which point it was recreated in Portland stone. Lacking both vertical and horizontal lines, and more significantly any specific religious, historical or martial symbols, its power comes from its admirable reticence and its longevity from the adoption by Lutyens, the leading architect of Imperial Britain, of a refined style that is both timeless and chaste.

The same cannot be said of the buildings that surround it, the majority of which are very much of their own time. One particularly monumental group of three buildings, for example, are those which were erected between 1844 and 1915 on the opposite side to the Banqueting House. Their huge scale

and self-confident style reflect the need to accommodate growing numbers of civil servants as the business of government became increasingly complex, and at the same time a desire on the part of the establishment to underline through architecture the importance of the work and of those carrying it out.

Of these the largest is J. M. Brydon's confidently baroque Treasury, which occupies a commanding position on the corner of Parliament Square (under which entry a photograph can be viewed). This was completed in two phases (1908 and 1915) but unfortunately required the wholesale demolition of Charles Barry Junior's Institution of Civil Engineers in Great George Street – a mere fourteen years after its completion – and of a handsome collection of first rate Georgian houses that for decades had housed government workers. A number of the smaller professional institutions also disappeared at this time.

HM Treasury occupied the new building from 1940 onwards, and still does, prior to which it had housed the Board of Education, the Local Government Board and part of the Ministry of Works. In style it is an early

The Cenotaph and the Foreign and Commonwealth Office, Whitehall

exercise in Edwardian Baroque Revival. It is of course not open to the public excepting that portion of the heavily armoured basement now called the Cabinet War Rooms. This falls under the control of the Imperial War Museum, occupies a very small part of an incredible complex of more than six acres of top secret offices excavated beneath Whitehall prior to the Second World War, and is protected by a concrete layer more than seventeen-feet thick. (The entrance is on Horse Guards, on which page a photograph can be viewed.)

With its picturesque tower on the park side, the Foreign and Commonwealth Office by George Gilbert Scott (with some interiors by Matthew Wyatt) was constructed from 1862–75, at which time the Home and Colonial Office occupied those chambers on the Whitehall front with the India Office behind. The architect originally favoured a Gothic design, and produced one, but was persuaded to follow the prevailing style of Whitehall offices, which was firmly Classical.

In keeping with the original occupants' areas of influence the elaborate allegorical sculptures on the street façade represent Literature, Commerce, Manufacture, Science, Art, Agriculture and Law as well as Government, Europe, Asia, Africa, America, Australasia and Education. Its many highlights include the Durbar Court in the former India Office, by Wyatt, which was originally open but has now been glazed, and the State Stair in the original Foreign Office, which Pevsner describes as '*Pax Britannica* at its proudest, glowing with marbles, mosaic, granites and gilding'.

Occupying the site of another (Tudor) cockpit, the Old Treasury at no. 70 – now the Cabinet Office – was completed by Sir Charles Barry in 1847 but conceals a number of eighteenth and early-nineteenth century fragments, including a frieze and columns by Sir John Soane, work by William Kent, and the remains of Henry VIII's tennis court. When it was first converted to a private residence it was for the future Queen Anne. Following her accession she presented the building to the Duke and Duchess of Marlborough, the latter having once been held prisoner there by James II before he was forced to flee. By 1719 it was in the hands of the Cabinet Office, and nearly three hundred years later is still is.

Concealed from the street by a large blank wall, Dover House (now the Scotland Office) is another rare survivor, this time of that species of aristocratic palace which once clustered around the sovereign before Whitehall was lost to office space and civil servants. The original apartments on the site were assigned as lodgings to the first Duke of Ormonde, whose grandson and heir was later charged with treason, attainted and deprived of the house after joining forces with the Old Pretender. An early Scottish connection thus confirmed the place was then rebuilt to the designs of the prolific Palladian James Paine for Sir Matthew Featherstonehaugh, an undistinguished baronet who acquired a country estate at the same time – Uppark, in Sussex – as one of

the conditions he had been required to meet in order to inherit £400,000 from a kinsman.

In 1787, however, what was then Featherstonehaugh House was substantially remodelled by Henry Holland for the Regent's brother, Frederick, Duke of York and Albany. He shortly afterwards exchanged it for Lord Melbourne's house in Piccadilly, now known as Albany (see Mayfair chapter). Holland's work on his behalf was nevertheless a triumph, his masterstroke being the creation where the front courtyard had been of a one of London's most magnificent entrance halls. A splendid drum beneath a shallow saucer-like dome, it was top-lit by a circular lantern and concealed behind a grand Greek portico with four Ionic columns attached to an otherwise and unusually blank rusticated screen facing onto the street.

The result of this was not just to shift the focus away from the rear – where behind a simple but dignified façade the main rooms looked across Horse Guards Parade – but also to provide an entrance and indeed an address more suited to a younger brother of a future king. The key component of what Pevsner describes as the 'the most elegant piece of architecture to the whole of Whitehall', the circular hall is encircled by eight Tuscan columns in scagliola, the finish one of pink Siena marble set against pale green walls. Its stone staircase, incidentally, is the one up which a clubfooted Byron would have limped for his first assignation with Lady Caroline Lamb in the spring of 1812.

Lofty, imposing, deliciously spare in its ornamentation, and as a consequence incredibly grand, it has since been suggested that had Dover House been slightly less splendid it might in time have become the new 'No.10'. Prime Minister Gladstone valued his privacy and is thought to have turned it down because he felt its size would oblige him 'to receive', and more recently, when the establishment of the Scottish Parliament threatened to make the Scottish Office redundant, it was suggested that the Blairs might like to move out of their confining flat at no.10.

At no. 26 a completion date of 1726 for the Old Admiralty by Thomas Ripley makes it the oldest government office on Whitehall for what at the time would have been the largest department. Once again the building is hidden by a wall – a Roman Doric screen designed in the 1750s by Robert Adam – but behind this the somewhat disappointing three-storey building in yellow brick was conceived as the official residence of the First Lord of the Admiralty. With its neo-classical interiors it served as such until 1964, Winston Churchill being one of its better-known occupants.

Crossing back over Whitehall once more, there is less of interest on the river side and where there is something worthy of note it dates from more recent times. At no. 79, Richmond House, home of the Department of Health since 1987, is by William Whit-field and Partners. A boldly banded façade of brick and stone, perpendicular and emphatically asymmetrical, its lively styling contrasts strongly with the nearby Ministry of Defence. The latter was designed during the First World War by Vincent Harris, and building started on the eve of the Second, but it was not finally completed for another twenty years. An enormous wedge, strangely blank but for the top-floor colonnades and pedimented corner blocks, its windows honour Georgian proportions but at eight storeys (ten with the roof-top pavilions) it is too high and too prominent except perhaps when viewed from the London Eye.

On the river side the stone fragments in the garden are small remnants of the Palace of Whitehall, and Queen Mary's Steps installed by Wren to provide access to the pre-Embankment Thames.

Whitehall Place

This is dominated by the almost fairytale French Renaissance architecture of Thomas Archer's Whitehall Court, an eight-storey complex of hotel and apartments that is linked at one end to the National Liberal Club and at the rear overlooks the river. Designed in the 1880s by Alfred Water-house, and in its day easily London's largest private club, the latter counted William Gladstone among its members and his famous axe is still shown to visitors. White-hall Court itself, rising to eleven storeys, was one of the first residential buildings in England to have lifts.

In truth the complex as a whole is perhaps best glimpsed from a distance, either from St James's Park (see overleaf) as previously noted or from the far side of the river, where the pyramids and ornate balconies provide a wonderful contrast with the monolithic bulk of the Ministry of Defence further upstream. That said the interior of the Gothic club-house, whilst too large to be intimate, contains some attractive wood panelling, a good deal of what at the time was very fashionable glazed tile work – Lord Chancellor Birkenhead, a Tory, affected to believe it was London's largest public lavatory – and a breathtaking oval spiral staircase designed by the émigré architect Berndt Engle to replace one lost to German bombing.

Whitehall Place from St James's Park

BELGRAVIA

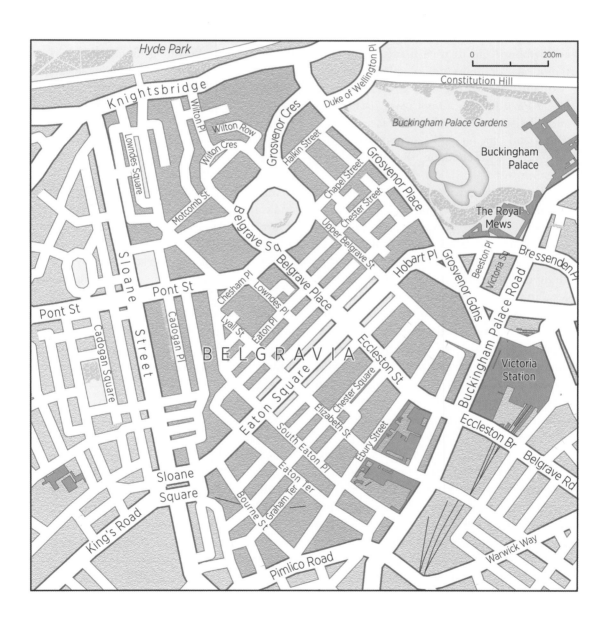

In 2010 in a declining property market many Londoners were astonished to read of a house in their city – a terraced house – being offered for sale at £100 million. Its Belgrave Square location will have come as less of a surprise, however, as prices in this corner of the capital have remained among the world's highest ever since a special Act of Parliament was passed in 1826. The Act permitted the ground landlord, the 2nd Earl Grosvenor, to develop an area then infested with footpads and robbers and to turn it into what contemporaries called a 'city of palaces'. Nearly two centuries on the area stretching from Hyde Park Corner down towards Pimlico and Chelsea still matches that last description, and it is still owned by Lord Grosvenor's descendant, the 6th Duke of Westminster.

The work required to transform this part of the Grosvenor inheritance of 'Five Fields' into what is by far London's most exclusive and expensive suburb was considerable. In specific terms, the Act permitted the Earl to 'drain the site, raise the level, and erect bars, &c.,' in short to do whatever his advisers felt was necessary to liberate an area that for centuries had been little more than a lagoon in the Thames – and which by the early nineteenth century had become heavy-clay swamp of seemingly little or no promise. Once work started, however, the progress towards that celebrated city of palaces was to be astonishingly rapid.

By 1831 it was already noted that 'during the late reign – that of George IV – Lord Grosvenor has built a new and elegant town on the site of fields of no healthy aspect, thus connecting London and Chelsea, and improving the western entrance to the metropolis, at a great expense'. Grosvenor's genius lay not just in the scale of his opera-

tions but in the appointment as master builder of Thomas Cubitt (1788–1855) the inspired and industrious son of a Norfolk carpenter of whom Queen Victoria said (after he had completed her beloved house at Osborne on the Isle of Wight) 'a better, kinderhearted or more simple, unassuming man never breathed' (see panel).

Belgravia's close proximity to the sovereign's new Buckingham Palace was obviously heavily in its favour, but the land itself was low-lying and prone to flooding. It was also crossed by two large and noxious sewers, the Ranelagh and the deceptively pleasant-sounding King's Scholar's Pond, the courses of which in the words of an official report some years later abounded 'in the foulest deposits, in many cases stopping up the house drains and emitting the most digusting effluvium'. Amidst the area's mix of swamp, rough pasture and poor quality orchards Londoners had also long been in the habit of dumping the city's rubbish.

Cubitt was undeterred, however, and as one observer put it 'perceiving the disposition of the fashionable world to follow in the wake of Royalty,' he set out completely to transform the area. Expensively rerouting, relaying and enlarging the sewers, and draining the worst of the marshland, he quickly laid and paved a network of new roads across more than 140 acres. The acreage he needed to build he leased from Earl Grosvenor's holding of more than two hundred, initially paying just £6 an acre for it but with this cost rising to £150 as he himself poured in the money, manpower and other resources needed to improve it. Like any investment this was not without its risks, but it made sense to a man keen to profit from the London property boom that characterised the decades following the defeat of

THOMAS CUBITT, MASTERBUILDER

From his workshops in Gray's Inn Road, Holborn the indefatigable Cubitt had already been working on the Duke of Bedford's London estate since 1820 (see Bloomsbury chapter) but by far his greatest achievements were to come at Belgravia, and we are fortunate that the vast majority of his work survives to this day. The scale on which he worked was enormous, and such that following a fire in 1854 it is estimated that a single one of his yards sustained £100,000 worth of damage. Unusually at a time when sub-contracting was very much the norm Cubitt also chose to employ everyone directly, some two thousand in all from draughts-men to labourers, bricklayers to masons, joiners, slaters, even paper-hangers.

By the time he died this son of a humble Norfolk carpenter was a millionaire, and his will the longest on record at 386 pages. If nothing else such statistics speak volumes for his talents as a builder, developer and businessman, although Cubitt modestly refused to consider himself anything but the first of these. His social ascent was nevertheless to be as impressive as anything he built using brick and stucco, with one of his sons being elected to the Commons (and later sent to the Lords as Baron Ashcombe) and the company he founded surviving until well into the twentieth century. At the height of the Cold War in the 1950s, for example, one of its subsidiaries was to be responsible for the construction of several top secret reinforced concrete 'pagodas', which were used for testing Britain's atomic weapons at Orford Ness on the Suffolk coast.

Cubitt himself had begun work as a roving ship's carpenter 150 years earlier, around 1806. The profits from this enabled him to rent some premises in Eagle Street, Holborn on his return in 1810 and asked to repair the roof of the Russell Institution on the Bloomsbury Estate his evidently fine work and professional approach led directly to his first major building contract. This was to construct a new London Institution, designed by architect William Brooks 'for the

Advancement of Literature and the Diffusion of Useful Knowledge' and intended for a site at Moorfields. It was a commission worth around £20,000, a truly enormous undertaking for a man with barely five years' experience, but Cubitt relished the challenge and by employing rather than subcontracting his labour he was able to complete the project on time, within budget and to the required high standard. The building stood until 1936, Cubitt observing that it was better 'to submit to paying rather more for the labour than to submit to the other evil of having it badly done'.

This unusual method was one he was to employ again and again, always preferring to shoulder the additional upfront costs and associated risks in order to maintain close control over the timing and quality of everything he built. He also chose to develop his business as a speculative builder, a venture that was then without the pejorative associations it has since acquired, and one that simply meant building houses and finding tenants (or buyers) rather than building to order. Quality was his top priority and it is interesting to note that the accommodation he built for his own workforce by his new yard on the Grays Inn Road was sufficiently well constructed to be still in use some two-and-a-half centuries later.

His work for the London Institution introduced Cubitt to influential men, and he was quick to grasp the opportunities this gave him. Its president, for example, was the 1st Lord Carrington, a banker who helped secure funding for many of his future projects. One of its governors was J. W. Freshfield MP, the founder of the eponymous law firm, who was quick to invest in some of Cubitt's earliest schemes and introduced him to landowners such as Lord Calthorpe who leased him land on which to build.

For the time his was the perfect business model and, even now, it is probable that no-one alive or dead built more of London than Thomas Cubitt, or did a more thorough job. (Above ground, anyway, as Sir Joseph Bazalgette may have an equal claim when it comes to the subterranean.) In Bloomsbury and Highbury he built smart homes for the aspiring middle classes. South of the river, in Clapham, larger houses were erected for professional and City men and a country house for himself. And in Belgravia he planned some of the largest houses in streets and squares finer than any London had yet seen.

These were intended for the titled, wealthy and most fashionable elites of late-Georgian and early-Victorian society, whereas neighbouring Pimlico Cubitt set aside for artisans and clerks. In an era when land close to the stink of the Thames was considered inferior the latter was a much less salubrious one than it might now appear. (It is interesting to note as well that when the 2nd Duke of Westminster decided to sell Pimlico in the 1950s one of his reasons for doing so was that he was fed up at the regularity with which the area – and so his family name – cropped up in prosecution cases mounted against local prostitutes.)

Of these several areas where Cubitt's men were active for much of the nineteenth century, Belgravia – the name derives from Viscount Belgrave, a subsidiary Grosvenor title relating to a village on the family estate near Chester – provided what was to be by far the greatest challenge, but it was also to be the builder's greatest triumph and is today his greatest legacy. Greater than Osborne House, which he built for his sovereign, greater than the purchase for the public at his behest of Battersea Park in 1853, and certainly greater than his work at Buckingham Palace where he created for Her Majesty a new east front and two new wings. This last project he cleverly helped fund by negotiating the sale to the people of Brighton of her late uncle's exotic, oriental Pavilion, a building Victoria and Albert used only very rarely and considered altogether too louche.

Napoleon. Even so, his certainty that it would come right would probably horrify many present-day speculators.

Ingeniously, whilst draining the aforementioned lagoon to reclaim land lost to the river, Cubitt ordered the wet clay to be dug out and made on site into bricks. The underlying gravel was to provide a more solid base on which his men could build, and as at Pimlico additional material was transported from the other side of London where the huge St Katherine Docks were being excavated. The spoil from this was carried upriver by barge and unloaded at Millbank, an area hitherto good for little more than duck-shooting. In this way Belgravia was raised up although it is still unusually low-lying and the attic storey of a typical Cubitt house here is at about the same elevation above the high-water mark as the basements or ground floors of houses in Westbourne Terrace on the other side of Hyde Park.

When at last he began work on the houses themselves he started with Belgrave Square, then as now the heart of what remains one of the most coherent and unified pieces of town planning anywhere in England. Today like much of the rest of Belgravia the square is remarkable not just for its grandeur, self-confidence and elegance but also because so much of it has survived in its original form; a tribute both to Cubitt as builder and the Grosvenor Estate as landlord. From the start it seemed destined to be a success, and indeed the sovereign herself was among the earliest customers for one of the square's ample and spacious terraced houses. Seeking a house close but not too close to the Palace for her meddling and conniving mother, Queen Victoria leased no. 36 for the Duchess of Kent.

Even so, Benjamin Disraeli deplored much of what Cubitt had achieved, describing the new development as being 'as monstrous as Marylebone and so contrived as to be at the same time insipid and tawdry'. Nor was his an entirely lone voice, for the Victorian preference for what at this stage was still essentially Georgian architecture was never as marked as our own. The General Post Office was also somewhat sniffy about the new addition to London, refusing initially to accept the name 'Belgravia' and redirecting any letters so addressed to Vienna in the supposed belief that it sounded too middle-European to be anywhere in England.

The rich and titled were nevertheless very quick to populate Cubitt's streets, crescents and squares, a network assembled in such a way as to blend perfectly the stately and the picturesque as indeed it still does today.

It is true that the greatest houses have in recent decades become embassies, and blocks of flats have managed gradually to invade Chesham Place and Lowndes Square. But there is still no streetscape in London to match the visual impact and harmony of the stuccoed streets and squares of Belgravia. Nor is there another area where the very few pubs that exist are almost without exception missing from their normal prominent corner sites and instead hidden away in the mews and courtyards where once only servants lived. (Shops and other traders were similarly tidied away, restricted to specific streets and lanes.)

Belgravia was also to be a place where nothing so vulgar as a Tube station would be allowed to intrude, and indeed its prestige is still such that even the residents of nearby Knightsbridge may be heard wistfully paraphrasing the playwright Jack Rosenthal as they describe their own neighbourhood as abutting the borders of Belgravia.

Beeston Place

In 1910 Otto Richard Goring opened his eponymous private hotel a polite distance from the rail terminus at Victoria. It was the last to be built in the reign of Edward VII, and, according to his descendants who still own and run it, the first in the world to provide en-suite bathrooms for every bedroom. It replaced the old Sun Pub and an undistinguished row of houses and a little over a hundred years later images of its variegated redbrick facade flashed round the world as Kate Middleton, accompanied by her father, left this ordinarily quiet and self-effacing establishment for Westminster Abbey and a new life as Her Royal Highness, the Duchess of Cambridge.

In fact with its charming Edwardian architecture (and a small private garden acquired from the present Duke of Westminster as recently as 2005) the hotel is no stranger to royalty. Queen Mary was a frequent visitor in the 1920s and half a century later so too was Queen Elizabeth the Queen Mother. Between times the hotel was fond of quoting the Norwegian Crown Prince, who checked in for the 1937 Coronation, saying he was doing so because

Goring Hotel, Beeston Place

if he stayed at Buckingham Palace he would have to share his bathroom with as many as five other guests.

Belgrave Place

The Royal Norwegian embassy correctly belongs to Belgrave Square, although as no. 25, an end of terrace, it has an entrance onto Belgrave Place either side of which are two decidedly un-Nordic eighteenth-century plaques in Coade Stone. Dating back to 1776 these show cherubs engaged in a variety of artistic pursuits and originally formed part of the old Danish-Norwegian consulate in Wellclose Square in Stepney, East London. Further south a number of much smaller low-rise houses are typical of the thoughtful and meticulous planning of the Belgravia estate, matched pairs of these forming quiet but dignified entrances to Eccleston Mews and Belgrave Mews South. These would once have served the very substantial houses on Eaton Square and in Eaton Place, but with their small-scale and delightfully varied architecture they are themselves now highly sought-after residential enclaves.

Belgrave Square

From the start his 'great showpiece,' the conceit of Belgrave Square was clearly Cubitt's own but its execution in a powerful Graeco-Roman style was largely the work of Disraeli's nephew Elias George Basevi (1794–1845).

Personally cold and haughty, but a brilliant pupil of Sir John Soane, Basevi travelled widely in Italy and Greece before establishing his own practice and naming his son Palladio. For the main square of nearly ten acres, Basevi's magisterial scheme called for four vast terraces, three of them comprising eleven immense white-stucco houses while the fourth, the southernmost, was made up of twelve. Architecturally the most ambitious speculative developments ever undertaken in London – each house is of more than twenty thousand square feet – the first to be built were the north and east ranges. The more elaborate south and west terraces followed only once it was apparent that plan was going to be commercially secure, the financing coming from a largely Swiss consortium headed by a well-connected director of the Bank of England.

With their subtle variations of scale and prominence the terraces are four storeys high, with the top floor above the cornice. Each side of the square was designed as a single entity but with small deviations from one to another so that, for example, the

north and east ranges have six-column central blocks, whereas the south side has eight and the west just four with two square piers. On all four the rich balustrading, entrance porches, and Giant orders of engaged columns and pilasters clearly benefited from Basevi's travels around the Mediterranean, in this case much of his style being derived from the Tower of the Winds in Athens. With richly treated end elevations, each block of houses also has a raised and more ornate attic storey above a Corinthian centre and different ground-floor treatments – features designed to distinguish one from another without disrupting the overall symmetry and unity of their unified palazzo façades, and indeed of the square itself.

At three of the four corners to break up the regularity of the design the original

Seaford House, Belgrave Square

square was graced by even larger, detached houses, each one placed diagonally and looking onto an immense private garden at the centre. A fourth came later, no. 49 in 1851, which was built by Thomas Cubitt for Sidney Herbert. This is now the residence of the ambassador of Argentina, and with the other three provides an attractive solution to the difficulty of having two streets at each of the four corners threading into the square.

By far the largest of the four is no. 37, Seaford House (1842), which is now missing its portico but was designed for the 3rd Earl of Sefton by Philip Hardwick, architect of the City of London Club, much of Lincoln's Inn and of Goldsmiths' Hall. From 1902 until the Second World War it was occupied by the 8th Lord Howard de Walden, who chose to live here rather than on his own Portland Estate, which is centred on Harley Street. The name is a reference to a subsidiary title, no longer in the family, of Baron Seaford but following the war few families were able or prepared to take on such large properties and in 1946 it was taken over by the Royal College of Defence Studies. Prior to this, considerable interior work was carried out for de Walden, including the installation of a green marble and onyx main staircase and lavish Edwardian panel work. The house is only very rarely open to the public, but the interior can be glimpsed in the film *Titanic* where some of its showiest elements were used as a backdrop for the first-class passenger accommodation on board the doomed liner.

No. 24 is now the Spanish embassy and was designed by H. E. Kendall for Thomas Kemp, who had separately commissioned Cubitt to build his own development of Kemp Town at Brighton. Like no. 12, by the architect of the British Museum, Sir Robert

Stucco perfection, Belgrave Square

Smirke, it was conceived on a slightly smaller scale than the terraces and has a neo-Greek porch.

As previously noted Queen Victoria rented a house in Belgrave Square for her mother (no. 36, at £2,000 per annum). Other notable residents included another great London landlord the Duke of Bedford at no. 15, the Earl of Essex at no. 9 (who attracted so many other aristocratic residents he was nicknamed 'the decoy duck') the Duke of Connaught at no. 41 and the Earls of Faversham at no. 19. Sir Henry 'Chips' Channon MP, the celebrated twentieth-century socialite and diarist, lived at no. 5 with his wife, the Guinness heiress, but today – but for the inevitable Russian oligarchs and a handful of others – the square is no longer residential. Nearly a dozen properties are foreign embassies or high commissions, while several others have passed into commercial, cultural or institutional use.

Strange as it may seem, after nearly two hundred years there is only one blue plaque in Belgrave Square – commemorating the Dunkirk commander Field Marshal the Viscount Gort VC, who lived at no. 34 – but there are a number of statues including ones of Christopher Columbus, Simón Bolívar, Prince Henry the Navigator, and the 2nd Earl Grosvenor, 1st Marquess of Westminster. There is also a bust of George Basevi, who died young after falling from the tower of Ely Cathedral, and a sculpture entitled *Homage to Leonardo, the Vitruvian Man* by the Italian Enzo Plazzotta.

Chapel Street

First laid out in 1775, and completed by 1811, the name is derived from a chapel attached to the London Lock Hospital in nearby Grosvenor Place. This was a charitable institution established in the 1746 for 'females suffering from disorders contracted by a vicious course of life' – or as we would call them today, sexually transmitted diseases. (The term 'lock' is itself derived from the hospital's earlier incarnation as a lazar house or leprosy hospital, locks or rags being used to conceal the unfortunate patients' lesions.)

One of very few buildings in the area before Lord Grosvenor decided to develop, the hospital was demolished in 1842 and the patients removed to Westbourne Grove. By that time Chapel Street's smart Georgian brick terraces would have looked much as they do today, many of the original houses still standing and with nos. 9–11 dating back to 1787. The last of these provides a particularly attractive feature to the street, with its slightly later glazed first-floor balcony, and no. 24 is where former Beatles manager Brian Epstein was found dead (see panel below).

Groom Place, Chapel Street

Chapel Street also gives on to a number of charming backwaters, including Groom Place where the Horse and Groom pub illustrates the clever way in which early planners were able to provide for the servant class without disturbing the elegance and style of the neighbourhood as a whole. On the other side of the street, arrow-straight Montrose Place and Headfort Place each displays a cheerfully diverse yet typical array of mews architecture, old and contemporary. With most of the traditional Belgravia mansions now in commercial or institutional hands it is to places such as these that any families able to remain in the neighbourhood have migrated.

Chesham Place

Historically that small portion of Belgravia not owned by the Dukes of Westminster belonged to the Lowndes family, a family

Finnish Embassy, Chesham Place

might not look out of place as part of any post-war European airport. On the other a long stucco terrace is rather more appropriate to the surroundings, with an early plaque at one end recording the occupation of the end house by Lord John Russell, 1st Earl Russell, who served twice as prime minister during the nineteenth century. When his parlous financial situation meant that he was eventually forced to move out and lease the house, Queen Victoria kindly offered him a house in Richmond Park, although his new accommodation was at the expense of his social life as it 'obliged us to give up most dinner engagements in London'.

claiming descent from the Seigneur de Lounde who arrived with William the Conqueror in 1066. More recently based in the Buckinghamshire town of Chesham, they include William Lowndes (1652–1724) who sat in Parliament under three sovereigns – William III, Anne and George I – and was Secretary to the Treasury to the first of these.

Today one side is dominated by the Finnish embassy at no. 38, a large detached Cubitt property of 1840 that would not look out of place in Belgrave Square, and the contrastingly brutal consular department of the German embassy, which, by the same token,

Chester Square

Like nearby Chester Row another reference to Cheshire estates of the dukes of Westminster, Chester Square dates from the late 1840s but with its immaculate magnolia stucco displays the same dignity and quiet elegance of Belgravia's earlier and larger-scale developments. Much of this depended on the careful maintenance of uniformity across the individual house designs although as elsewhere in Belgravia slight variations – ranging from, for example, balconettes to Doric porticoes – shows some deference to the changing tastes of owners.

Much like a smaller version of Eaton Square – meaning it is not square at all – its dominating feature is the church of St Michael by Thomas Cundy the Younger (1790–1867). Cundy built it wide and spacious using Kentish ragstone and Bath stone dressings, an unusual choice of materials for this part of London. With its 150-foot spire it was built on a site originally intended for a mews, which explains its unusual shape, the change of use possibly

THE DEATH OF BRIAN EPSTEIN

The body of Beatles manager Brian Epstein was found at his flat in Chapel Street on 27 August 1967. He had been at a weekend party in his home in Sussex, but had driven back to Belgravia in the early hours of Sunday morning. When his housekeeper couldn't get a reply to her knocks on his bedroom door friends were called and they broke into the bedroom, finding his body. Epstein, who was only thirty-two, was in the flat on his own at the time, and officially his demise was attributed to alcohol and an overdose of Carbitral, a barbiturate form of sleeping pill that was widely used in the Sixties.

Although the official cause of death was recorded as an accidental overdose some have speculated that he took his own life. The reasons given for committing suicide involve a combination of his gay lifestyle (homosexuality was still illegal in 1967), gambling debts, recent ill health and the death of his beloved father a few months beforehand. On balance it is likely that his death was indeed accidental. He had appeared cheerful and relaxed at the party in his country house the night before and he had been looking forward to seeing the Beatles in Wales. It is also the case that he took a huge array of prescription medicines, as the police discovered when they turned up at the house in Chapel Street. Whatever the reason, the sudden death of Britain's most successful and high-profile pop-music entrepreneur caused a media sensation, featuring on many newspaper front pages.

Brian Epstein was the son of a successful Liverpool businessman and he originally wanted to be an actor, studying for a year at RADA before deciding that treading the boards was not for him. Shortly thereafter he opened a record department in his father's furniture store and it quickly became a huge success. He boasted that he could get any record and it was when he got a request for a disc entitled 'My Bonnie', by the Beatles, that he first met the Fab Four. Tracing the record to Germany he discovered to his surprise that the band was from Liverpool and that it was now playing at the Cavern Club. The rest, as the saying goes, is history.

There can be no doubting Epstein's influence on his four young protégés. He encouraged them to ditch their jeans and leather jackets, to wear smart suits on stage and to stop swearing and smoking during performances. He also worked tirelessly to secure a record contract, a process that was successfully concluded in 1962 when the Beatles signed up with Parlophone, a small label owned by EMI, after being rejected by almost every record company in London. Epstein was also available to do the group's dirty work, such as the sacking of the original drummer, Pete Best, who was replaced by Ringo Starr. Beatlemania, which lasted from 1963 to 1966, made the four Beatles rich beyond their wildest dreams, but it also enabled Epstein to accumulate a substantial fortune through his stake in Northern Songs, which owned the copyright to the Lennon-McCartney song catalogue. He also managed a string of other highly successful acts, including Cilla Black, Billy J. Kramer and Gerry and the Pacemakers.

The death of their friend and manager shocked the Beatles, who were in Bangor, north Wales for a meeting of the International Meditation Society. Epstein was to have travelled to Bangor on the day he was found dead to join the IMS. On being told the grim news the four members of the group immediately broke off from the meeting and drove back to London. Paul McCartney said, 'It is a great shock and I am very upset,' while John Lennon stated that, 'Our meditations have given us confidence to stand such a shock.' George Harrison, of the four perhaps the strongest believer in meditation, was even more philosophical: 'There is no such thing as death, only in the physical sense. He will return because he is strong and he is striving for happiness and desired bliss so much.'

In the years since, however, many commentators have drawn uncomfortable parallels between this death and those of the murdered playwright Joe Orton and the pop producer, Joe Meek, a friend of Epstein's. The similarities are striking: all three worked in the field of entertainment; all three were flamboyant gay men; all three had a grisly demise in London in the same year of 1967. Epstein, Orton and Meek were talented young men at the peak of their careers, but they lived with the pressure of exposure and imprisonment at a time when their gay lifestyles were not only considered socially unacceptable but also constituted a criminal offence.

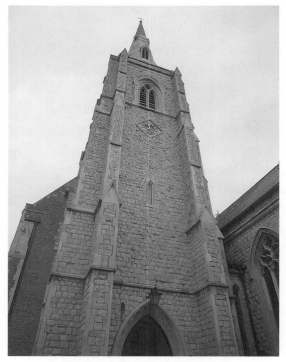

St Michael's, Chester Square

number of famous residents including the poet and critic Matthew Arnold at no. 2 and Queen Wilhelmina of the Netherlands who spent much of the war years in exile at no. 77. More recent residents of the square have included at least two Conservative prime ministers, Harold Macmillan and Baroness Thatcher (the latter until her death in April 2013), the musician Sir Yehudi Menuhin, and the traitor Guy Burgess who for five years leased the top floor of no. 38. The author of *Frankenstein*, Mary Shelley, lived and died at no. 24, but for years she had no plaque as the house was a vicarage and it was thought inappropriate to have the word 'Frankenstein' so prominently displayed. Eventually an accommodation was found, and in 2003 a plaque was duly unveiled by the English novelist (and Shelley biographer) Miranda Seymour.

resulting from the loss of the aforementioned Lock Hospital chapel, which left the area without a place for worship. Like his father before him Cundy was the Grosvenor estate surveyor, and was in turn succeeded by his own son. In 1921 the church was extended by Giles Gilbert Scott. Scott, the architect of Battersea power station and the designer of the iconic red 'K2' telephone box, added a new memorial chapel to the north side commemorating those parishioners who had fallen in the Great War. For years a feature of the chapel, with its tall lancet windows and stain glass, was the flag carried in the retreat from Mons by Sir Henry Wilson (see Eaton Place), and among the regular worshippers was Queen Mary, widow of George V.

In the square itself, blue plaques record a

Chester Street

Largely comprised of early-nineteenth-century terraced houses of brick with stucco ground floors, Chester Street nevertheless benefits from variety with much larger houses at the Upper Belgrave Street end – the largest being the embassy of the Ivory Coast – and smaller properties at the entrance to Wilton Mews. From the street there is a charming view into the self-contained 'village' of Groom Place, and the doorway to the house at no. 3 is particularly attractive.

Cliveden Place

The address of course commemorates Cliveden, Charles Barry's large country house near Taplow in Berkshire, an Italianate *palazzo* positioned above what is arguably the most beautiful stretch of the Thames and now owned by the National Trust. These days the most famous British political scandal of the 1960s ensures that it is John Profumo's name that is most closely associated with Cliveden House, although long before his hosts the Astors took up residence it had passed through several more illustrious families. Created for one duke, let to another, rebuilt by a third, and bequeathed to a fourth – respectively the dukes of Buckingham, Gloucester, Sutherland and Westminster – the name of Cliveden Place commemorates the last of these although when he inherited the Berkshire estate Hugh, 1st Duke of Westminster, felt no need of yet another vast country house and quickly sold it on.

Linking Eaton Square to Sloane Square, the houses that line this western approach to Belgravia are handsome and uniform in character. They are nevertheless modest by local standards and with their unadorned brick façades clearly inferior – and intended to be so – to the great stucco mansions and terraces of Eaton Gate and Eaton Square.

Eaton Place

For nearly six hundred years, the Grosvenor family has had its seat at Eaton Hall in Cheshire, Rauf Grosvenor marrying Joan of Eaton around 1440 and his descendants rapidly ascending through the ranks from baronet to baron, through viscount, earl and marquess, to duke. Given this exceptionally long tenure it is unsurprising that such a cherished name is referenced frequently on this part of the 6th Duke's London estate. In appearance today Eaton Place is perhaps the definitive Belgravia streetscape of tall and substantial brick-and-stucco houses, immac-

ulately maintained and still largely residential although many of the houses have long since been converted into apartments. No. 65 will be familiar to viewers of the hugely popular 1970s television period drama *Upstairs Downstairs*. Renumbered 165 (there is no such address) for filming purposes, in a bid to give the occupants a degree of anonymity, it served as the Bellamy house although interior scenes were naturally shot on sets constructed elsewhere. The story of the series appears in the panel.

Things have changed very little since the street was first developed in 1826, a tribute not just to the Grosvenor stewardship of

The 'Upstairs Downstairs' house, Eaton Place

their estate but also to the quality, soundness and solidity of everything that Cubitt undertook. His painstaking attention to detail was unusual and wholly laudable, particularly when compared to the famously shoddy construction undertaken at John Nash's behest in Regent Street and the adjacent park. The earliest houses are at the eastern end, most likely designed by Cubitt's youngest brother Lewis, and the first occupiers were settled here by 1828. However, it took nearly twenty years to complete the remainder, which perhaps explains the variety of small detail changes from one house to the next, although, as in Belgrave Square, the pleasing classical uniformity of Eaton Place has not been sacrificed.

A blue plaque at no. 15 commemorates the tenure there of Lord Kelvin OM (1824–1907), the academic, scientist and innovator now buried besides Sir Isaac Newton in Westminster Abbey. Frédéric Chopin gave his first recital in London in 1848, at no. 99, and in 1922 outside his home at no. 36 the popular field marshal, Sir Henry Hughes Wilson, was gunned down by two Irish nationalists. Sir Henry – who harboured such a violent dislike of taxis that when on leave he would prowl the streets of London in his Rolls-Royce looking for cabs he could force onto the pavements – had just returned from unveiling a memorial to the fallen of the Great War at Liverpool Street station.

The old soldier made an attempt to draw his sword and fight back but, having been hit by seven bullets, fell face first onto the pavement and died. The perpetrators of what *The Times* called 'the foulest in the foul category of Irish political crimes' were quickly caught – one of them had a wooden leg, and made it no further than Ebury Street – and subsequently hanged. Their

36 Eaton Place

motive, presumably, was that Wilson – by this time a Conservative MP for an Ulster seat – was an outspoken opponent of Home Rule for Ireland.

At its continuation at South Eaton Place the house at no. 16 is unusual in that it has two blue plaques, one to Viscount Cecil of Chelwood (1864–1958) and a later one to his friend Philip Noel-Baker (1889–1982). Lord Cecil was instrumental in creating the League of Nations, the forerunner to the United Nations, while Noel-Baker is recalled as the only winner of an Olympic medal to win a Nobel Prize. After captaining the British team in 1920 – and taking silver in the 1,500 metres – he went on to pen the highly influential *The Arms Race: A Programme for World Disarmament* and was awarded the Nobel Peace Prize for 1960. In 1977 he was made a life peer, although the plaque does not record this.

THE *UPSTAIRS DOWNSTAIRS* STORY

When two friends sat down to pore over old photographs they could never have imagined that the seed had been sown for one of the most successful and acclaimed television series of all time. Jean Marsh and Eileen Atkins, both actresses, were thumbing through the Atkins family album when they came across a snap taken on a servants' outing. That led directly to the phenomenon that was *Upstairs Downstairs*.

Both women had family members who had been in service: Atkins's father was an under-butler and her mother a needlewoman, while Marsh's mother was a housemaid. They knew that the lives of the many millions who had worked as servants were rarely, if ever, portrayed in films or on television. It was therefore not only an opportunity to set the record straight but also to produce something genuinely innovative. The original idea was to focus solely on those below stairs but they quickly realised that 'upstairs' would have to be included. After all, the butlers, housemaids, cooks and valets had to serve someone.

The two friends took their idea to a production company, where one of the first tasks was to come up with an appropriate name for the drama. Many were considered, such as *The Servants' Hall* and *Below Stairs*. However, no doubt for solid commercial reasons, it was decided a title that evoked Belgravia, with its connections to wealth and power, would be preferable. One suggestion was *75 Eaton Square* but that was ditched in favour of *165 Eaton Place*, which was the working title as filming drew near. In fact it was only when production began that the name *Upstairs Downstairs*, perfect in its simplicity, was seized upon. A decision was also taken to set the action in the Edwardian era, a time of great social and political upheaval and therefore full of dramatic possibilities.

Upstairs Downstairs was the story of the Bellamy family and their servants, who lived at 165 Eaton Place in Belgravia. Richard Bellamy, a Conservative MP, was the patriarch and he was married to Lady Marjorie, the daughter of a wealthy earl. The Bellamys had two children, James and Elizabeth, and a retinue of servants that included Hudson, the butler, Mrs Bridges, the cook, and Sarah, the under-housemaid. From the start the emphasis was on quality in terms of script, production values and acting talent. The writers, who meticulously researched the politics and history of the period, counted the acclaimed novelist Fay Weldon among their number.

The cast was equally distinguished: David Langford as Richard Bellamy, Rachel Gurney as Lady Marjorie, Angela Baddeley as Mrs Bridges, Pauline Collins as parlourmaid Sarah and Jenny Tomasin as slow-witted kitchen-maid Ruby. Jean Marsh also found a pivotal role as Rose Buck, the head parlourmaid, but Eileen Atkins, her co-creator, could not take part due to her stage commitments. However, the star of the show was undoubtedly the veteran Scottish actor, Gordon Jackson, who played butler Angus Hudson, although this inspired piece of casting came rather late in the day. As Richard Marson explains in his admirable book on the programme (*Inside Updown: the Story of Upstairs Downstairs*) the original intention had been for another distinguished British character actor, George Cole, to play the butler, but as 'Frank Hudson'. Cole, who would later star in the popular *Minder* series as dodgy Cockney businessman Arthur Daley, would certainly have brought his unique sensibilities to the part. But instead, Jackson became Hudson, a typical Scots Presbyterian, ever meticulous about grace and reading the Bible.

The first episode of *Upstairs Downstairs* was broadcast by London Weekend Television on 10 October 1971 in the 'graveyard' slot of a late Sunday evening. But the unpromising scheduling could not hinder it; the show became an immediate critical and ratings success. The elegant backdrop of Belgravia undoubtedly helped: 65 Eaton Place, which was renumbered 165 during filming, features in many of the outside shots. Viewers across the world loved it, especially in the United States, where it was shown on the Public Broadcasting Service as part of its Masterpiece Theatre. For the actors it was something of a goldmine: David Langdon appeared in a film with Paul Newman, Jean Marsh secured a part in *Frenzy*, a movie directed by Alfred Hitchcock, while Pauline Collins and John Alderton would become two of the biggest stars on television.

Running to five series, *Upstairs Downstairs* was garlanded with awards. Most prominent among them was a Bafta for best drama series and an Emmy for outstanding drama series. There were also awards, in a number of different categories, from the Golden Globes, the Royal Television Society, the American Drama Critics' Circle, the Variety Club of Great Britain, the Writers' Guild and many more besides. Jean Marsh, whose idea it had been, was honoured with the 1975 Emmy for outstanding lead actress. Even the critics were sorry to see it end: Alan Coren, writing for *The Times*, observed that 'I cannot think of a popular series which maintained so consistently high a standard for so long, or one which more entertainingly served the wildly diverse demands of a contemporary audience.'

Eaton Square

Built around no fewer than six private gardens and comprising 104 houses, Eaton Square is nothing of the sort but rather what Cubitt called a great 'parkway', being substantially more than 1,600 feet in one direction and barely 370 in the other. In fact it seems rather longer, most obviously because it is bisected along its main axis by the continuation of Chelsea's noisy King's Road with a number of other streets crossing it laterally. The gardens naturally insulate the houses from the road, but at the same time make it hard if not impossible to view the square as a whole – it covers nearly fifteen acres – except, obviously, from the air. Despite the traffic it is probably the most prestigious address in Belgravia, with Belgrave Square its only possible rival. Development began in 1826, with what are now nos. 103–18, and completion coincided

with the death of Thomas Cubitt in 1855. As at Eaton Place this long gestation has left its mark today in a proliferation of irregular detailing although, once again, to the casual viewer, the overall impression is one of great and unmatched uniformity.

With a parade of more than a hundred columns running down one side the finished effect has been called pretentious, and certainly there is nothing whatever of the modesty and reticence – in either design or execution – which one looks for in the best examples of sophisticated Georgian town planning. Mostly though Eaton Square is properly grand and quite magnificent, and as such it speaks volumes for the painstaking way in which Earl Grosvenor and Cubitt and his collaborators undertook their conversion of such an unpromising site. Everything by Cubitt was done according to a well-conceived blueprint, from the

Eaton Square

drainage to the rerouting of new sewers, through the laying out of wide roads (and even the choice of surfaces) to the planning and planting which has created the 'city of palaces' we see today. Such thoroughness may not have been the only reason for Belgravia's desirability in the 1830s, but to a great degree ensures that it still is today.

Along each of its long sides the square comprises three vast blocks, the central one of each trio differentiated by a richer, more ornate treatment. Those on the north side were developed by Cubitt himself, starting at the western end and working eastwards with increasing emphasis on grandeur and scale. The earlier terraces, for example, are not dissimilar to his work in Bloomsbury but the later work is more Italianate and closer in style to Charles Barry. The change is in part explained by the time it took to complete the square, Cubitt being required to wait for some market-garden leases to expire on the north side of the square.

The opposing range is by a lesser-known architect, W. H. Seth-Smith of Mayfair, who sought assistance from the South Kensington developer Sir Charles James Freake when it became apparent he had taken on rather too much. Like Cubitt, Seth-Smith began with stock brick and stucco dressings albeit with stronger Corinthian motifs than the Norfolk man. His work was completed over a much shorter time period, as little as five years, but as fashions changed he too moved more towards stucco, modifying the details as tastes leaned towards shallower ornamentation, elegant balconettes and projecting porches.

Once again there are relatively few blue plaques in the square, just six, almost certainly restricted to preserve the dignity of the terraces since at such an enduringly

fashionable address it would be possible literally to plaster the ground-floor façades with such things. For example early residents included the eminent brewer W. H. Whitbread, at least one of William IV's numerous illegitimate children and Prince Metternich who received Wellington and Disraeli at no. 44. The American philanthropist and friend of Britain George Peabody lived at no. 80 and, at various times, the square has been home to at least three prime ministers in Earl Russell (no. 48) Neville Chamberlain (no. 37) and Stanley Baldwin (no. 93).

In 1939 records show that 95 per cent of the houses were in single family occupation but during the war years a majority were requisitioned or converted to institutional use. In the years following many, if not the majority, were remodelled again into large apartments: some of the redevelopment was done laterally, to encompass multiple houses designed for a new generation of super-rich that does not wish to live on five, six or seven storeys. Two more are now embassies, with Bolivia at no. 106 and Belgium at no. 103, a plaque on the last of these recording the sacrifice of the many residents of that country 'who volunteered during World War Two to fight with their allies on land, sea and air'. It was unveiled by Queen Elizabeth the Queen Mother in 1964.

The only classical church in Belgravia, St Peter's, at what one might call the London end of the square, is a Greek Revival structure. It has a modern interior as the original – somewhat gloomy with its iron chancel screen – was burned out (for the second time) in the 1980s. It was designed by John Henry Hakewill in 1824, rebuilt by him after the first fire in 1836 but then remodelled and extended by Sir Arthur

Blomfield in the 1870s. The Trafalgar hero Admiral Codrington, who died at no. 92, was buried in the church in 1851. Later churches in the neighbourhood were to be Gothic, which was increasingly fashionable, considered more pious and rather cheaper to build.

Ebury Street

In an historical sense the southern boundary of Belgravia, Ebury Street takes its name from the ancient Eia or Ebury Farm, once the property of Elizabeth and the origins of the Grosvenors' Five Fields. It was mostly laid out during the period 1815–60, although the properties at what was once called 'Five Fields Row' (where no. 180 is now), predate this.

This was where the Mozart family lived for a while when the child prodigy came to London in 1764 and where he wrote his first symphony. The 8-year-old, together with his father Leopold and his sister, was engaged in a musical tour of Europe. They lodged with a Dr Randal at what, in those days, would have been an address well outside London with a convincingly rural outlook.

Leopold was ill for much of their stay here, and in order to hasten his recovery the children were forbidden to play musical instruments until his health improved, enabling them to move back into London (see Soho). According to his sister, Wolfgang Amadeus, 'in order to occupy himself . . . composed his first symphony for all the instruments of the orchestra, especially for trumpets and kettledrums'. Sadly, the piece is now thought lost although that known as K.16 in E flat major was written around the same time.

Some two-and-a-half centuries later the

Former Pimlico Grammar School, Ebury Street

architecture of Ebury Street is generally homely and small-scale rather than impressive or distinguished, a mostly pleasant mix of domestic and retail properties interspersed with bars and private hotels. Only some of the street has the authentic feel of Belgravia: for example some of the terraces on the western side and also the former Baptist chapel, which subsequently became Pimlico Grammar School, at no. 22 (and later still the Pimlico Literary Institute). With its Greek Doric portico and pediment, this was built in 1830 by J. P. Gandy-Deering. As one travels north, much of this feeling is lost so that the remainder (including several of the simpler terraces with stucco ground floors and plain brickwork above) seems somewhat out of place here, and might be better suited to Pimlico. The properties at nos. 162–70 also hint at Chelsea and indeed, at this point, Belgravia is beginning to peter out and much of Ebury Street feels positively raffish in comparison.

A blue plaque on the aforementioned institute shows that it has long been flats: the author Ian Fleming lived here for more than a decade from 1934. Alfred Lord Tennyson lived at no. 42 before relocating in 1880 to somewhat more prestigious quarters in Upper Belgrave Street, specifically to a house large enough to require a retinue of ten indoor servants. Other litterateurs who made their homes in Ebury Street included the brittle and snobbish Vita Sackville-West and her husband Sir Harold Nicolson at no. 182, and George Moore at no. 121. The actress Dame Edith Evans lived at nos. 109–11, and no. 50 was where incriminating papers belonging to Sir Roger Casement were found. These so-called Black Diaries led to his execution for treason at Pentonville in 1916.

Eccleston Street

The name of the street (and of Eccleston Place on the other side of Ebury Street) commemorates another village on the Grosvenors' Cheshire estate, the parish church of which, dedicated to St Mary, contains important memorials to the 1st and 4th Dukes of Westminster and a number of other Grosvenor family members.

The street with its large but unpretentious stucco terraces was laid out by Cubitt in 1835 and before the coming of the railways would have continued through Eccleston Place into Pimlico. For a while the latter, while as previously noted far less prestigious, thus formed a contiguous whole with Belgravia. Indeed Pimlico even has an Eccleston Square, home to Winston Churchill from 1908–11 at an address (no. 33) which – not without irony – was to be used by the Labour Party as its London headquarters during the General Strike.

Given this it is perhaps unsurprising that, as the new London, Chatham and Dover Railway was to cut right through his territory, Cubitt and his lawyers fought long and hard to prevent the building of Victoria station on sixteen precious acres. Of course the battle was lost, but the social and political prominence of many of Belgravia's residents meant they were at least able to insist on the construction of a vast iron-and-glass roof. Required by a special Act of Parliament, this expensive addition was to run over the rails from the terminus to the river in order to maintain the purity of the air in their part of town.

Elizabeth Street

Very much the high street of south Belgravia (as Motcomb Street is to the north) and, as this suggests, somewhat noisier and more

Thomas Cubitt pub, Elizabeth Street

jumbled than much of traditional Belgravia. The Thomas Cubitt pub at no. 44 commemorates the great builder, and is clearly faring somewhat better than its east London sister, the Cubitt Arms on the Isle of Dogs, which closed a few years ago and is now decrepit. At the Eaton Square end some smart terraces remain, and the mews to the square are as charming as ever. Unfortunately, much of the new building in Elizabeth Street is less successful, for example the block on the corner of Boscobel Place, which mimics the terrace opposite but in a manner that is cheapening and wholly unsuccessful. Further south there are some lively shop conversions, however, with particularly attractive fronts at nos. 45, 57 and 59.

Graham Terrace

Belgravia on a much reduced scale, Graham Terrace runs parallel to Ebury Street and largely comprises compact terraced houses of a size and style that are now much sought after by families. Mostly of two storeys with basements, the ground floors of stucco and the remainder of London stock brick, they are the epitome of relatively modest (but now very costly) late Georgian London townhouses. The builder in 1822 was a local man, William Graham, on land leased from the Grosvenors, but at the southern end the red-brick church of St Mary's Bourne Street is substantially later.

In fact, St Mary's was built in 1874 to the designs of the Somerset-born architect Robert Jewell Withers (1824–94), a man recognised in his obituary as building 'a good cheap type of brick church', which was what the area needed as its population grew. Originally intended as a chapel-of-ease

attached to St Paul's, Knightsbridge, his chosen style here was a form of Early English, using machine-made red bricks to create a spacious, lofty nave with two aisles and an apsidal chancel. What the *Church Times* called 'an excellent specimen of an inexpensive church' – discounting interior

St Mary's Bourne Street, Graham Terrace

features such as the reredos and altar, the building had cost £4,500 – was subsequently extended in the 1920s by Harry Stuart Goodhart-Rendel, who added buttresses and a vestry. At the time of this commission, Goodhart-Rendel was young and relatively unknown, but he was subsequently appointed Oxford University's Slade Professor of Fine Art and served as president of the Royal Institute of British Architects from 1937 to 1939.

Grosvenor Gardens

In architectural terms a continuation of Grosvenor Place – and therefore similarly if unexpectedly French Renaissance in style – Grosvenor Gardens, Upper and Lower, is built around two small triangular open spaces.

These are still owned by the Grosvenor Estate but for some years have been open to the public. Heavy traffic into and around the railway terminus at Victoria means they are noisy places to visit, but both gardens are popular with office workers and others wishing to relax for a few minutes. The southernmost space is the more interesting, with a large bronze of France's Maréchal Foch, who famously saluted the casket as Britain's 'Unknown Warrior' was carried up the gangway of the destroyer HMS *Verdun* on the journey from the Western Front to Westminster Abbey.

There is also a pair of small *fabriques* or follies, too small to be considered cottages ornée but attractively decorated with shells and stones. They are used by the gardeners to store their tools and were presented to London in the early 1950s in memory of the Maréchal and to celebrate Anglo-French cooperation in two world wars.

Maréchal Foch, Grosvenor Gardens

Shell house, Grosvenor Gardens

Upper Grosvenor Gardens contains a large and striking memorial to the Rifle Brigade which was unveiled in 1920. Looking towards Buckingham Palace it commemorates the 11,576 officers, non-commissioned officers and men of the Brigade who fell in the Great War. More recently the garden has become the location of a contemporary representation of a lioness attacking a kudu, a copy of a work by Surrey sculptor Jonathan Kenworthy that was commissioned by the present Duke of Westminster for the gardens at Eaton Hall, Cheshire.

Grosvenor Gardens is also the location of one London's distinctive green cabmen's shelters, although the number of these has now dwindled to around just thirteen since the first was erected in 1875. All are now Grade II listed. Originally they numbered sixty, the brainchild of Captain George

Rifle Memorial, Grosvenor Gardens

Bronze lioness, Grosvenor Gardens

Cabmen's shelter, Grosvenor Gardens

Armstrong, late of the Indian Army and now managing editor of the *Globe* newspaper, who one night found plenty of vacant hackney carriages on the stand, but no drivers as the cabbies had all gathered in a nearby tavern.

Propelled by typically Victorian good intentions, Armstrong set out to devise a practical alternative, somewhere to provide the same shelter and companionship, but without the temptation of liquor. His solution also included stoves on which to cook and a selection of books and newspapers, although there were to be strictures against the cabbies discussing union business while inside. The Metropolitan Police similarly decreed that, as the shelters were to occupy space on the Queen's Highway, each should be no larger than a horse and cab which is why, even now, they are so compact.

Strictly speaking they are permitted to serve only cabmen, although it is said that, occasionally, guests are favoured including the explorer Sir Ernest Shackleton, who, prior to the Great War, used to drop into one of them and 'bring down great big books of photographs, and talk all night about his travels'.

Aside from this curious survivor, the buildings that surround both gardens are now all offices but no. 32 was for many years the home of the statesman and barrister Frederick 'F. E.' Edwin Smith, 1st Earl of Birkenhead (1872–1930). He was known for his wit rather than for his patience, as this anecdote proves: after a lengthy and tedious introduction at a public meeting concluded with the words 'Mr Smith will now give his address,' the great man approached the lectern and announced '32 Grosvenor Gardens, London' before walking off the stage and hailing a cab.

Halkin Street

Much of the wealth that enabled the Grosvenor family to prosper in the early days came from mining interests in Flintshire, north Wales. In particular the family's Halkyn estate – 1,800 acres of which it still owns after many hundreds of years – was one of Britain's most important sources of lead and zinc and remained so until prices crashed in 1957. Prior to this collapse, the revenues from their extraction and sale provided Sir Thomas Grosvenor with the £30,000 required to pay for the dowry of Mary Davies in 1677, the bulk of this being the aforementioned Five Fields. As previously noted their marriage gave him, and his heirs, title to the land which was subsequently developed to form much of Belgravia, Mayfair and Pimlico.

At the time of writing the largest house on the street (and so one of the largest in London) is being redeveloped as a private home. Nine bays wide and of yellow brick, Forbes House, with its carriage drive, mature trees and gate-lodge occupies what appears to be the largest and most enviable plot in the whole of Belgravia, although for many years it was offices with much of its extensive garden lost beneath a car park. Next to it, no. 9 is neo-Georgian and robustly red brick and replaced the neo-classical St John's chapel in 1912. The house was designed by Detmar Blow (1867–1939) who was employed by the 2nd Duke of Westminster as estate manager until the two fell out over an accusation that the architect was embezzling funds. He designed chiefly in the fashionable Arts and Crafts style, and no. 9 is a fine example of his work. It was completed in 1907 for the distiller Hugh Morrison, who owned much of Islay. Since 1946 it has been home to the Caledonian

Forbes House, Halkin Street

Club, which was established in 1897 but bombed out of its premises in St James's Square in 1941. Unsurprisingly, it is said to have the largest collection of whiskies of any London club.

On the other side of Belgrave Square the names of well-preserved West Halkin Street and Halkin Place have similar origins. An archway on one side of the latter gives onto Belgrave Mews West, where the Star Tavern is neatly hidden away in a manner which will by now be familiar in this part of the capital. The Star was once a popular rendezvous for the so-called Great Train Robbers, who, in August 1963, hijacked the Glasgow–London mail train when it was passing through Buckinghamshire. After violently attacking the driver the gang stole £2.6 million, but were soon caught, convicted and imprisoned.

West Halkin Street, something of an afterthought in 1830 to provide better access into Belgrave Square, was home to a

Presbyterian (and later Spiritualist) chapel at no. 118. In the 1920s this Victorian Gothic building was converted into an extraordinary eight-bedroom private house – complete with organ – and it is now a private dining club.

Hobart Place

Robert Hobart, 4th Earl of Buckingham-shire (1760–1816), was secretary of state for war and the colonies and gave his name to the capital of Tasmania as well as to Hobart Place. Today one side is dominated by the aforementioned church of St Peter and the wholly unremarkable modern premises of the consular section of the Italian embassy. The other side provides an attractive prelude to Eaton Square, however, with small, elegant brick-and-stucco terraces and an appealing but almost comically narrow exercise in French Renaissance style immediately to the left of the entrance into Eaton Row.

In 1823 the junction with Grosvenor Place was the scene of an unusual double tragedy when a young man called Abel Griffiths killed himself after murdering his father. As was the custom at that time, when suicide was technically a capital offence, the offender's body was buried at a crossroads with a stake through the heart. This reportedly so annoyed George IV, who was building his new palace across the road, that on 8 July an Act of Parliament was passed abolishing this strange and cruel punishment, although suicide remained a serious crime until well into the 1960s.

Lowndes Place

In the 1720s the aforementioned William Lowndes was able to purchase a pair of empty fields situated to the west of London. A century later, albeit on a much smaller scale, his grandson (also William) set out to develop this inheritance in a manner not unlike that of his neighbour, Earl Grosvenor. Lowndes Street is thought to occupy the narrow strip of land that once joined his grandfather's two fields. The long and narrow Lowndes Square was built on the northernmost portion – with work starting in the mid-1830s – and Chesham Place (see above) and Lowndes Place on the southernmost.

Lowndes Place is a charming but orderly jumble of mostly low-rise private houses, clearly not one of Belgravia's prime addresses although in an age when live-in servants are not the norm these smaller but detached or semi-detached properties have become enormously sought after. The most intriguing is no. 8, known as Lowndes Cottage. With two sets of curved steps up to the front door, it was for some years home to

Lowndes Cottage, Lowndes Place

the composer and conductor Sir William Walton – his time here is now marked by an official blue plaque – and subsequently of Harry Saltzman, co-producer of much of the James Bond movie canon.

Lowndes Square

Approaching Knightsbridge at its northern end – where it is spoiled by a number of late-twentieth-century developments – the square is dominated by the broadly circular, yet angular, bulk of the Sheraton Park Tower Hotel. This was built in 1971 on the site of Wontland's, a once fashionable department store that was developed from a former servants' bazaar. Views from the top of the hotel are spectacular, both towards Hyde Park and across Belgravia, and of course from inside one is spared the sight of the building itself.

Things improve markedly as one moves away from the Sheraton, however, and towards the southern end of the square, on the western side, are a number of well-preserved townhouses in the neighbourhood's characteristic white stucco. Their Greek Doric and Tuscan porches are typical of the

Lowndes Square South

a search of the premises revealed evidence of drug use and 'implements of fetishism and perversion'. There was no doubt who had pulled the trigger but Mrs Barney was acquitted and four years later she was found dead in a hotel room in France, her demise being attributed to the effects of a lifetime of alcohol and narcotics abuse.

Lyall Street

Charles Lyall was a business partner of William Lowndes, and one of his estate's trustees. The street that carries his name runs down from the junction with Chesham Place across Eaton Square and joins Elizabeth Street. Unlike the latter, it is still entirely residential, although many of the houses have been broken up into apartments. To one side the houses backing onto Lyall Mews are modest by Belgravia standards, but on the western side most are of five or even six storeys. One of these indeed is where Cubitt himself chose to live (there is a blue plaque to this effect on the façade of no. 3) and a much smaller property in the mews to the rear still calls itself Cubitt Lodge. Towards Eaton Square, attractive rusticated archways, one of which ingeniously incorporates the doorways of the adjacent houses, give on to the quiet mews that would once have served the much larger houses on the north side of the square.

area, but a few of them display some of the stranger manifestations of Victorian taste, including curious round-headed windows and heavily faux 'Jacobethan' balustrades.

Nearby Harriet Walk and Harriet Street are named after the wife and sister of William Lowndes, who shared the same forename. On the opposite side of the square the rebuilt 21 William Mews is where, in 1932, the socialite Elvira Barney shot and killed her lover Michael Scott Stephen. The case caused something of a scandal at the time, not simply because Barney was married and her parents titled, but also because

Motcomb Street

Chic and busily commercial, Motcomb Street is very much the northern counterpart to Elizabeth Street. A thriving, buzzing little street of acutely fashionable retailers and sleek restaurants and bars, the name comes from the manor of Motcombe in

Dorset and an estate there which was owned by the 2nd Marquess of Westminster – the 1st Duke's father – in the 1880s. Many of the original nineteenth-century houses have survived, despite being considered third rate when first built, and becoming commercial premises within ten or twenty years. It is fortunate that cast-iron first-floor balconies, allied to a certain uniformity, mean that even those with newer shop fronts still look smart and dignified.

However, the most outstanding building in Motcomb Street is the Pantechnicon, which was completed in 1830 by one of Seth-Smith's collaborators, Joseph Jopling. At one time this covered two acres and offered local residents secure 'fire-proof' storage within its labyrinthine vaults for their personal effects, including horses, carriages and wine. It was nevertheless more or less destroyed in a fire barely forty years later, leaving just the screen we see today – of double-height Greek Doric columns – which Pevsner likens to a more austere version of the screen at the Royal Institution

(see Mayfair chapter). Rebuilt following the fire, the new Pantechnicon was smaller and occupied a much-reduced site, and much of what remains has now been redeveloped into an attractive public house. The gleaming stucco extension directly opposite, also by Jopling, extends all the way to West Halkin Street. Irregular in shape, it is original and highly unusual – eight bays wide and with two vast round-headed windows – and now houses a supermarket.

At the far end of the street, and so almost certainly technically a part of Chelsea, the curved façade of semi-circular Chelsea House (by Thomas Tait) looks much younger than its mid-1930s date and nicely closes the view to the west.

Upper Belgrave Street

With its extension in Lower Belgrave Street this is perhaps the smartest of the roads crossing Eaton Square. Its houses share many features and details with Belgrave Square, including giant pilasters and, in

The Pantechnicon, Motcomb Street

Upper Belgrave Street

places, monumental columns. Of particular note is the central portion of the terrace on the north-east side. At nos. 6–8 a massive porch serves all three houses with paired Ionic columns and a heavy balustrade is clearly intended to enhance the view from Eaton Place and does so. The remaining houses have more conventional individual porches, and diagonally opposite the quite extraordinarily low-rise Belgrave Cottage (one storey above a basement) sits in front of Eccleston Mews.

While living at no. 9, Alfred Lord Tennyson was painted by John Millais. He hated the result, although Millais regarded it as one of his most successful portraits. From 1861–70 Walter Bagehot lived at no. 12, one of a pair of stuccoed houses built around 1830. The sometime editor of *The Economist*, Bagehot wrote *The English Consti-*

tution, a highly influential book that explores the relationship between the monarchy, the legislature and the executive and also contrasts the British form of government with its American counterpart. Considered a masterpiece of political analysis, it is still widely read today.

In Lower Belgrave Street is a rare thing for Belgravia, a pub that is not hidden away in a yard or mews. The Plumber's Arms was, even so, largely unknown except to the locals, but all that changed on 7 November 1974 when it became the focus of one of the greatest unsolved mysteries in British criminal history: the disappearance of Lord Lucan after the family's nanny had been brutally murdered (see panel, p. 344). Today, with more brick than stucco, Lower Belgrave Street appears more modest than Upper; but with four storeys above a basement – and very few commercial conversions – the houses on both sides of the road are still impressively intact.

Victoria Square

Small and attractive, Victoria Square is the work of Matthew Wyatt – son of Matthew Cotes Wyatt (see Hyde Park Corner) – and was built in 1838–9. Its compact size in part explains its relative anonymity but it is also somewhat cut off from Belgravia proper by heavy traffic along Grosvenor Gardens. Its name and date mean of course the architecture is no longer Georgian, but to the casual visitor the air of the creamy and sober terraced houses with their decorative ironwork is very much one of the Regency, and even of Brighton. Ian Fleming purchased the house at no.16 in 1953, just before the publication of his first novel, *Casino Royale*, which introduced James Bond to the world.

THE LORD LUCAN MYSTERY

It was a quiet Thursday night at the Plumber's Arms, a pub in Lower Belgrave Street, in the heart of Belgravia. A dozen regulars were enjoying their pints, when, at about twenty to ten, a woman came in through the front door. Blood was pouring from deep cuts in her head and, as she staggered about the bar, hardly able to stand, she began to scream and shout: 'I have just got away from being murdered. He's murdered my nanny. My children. My children!'

The date was 7 November 1974 and it was the opening act in a drama that has baffled the police, press and public for the best part of forty years

The woman in question was the Countess of Lucan, who lived in a discreetly smart terraced house at 46 Lower Belgrave Street with her three children, aged ten, seven and four. She was separated from her husband, 7th Earl of Lucan, who now lived a few minutes' walk away in Elizabeth Street. Police were called and when they forced entry to no. 46 they carried out a thorough search of the house, finding the three Lucan children in their bedrooms and unharmed.

The basement, which consisted of a breakfast room and kitchen, was a different story: the walls were covered in blood and there was also a pool of blood on the floor, which a man had walked through and left his footprints. There was a sack in the corner of the room, which they could see contained a bulky object. Opening the sack the police made a gruesome discovery: the body of 29-year-old Sandra Revitt, nanny to the Lucan children. Detectives realised immediately that the unfortunate young woman had been battered to death with the proverbial blunt instrument, a conclusion that was confirmed when they found a length of lead pipe, bent out of shape and covered in bloodstains. When Lady Lucan was able to make a statement to police she named her husband as her attacker and as the killer of Sandra Revitt. The problem for Scotland Yard was that of Lord Lucan there was no sign.

Richard John Bingham, Lord Lucan, was a character who might have stepped from the pages of a Graham Greene novel: handsome, dashing, aristocratic, but with a talent for dissolution. Born in 1934 Richard Bingham had the classic background of the British upper classes: prep school, Eton, the Coldstream Guards and the City, where he worked as merchant banker. With his looks and charm he would not have looked out of place as a leading man on the silver screen and in fact he was courted by directors keen to cast him in their movies; it is said that he was even screen-tested for the role of James Bond in *Dr No*, before Sean Connery was offered it. Richard Bingham might have had a highly productive life but he had been a reckless gambler from an early age. Although he was a skilled back-gammon player he was obsessed by *chemin de fer*, the most addictive gambling game of them all. It may have been a weekend in a Le Touquet casino that fired his passion for 'chemmy': he won £20,000 playing the game, earning him the nick-name 'Lucky'. After that gambling became his life, leading him to give up his City job and become a professional gambler.

In 1964 he married Veronica Duncan, the daughter of an army officer, but his new responsibilities as first a husband and then a father did little to curb his enthusiasm for the high life. He was now part of the Clermont Set, named after the Clermont Club in Berkeley Square, an exclusive group of playboys and rich businessmen that included John Aspinall and James Goldsmith. His gambling became yet more high risk, even reckless, and he began to lose heavily. The Lucky sobriquet he had earned in Le Touquet was now a sad joke as he squandered his fortune on the tables. Not surprisingly, his wife was beside herself with worry about the losses and they fought bitterly when he refused to seek treatment for his addiction. It was hardly surprising when they separated in late 1972, with care and control of the children being granted to Lady Lucan against her husband's wishes.

Lord Lucan's life began to spiral out of control. Despite the support of the Clermont Set, he became increasingly angry at the hand life had dealt him. He was bankrupt, owed substantial sums to moneylenders and had very little hope of ever getting his children back. According to one account, his relaxation now consisted of reading Hitler's *Mein Kampf* and listening to recordings by its author, sessions that were accompanied by copious amounts of alcohol. One chronicler of his life asserts that during this time he talked openly about murdering his wife.

We will never know for sure what happened on that fateful November night. According to Lord Lucan himself – in account given to a friend on the day after he disappeared – he was passing his wife's house when he spotted an intruder, let himself in through the front door and went down to the basement where he slipped in the pool of blood. Realising what had happened Lucan tried to help and comfort his wife, but she ran out of the house screaming 'murder'. His justification for fleeing was that the police, who would of course find out about the marital discord, would never believe his story. However, at the inquest Lady Lucan told a very different story. She named her husband as the murderer and stated that he had also tried to kill her, only desisting when she squeezed his testicles. The jury had no doubt, naming Lord Lucan as the killer after deliberating for only thirty-one minutes (it was, incidentally, the last time an inquest jury was legally able to name a murderer).

The only positive thing one can say about the 7th Earl of Lucan is that despite the best efforts of the police he has never been seen since, apart from a two-day stay with friends in Uckfield, Sussex immediately after the murder. The police did find the car he was driving that night, a Ford Corsair, which he had abandoned in Newhaven, a ferry port on the English Channel. Theories abound as to his fate: the most obvious, and perhaps the most credible, is suicide; another has it that his rich friends helped him start a new life on the Continent or further afield, which of course ties in with the dozens of 'sightings' of the elusive peer over the years; a third, more outlandish, holds that he was spirited out of the country by a rich international financier, but who then found him too hot to handle and had him killed. Lord Lucan was declared dead in 1999, although reports that he has been spotted at both home and abroad continue to be reported in the media.

Wilton Crescent

In 1831 Robert Grosvenor, 1st Marquess of Westminster, married Eleanor, the only child of Sir Thomas Egerton. Sir Thomas later became the 1st Earl of Wilton, a title subsequently commemorated in a number of Belgravia addresses as it has been closely connected to the Grosvenor family in the years since. The Crescent was created jointly by Cubitt and the aforementioned Seth-Smith in 1827, an elegant and conspicuously grand feature lying to the north of Belgrave Square. It is one not necessarily enhanced by the stone façade added to its twin curves between 1908 and 1912, a modification that is reminiscent of Bath or Edinburgh New Town, but seems curious here. That said the uniformity of the lofty terraces (each of five storeys between a basement and continuous balustrade) nevertheless makes this a spectacular entry into Belgravia for anyone

Wilton Crescent

turning from Knightsbridge into Wilton Place.

The southern portion of the Crescent gives a better impression of what was first intended, and with its stucco finish, giant pilasters and balconettes it is immediately more traditional of this area. The newer stone facades are smart but somehow colder, and perhaps inevitably two are now embassies. Otherwise no. 33 was home to President Alfonso Lopez-Pumarejo of Colombia (1886–1959) during his time as that country's ambassador to the Court of St James's and – of more immediate interest to most visitors – the house at no. 2 was owned by Earl Mountbatten of Burma from 1950 until his murder by the IRA in 1979.

Wilton Place

Wilton Place is slightly older than the Crescent, and looks it. The original entrance into Belgravia from Knightsbridge – Grosvenor Crescent came later, bringing traffic with it – the narrow brick and stucco houses on the west side were completed around 1824–5. Those opposite date from the 1840s, and if neighbouring Kinnerton Street today looks more like a mews than a street this is because originally that is what it was.

Built to service the much larger houses of Wilton Place, and unpleasantly close to the old Ranelagh sewer (which remained open to the skies until 1844) Kinnerton Street was for a while little better than a slum. A decade later rent rolls show a saddler, two tailors, a plumber and wheelwright as tenants, and a hundred years ago a six-room house could still be rented for no more than £40 per annum. A number of pubs can still be seen in the street today – including the Wilton Arms of 1826 – as if to underscore its lower status.

Before Wilton Place was developed this northern extremity of the Five Fields was known as Porter's Lane and much of it was occupied by a dairyman's yard. In about 1758 part of the site was let on a long lease to the War Office, and until the 1840s a large portion of the eastern side of Wilton Place was occupied by the barracks and offices serving the Foot Guards. When these were demolished they were replaced by houses, and then, in the 1960s, the site was cleared once again for a new hotel designed by Brian O'Rourke to be built on the corner with Knightsbridge. This is the Berkeley and as the name suggests the original had been in Mayfair, at the junction of Berkeley Street and Piccadilly. On its completion in 1971 it was described as 'large and inappropriate', and looking at the site more than four decades later the impression given is much the same.

Dedicated to St Paul the church on the eastern side contrasts strongly with both hotel and houses, designed in the Perpendicular style by Thomas Cundy the Younger and completed in 1843. The interior features a magnificent open timber roof, and a rood and screen by the Gothic revivalist and Royal Academician George F. Bodley. There are also memorials to the women of the wartime Auxiliary Transport Service and the First Aid Nursing Yeomanry (FANY). Among the more than fifty names commemorated on these is that of the secret agent Violette Szabo who received a posthumous George Cross after being tortured and executed by the Nazis at Ravensbrück concentration camp. She was twenty-three and had lived in Stockwell.

A blue plaque on the façade of no. 25 marks it as the home of George Bentham (1800–1884) the long-lived nephew of the

St Paul's, Wilton Place

philosopher Jeremy Bentham and a formidable figure in the world of botany. Active in the Linnaen Society (of which he was president) and at Kew Gardens where he laboured daily, Bentham co-authored the *Genera Plantarum*. A rigorous model of scientific accuracy, this brilliantly revised the accepted definitions of every known genus of flowering plant and remained current for the following hundred years.

a regular here (another popular myth) for while the Iron Duke lived nearby at Apsley House he was notably ill-disposed towards gambling and drinking in public. He was also a member of numerous clubs – including the Athenaeum, the 'Rag', the 'Senior', the City of London, the Oxford & Cambridge and the Guards (with sixteen subscriptions only Lord Mountbatten seems to have belonged to more) – leaving one wondering why he would leave the safe embrace of St James's to play a few hands with the lower ranks in what was, for all its charm today, merely a common tavern.

Grenadier pub, Wilton Row

Wilton Row

Originally called Crescent Mews, Wilton Row is among the best-known addresses in the whole of Belgravia almost entirely because of the famous pub that lies hidden halfway along its length. This is the Grenadier, which was built around 1830 when the cobbled, serpentine alleyway was constructed to serve the eastern side of Wilton Row, and, later, the houses on Grosvenor Crescent. According to legend it originally formed part of the officers' mess for the aforementioned barracks, but this is not true although the sentry box outside appears genuine. It is nevertheless said to be haunted by the ghost of a young subaltern who was caught cheating at cards and flogged to death by his outraged companions.

Nor is it at all likely that Wellington was

INDEX